Penguin Education

International Investment

Edited by John H. Dunning

Penguin Modern Economics Readings

International Investment

Selected Readings

Edited by John H. Dunning

Penguin Books

Penguin Books Ltd, Harmondsworth,
Middlesex, England
Penguin Books Inc, 7110 Ambassador Road,
Baltimore, Md 21207, USA
Penguin Books Australia Ltd,
Ringwood, Victoria, Australia

First published 1972

Made and printed in Great Britain by
Richard Clay (The Chaucer Press) Ltd,
Bungay, Suffolk
Set in Monotype Times

Contents

Introduction

These Readings have been chosen to reflect the main stream of research and writing on the subject of international investment in the post-Second World War era. All but one of the contributions have been written in the last twenty years, and most since 1965.

The emphasis of the essays is largely directed to international *direct* investment, that is, investment undertaken by companies in foreign ventures in which they have a controlling and managing interest. Apart from official capital outflows – mainly to provide the necessary infra-structure for economic development – more than three-quarters of the foreign investment undertaken since 1950 has been direct investment, although, more recently, as Professor Cooper shows in Reading 9 there has been somewhat of a resurgence in portfolio investment. These Readings sketch the historical background of international capital movements and after summarizing some of their theoretical implications trace out some of their effects on both investing and host countries.

There are many fine contributions which we have not been able to include in this volume. Some we hope to publish in a later volume on the multinational enterprise. Others like Ragnar Nurkse's (1954) excellent essay on international investment have been incorporated in another volume in the Penguin Modern Economics series – *International Finance*, edited by R. N. Cooper, 1969. Again, a somewhat different orientation would have certainly included more essays on the financial aspects of capital movements.

As a background to what follows, the rest of this introduction distinguishes between the various forms of private foreign investment, and then outlines the main determinants of direct investment and work which has recently been done on this subject.[1]

1. Part of this introduction was originally published by the editor in his *Studies in International Investment*, Allen & Unwin, 1970.

The history of international capital movements

In 1914, 90 per cent of all international capital movements took the form of portfolio investment, that is, the acquisition of securities by individuals or institutions, issued by foreign institutions without any associated control over or participation in their management. It is true that several American and European companies, for example, Lever, Singer, General Electric, Courtaulds, Nestlés, already owned sizeable foreign manufacturing ventures, but these were the exception rather than the rule and they rarely accounted for a major part of the enterprise's total activities. In a world operating under the gold standard, capital normally moved across national boundaries in response to interest rate differentials. The classical and neo-classical theories of international investment were both largely concerned with explaining the balance of payments adjustment process of these capital movements and their effects on the money supply, relative prices and the level of economic activity in the lending and borrowing countries.[2]

Later, the Keynesian revolution and the economic circumstances of the inter-war period changed the complexion, though not the principles, underlying the earlier theories. New approaches were introduced to deal with capital movements under a paper standard, fixed exchange rates and controls on both the movement of goods and capital; and new ideas, for example, that the purchasing power generated by the transfer process might be greater or less than the amount of capital actually involved, advanced. But economists still sought to answer basically similar questions as they did in the past, and the theme of Carl Iversen's (1936) comprehensive study was little different from that of the classicists nearly a century earlier. Even J. M. Keynes (1924), in his very derogatory remarks about foreign investment, confined his remarks largely to movements in portfolio capital.

Gradually, however, the centre of interest was shifting. The collapse of the world monetary system in 1930 caused a profound

2. However whereas the classicists, notably Ricardo, Hume and Mill considered that the adjustment process was brought about mainly by changes in relative prices, the neo-classicists, such as Taussig, Viner and White focused attention on the effect of capital movement on income levels and their effects on the balance of payments through the marginal propensity to import. For a comprehensive discussion see Ohlin (1933).

change in both attitudes and policies towards international investment (United Nations, 1949). The immediate consequence of the depression was to curtail the flow of capital movements to a trickle and to reduce substantially the real value of those still outstanding. Compared to a substantial net outflow of capital from the leading capital exporters between 1905 and 1914 and 1919 and 1929, there was a net repatriation between 1929 and 1939. At the same time, direct investments came through the depression reasonably well and even increased in value (Lewis, 1938): by 1939, most of today's leading multinational enterprises had already established, albeit in a small way, foreign branches and/or subsidiaries.

Since 1930, there has never been a free international capital market, nor have interest rates solely reflected the outcome of market forces. In consequence, and for politcal reasons too, investors have remained a good deal more cautious in their attitudes to foreign securities than once they were. Nowadays, the greater part of private foreign investment takes the form of foreign operations by business corporations, while public or semi-public institutions have replaced private investors in supplying funds for those types of projects which previously accounted for the bulk of capital exports in the early nineteenth century.

In the last decade, there has been a noticeable recovery in the international bond market: between 1958 and 1968 foreign bond issues in Europe and American recorded a four-fold increase. In addition, new markets, for example, the Euro-dollar and Euro-bond market have been evolved, while existing markets have become more closely integrated as capital mobility has increased. Nevertheless, private portfolio investment still accounts for less than one-fifth of all international investment. Its movements – both short and long term – can still be explained by the tools of international economics. Flows in direct investment are differently determined; it is now recognized that an understanding of these movements lies more in the theory of the growth of the firm (Hymer, 1960).

Direct and portfolio investment

The main distinguishing feature of direct foreign investment is that, unlike portfolio investment, the investing unit (usually a business enterprise) purchases the power to exert some kind of control over the decision-taking process of the invested-in unit (again, usually, a business enterprise). This immediately suggests that something other than money capital is (or may be) involved in direct investment. This might simply be informal managerial or technical guidance; or it could incorporate the dissemination of valuable knowledge, in the form of research and development, production technology, marketing skills, managerial expertise, and so on; none of which usually accompanies portfolio investment. Where such knowledge is not separately obtainable (for example, by licensing agreements) and is an important determinant of a company's competitiveness, this may be as vital a component of direct investment to the host country as the capital *per se*, as it will initiate not only an income-generating effect, but a 'technological-generating' effect which reflects directly in the superior knowledge of the investing country. (Compare, for example, a US investment in the French computer industry with that in the UK cotton textiles industry.) One interesting application of this difference is that while portfolio capital will normally move to those sectors within the recipient economy which, as revealed by their profitability, have a comparative advantage over their counterparts in the investing country, in the case of much direct investment, capital will flow to those industries in which the investing country (initially) has the comparative advantage but in which it is possible for the recipient country to gain.

The special characteristics of direct investment, then, are first that it buys, for the investing company, a power of control over decision taking in a foreign enterprise – the extent of which will vary according to its equity participation, particularly in relation to that of other investors.[3] Secondly, it is usually accompanied by the transference of other factor inputs, or the output of such inputs, in the form of knowledge and ideas. In some ways, the multinational enterprise is better regarded as a vehicle for the dissemination of other factor inputs and/or services than a provider of finance. From the viewpoint of the investing country, while portfolio capital is mainly supplied by individuals and in-

3. A 30 per cent ownership with no other individual shareholder holding more than 10 per cent of the total shareholding is likely to afford a more significant element of control than a 49 per cent shareholding where the remaining shares are held by one enterprise.

stitutions to different foreign individuals and institutions, through the mechanism of the capital market, direct investment, except where the purchase or part purchase of an existing enterprise is involved, is usually accomplished without any change in ownership at all. Essentially, it represents the vertical or horizontal geographical extension of a firm's activities and must thus be viewed in the light of its overall objectives, of which the expected profit rate of the new offshoots may be only one.

In general, direct investment, particularly direct manufacturing investment, is more likely to promote world economic growth than is portfolio investment. This is because it tends to be concentrated in the dynamic and technologically advanced sectors where the knowledge content of the investing firm is superior to that of local competitors. The distribution of the gains resulting from the investment between the host and investing country will depend *inter alia* on the extent of competition and government policy in the host country. Britain, in the nineteenth century, largely invested overseas in those outlets which yielded a safe return, but little capital growth. Outside trade distribution and certain resource industries, US firms today invest either to exploit certain economic advantages not possessed by competitors (or potential competitors) in host countries or where the pattern of market growth is likely to follow that of the US. Not only have these investments, in general, yielded high profits, but also a considerable capital appreciation.

Motives and determinants

Since foreign direct investment represents the territorial expansion of business activities, it may be assumed that, in principle at least, it is undertaken to advance the interests of the investing institution – whatever these interests may be. It is true that most firms are influenced in their behaviour by more than one objective and sometimes different values are placed on the same objectives. Moreover, not all firms view their overseas investments in the same light as their domestic investments. For example, one of the earliest theories of foreign direct investment suggested that businessmen were prepared to gamble more with their foreign investments than those at home simply because the former constituted such a small part of their total operations. This is no longer true; in 1969, for example, one-fifth of all plant and equipment expenditure by US manufacturing companies was undertaken by their foreign subsidiaries. It would then seem reasonable to suppose that the behaviour of firms in respect of overseas activities will be influenced by broadly similar objectives as domestic operations and that no specific theory of motivation is required.

There are, however, two qualifications to this statement. The first is that the decision takers in the foreign subsidiaries may not be the same people as those in the parent companies and may not be subject to the same economic pressures. An obvious example of a possible difference in objectives is where the foreign enterprise is partly owned by local interests, whose motives may not be the same as the foreign shareholders. The second qualification concerns the precise combination of the 'mix' of objectives which make up a firm's utility function; these may vary *inter alia* as to the type of investment being made and economic circumstances. Thus, at certain times, a firm may value security and a low profit relative to uncertain growth, and at other times the reverse. Income earned by a sales or distribution venture may be discounted at quite a different rate from that earned by a mining subsidiary. Since the environment facing the firm will differ between countries, it may well follow that its objectives will not be identical. The behaviour of a subsidiary of a US chemical company in Ghana may not be quite the same as its counterpart in Holland purely because of the difference in political and/or exchange risks in the two countries.

Most of the literature dealing with the theory of direct foreign investment has, however, been more concerned with the determinants of such investment rather than its objectives. Again, many of these determinants are common to domestic investment, although their importance may substantially differ. The principles influencing whether a New York based pharmaceutical company sets up a branch plant in California will be much the same as those which it takes into account in deciding whether or not to set up a similar subsidiary in France. There will, however, be certain considerations which apply in the French case and not in the Californian case (and sometimes vice versa). For example, free trade exists within the United States but a tariff is imposed on American pharmaceutical imports into France; there is always the possibility of an alteration in the exchange rate between the franc and the dollar, and there are always additional political-cum-environmental factors involved in investing in a foreign country which do not apply at a domestic level. In a number of cases too, domestic and foreign investment are complementary, rather than competitive with each other, and factors influencing investment abroad may not have any counterpart at home.

Studies so far undertaken on the determinants of foreign direct investment fall into three categories. First, there are those which try to evaluate, mainly from data supplied by individual businesses, the main factors influencing the decision to invest in a particular country and/or industry. The work of Basi (1966), Behrman (1962), the National Industrial Conference Board (1961) and Robinson (1961) fall into this group. Though the authors usually attempt to rank the various influences according to their importance, none has quantified their significance in any systematic way and, in some cases, the variables considered (either by the researchers or the enterprises in question) are not only loosely defined but interdependent of each other. It is difficult to summarize the findings of this kind of approach. Investments vary in type; they are undertaken for a variety of reasons, and economic conditions in one country are often very different from those in another. Sometimes, too, an investment is made to protect existing markets or avoid losses rather than to make profits; in other cases, it is more aggressively oriented. The determinants of a vertically integrated investment by a manufacturing company in a resource industry may be prompted by completely different factors than an investment by the same company in a subsidiary overseas to produce a similar line of products to those produced at home. The decision-taking process behind any foreign investment is often very complex and time consuming and involves many different personalities (Aharoni, 1966).

The second type of approach is more macro-oriented. This takes as its starting point such published data as are available on direct capital flows by one country either in various countries abroad or in particular industries, and seeks to establish some kind of functional relationship between this and possible determinants. Bandera and White (1968), for example, related US investment in Europe to profitability and growth in real output. A variety of econometric studies have also been undertaken by Moose (1968), Popkin (1965), Severn (1970), Stevens (1969) and others. The majority of these seem to support the 'accelerator principle' of investing overseas, which US economists have found to be dominant with respect to domestic investments (Jorgenson and Siebart, 1968), but as yet data are not sufficiently disaggregated on an industrial basis for conclusions of any practical value to be drawn. Other economists have attempted to evaluate the importance of particular variables affecting foreign investment. The writings of Balassa (1967), d'Arge (1969) and Scaperlanda (1967), on the effects of tariffs and customs unions, and those of Heckerman (1969), Hirshleifer (1964) and Stevens (1969), on exchange risks, fall into this category.

The third approach – which runs parallel to the two just described – is, perhaps, the most interesting intellectually. Essentially, it seeks to explain why foreign direct investment is preferred to other forms of resource allocation. For example, assuming overseas investment is considered worthwhile, why should it take the form of direct rather than portfolio investment? Second, why should direct investment be preferable to other ways of exploiting a foreign market, for example, exports of licensing agreements? Third, what is the cost of foreign investment in terms of forgone investment opportunities at home?

To answer these (and similar) questions let us first assume that a firm has a certain amount of capital available for investment and that it wishes to secure the highest rate of return on that investment. Then, it follows that it will choose to invest abroad by extending its own operations, rather than investing in a domestic company (or companies) operating in the country in which it is interested, as long as the income it expects to earn is greater. This will occur whenever the investing company possesses some advantages over its foreign competitor which are not readily available to it and are sufficient to compensate for the disadvantages of operating a subsidiary at a distance. These advantages, as described by Kindleberger (1969) may take various forms and include superior technology, patents, access to markets, entrepreneurial expertise and experience, economies of integration, and so on. A firm will wish to fully exploit these benefits rather than share them with potential competitors, and this encourages them to undertake direct rather than portfolio investment. The more significant the advantages, the greater the likelihood of monopoly profits being earned, and the more a firm is encouraged to engage in direct rather than portfolio investment, since, over the years, not only have technological advances become the key determinant of most countries' economic progress, but also the gap in knowledge between both countries and firms within particular industries has widened. This has meant that the incentive for direct, *vis-à-vis* portfolio, investment has become increasingly pronounced.

The above hypothesis does not, however, explain why enterprises should exploit their economic and technological advantages of owning assets denominated in one currency rather than another. Why, for example, should direct investment be preferable to other means of international involvement, for example, exports? The traditional theory suggests that where the (additional) cost of producing a certain quantity of output for export to a particular country, plus distribution and marketing costs, is greater than the cost of producing this same product in the country concerned, it will pay the exporting company to set up local production facilities. This tendency will be accentuated whenever there are external economies, or spillover effects, of producing abroad, which accrue to the investing company. In recent years, too, it has become increasingly difficult for many business enterprises to maintain, let alone advance their export markets. This has been due, partly to the tariff policy or other forms of import control imposed by host governments (and/or regional customs unions), and partly the ease at which technology and managerial expertise can be obtained by means other than direct investment. This point has been elaborated upon in various studies and is most frequently cited by businessmen as one of the key determinants of overseas investment.

International direct investment is then only likely to occur where there is an imperfect market in the dissemination of knowledge and where it is not profitable to exploit the foreign markets in question by alternative means. It is also likely to be encouraged wherever there are differential advantages in holding particular currencies.

There is, however, a third type of opportunity cost of foreign investment which still needs to be considered, namely, the return which could have been made had the capital been utilized domestically. We have discussed this issue elsewhere in so far as British experience is concerned (Dunning, 1966). From the viewpoint of the individual enterprise, both foreign and domestic investment will be profitable as long as the expected income from each exceeds the borrowing costs involved. Assuming that there is complete mobility of capital, this implies that, in equilibrium, subject to a discount for risk – including the risk of exchange depreciation – the marginal return on foreign investment should be equal to that of home investment. Where, however, there are constraints on the outlets for investment within the investing country, businessmen may invest more overseas than they might otherwise do if such restrictions were removed. The ease of capital mobility and government policy are, perhaps, the two most important factors influencing the level and structure of domestic investment and, thus, indirectly the level and direction of investments overseas. Most certainly, there is powerful evidence to suggest that domestic economic conditions do influence the rate of investment abroad. In the mid-1950s, for example, the share of new manufacturing investment undertaken by US companies at home and abroad accounted for by the European subsidiaries of such companies was rapidly expanding, as profit rates and growth prospects in Europe were more favourable than those in the US. More recently, improved US domestic economic conditions and restrictive government measures towards foreign investment have caused a deflection of new investment from Europe to domestic outlets.

To conclude this short discussion of the determinants of foreign investment, mention should be made of the work now being undertaken on the relationship between international trade and international investment. One approach pioneered by Raymond Vernon and his colleagues at Harvard suggests that US direct investment in manufacturing industry is part and parcel of a cycle in the goods it trades, and a means of ensuring the US's competitive position in the products it innovates (see Reading 12). However, we observe that these theories are less explanations of why foreign direct investment takes place and more an attempt to explain the role of direct investment in the international operations of enterprises and the relationship between the various strands of these activities.

The subject of international investment today

The study of international investment today, then, embraces both international economics and the theory of the business enterprise. As part of the wider discipline of international business, it stands in the same relationship as the economics of the firm does to business administration. This explains why until recently much of the writing on the microeconomic issues of international investment has been the work of business economists or business administrators – notably Farmer and Richman (1966), Fayerweather (1960), Kolde (1968) and Martyn (1964). In the last few years, a more rigorous approach to the subject has emerged as a group of younger scholars has tried to extend the tools of investment appraisal and financial analysis to international business. Both groups of writers, however, have in general been more concerned with functional questions of finance, ownership, organization, performance, management and marketing, and less with the economics of overseas activities and the broader environmental issues. As Professor Kolde points out international direct investment is – at a micro level at least – a narrower concept than the study of the multinational coporation. The former is concerned essentially with the economics of operating overseas activities which involve the transfer of capital, but is only incidentally concerned with organizational or administrative aspects. By contrast, a study of the multinational corporation is multi-disciplined and is more interested in the factors, political, legal and sociological as well as economic, influencing the process of decision taking as such.

Nevertheless, it is the macroeconomic implications of international investment which are currently attracting most attention from economists and policy makers. This is sometimes classified as the environmental approach which is concerned with the costs and benefits of the operations of international companies on the national economies of which they are part – be they host or recipient countries. The macro theory of foreign direct investment has been explored by several economists, notably Frankel (1965),

Jasay (Reading 4), Kemp (1962), MacDougall (Reading 5), Pearce and Rowan (Reading 7), Pitchford (1969) and Simpson (1962) – both from the angle of the host and investing countries. A selection of these contributions is presented in Part Two of this volume. These essays are followed by two others which illustrate some of the work done on portfolio capital movements.

From a practical viewpoint, there have been a number of issues in recent years, which have focused attention on the macroeconomic significance of international direct investment. We give three illustrations. First, in the 1960s, both the United States and the United Kingdom have been concerned about their balance of payments position and, in particular, about the impact of capital exports on that position. Governments of both countries have adopted policies to reduce outward investment as a means of improving the balance of payments in the short run, much to the criticism of business enterprise, which has directed its arguments more to the long-term gains of such investment. Until recently, little substantive evidence was available to support either (or both) views, but in 1967 and 1968 two reports – one British and the other American – were published which systematically attempted to evaluate the balance of payments implications both of investing and not investing overseas (Hufbauer and Adler, 1968; Reddaway, Potter and Taylor, 1967–8). These studies have commanded widespread attention in both business and academic circles. Part Five of this volume summarizes the main issues involved.

Second, since investment, particularly innovatory investment, is a key component of economic development, the importation of such knowledge capital, via the medium of multinational corporations, is of considerable interest to host countries. Various studies have already shown that the contribution of foreign subsidiaries to the technological advancement of host countries can be, and often is, an important one, but that less desirable effects may also be generated. The role of the multinational company as a disseminator of knowledge is only now being seriously investigated by economists. One aspect commanding particular attention is the 'technological gap' between Europe and the US. This and the general role played by foreign direct investment in developing countries forms the basis of Part Six of this volume.

Third, there is the whole question of the impact of foreign investment on the sovereignty of the nation states in which its investments are made. This issue is becoming increasingly important with the growing contribution of multinational enterprises to the output of various economies, and the tendency of such enterprises to become geocentric and more closely integrated in their activities. Moreover, the economic power of such companies is sometimes sufficient to thwart or interfere with government policy in the host countries whenever the objectives of the multinational companies conflict with those of the host countries. The welfare implications of the multinational companies have recently been analysed by Professor Harry Johnson (Reading 18) and by Professor Jack Behrman (1971). The issue is not only that the forces controlling decisions taken by subsidiaries of an international enterprise (including government policies of the investing country) may not always coincide with the economic strategy of the host country, but also that the latter can be side-stepped. This might show itself in various ways, for example, the manipulation of intra-group prices, anti-trust legislation, intra-group capital transfers, policy towards remittance of profits, export sharing agreements, and so on.

There are other fascinating areas of research into the causes and effects of international direct investment also being pursued. These include its impact on the industrial structure and efficiency of the host nation, and two of the most interesting contributions in this area are presented in Part Four. Work is also proceeding on the effects of the multinational enterprise on industrial relations and collective bargaining, on management training and methods of marketing, on import substitution, on its regional development and economic integration, and on the economic welfare of both investing and recipient countries. Detailed attention is being directed to patterns of organization of multinational corporations and alternatives to direct investment as a means of transferring the benefits of such investment. Some of the contributions to these topics will be included in a complementary volume to this one on the multinational enterprise.

This is an exciting and rapidly growing field of study. Indeed, probably more than half the words written on the subject are less than five years old. At the present rate of output, there is little doubt that the same will be true five years hence.

References

AHARONI, Y. (1966), *The Foreign Investment Decision Process*, Harvard University Press.

BALASSA, B. (1967), 'Trade creation and trade diversion in the European Common Market', *Econ. J.*, vol. 77, pp. 1–21.

BANDERA, V. N., and WHITE, J. T. (1968), 'US direct investments and domestic markets in Europe', *Economia internazionale*, vol. 21, pp. 117–23.

BASI, R. S. (1966), *Determinants of US Direct Investment in Foreign Countries*, Kent State University Press.

BEHRMAN, J. N. (1962), 'Foreign associates and their financing', in R. Mikesell (ed.), *US Private and Government Investment Abroad*, Oregon University Press.

BEHRMAN, J. N. (1971), 'Governmental policy alternatives and the problem of international sharing', in J. H. Dunning (ed.), *The Multinational Enterprise*, Allen & Unwin, pp. 289–302.

D'ARGE, R. (1969), 'Notes on customs unions and direct foreign investment', *Econ. J.*, vol. 79, pp. 324–33.

DUNNING, J. H. (1966), 'Further thoughts on foreign investment', *Moorgate and Wall Street*, Autumn, pp. 5–37.

FARMER, R. N., and RICHMAN, B. M. (1966), *International Business: An Operational Theory*, Irwin.

FAYERWEATHER, J. (1960), *Management of International Operations*, McGraw-Hill.

FRANKEL, M. (1965), 'Home versus foreign investment: a case against capital exports', *Kyklos*, vol. 18, pp. 411–32.

HECKERMAN, D. G. (1969), 'The exchange risk of foreign operations', Graduate School of Business, Chicago, unpublished.

HIRSHLEIFER, J. (1964), 'Efficient allocation of capital in an uncertain world', *Amer. econ. Rev.*, vol. 54, pp. 77–85.

HUFBAUER, G. C., and ADLER, F. M. (1968), 'Overseas manufacturing investment and the US balance of payments', *US Treasury Tax Research Policy Document*, no. 1.

HYMER, S. H. (1960), 'The international operations of national firms: a study of direct investment', unpublished doctoral dissertation, MIT.

IVERSEN, C. (1936), *International Capital Movements*, Oxford University Press.

JORGENSON, D. W., and SIEBART, C. D. (1968), 'A comparison of alternative theories of corporate investment behavior', *Amer. econ. Rev.*, vol. 58, pp. 681–712.

KEMP, M. C. (1962), 'Foreign investment and the national advantage', *Econ. Rec.*, vol. 38, pp. 56–62.

KEYNES, J. M. (1924), 'Foreign investment and the national advantage', *The Nation and the Atheneum*, vol. 35, pp. 584–7.

KINDLEBERGER, C. P. (1969), *American Investment Abroad*, Yale University Press.
KOLDE, E. (1968), *International Business Enterprise*, Prentice-Hall.
LEWIS, C. (1938), *America's Stake in International Investment*, Brookings Institution, Washington.
MARTYN, H. (1964), *International Business: Principles and Problems*, Free Press.
MOOSE, J. S. (1968), 'A study of US direct investment overseas in manufacturing and petrol industries', unpublished doctoral dissertation, Harvard University.
NATIONAL INDUSTRIAL CONFERENCE BOARD (1961), *Costs and Competition: American Experience Abroad*, NICB, New York.
NURKSE, R. (1954), 'The problem of international investment today in the light of nineteenth-century experience', *Econ. J.*, vol. 64, pp. 744–58.
OHLIN, B. (1933), *Interregional and International Trade*, Harvard University Press, rev. edn 1967.
PITCHFORD, J. D. (1969), 'Foreign investment and the national advantage in a dynamic context', unpublished research paper, Canberra.
POPKIN, J. (1965), 'Interfirm differences in direct investment behavior of US manufacturers', unpublished doctoral dissertation, University of Pennsylvania.
REDDAWAY, W. B., POTTER, S. J., and TAYLOR, C. T. (1967–8),' The effects of UK direct investment overseas: final report', *University of Cambridge, Department of Applied Economics, Occasional Paper.*, no 15.
ROBINSON, H. J. (1961), *The Motivation and Flow of Private Foreign Investment*, Stanford Research Institute, California.
SCAPERLANDA, A. (1967), 'The EEC and US foreign investment: some empirical evidence', *Econ. J.*, vol. 77, pp. 22–6.
SEVERN, A. K. (1970), *Investment and Financial Behaviour of American Investors in Manufacturing*, National Bureau of Economic Research.
SIMPSON, P. B. (1962), 'Foreign investment and the national economic advantages: a theoretical analysis', in R. Mikesell (ed.), *US Private and Government Investment Abroad*, Oregon University Press.
STEVENS, G. V. G. (1969), 'Fixed investment expenditures of foreign manufacturing affiliates in US firms: theoretical models and empirical evidence', *Yale econ. Ess.*, vol. 9, pp. 137–200.
UNITED NATIONS (1949), *International Capital Movements in the Inter-War Period*, New York.

Part One
Historical Aspects

The first two Readings trace the growth of international capital movements from the beginning of the nineteenth century to the present day. They should be read in conjunction with Ragnar Nurkse's (1954) classic overview of the differences between the current environment for international investment and that of a century ago.

The reader is also referred to a list of other writings which appears as a reading list at the end of each of the essays. The most comprehensive account of UK capital exports up to 1875 is that contained in the 1938 revision of Jenks (1927). For the nineteenth century as a whole, the works of Cairncross (1953), Feis (1930), Hall (1968) and Hobson (1914) all include useful material. For statistical estimates of the value of British investment overseas, the writings of Imlah (1958) and Simon (1967) should be consulted. Lewis (1938), North (1960) and Simon (1960) each provide data of US capital imports. An analysis of the relationship between movements in capital and those in trade and labour is contained in Brinley Thomas (1954) and Williamson (1964).

The literature of the post-First World War period is no less extensive. Perhaps the best reviews of the inter-war years are those of the United Nations (1949) and the Royal Institute of International Affairs (1937). For the post-1945 period, Raymond Mikesell's (1962) book supplements the various United Nations reports, while various studies of foreign investment in particular countries present a large amount of helpful data. A good general volume on capital movements is that edited by J. H. Adler, on behalf of the International Economic Association and published in 1967.

References

Adler, J. H. (ed.) (1967), *Capital Movements and Economic Development*, Macmillan.

Cairncross, A. K. (1953), *Home and Foreign Investment, 1870–1913*, Cambridge University Press.

Dunning, J. H. (1970), 'British investment in the United States, 1860/1913', in *Studies in International Investment*, Allen & Unwin.

Feis, H. (1930), *Europe: The World's Banker, 1870–1914*, Yale University Press.

Hall, A. R., (1968), 'Capital imports and the composition of investment in a borrowing country', in *The Export of Capital from Britain, 1870–1914*, Methuen.

Hobson, C. K. (1914), *The Export of Capital*, Constable, reissued 1963.

Imlah, A. H. (1958), *Economic Elements in the Pax Britannica*, Harvard University Press.

Jenks, L. H. (1927), *The Migration of British Capital in 1875*, Cape, revised 1938.

Lewis, C. (1938), *America's Stake in International Investment*, Brookings Institution, Washington.

Mikesell, R. (1962), *US Private and Government Investment Abroad*, Oregon University Press.

North, D. C. (1960), 'The United States balance of payments, 1790–1860', in *Trends in the American Economy in the Nineteenth Century*, Princeton University Press.

Nurkse, R. (1954), 'The problems of international investment today in the light of nineteenth-century experience', *Econ. J.*, vol. 64, pp. 744–58.

Royal Institute of International Affairs (1937), *The Problem of International Investment*, Cass.

Simon, M. (1960), 'The United States balance of payments, 1861–1900', in *Trends in the American Economy in the Nineteenth Century*, Princeton University Press.

Simon, M. (1967), 'The pattern of new British portfolio investment, 1865/1914', in J. H. Adler (ed.), *Capital Movements and Economic Development*, Macmillan.

Thomas, B. (1954), *Migration and Economic Growth: A Study of Great Britain and the Atlantic Economy*, Cambridge University Press.

United Nations (1949), *International Capital Movements in the Inter-War Period*, New York.

Williamson, J. G. (1964), *American Growth and the Balance of Payments, 1820–1913*, University of North Carolina Press.

1 Brinley Thomas

The Historical Record of International Capital Movements to 1913

Brinley Thomas, 'The historical record of international capital movements to 1913', in J. H. Adler (ed.), *Capital Movements and Economic Development*, Macmillan, 1967, pp. 3–32.

Problems of measurement

United Kingdom

It is now half a century since the appearance of C. K. Hobson's (1914) pioneering study, *The Export of Capital*. Published in the year when the First World War broke out, the book did not attract the attention it deserved until well into the inter-war period. Hobson's was the first systematic attempt to produce annual estimates of British capital exports for the period 1870–1912. The fact that later research has thrown doubt on some of his figures does not detract from the magnitude of what he achieved. It is convenient to take this work as our starting-point in considering the quality of the sources and the extent to which the main problems of measurement have been overcome.

It is illuminating to compare Hobson's results for the period 1870–1912 with those presented by Imlah (1958, ch. 3) in his authoritative work published in 1958. According to Hobson, the aggregate of the annual net outflows of British capital for this period amounted to £2332·8 million, whereas Imlah estimated this aggregate as £3073·0 million. Cairncross (1953, pp. 170–86), paying special attention to shipping earnings and the yield of investments abroad, arrived at a total of £2220 million, even lower than Hobson's. This is a serious divergence, even though it does not materially affect the time-shape of the series. There can be no doubt that Hobson overestimated the size of Britain's creditor position in the 1870s by adopting A. L. Bowley's (1905, pp. 76–7) estimate of £1400 million as Britain's foreign investment in 1875, a figure which must be rejected as too high. A careful calculation by Giffen in 1878 showed that the income on British capital invested abroad was about £65·5 million in the fiscal year 1874–5. By capitalizing at appropriate rates, he estimated the value of the stock of investments at £1048·3 million. When this figure is adjusted to make it comparable with Imlah's estimates, it becomes £1038 million, which is very near to Imlah's figure of £1013·8 million for the end of 1874. A detailed examination of Hobson's estimates for the various components of the balance of payments indicates that he erred on the low side in regard to interest and dividends, earnings of shipping, and commissions, insurance and banking charges. The main reason was his failure to take into account the profits on foreign trade (Imlah, 1958, pp. 76–8).

A major item in the invisible balance was the net earnings from shipping, including the outlays of foreign and colonial ships in British ports; up to the 1870s it was bigger than income from foreign investments. Much depends on the margin of error in calculating this item. Fortunately this problem attracted the attention of Robert Giffen when he was head of the Statistical Department of the Board of Trade, and his pioneering study has had a profound effect on subsequent work in this field (Giffen, 1882). His method was based on samples of freight earnings and of outlays abroad from a number of shipping firms at selected years, e.g. 1880 and 1898. Hobson followed his example in some respects but added a great deal that was original, especially his 'increasing efficiency factor', which led him to allow 4 per cent per annum for increased earning capacity due to technical progress between 1870 and 1912. Imlah went over the ground thoroughly and produced annual estimates of net credits from shipping from 1816 to 1913. In doing so he admits that he had to resort to the dubious expedient of using an import price index which is of necessity '. . . only a crude measure of the ups and downs of freight rates' (Imlah, 1958, p. 53). Douglass North and Alan Heston (1960), in a penetrating review of the whole subject, have shown that many difficulties still remain unsolved. Given the primary data available, it is an open question whether a more accurate series can be attained.

As we go back through the nineteenth century from 1870 the difficulties of statistical estimation become more numerous. An outstanding work on British capital exports in that period is that of Leland H. Jenks (1927), whose profound researches threw a flood of light on the subject. Basing himself on the work of Giffen, Newmarch and others, Jenks constructed a table of Great Britain's international accounts for the period 1854–80 (Jenks, 1927, p. 414). The calculation indicated an aggregate net export of capital from 1854 to 1874 inclusive amounting to £332 million. Jenks paid particular attention to the problem of estimating the stock of British foreign investment at 1854 and came to the conclusion that Bowley's (1905, p. 76) estimate of £550 million was far too high; he substituted it for a total of £195 to £235 million of British holdings of foreign publicly issued securities. This was ditsributed as follows (Jenks, 1927, p. 413):

	£ million
United States	50–60
French, Belgian, Dutch and Russian government securities	45–55
Spain and Portugal	35–45
Latin America	35–40
French railways	25–30
Belgian railways	5
	195–230

This estimate is the best available for mid-century and it is reasonably consistent with the equally trustworthy one made by Giffen for the mid-1870s.

By his original research into the actual security issues Jenks drew a big question-mark over the ideas current about the extent of British capital exports in the first half of the nineteenth century. It was Imlah, through his notable work on Britain's trade statistics, who finally demonstrated how wildly inflated were the estimates of foreign lending in the decades after the Napoleonic wars. To quote his words:

For the first part of the century, the size of British credit balances and of the amount of capital export have generally been exaggerated, partly because of the assumption, which the 'official' valuations of merchandise trade seemed to confirm, that British factories produced huge export surpluses at this time. Even when the merchandise trade statistics had greatly improved, after 1853, the uncertainty concerning the 'invisibles' which offset the huge trade deficits left room for some very large errors. It is possible to be much more definite in these matters. By drawing on the findings and procedures of investigators who have worked on various facets of the problem by extending them over a longer period, and by filling in the remaining gaps on the basis of more or less guided assumptions and conjectures, one can construct annual balance of payments statements for the United Kingdom beginning with the year 1816 with some assurance that the main items are measured fairly closely and that other items are adequately allowed for. The balances so constructed measure the growing volume of foreign investment which, in turn, can be checked at certain points with the more credible results achieved by other investigators who have made different approaches to the problem (Imlah, 1958, pp. 42–3).

Economists and historians are deeply indebted to Imlah for providing this indispensable groundwork. Errors in some components are likely to be cancelled by compensating errors in others; and, even if there may be doubts about the figures for some individual years, there is every reason to rely on the long-term movement and the long cycles.

A final check on the validity of Imlah's methods may be made by referring to Sir George Paish's well-known estimates for the end of the period, i.e. 1907–13. According to Paish (1909), the amount of British capital placed abroad in publicly issued securities at the end of 1907 was £2693·7 million. In addition, it was calculated that private placings, e.g. investment in unincorporated businesses and deposits in foreign and colonial banks, came to about £500 million. Of the interest and dividends assessed to income tax in 1906–7 about 10 per cent was paid out to foreigners; accordingly Paish inferred that one-tenth of the publicly issued securities was foreign-owned. To establish Britain's net creditor position in 1907 it is necessary to subtract from the gross total of British foreign investment an amount to cover holdings of British assets by foreigners; there is reason to think that this deduction should be about 10 per cent. In this way the Paish estimates give the size of Britain's net creditor position at 1907 as £2874 million which is not very different from the accumulating balance of credit abroad of £2913·7 million arrived at by Imlah.

Paish's estimates for the end of 1913 brought out the striking fact that in six hectic years the aggregate of British holdings of publicly issued foreign securities had grown by over £1000 million to £3714·7 million (Paish, 1914). Even this figure, according to Herbert Feis, was an underestimate, in that too little had been allowed for Russian and Turkish loans; he raised Paish's estimate for investments in Russia from £66·7 million to £110·0 million and in Turkey from £18·7 million to £24·0 million (Feis, 1930, pp. 23–4). When Imlah, at the conclusion of his exhaustive statistical exercise, compared his estimate of Britain's net creditor position on the eve of the First World War with that of Paish, as amended by Feis, he had ample reason to be satisfied. The latter, based on a survey at a point of time, yielded a figure of £4014 million as against his own estimate of £3989·6 million, resulting from an assessment of the component series over time; the disparity was merely 0·6 per cent (Imlah, 1958, p. 80).[1]

The United States, Canada and Australia

The difficulties raised by the unknown degree of error in the merchandise trade figures and the main components of the invisible account in the nineteenth century are as serious, if not more so, in the United States as in the United Kingdom. The section on the international transactions of the United States for 1821–41 and 1850–1918 in the authoritative abstract of historical statistics (Bureau of the Census, 1949, pp. 242–3) issued by the Department of Commerce reproduces the well-known estimates of C. J. Bullock, J. H. Williams and R. S. Tucker published in 1919. The text contains a warning that '. . . the data for the period prior to 1914 are admittedly far less satisfactory than the data for the later period because, with the possible exception of merchandise trade, very few data are available for this early period to provide a basis for estimating international transactions' (Bureau of the Census, 1949, p. 237).

Fortunately the situation has changed in recent years as a result of new researches on original sources and the application of more refined methods. Thanks to the enterprise of Douglass North (1960) and Matthew Simon (1960), we now possess a detailed quantitative record of the balance of payments of the United States from 1790 to 1900. These two studies are the first systematic attempt to apply the residual method to American data; these new annual estimates are an indispensable counterpart to the corresponding estimates for the United Kingdom by Imlah.

1. For a re-examination of the original data in *The Investor's Monthly Manual*, see Segal and Simon (1961).

In introducing his results for the period 1790–1860, North is careful to emphasize the limitations of the data.

The relative neutrality of the errors and omissions requires both confidence in the accuracy of the trade and invisible items and an intimate knowledge of the period and of the country's international economic relations. Reliable contemporary direct estimates of the individual items and particularly of the total debt (or credit) position of the economy provide the best indication of the degree to which errors and omissions are counterbalancing. But anyone who has calculated historical balance of payments is aware of the way small changes in the interest charge or in the initial debt figure become large changes over time. Even when the data are very good, it would be ridiculous to assert that the absolute figures are always accurate (North, 1960, pp. 574–5).

According to North's calculations there were marked long cycles in the inflow of capital with peaks in 1816, 1836 and 1853 and these were accompanied by similar swings in immigration, building, land sales, and transport and incorporations. The cumulative balance of indebtedness rose from $86·7 million in 1820 to $379·2 million in 1860.

In his exhaustive analysis of the period 1861–1900, Matthew Simon found much to criticize in previous estimates. He indicates his own approach in the following words:

Since the international economic transactions of the United States during the late nineteenth century developed an extraordinary complexity, it is necessary to overcome the limitations of the fragmentary approaches to balance of payments estimation by employing an alternative method. Scientific procedure requires that each of the many components be properly identified and distinguished from other parts of the balance of payments. The best possible series must be constructed to mirror the impact of the secular, cyclical and extra-economic pressures operating on the magnitude of the particular economic variable over the forty-year span. This does not permit lumping two or more items together or into a 'miscellaneous category' or assuming that one or more items on the credit side can exactly offset specific items on the debit side for one or for forty years (Simon, 1960, p. 630).

He has shown that it is possible to construct series for nearly all the distinct items in the balance of payments on current account. Among the outstanding contributions to knowledge resulting from the work of North and Simon are the carefully calculated annual estimates of shipping earnings, and immigrants' funds, remittances and tourist expenditures. From what is established about the time-shape of Britain's capital outflow, it is not surprising, in view of the large proportion of it which went to the United States, to see the long swings firmly confirmed in Simon's figures, with peaks in 1872 and 1888. The net accumulating balance of indebtedness of the United States is estimated to have grown from $483·6 million in 1861 to $3338·0 million in 1896 and $2490·0 million in 1900.

The annual estimates of net international capital movements for the United States over the period 1820–1913 can be checked in various ways. The task has been well carried out by Jeffrey G. Williamson who found, over the long swing, '. . . general conformity in direction, timing and amplitude between available indirect and direct estimates of net capital movements, and general conformity among *all* independent estimates published in recent years' (Williamson, 1964, app. A, pp. 234–54). The conclusion is corroborated after a critical look at the merchandise trade and service balances and the net gold movements.

We must briefly refer to recent research on two other important capital-importing countries, Canada and Australia. Annual estimates of the Canadian balance of payments for 1868–99 have been produced by Penelope Hartland (1960); thus, with estimates previously available from 1900 onward, we now have an unbroken series covering almost a century. The gross inflow of capital accounted for 26 per cent of gross domestic investment in 1900–1905 and 38 per cent in 1906–10. For Australia in the period 1861–1900, N. G. Butlin has presented annual estimates of British investment as well as the net proceeds of government loan raisings overseas, by colony. Butlin's comprehensive researches (1962, pp. 405–44; 1964, pp. 334–51) have added greatly to our understanding of the relation between capital movements and Australian economic development.

The world investment picture in 1913

The great era of accumulation and international lending which ended in 1913[2] had created a world sharply divided into creditor and debtor nations, as shown in Table 1.

2. The analysis in this paper is restricted to long-term capital. No account is taken of short-term capital movements.

Britain's gross creditor position in 1913 amounted to $18 billion, or 41 per cent of the world total of $44 million. This mirrored the prominent part played by British long-term lending in the nineteenth century. At first glance it is remarkable that the five continental creditor nations, France, Germany, Belgium, the

Table 1 Main Creditor and Debtor Countries, 1913

	Gross credits			*Gross debts*	
	$000 million	*%*		*$000 million*	*%*
United Kingdom	18·0	40·9	Europe	12·0	27·3
France	9·0	20·4	Latin America	8·5	19·3
Germany	5·8	13·2	United States	6·8	15·5
Belgium, Netherlands and Switzerland	5·5	12·5	Canada	3·7	8·4
United States	3·5	8·0	Asia	6·0	13·6
Other countries	2·2	5·0	Africa	4·7	10·7
			Oceania	2·3	5·2
	44·0	100·0		44·0	100·0

Source: United Nations (1949).

Netherlands and Switzerland, had between them built up a creditor position of $20·3 billion, over $2 billion larger than that of Britain; even France by herself seemed to be half as important as Britain. This simple comparison, however, is misleading. There were profound differences between continental and British outflows of capital, in terms of quality, motivation and consequences. Private enterprise subject to the mildest of British government regulation was the mainspring in England, whereas in France and Germany foreign investment was an instrument for the attainment of national objectives.

French long-term foreign lending increased threefold between 1880 and 1914 when the aggregate reached 45 billion francs. The geographical distribution is set out in Table 2.

The political designs of the French government resulted in the equivalent of £500 million being invested in Russian bonds and the Russian Government was spending half the proceeds on armaments. Similar ill-fated loans were made to Turkey, Austria–

Hungary, the Balkan States and Latin America. The yield was lower than that on domestic securities and the borrowing countries did not increase their demand for French exports. Nearly all the loans were ultimately repudiated. It is estimated

Table 2 Geographical Distribution of French Foreign Long-Term Investment, 1900 and 1914

Country	*1900*	*1914*
Russia	7·0	11·3
Turkey (in Asia and Europe)	2·0	3·3
Spain and Portugal	4·5	3·9
Austria–Hungary	2·5	2·2
Balkan States	0·7	2·5
Italy	1·4	1·3
Switzerland, Belgium and Netherlands	1·0	1·5
Rest of Europe	0·8	1·5
Europe	19·9	27·5
French Colonies	1·5	4·0
Egypt, Suez and South Africa	3·0	3·3
United States and Canada	0·8	2·0
Latin America	2·0	6·0
Asia	0·8	2·2
Outside Europe	8·1	17·5
Grand total	28·0	45·0

Source: Feis (1930, p. 51).

that French investors lost no less than two-thirds of the capital placed in foreign bonds, an amount equal to six times the German indemnity of 1870.

Germany experienced rapid economic expansion in the period 1871–1913. The domestic rate of interest was higher than in Britain and France, and the government was determined that foreign investment should be subordinated to the needs of the German economy. The priorities to be observed were described by a contemporary writer as follows:

1. The issue of foreign securities in the domestic market, like the establishment of branches of domestic enterprises and participations abroad, is permissible only after the domestic demand for capital has been fully

satisfied, since the first duty of the banks is to use the available funds of the nation for increasing the national production and purchasing power and for strengthening the home market.

2. International commercial dealings as well as international flotations ought to be but the means for attaining national ends and must be placed in the service of national labor.

3. Even when the two foregoing conditions have been fulfilled, the greatest care will have to be used in selecting the securities to be floated (Reisser, quoted in Feis, 1930, p. 162).

In interpreting the national interest the German banks had an important influence on the volume of foreign investment and there is evidence that, particularly up to 1900, they were to a large extent engaged in 'borrowing short' in London and Paris and 'lending long' in foreign countries. Germany's foreign lending was much greater than the surplus in her trade and services account. On the eve of the First World War a little over half of the total of $5·8 billion of foreign investment was in Europe, partly inspired by the desire to increase the military effectiveness of her allies. The flow of capital to her colonies was very small; nearly a third of her total foreign assets was in North and South America (Feis, 1930).[3]

We may thus conclude that the state-controlled lending activities of France and Germany in the forty years before the First World War, although considerable in scale, had a negligible effect on the growth of the international economy. The dominant influence was the flow of long-term capital from Great Britain.

The distribution of Britain's oversea investments in publicly issued securities, by country and by category, is shown in Tables 3 and 4.

In the early phase Britain lent a great deal to governments; it is estimated that of the £1150 million of foreign assets in 1880 nearly a half (£500 million) was in foreign government loans and guarantees, and about a fifth (£240 million) in railways in Europe, the United States and South America. British entrepreneurs like Thomas Brassey had been responsible for a large-scale direct investment in railway-building on the continent of Europe. In

3. For an excellent summary of the influence of government policy on foreign lending in France and Germany up to 1914, see Feis (1930, pp. 118–88).

Table 3 British Oversea Investments in Publicly Issued Securities, December 1913, by Country

	£ million	*%*
Canada and Newfoundland	514·9	13·7
Australia and New Zealand	416·4	11·1
South Africa	370·2	9·8
West Africa	37·3	1·0
India and Ceylon	378·8	10·0
Straits Settlements	27·3	0·7
British North Borneo	5·8	0·2
Hong Kong	3·1	0·1
Other British Colonies	26·2	0·7
British Empire	1780·0	47·3
United States	754·6	20·0
Argentina	319·6	8·5
Brazil	148·0	3·9
Mexico	99·0	2·6
Chile	61·0	1·6
Uruguay	36·1	1·0
Peru	34·2	0·9
Cuba	33·2	0·9
Other Latin American States	25·5	0·7
Latin America	756·6	20·1
Russia	110·0	2·9
Spain	19·0	0·5
Italy	12·5	0·3
Portugal	8·1	0·2
France	8·0	0·2
Germany	6·4	0·2
Austria	8·0	0·2
Denmark	11·0	0·3
Balkan States	17·0	0·5
Rest of Europe	18·6	0·5
Europe	218·6	5·8
Egypt	44·9	1·2
Turkey	24·0	0·6
China	43·9	1·2
Japan	62·8	1·7
Other countries	77·9	2·1
All foreign countries	1983·3	52·7
Grand total	3763·3	100·0

Source: Feis (1930, p. 27). Investments in shipping are excluded.

Table 4 British Oversea Investments in Publicly Issued Securities, December 1913, by Category

	£ *million*	%
Dominion and colonial governments	675·5	17·9
Foreign governments	297·0	7·9
Overseas municipalities	152·5	4·1
Government and municipal	1125·0	29·9
Dominion and colonial railways	306·4	8·1
Indian railways	140·8	3·7
United States railways	616·6	16·4
Other foreign railways	467·2	12·4
Railways	1531·0	40·6
Electric light and power	27·3	0·7
Gas and waterworks	29·2	0·8
Canals and docks	7·1	0·2
Tramways	77·8	2·1
Telegraphs and telephones	43·7	1·2
Other public utilities	185·1	5·0
Coal, iron and steel	35·2	0·9
Breweries	18·0	0·5
Other commercial and industrial	155·3	41·0
Commerce and industry	208·5	5·5
Mines	272·8	7·2
Nitrates	11·7	0·3
Oil	40·6	1·1
Rubber	41·0	1·1
Tea and coffee	22·4	0·6
Raw materials	388·5	10·3
Banks	72·9	1·9
Financial, land and investment	244·2	6·5
Banks and finance	317·1	8·4
Miscellaneous	8·1	0·3
Total	3763·3	100·0

Source: Feis (1930, p. 27). Investments in shipping are excluded.

1913 the aggregate of investments in publicly issued securities amounting to £3763·3 million was distributed geographically as follows: 47 per cent in the British Empire, 20 per cent in the United States, 20 per cent in Latin America and 6 per cent in Europe. The large part played by investment in railways is clearly brought out in Table 4; it amounted to no less than £1531 million, or 40 per cent of the total. Government and municipal securities at £1125 million accounted for 30 per cent. Of the £1780 million invested in Empire countries, 47 per cent comprised holdings of government and municipal bonds, and 25 per cent were in railway securities. The net income from foreign investments had grown from £58 million in 1875 to £200 million in 1913.

The great era of British foreign lending had been unique. At the end of the period her capital exports were at the rate of 9 per cent of her national income. It had been largely portfolio rather than direct investment and mainly in securities yielding a fixed return; the plantation type of investment associated with colonies did not occupy a prominent place. Most of the capital went to developing countries of new settlement, particularly the overseas descendants of Western Europe – the United States, Canada, Australia and New Zealand – which are now in the world's top income bracket. Much of their infra-structure was built up on the savings of the British private investor. The leading creditor country had a high propensity to import; and the growth of the Atlantic economy was marked by alternating phases in which Britain was putting her money back into world circulation either through a wave of lending or an upsurge of imports. Under this regime it was possible for the effects of differential productivity increases to be transmitted internationally without serious disequilibrium.

The time-shape and capital movements

In the nineteenth century the international flow of capital fluctuated with a periodicity of about eighteen years from peak to peak. This long swing was quite clear in the series for 1870–1912 published by C. K. Hobson in 1914, but it was many years before its economic significance was appreciated. Recent work by Douglass North (1960) has filled in the gap for the United States in the first half of the century; it is now established beyond doubt that net capital inflow into the United States exhibits five prominent long swings between 1820 and 1913, with peaks in 1836, 1853, 1872, 1888 and 1910, and troughs in 1827, 1840, 1858, 1878 and 1900. The record can be summarized as follows:

Table 5 United States Net Capital Movements*

	Year	*$ million*
Trough	1827	−10·0
Peak	1836	+62·2
Trough	1840	−30·8
Peak	1853	+55·6
Trough	1858	−23·1
Peak	1872	+224·8
Trough	1878	−161·9
Peak	1888	+285·0
Trough	1900	−296·4
Peak	1910	+51·1

* For sources see Jeffrey G. Williamson (1964, pp. 255–7).

We shall follow the example of workers in this field by referring to this type of fluctuation as the Kuznets cycle, since it was Kuznets (1930) who first drew attention to its importance as a general feature of economic growth. In a recent work he has presented a comprehensive analysis of long swings in population growth, capital formation and national product in the United States since 1870 (Kuznets, 1961).

Any attempt to explain the ebb and flow of international factor movements must concentrate on the process of interaction within the Atlantic economy (Thomas, 1961). This can be shown by referring to Schumpeter's (1939) monumental analysis of the capitalist process in the nineteenth century. His method was to set up a model of economic growth in a closed system and then to seek verification in the economic time-series of each of his countries – England, the United States and Germany – taken separately. International factor movements were regarded as 'external' or exogenous influences, i.e. not inherent in the working of the economic organism itself. He argued cogently that, in the light of his statistical testing, the rhythm of economic evolution postulated in his model could be observed *simultaneously* in the history of the three countries. Unfortunately, there was one irritating exception and it could not be brushed aside as peripheral. Schumpeter conceded that 'England's economic history from 1897 to 1913 cannot, owing to the comparative weakness of the evolution (in our sense) of her domestic industries, be written in terms of our model – the only case of this kind within the epoch covered by our material' (Schumpeter, 1939, vol. 1, p. 435). One cannot help wondering why perifidious Albion failed to toe the line in this period. Was it the exception which proved the Schumpeterian rule? There is a significant clue in volume 2 of *Business Cycles* where the reader is reminded that 'the cyclical aspects of international relations . . . cannot receive due attention within this book' (Schumpeter, 1939, vol. 2, p. 666). Then comes this important admission:

> Of all the limitations imposed by the plan and purpose of this book, this is the most serious one. Not only do cycles in different countries systematically affect each other, so much so that the history of hardly any one of them can be written without reference to simultaneous cyclical phases in other countries, but cycles really are, especially as regards the great innovations which produced the Kondratieffs, international phenomena. That is to say, such a process as the railroadization or the electrification of the world transcends the boundaries of individual countries in such a way as to be more truly described as one worldwide process than as the sum of distinct national ones. Capitalism itself is, both in the economic and the sociological sense, essentially one process, with the whole earth as its stage (Schumpeter, 1939, vol. 2, p. 666).

This is a crucial point. If the phenomena under review were 'one worldwide process' and not 'the sum of distinct national ones', one would have thought that Schumpeter might at least have indicated that his mode of verification, based on the notion that the process *was* the sum of distinct national ones, was to be regarded as an interim judgement. Instead of that, he went on to say that

> . . . both reasons – interactions and supernational unity of fundamental processes – explain why in our historical survey the cycles in our three countries were found to be so much in step. The fact that they were is not more obvious than the mechanism that produced it and also – in principle, at least – the manner in which these relations affected the working of pre-war central banks and the pre-war gold standard (Schumpeter, 1939, vol. 2, p. 666).

Schumpeter was bent on having it both ways.

What happens when the basic postulates are changed? First, let us regard international factor movements as endogenous and the countries concerned as an entity, the Atlantic economy. Secondly, let us transfer attention from the Kitchin, Juglar and Kondratieff fluctuations to the Kuznets cycle. In other words, we conceive the evolution of capitalism (as Schumpeter said we ought to) as a process transcending national boundaries, and we drop his three-cycle scheme.[4] As soon as we regard the individual nations as regions comprising an aggregate and we ask what are the conditions under which the rate of growth of income in this aggregate can be maximized over time, there is no reason to expect each of the parts to pass through identical and simultaneous phases according to a theory of a closed system. Secular growth entails internal shifts within the aggregate via international factor movements; the expansion of the whole is likely to express itself through disharmonious rates of growth in the parts. It is now generally agreed that this is what happened in the Atlantic economy between the middle of the nineteenth century and the First World War. There were four major outflows of population and capital from Europe – 1845–54, 1863–72, 1881–90 and 1903–13, and there was an inverse relation between the long swings in capital formation in the United Kingdom and in countries of new settlement overseas. A wave of home construction in the United Kingdom drew the rural surplus into urban employment at home; a wave of foreign investment drew the rural surplus into urban employment abroad. International movements of labour and capital were a pivotal element in determining the time-shape of economic development in the sending and receiving countries. One may summarize the process as an inter-regional competition for factors of production within the Atlantic economy, with the Old World and the New World alternating in their intensive build-up of resources. This is the essential characteristic which distinguishes these long swings from short business cycles. Long swings are fluctuations in the rate at which resources are developed, whereas the short business cycles are fluctuations in short-term investment in producer durables and inventories. From this analysis it is clear that Schumpeter

4. This was the starting point of my *Migration and Economic Growth* (Thomas, 1954).

was not justified in claiming that 'interactions and supernational unity of fundamental processes' gave added support to his finding that the cycles of his three countries were in step. On the contrary, this particular approach uncovers the inverse long swings and leads to the conclusion that the United States economy had fluctuations of a greater amplitude than the United Kingdom because in the latter country movements in home investment were partly counterbalanced by opposite movements in foreign investment and this was not the case in the United States. There was a clear long swing in real income per head in Britain in the period 1870–1913, inverse to the more violent swing in real income per head in the United States (Thomas, 1954, p. 111).

Some of the important statistical findings relating to the mechanism of this inverse relation, mainly over the period 1870–1913, may be briefly noted. The main series are plotted in Figure 1.

United States

1. Population-sensitive capital formation (non-farm residential construction and durable capital expenditure by railroads) display long swings coincident with (or lagging slightly behind) those in population additions, immigration and internal migration (Kuznets, 1961, ch. 7).

2. Between 1817 and 1917 there were five long swings in net capital inflow and merchandise imports, with an average span of about eighteen years. Deflated imports tend to lag behind domestic activity and the rate of capital inflow tends to be synchronous with domestic activity at troughs and to lead by about a year at peaks (Williamson, 1964, pp. 75 and 96).

3. From 1870 to 1914 between 55 and 60 per cent of the net foreign investment in the United States was contributed by Britain (Williamson, 1964, p. 145).

4. The gross volume of population-sensitive capital formation was over 40 per cent of total capital formation in the 1870s, and even in the first decade of the twentieth century it was still 25 per cent of the total (Kuznets, 1961, ch. 7).

5. Long swings in population-sensitive capital formation were inverse to those in other capital formation (i.e. net changes in

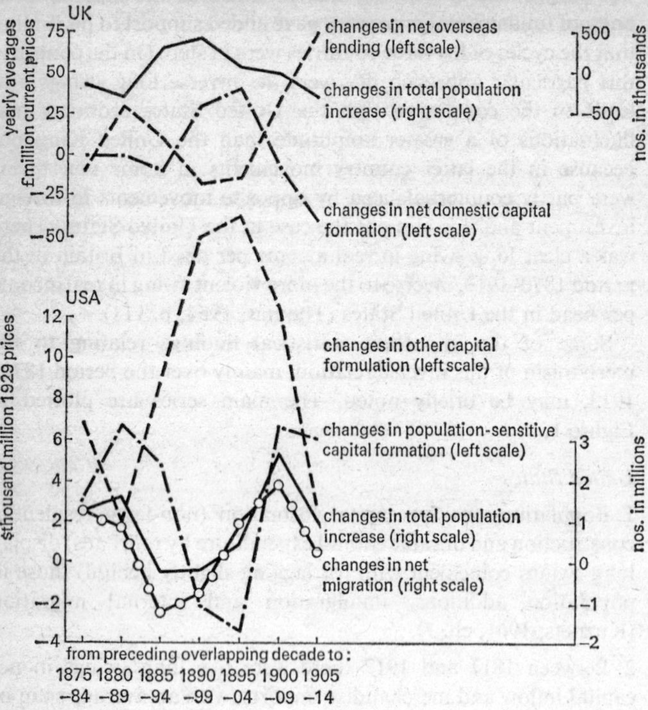

Figure 1

Definitions and sources: United Kingdom – net overseas lending, population increase and net domestic capital formation in current prices, in overlapping decades, 1870–79 to 1905–13 (Jeffreys and Walters, 1955).
United States – net additions to total population; net migration; gross population-sensitive capital formation (i.e. non-farm residential construction plus railroad capital expenditures); other capital formation (i.e. net changes in inventories, foreign claims and producer durable equipment) (all in overlapping decades, 1870–79 to 1905–13) (Kuznets, 1958)

inventories, foreign claims and producer durable equipment). This inverse relation ceases and becomes a positive association from the 1920s (Kuznets, 1961, ch. 7).

United Kingdom (Thomas, 1954; 1964)

1. From 1870 to 1913 there were long swings in additions to population inverse to those in the United States.

2. The long swings in British domestic capital formation were inverse to those of population-sensitive capital formation in the United States.

3. Long swings in British capital exports and in British and European oversea migration were coincident with the long swings in population-sensitive capital formation in the United States.

4. Long swings in British imports at constant prices were positively related to swings in British domestic capital formation and in American 'other capital formation', and negatively related to swings in American population-sensitive capital formation.

5. Swings in British internal migration were inverse to those in the United States.

A satisfactory interpretation of this complex set of interactions must await further research. We might suggest the following as the basis of a two-country model, A being capital-exporting and B capital-importing, and each divided into a domestic capital-formation and an export sector. The word 'period' refers to either the upward or downward phase of the Kuznets cycle.

1. A substantial part of domestic capital formation is population-sensitive, i.e. varies with the rate of population additions.

2. The rate of population additions is due mainly to the rate of change in net migration.

3. The expected growth of sales in the export sector in a given period depends on the marginal efficiency of investment in the domestic capital-formation sector of the other country in the same period.

4. There is an inter-temporal relation between the output capacity of the export sector in a period and the growth of investment

in the domestic capital-formation sector of that country in the previous period (Thomas, 1958a).[5]

A model based on these relationships can be tested in the light of the more abundant statistical data now available (see Abramovitz, 1964; Easterlin, 1964; Gottlieb, 1964; Simon, 1964). Deeper research may reveal that the operative variable was population growth.[6] The valuable work done by Jeffrey G. Williamson on American growth and the balance of payments in the nineteenth century shows how necessary it is to take fully into account the interaction between conditions in the United Kingdom and the United States. His analysis leads him to

> . . . underline the apparent importance of supply conditions in supporting and partially controlling the long swing in net capital imports into the United States. . . . Clearly, the severity of amplitude of these long swings in net capital inflow associated with the rate of transportation development in the United States is in part due to the inverse nature of British investment opportunity (Williamson, 1964, pp. 157–8).

A complete diagnosis must also take in the fluctuations in capital flows to other countries of new settlement such as Canada, Australia, New Zealand and Latin America.

Capital movements and the terms of trade

It is natural that the underdeveloped countries of today should be interested in the experience of their counterparts in the nineteenth century. The lessons drawn from that experience can have an important effect on the policies pursued by the governments of countries which have passed from colonial to independent status. One of the ideas which has been fairly widely accepted is that the underdeveloped countries of the second half of the nineteenth century had the worst of both worlds, as consumers of manufactured goods and as producers of food and raw materials. If this proposition is true, one can hardly blame the peoples of the

5. This relationship is well brought out by the behaviour of 'other capital formation' in the United States in Figure 1, since it contains a large component of foreign claims. See Thomas (1958a).

6. It has been shown that damped Kuznets cycles are generated by the Klein–Goldberger econometric model of the United States, with population growth as an exogenous variable. See I. Adelman (1963). Further testing is required with population growth as an endogenous variable.

poorer countries for wishing to make certain that a similar fate will not befall them in the second half of the twentieth century.

The doctrine is based on a theoretical analysis of the distribution of gains between investing and borrowing countries. It is clearly set out in a well-known article by H. W. Singer (1950). There are two main strands which I shall call the lop-sided multiplier effect and the lop-sided terms of trade effect. The former is put by Singer in the following words:

> Could it not be that in many cases the productive facilities for export from underdeveloped countries, which were so largely a result of foreign investment, never became a part of the internal economic structure of those underdeveloped countries themselves, except in the purely geographical or physical sense? Economically speaking, they were really an outpost of the economies of the more developed investing countries. The main secondary multiplier effects, which the textbooks tell us to expect from investment, took place not where the investment was physically or geographically located but (to the extent that the results of these investments returned directly home) they took place where the investment came from (Singer, 1950, p. 475).

The argument on the terms of trade rests on the high income and price elasticity of demand for manufactured goods and the low income and price elasticity of demand for primary products. It is asserted that, because the rise in productivity was taken out in increased factor incomes in the investing countries, the latter took the lion's share of the fruits of technical progress at the expense of the primary-producing countries.

When pressed for a definition of 'underdeveloped', Singer simply said that he had in mind 'countries which are poor for reasons other than war destruction'; he did not mean 'countries which are not at present industrialized'. 'An underdeveloped country', he added, 'is like a giraffe – difficult to describe, but you know one when you see one.'[7] I suggest that if Singer had been looking for giraffes round about 1860 he might well have picked on, say, Canada, Japan, Australia, Ireland and Denmark. He is being wise after the event when he assures us that he does

7. These quotations are from Dr Singer's reply to Dr A. N. McLeod (1951).

not consider Saskatchewan, Iowa, Denmark or New Zealand to be 'underdeveloped'. His whole thesis is about the era of large-scale private foreign lending and he himself argues that '. . . ever since the seventies the trend of prices has been heavily against sellers of food and raw materials and in favor of the sellers of manufactured articles' (Singer, 1950, p. 477). To establish his case he must include all countries which would have been regarded as underdeveloped about the middle of the nineteenth century.

Let us first take the underpopulated areas of new settlement, such as Canada, Australia and New Zealand. The rate of economic growth in these 'outposts' in the half-century before the First World War was much higher than in the creditor country. Real national product per head in Canada, for example, went up 24·7 per cent per decade as against 12·5 per cent in the United Kingdom (Kuznets, 1956, p. 13). It cannot be denied that the export of capital and labour from Britain to these countries had a cumulative effect on their productive capacity; they would never have grown as rapidly as they did if the secondary multiplier effects had been felt mainly in the investing country.

Careful work on the statistics of the terms of trade leaves room for serious doubt. Kindleberger concludes that

. . . there is no long-run tendency for the terms of trade to move against primary products in favour of manufactures. On the contrary, if allowance is made for the unprovable but generally accepted fact that the improvement in the quality of manufactures over the past eighty years has been greater than that of primary products, the terms of trade may have turned against manufactures and in favour of raw materials per unit of equal quality, however that may be defined (Kindleberger, 1956, p. 263).

Theodore W. Morgan also failed to find any conclusive evidence of a general worsening of the price position of primary producers; he was impressed by the wide variety of experience of different nations (Morgan, 1959). It is dangerous to generalize from what has happened to particular countries. For example,

. . . the rising terms of trade for agriculture in the Indian and New Zealand data, from the 1860s to the first decades of the twentieth century, suggest that falling world and local transport costs were then exerting a strong upward pull on farm prices in producing areas and a downward push on manufactured prices in distant consuming areas. Increasing industrialization could weaken this effect later (Morgan, 1959, p. 17).

The argument about factor incomes in relation to productivity in the investing country is not borne out by an analysis of the course of wage rates and export prices in the United Kingdom (Meier, 1952–3); there is no evidence that increases in the productivity of British industry were taken out to any marked extent in rising money wages (Phelps-Brown and Hopkins, 1950). The real issue is why some underdeveloped countries in the nineteenth century remained poor while others had a rapid increase in real product per head. Why did some of them plough back part of the yield of their export booms into an expansion of domestic manufacturing, while others did not? The average rate of increase per decade in real national product *per capita* in the forty or fifty years up to the First World War was 12·5 per cent in the United Kingdom compared with 17·9 per cent in Ireland, 19·3 per cent in Denmark, 24·7 per cent in Canada and 33·7 per cent in Japan (Kuznets, 1956, p. 13). Why then did the 'backward export economies' of South-East Asia, West Africa and Latin America fare so much worse? Was it because of an 'export bias' forced on them by the rich industrial countries? The real reasons are to be found not in the process of international investment or in international division of labour but in the internal economic and social structure of these countries, and the colonial powers were partly responsible for the maintenance of these conditions. Perhaps the chief impediment was the cheap labour policy based on the fact that labour was available to the capitalist sector in perfectly elastic supply. In these conditions the wage became frozen at the level needed for subsistence and the expansion of the capitalist sector raised the share of profits in the national income but not wages. The scarcity of entrepreneurs and skilled labour was often aggravated by non-competing groups and immigration. As Professor Myint has shown,

. . . in the latter half of the nineteenth century immigrant labour, particularly from India, may really be regarded as an international commodity having a uniform price rather than as a factor of production.

Wherever it was imported, it decisively pulled down wages and incomes in the 'semi-empty' countries to the very low level appropriate to the overpopulated countries instead of giving them a chance to rise a part of the way towards the high wage levels of the 'empty' continents of North America and Australia (Myint, 1954–5, p. 135).

There is plenty in this record to justify resentment on the part of the poorer countries, but the real culprit was not the system of international lending (Thomas, 1958b).

Let us now pass from the long-run trend to fluctuations in the terms of trade. Was there a causal relationship between these fluctuations and those of capital movements? Cairncross, in his analysis of British experience between 1870 and 1913, concluded that '. . . it was upon the terms of trade that the distribution of investment between home and foreign, as well as the course of real wages, ultimately depended' (Cairncross, 1953, p. 208). On this reasoning, when the terms of trade moved against Britain and in favour of the countries supplying her with imports, British capital was attracted to these countries; the downswing in capital exports would be brought about by a movement of the terms of trade against the oversea countries. In seeking to verify this thesis, Cairncross was troubled by the fact that the great upswing in foreign investment in the 1880s was accompanied by a movement of the terms of trade *in favour of* Britain, and he had to go to considerable pains to explain this away (Cairncross, 1953, pp. 192–5). Since the same phenomenon is to be observed during part of the other two upswings in foreign investment, 1863–72 and 1902–13, it is necessary to examine these phases more closely. There may be an alternative explanation which better fits the facts.

There are serious objections to using the net barter terms of trade as an indicator of the distribution of gain between trading countries. What is significant is not so much the ratio between the average price of exports and the average price of imports as the quantities – factor movements, volumes of exports and imports, and rates of productivity – lying behind the ratio. A glance at Figure 2 shows that the three major upsurges in foreign investment between 1860 and 1913 shared one common feature; in the second half of the boom when capital exports were at their heaviest and moving towards the peak, the terms of trade were

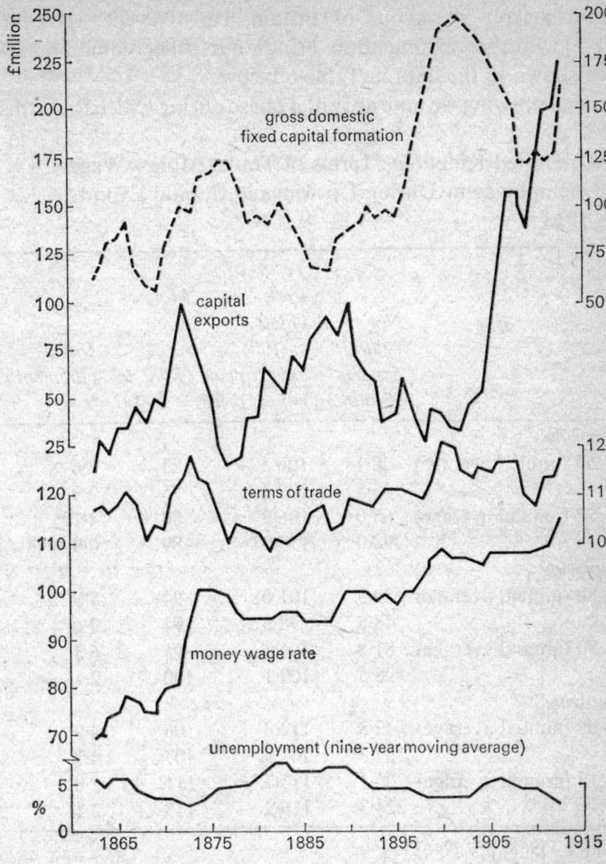

Figure 2

Definitions and sources: United Kingdom, 1862–1913, annual data. Balance on current account (Imlah, 1958, pp. 72–4). Net barter terms of trade (export price index divided by import price index) (Imlah, 1958, pp. 96–8).

Gross domestic fixed capital formation, in current prices (Feinstein, 1961, p. 374).

Money wage rate (1890–99 = 100) (Phelps-Brown with Hopkins, 1950, p. 276)

moving sharply in favour of Britain, i.e. 1868–72, 1883–90, 1910–13. Further examination brings out other common elements shown in the data in Table 6 below.

In each upswing we note an initial phase during which the terms

Table 6 United Kingdom: Terms of Trade, Money Wages and Unemployment During Upswings in Capital Exports, 1863–1913

	Net capital exports (£ million)*	*Terms of trade† (1880 = 100) export price / import price*	*Money wage rate‡ (1890–99 = 100)*	*Unemployment§ %*
1st upswing				
1863–65 (annual average)	28·1	106·3	73	3·6
1868	36·5	100·3	75	7·9
1869–72 (annual average)	65·0	106·9	80	4·1
1872	98·0	113·0	89	0·9
2nd upswing				
1878–80 (annual average)	29·3	101·0	94	7·9
1883	48·8	98·5	94	2·6
1884–90 (annual average)	81·8	104·1	95	6·3
1890	98·5	109·1	100	2·1
3rd upswing				
1902–04 (annual average)	43·3	112·8	106	4·9
1910	167·3	107·9	107	4·7
1911–13 (annual average)	206·1	113·7	111	2·8
1913	224·3	116·2	115	2·1

* Imlah (1958, pp. 72–5).
† Imlah (1958, pp. 96–8).
‡ Phelps-Brown and Hopkins (1950, p. 276).
§ Mitchell and Deane (1962, pp. 64–5).

of trade move against Britain and there is a moderate revival in capital exports; then the terms of trade turn in favour of Britain and it is in this second phase that the rate of capital outflow is greatest. It is significant that the absorption of capital by oversea countries was at its height during years when the terms of trade were moving against them. Those who believe that the terms of trade played a decisive causal role will find it hard to explain this phenomenon. Perhaps an explanation can be found if we look behind the ratio. Given the inverse relation between home and foreign investment, the beginning of an upswing in foreign lending and exports is accompanied by a fall in the level of activity in domestic capital formation. Thus, during the first phase of a lending-export boom there is a high elasticity of supply of factors for the export sector due to the downturn in the construction sector. Unused labour and existing equipment are being reabsorbed in the export sector; this entails a rise in productivity, and money wages and export prices are kept down. As the boom gathers momentum, a turning-point is reached; marginal costs rise sharply under the influence of bottlenecks at the higher level of employment in the export sector, while demand is running high in oversea construction activity; productivity has now ceased to rise and may be falling, hence a steep rise in export prices relative to import prices. Although the statistics at our disposal are inadequate for the measurement of productivity, the figures in Table 6 are a rough guide. In the 1863–72 upswing the first phase saw the terms of trade move against Britain (from 106·3 to 100·3), money wages rose only slightly and unemployment was heavy. Then in the second phase, 1868–72, the terms of trade moved sharply in Britain's favour (from 100·3 to 113·0), wages rose by nearly 20 per cent and unemployment fell to 0·9 per cent. A similar pattern is seen in the 1878–90 and 1902–13 upswings in capital exports. Between 1880 and 1887 British export prices fell by 30 per cent while money wages remained constant; this is a strong suggestion of rising productivity in the export sector which did not lead to higher money wages. Then between 1887 and 1890 export prices rose by about 18 per cent and money wages went up by 8 per cent; we may infer that in those years productivity declined. On this reading of the interaction between the terms of trade and the inverse swing in home and foreign investment, one is led to regard movements in the net barter terms of trade as a *consequence* of the fundamental forces at work rather than a causal factor determining the distribution of the flow of capital between home and foreign investment.

This is consistent with what was suggested in the previous section about the inverse relation between long swings in domestic capital formation in the lending and borrowing countries. In each country, the capacity of the export sector in the upswing phase is a function of the rate of home construction in that country in the previous phase. The export performance of the underdeveloped country in a given period is based upon the amount invested by the creditor country in its construction sector in the previous period; and the ability of the industrialized country to expand its own construction in a given period is promoted by the increased flow of food and raw materials from the underdeveloped country. Given these intertemporal relationships, there was a fundamental long-run community of interest between lender and borrower which should not be overlooked.

The Edwardian climax

As the financial centre of the world, London had acquired an unrivalled expertise. *The Economist* proudly declared on 20 February 1909 that '. . . we enjoy at present an undisputed right to place our money where we will, for Government makes no attempt to twist the stream into a given channel, and every borrower – native, colonial and foreign – has an equal opportunity of satisfying his needs in London'. The great upsurge in Britain's foreign lending in the years 1903–13, following the boom in home construction in the 1890s, was a continuation of the rhythm which had marked the country's growth over most of the nineteenth century. But this time there was a subtle difference. After the turn of the century there were ominous signs, though not yet perceived amid the pomp and glitter of the Edwardian age, that foreign investment was proving to be too much of a good thing.

Between 1907 and 1913 the outflow of British capital averaged £176 million a year as compared with average gross domestic fixed capital formation of £132 million a year. This was the climax of the age described by Keynes in 1919 as the 'economic Eldorado' in which the inhabitant of London

. . . could secure forthwith, if he wished it, cheap and comfortable means of transit to any country or climate without passport or other formality, could despatch his servant to the neighbouring office of a bank for such supply of the precious metals as might seem convenient, and could then proceed abroad to foreign quarters, without knowledge of their religion, language or customs, bearing coined wealth upon his person, and would consider himself greatly aggrieved and much surprised at the least interference. But, most important of all, he regarded this state of affairs as normal, certain and permanent, except in the direction of further improvement, and any deviation from it as aberrant, scandalous and avoidable (Keynes, 1920, pp. 9–10).

Some statesmen were dimly aware that there was a serpent in this paradise; Balfour and Joseph Chamberlain thought they recognized it in the shape of insular free trade. But there was no one who asked whether Britain, by investing so much abroad, was paying too high a price in terms of domestic productivity and employment.

The period 1897–1913 saw a wave of fundamental innovations in electricity, chemistry and the automobile industries. Countries such as the United States, Germany and Sweden took full advantage of this technological revolution; their domestic investment and the physical productivity of their industries rose rapidly between 1900 and 1913. One cannot escape the conclusion that the technical efficiency of the British economy lagged behind in this period. It would be wrong to try to demonstrate this by analysing the preponderance of foreign issues on the London market. At the turn of the century the typical domestic entrepreneur was still a private company or a family business which had hardly any access to the new issue market. Cairncross (1953, p. 145) has estimated that in 1907 the aggregate capital of manufacturing industry was about £1000 million and net industrial investment about £50 million. If two-thirds of the latter came from profits, and only one-tenth from new issues, the remaining quarter must have come from other sources of borrowed capital. The fact remains that adequate facilities for industries to avail themselves of the benefits of technical innovation were lacking. The domestic rate of interest rose from 2·76 in 1900 to 3·39 in 1913. There was a pronounced shift to profit and, unlike the 1880s, real wages were falling; and there was bitter industrial warfare. The pursuit of private investment profits overseas had become inconsistent with the long-run social productivity of the British economy in a changed environment. The technical performance of British industry and the welfare of the wage-earners would have been improved if foreign lending had been on a smaller scale, with the domestic rate of interest reduced to the level consistent with full employment of home resources.

References

ABRAMOVITZ, M. (1964), *Evidences of Long Swings in Aggregate Construction since the Civil War*, Columbia University Press for the National Bureau of Economic Research.

ADELMAN, I. (1963), 'Long cycles: a simulation experiment', *Proceedings of Conference on Simulation.*

BOWLEY, A. L. (1905), *England's Foreign Trade in the Nineteenth Century*, Sonnem Schein.

BULLOCK, C. J., WILLIAMS, J. H., and TUCKER, R. S. (1919), 'The balance of trade of the United States', *Rev. Econ. Stat.*, vol. 1, pp. 215–66.

BUREAU OF THE CENSUS (1949), *Historical Statistics of the United States, 1789–1945*, Department of Commerce, Washington.

BUTLIN, N. G. (1962), *Australian Domestic Product, Investment and Foreign Borrowing, 1861–1938/9*, Cambridge University Press.

BUTLIN, N. G. (1964), *Investment in Australian Economic Development, 1861–1900*, Cambridge University Press.

CAIRNCROSS, A. K. (1953), *Home and Foreign Investment, 1870–1913*, Cambridge University Press.

EASTERLIN, R. A. (1964), 'Long swings on US demographic and economic growth: some findings on the historical pattern', revised and shortened version of a report presented at the Meeting of the Population Association of America, San Francisco, June.

FEINSTEIN, C. H. (1961), 'Income and investment in the United Kingdom, 1856–1914', *Econ. J.*, vol. 71, pp. 367–85.

FEIS, H. (1930), *Europe: The World's Banker, 1870–1914*, Yale University Press.

GIFFEN, R. (1878), 'On recent accumulations of capital in the United Kingdom', *J. Roy. Stat. Soc.*, vol. 41, pp. 1–39.

GIFFEN, R. (1882), 'The use of import and export statistics', *J. Roy. Stat. Soc.*, vol. 45, pp. 206–23, 259–70.

GOTTLIEB, M. (1964), *Estimates of Residential Building, United States, 1840–1939*, National Bureau of Economic Research.

HARTLAND, P. (1960), 'Canadian balance of payments since 1868', in *Trends in the American Economy in the Nineteenth Century*, Princeton University Press, pp. 717–53.

HOBSON, C. K. (1914), *The Export of Capital*, Constable, reissued 1963.

IMLAH, A. H. (1958), *Economic Elements in the Pax Britannica*, Harvard University Press.

JEFFREYS, J. B., and WALTERS, D. (1955), 'National income and expenditure in the United Kingdom, 1870–1952', in *Income and Wealth*, series 5, Bowes and Bowes.

JENKS, L. H. (1927), *The Migration of British Capital in 1875*, Cape, revised 1938.

KEYNES, J. M. (1920), *The Economic Consequences of the Peace*, Macmillan.

KINDLEBERGER, C. P. (1956), *The Terms of Trade: A European Case Study*, Wiley.

KUZNETS, S. (1930), *Secular Movements in Production and Prices*, Houghton Mifflin.

KUZNETS, S. (1956), 'Quantitive aspects of the growth of nations: I. Levels and variability of rates of growth', *Econ. Devel. cult. Change*, vol. 5, pp. 5–99.

KUZNETS, S. (1958), 'Long swings in the growth of population and in related economic variables', *Proc. Amer. Phil. Soc.*, vol. 102, pp. 25–52.

KUZNETS, S. (1961), *Capital in the American Economy: Its Formation and Financing*, Princeton University Press for the National Bureau of Economic Research.

MCLEOD, A. N. (1951), 'Trade and investment in underdeveloped areas: a comment', *Amer. econ. Rev.*, vol. 41, pp. 411–19.

MEIER, G. M. (1952–3), 'Long-period determinants of Britain's terms of trade, 1880–1913', *Rev. econ. Stud.*, vol. 20, pp. 122–5.

MITCHELL, B. R., and DEANE, P. (1962), *Abstract of British Historical Statistics*, Cambridge University Press.

MORGAN, T. (1959), 'The long-run terms of trade between agriculture and manufacturing', *Econ. Devel. cult. Change*, vol. 8, pp. 1–23.

MYINT, H. (1954–5), 'The gains from international trade and the backward countries', *Rev. econ. Stud.*, vol. 22, pp. 129–42.

NORTH, D. C. (1960), 'The United States balance of payments, 1790–1860', in *Trends in the American Economy in the Nineteenth Century*, Princeton University Press.

NORTH, D. C., and HESTON, A. (1960), 'The estimation of shipping earnings in historical studies of the balance of payment', *Canad. J. Econ. polit. Sci.*, vol. 26, pp. 265–76.

PAISH, G. (1909), 'Great Britain's capital investment in other lands', *J. Roy. Stat. Soc.*, vol. 72, pp. 456–80, and discussion, pp. 481–95.

PAISH, G. (1914), *The Statist*, supplement, 14 February, pp. 5–6.

PHELPS-BROWN, E. H., and HOPKINS, S. V. (1950), 'The course of wage rates in five countries, 1860–1939', *Oxf. econ. Pap.*, vol. 2, pp. 226–96.

SCHUMPETER, J. (1939), *Business Cycles: A Theoretical, Historical and Statistical Analysis of the Capitalist Process*, McGraw-Hill, vols. 1 and 2.

SEGAL, H. H., and SIMON, M. (1961), 'British foreign capital issues, 1865–1894', *J. econ. Hist.*, vol. 21, pp. 566–81.

SIMON, M. (1960), 'The United States balance of payments, 1861–1900', in *Trends in the American Economy in the Nineteenth Century*, Princeton University Press.

SIMON, M. (1964), 'Some dimensions of the American commercial invasion of Europe, 1871–1914: an introductory essay', *J. econ. Hist.*, vol. 24, pp. 591–605.

Singer, H. W. (1950), 'The distribution of gains between investing and borrowing countries', *Amer. econ. Rev., Proc.*, vol. 40, pp. 473–85.

Thomas, B. (1954), *Migration and Economic Growth: A Study of Great Britain and the Atlantic Economy*, Cambridge University Press.

Thomas, B. (1958a), 'Migration and international investment', in *Economics of International Migration*, Macmillan.

Thomas, B. (1958b), 'The alleged exploitation of underdeveloped countries: a review of the evidence', *Proceedings of the 33rd Conference of the Western Economic Association.*

Thomas, B. (1961), 'The rhythm of growth in the Atlantic economy', in H. Hegland (ed.), *Money Growth and Methodology and Other Essays in Economics in Honour of John Aberman, March 31, 1961*, Gleerup, Lund, Sweden, pp. 39–48.

Thomas, B. (1964), 'Long swings in international migration and capital formation', *Bull. Int. Stat. Inst., Proc. 34th Sess.*, Toronto, vol. 40, pp. 398–412.

United Nations (1949), *International Capital Movements in the Inter-War Period*, New York.

Williamson, J. G. (1964), *American Growth and the Balance of Payments, 1820–1913*, University of North Carolina Press.

2 John H. Dunning

Capital Movements in the Twentieth Century

Excerpts from John H. Dunning, 'Capital movements in the twentieth century', *Lloyds Bank Review*, April, 1964. Revised version in J. H. Dunning, *Studies in International Investment*, Allen & Unwin, 1970, ch. 1.

The half-century prior to the First World War was a period uniquely favourable to the free movement of international capital. There were several reasons for this. In the first place, the world was sharply divided into capital-exporting and capital-importing countries whose needs and opportunities ideally complemented each other; a rapidly increasing demand for loanable funds by a group of nations at or around the 'take-off stage' in their development was matched by a no less remarkable expansion of savings available for foreign investment by the mature industrial nations. Second, during these years there were virtually no impediments to the international mobility of productive factors; indeed, both lending and borrowing countries actively encouraged the migration of capital and people between them. Third, due to the secure anchoring of the world's currencies to gold, there were few foreign exchange problems and no transfer difficulties; at the same time, the institutional machinery through which international investments were arranged was more highly developed and better equipped than its counterpart for financing domestic enterprise. Fourth, the movement of capital was paralleled, on the one hand, by a no less spectacular migration of population and, on the other, by a striking expansion of trade between debtor and creditor countries. While the former gave added stimulus to foreign investment, the latter helped to ensure the ready servicing of its debt. Lastly, these were years of unrivalled political stability, coupled with revolutionary developments in ocean-going transport. [. . .]

After the First World War

Even before 1914, certain changes were taking place in the character and industrial distribution of international capital movements. The war not only accelerated this process by dramatically altering the position of the leading participants, but heralded an era which eventually had a fundamental effect on the whole climate of international capital movements. In the twenties, however, there were few signs of the upheaval to come and, by 1929, the total international debt was of the same order as that in 1913. On the face of it, the main change which had occurred was the emergence of the US as the prime lender and the transformation of continental Europe from a substantial creditor into a substantial debtor. Even by 1919, the US had invested $6·5 billions abroad, excluding the large war loans to the Allies. In the following decade, her foreign investments rose by $8·3 billions – about two-thirds of the world total of new investment – raising America's total capital stake in 1930 to $15·7 billions. By contrast, most European countries were forced to relinquish large quantities of their foreign assets during the war; the UK gave up 15 per cent of hers, France over half of hers and Germany nearly the whole. Germany, in fact, was by far the largest borrower in the twenties and by the end of the decade owed $7·5 billions, mostly to the US. The UK recovered her international status in the late twenties and in 1930 her long-term investments were only fractionally less in value than those in 1913. France was then the third largest international creditor, with investments worth $2·5 billions, while the Netherlands, Switzerland, Belgium and Sweden were also net lenders.

The character of foreign investment of the 1920s differed from that of the earlier period in two other major respects. First, a somewhat larger share, about a quarter, took the form of direct investment, i.e. investment by companies in overseas subsidiaries and branches. But this was about equalled by the proportion of new capital going to finance relief, reconstruction and stabilization programmes in Europe. While the former, with the portfolio investment in primary-producing countries, was largely devoted to income-creating activities and thus helped service its own debt out of increased exports (or reduced imports), this was not the case with the European loans, which were often allocated to non-productive projects.

Investment of the latter kind was no less a feature of loans made to some South American States, for the US had neither the machinery nor the discriminating experience accumulated by the UK in this field, and there was a good deal of extravagant and imprudent lending (Mikesell, 1962). Moreover, the US proved an extremely poor market for some of the countries to which she lent capital, such as Germany, whose exports were competitive with, rather than complementary to, the American home economy. This, together with the collapse in raw material and foodstuff prices in the twenties, not only reduced the ability of borrowing countries to service their debts but seriously undermined the stability of the international capital market as a whole. A climate of investment so radically different from that of pre-war days, combined with substantial short-term capital movements, powerfully contributed to the world economic collapse of 1931 and its aftermath.[1]

The depression: a dividing line

With this collapse, the whole edifice of the international capital market tumbled and the depression which followed constituted a dividing line in the history of foreign investment. Not only were its immediate effects far more serious than anything which had occurred before – as shown by the wholesale defaults of debtor countries and sales of assets by creditor countries. The crisis itself was but a prelude to a series of events which were cumulatively disastrous for the international savings/investment process as it was then organized. The gold standard and free convertibility of currencies were replaced by exchange controls, and free trade gave way to import restrictions and bilateral trading. Trade in goods fell and the flow of foreign investment was virtually halted; when it was resumed after the Second World War its character was completely different.

As the US was the main supplier of non-resident capital in the 1920s, so it suffered most from the retrenchment which followed. In 1938 America's (gross) overseas investments were worth \$3·8 billions less than in 1930; nearly 90 per cent of this fall in value was due to the liquidation or depreciation of portfolio investments. Direct investments proved more resilient and indeed

1. For a comprehensive review of Britain's capital exports in the 1920s see Atkin (1968).

recovered slightly in the later thirties. The UK suffered to a lesser degree, due to the wider and better placing of her loans, but with other creditors she, too, was adversely affected by the declining fortunes of the primary countries as they sought to reduce the burden of their debts in various ways.

Unfortunately, such a loss of income only aggravated the position of the creditor countries and forced them to cut back imports from the debtor countries even more. The ultimate effect was to destroy the marketability of portfolio capital, as lenders became suspicious of the credit standing of borrowers who, in turn, were reluctant to borrow in case they could not service their debts. Indeed, the conditions for international investment in 1939, in a world riddled with tariffs, exchange controls and bilateral trading, were as different from those prevailing in 1914 as it is possible to imagine.

Nevertheless, an estimate of the international investment position in 1938 reveals that aggregate world indebtedness on long-term account at that date amounted to $55 billions. Though this estimate is not directly comparable with earlier ones, it is interesting to relate the position of the main creditor and debtor countries in that year with that in 1913. Table 1 shows the dominating role of the UK in both years, the growing significance of the US and the decline of France and Germany as leading creditor nations. Of the debtor countries (or areas), Canada, Asia and Oceania are seen to have increased their independence of foreign capital relative to Europe and Africa. Of the *net* creditors, the importance of the UK is even more marked, while Latin America, Asia and Canada are seen to be the major net importers of capital.

Changes during the last war

The war which followed had much the same effect on the foreign investments of the belligerents as did the First World War, save that losses suffered by the leading creditor nations (including the US) were much more devastating. Indeed, in 1945, neither of the two leading lenders of 1938 were net creditors. While there was a slight increase in the long-term assets of the US during the war years, this was more than offset by the increase in American short-term obligations, due both to the expenditure of her government and armed services abroad and to the accumulation of trade credits by foreigners.

The UK, from being a net creditor of $21·6 billions, emerged from the war owing about as much as she was owed, but within two years had become a net debtor to the tune of $2·6 billions.

Table 1 International Investment Position 1913 and 1938
(a) Leading Creditor Countries

	Gross credits				*Net credits*	
	1913 *$000 million*	*%*	*1938* *$000 million*	*%*	*1938* *$000 million*	*%*
United Kingdom	18·0	40·9	22·9	43·3	21·6	64·9
France	9·0	20·4	3·9	7·4	3·3	10·0
Germany	5·8	13·2	0·7	1·3	−2·0	−6·0
United States	3·5	8·0	11·5	21·8	4·5	13·5
Belgium, Netherlands and Switzerland	5·5	12·5	7·7	14·6	7·5	22·5
Other countries	2·2	5·0	6·1	11·6	−1·6	−4·8
	44·0	100·0	52·8*	100·0	33·3	100·0

(b) Leading Debtor Countries

	Gross debts				*Net debts*	
	1913 *$000 million*	*%*	*1938* *$000 million*	*%*	*1938* *$000 million*	*%*
Europe	12·0	27·3	10·3	18·8	—	—
Latin America	8·5	19·3	11·4	20·8	11·3	33·9
United States	6·8	15·5	7·0	12·8	—	—
Canada	3·7	8·4	6·6	12·0	4·7	14·1
Asia	6·0	13·6	11·2	20·4	9·3	27·9
Africa	4·7	10·7	4·0	7·3	3·9	11·7
Oceania	2·3	5·2	4·4	8·0	4·1	12·3
	44·0	100·0	54·9*	100·0	33·3	100·0

* The discrepancy between the total figures is due to certain inconsistencies in the data reported by investing and recipient countries.

Sources: Lewis (1948) and United Nations (1949).

This dramatic change in Britain's position was due to three main factors: (a) the sale of \$6·5 billions' worth of long-term investments, (b) an increase in long-term obligations (mostly to the US and Canada) of \$7·1 billions, and (c) an enormous increase in short-term liabilities (almost entirely sterling balances) of \$14·1 billions. On long-term account alone, the UK was a *gross* creditor of \$20·1 billions and a *net* creditor of \$10·8 billions (Lewis, 1948). The Netherlands, Belgium, Switzerland, Sweden and Portugal each retained their creditor status in spite of war losses.

On the other side of the balance sheet, there was a marked fall in the obligations of the debtor nations. The countries of the British Commonwealth reduced their debts by about \$12·5 billions, mainly the result of an accumulation of sterling balances arising out of Britain's large war-time expenditures. The Latin American countries similarly benefited from an increased demand for strategic and essential materials by the US. Since their imports rose much less quickly, these latter countries were able to reduce their total foreign indebtedness from \$11 billions to \$5 billions.

As a result of the war, then, aggregate *net* international obligations (long- and short-term) fell from \$25 billions to well under \$10 billions. The *gross* value of long-term investments declined rather less, from \$55 billions to between \$35 and \$40 billions.

Expansion since 1945

Since the war, a remarkable resurgence has taken place in international capital movements, the volume of which has risen much faster than that of world trade and industrial production during the last fifteen years. The most comprehensive source of material available is, perhaps, the various United Nations publications on international capital flows, from which the statistics contained in the next few paragraphs have been derived (United Nations, 1953, 1956, 1959, 1961, 1963, 1966).

In the period 1946 to 1950 the *net* flow of *private long-term capital* from the traditional *capital-exporting* countries averaged \$1·8 billions per annum (equal to one-half of the average for the 1920s). In the following decade it rose to \$2·9 billions per annum, reaching a peak of \$3·6 billions in 1958; since then it has fallen somewhat to less than $2 billion in the early 1960s. To these figures must be added the value of *official donations and long-term capital.* While no estimate of the total of these is available for the period 1946/50, in the following ten years such exports averaged $3·4 billions a year, and by 1961/4 were running at the rate of $5·8 billions per annum. This gives a total *net* international investment for the period 1951/60 of $63 billions, or $6·3 billions a year, and for 1961/4 of $31 billions or $7·7 billions a year (United Nations, 1966).

Table 2 Net Flow of Long-Term Capital and Official Donations from Capital-Exporting Countries 1946–64

	Private		*Official (donations and capital)*		*Private and official together*	
	Total $ million	*Per annum $ million*	*Total $ million*	*Per annum $ million*	*Total $ million*	*Per annum $ million*
1946–50	9145	1829	n.a.	n.a.	n.a.	n.a.
1951–5	9675	1935	12,970	2594	22,645	4529
1956–9	14,760	3690	16,416	4104	31,176	7794
1960–61	6213	3106	11,174	5582	17,377	8689
1961–4	5310	1770	17,427	5809	22,737	7579
1946–64	45,103	2374	n.a.	n.a.	n.a.	n.a.
1951–64	35,958	2568	57,977	4141	93,935	6710

As can be seen from Table 2, the trend of international capital movements moved steadily upwards until 1960, but after that fell back to its level in the mid 1950s. Nevertheless, in the two years 1963 and 1964, the average annual flow amounted to $7·6 billion, an amount considerably greater, in real terms, than the corresponding average in the 1920s.

The figures so far quoted refer to the value of *net* capital movements of the *capital-exporting* countries. But a better guide to the role of international investment in world economic development is, perhaps, provided by the value of *gross* capital flows for *all* countries. Unfortunately, data on such flows are available only for the period between 1958 and 1960, and for a group of selected developed countries (which, however, includes all but France and Switzerland among the important capital importers and exporters). Over the years in question, their *gross* outflow of capital averaged \$5·4 billions a year, compared with a *net* outflow of \$3·3 billions. At the same time, the 'gap' between *gross* and *net* capital outflows appears to be widening. This reflects the growing importance of capital transactions *between* the main capital exporters – a trend which we shall discuss in more detail later.

Adding the flow of official capital and donations to the *gross* export of private long-term capital, we obtain an aggregate long-term international investment of the order of \$12–\$13 billions per annum and increasing steadily each year. Finally, with the restoration of full or partial convertibility of many European currencies, the movement of short-term capital has also risen markedly in recent years. In 1960, it amounted to \$2·4 billions (gross) between the main developed countries.

Taking all these factors into account, there seems little doubt that the value of external capital movements each year is now running at three to four times that of fifteen years ago and in 1964 was about 10 per cent of the value of world trade. Private and official capital together (net) in 1964 was estimated at around 9·5 per cent of world trade.

No estimate of the current value of *total* international indebtedness is available. We do know, however, that the US and UK between them owned long-term foreign assets with a book value of \$125 billions at the end of 1966. Since these countries accounted for three-quarters of world investment, income receipts in 1964 (Committee on Invisible Exports, 1967) and in 1964/5 were responsible for four-fifths of all private capital exports (International Monetary Fund, 1968), it might reasonably be assumed that world international indebtedness was around \$160 billions in 1966 and is probably now (1969) close on the \$200 billion mark. Book values of US and UK assets 1965 were approximately \$130 billion (US \$100 billion and UK \$30 billion). This estimate excludes, of course, the official and private *donations* which between 1951 and 1965 alone totalled over \$40 millions (*net*). Moreover, it considerably underestimates the *market* value of the investments.

To appreciate further the reasons for the trends described above and their implications for world economic development, we shall discuss the main features of post-war international capital movements under four headings:

1. The changing media or forms of international lending, with particular reference to the growing significance of official donations and capital.

2. The growing multilateralism of foreign investment transactions, as shown by the trade in capital *between* developed industrial nations.

3. The emergence of the international business venture as the dominant form of private overseas investment and its expanding contribution to economic growth.

4. The attitudes adopted by lending and borrowing countries to foreign investment, viewed in the light of private and social costs and benefits of such investment.

The changing media of capital transactions

Like domestic investment, international capital transactions may involve three types of participants: lenders, financial intermediaries and borrowers. Any one, or all, of these may be (a) private individuals or business enterprises, or (b) public bodies. Up to 1914, both savers and intermediaries in the international capital market were almost entirely private persons or companies, while the borrowers were either public bodies or private corporations such as railways and public-utility undertakings.

In the 1920s, there were a number of bilateral government transactions – e.g. between the US and Germany – and in the following decade, the Export–Import Bank of Washington was formed to lend to both foreign governments and private enterprise. Only in the last two decades have public agencies, both national and international, become of dominating importance as lenders and intermediaries. Today, within a variety of lender/intermediary/borrower relationships, three broad groups may be distinguished, differing from each other in kind, purpose and effect. They are:

1. Private *direct* and *portfolio* investment, in which lender, intermediary and borrower are either business enterprises or individuals.

2. Bilateral inter-government loans and donations transacted directly between lending and borrowing countries.

3. Private and official loans channelled through international financial agencies.

In the period 1951/64, about 38 per cent of the *net* capital exports of the developed countries were private, about 51 per cent bilateral government transfers and about 11 per cent made through international financial agencies. In the last decade, the role of intergovernment loans has steadily increased relative to that of the other two sources. Of the private investment, at least four-fifths took the form of business capital for the establishment and operation of overseas enterprises and branch plants. Donations accounted for two-thirds and loans for one-third of the intergovernmental transfers. Just under two-fifths of official long-term capital and one-tenth of private capital was channelled through such bodies as the International Bank and its affiliates (the International Finance Corporation and International Development Association), the International Monetary Fund, the Export–Import Bank, the EEC Development Fund and the EEC Investment Bank. While virtually all these loans and intergovernment donations were absorbed by the underdeveloped areas, such areas attracted less than one-third of private capital in 1966.

Figures of *net* capital outflow, however, understate the role of private foreign investments, where offsetting movements of capital in opposite directions are greater than in the case of official capital. It is also worth noting that only about one-twentieth of international investment today is of the kind which predominated a half-century ago: namely, the purchase of foreign government, municipal or corporate securities by individual investors, usually through the medium of the stock market or specialist issuing houses. Security investment has been replaced as the main type of lending by entrepreneurial capital exports and official loans, either direct or through international agencies. Both, and particularly the former, are, in general, more income-stimulating than their nineteenth-century counterpart, in that they usually comprise a 'package' deal of finance, entrepreneurship, management and technical knowledge – four of the essential ingredients of economic growth.

These changes in investment media reflect, partly the structural developments which have taken place in both capital-exporting and importing countries, and, partly, the growing recognition by governments of the wealthier nations of their responsibilities towards the less developed nations.

The growth of direct investment essentially represents the *horizontal* or *vertical* extension of business enterprise across national boundaries, motivated by purely commercial considerations. Such capital exports (including reinvested profits) are directed mainly towards industrially advanced countries or (like their nineteenth century equivalent) to countries rich in natural resources. Public or official investment is influenced by different reasons. Initially, such institutions as the Export–Import Bank were intended to fill part of the vacuum left by the break-up of the international capital market in the thirties. In 1944, the World Bank (IBRD) was established as part of the Bretton Woods agreement to help the reconstruction of war-ravaged countries and to promote long-term development. In the last few years, attention has been directed mainly to this latter end, particularly in respect of the underdeveloped nations whose capital needs have been growing all the time.

With the private capital market in both Europe and the US largely closed to such countries, and with international business finding more profitable outlets elsewhere, it is only loans and grants from governments and the growth of multinational financial intermediaries that have made such development possible. Capital exports of this kind have been directed largely to 'basic development' or infrastructure projects which often have no inherent earning capacity, but which are an essential prerequisite to private investment. Official grants and loans are thus not only helping to finance projects which the private international capital market is unable or unwilling to finance; they also act as a catalyst for entrepreneurial investment by providing the necessary basic services and economic framework for growth.

International agencies

International and regional financial agencies have mushroomed in recent years: there are now, at least, a dozen of these, either publicly or privately sponsored, of which the World Bank (IBRD) is by far the largest. It is financed both from private and public sources and makes untied loans on the guarantee of the borrowing state, to both governments and private enterprise. Two-thirds of its 552 disbursements, which up to June 1968 had totalled $11·2 billions, have so far been in the field of communications, power and agriculture.

The International Finance Corporation (IFC) is a complementary body, set up in 1956 to help finance industrial and commercial ventures in developing areas. The unique feature of this intermediary is that it provides equity capital rather than fixed-interest loans and participates only in projects for which private enterprise subscribes at least one-half of the capital. In the last twelve years, the IFC has made commitments of $272 millions in thirty-nine countries. A third World Bank affiliate – the International Development Association (IDA) – was established in 1960, to meet the needs of a growing number of developing countries whose balance of payments position made it difficult for them to service conventional loans. The IDA issues long-term credits at very low or zero rates of interest; amortization begins after a ten-year period of grace and all loans are repayable in local currencies. It has so far made 127 commitments with a combined value of $1·8 billions.

Supplementing these international intermediaries is the United Nations Special Fund – formed in 1959 to provide technical assistance and funds for basic development projects such as roads, harbours, schools and hospitals in the underdeveloped areas – and several regional agencies such as the Inter-American Development Bank, which provides socio-economic development funds for Latin American states, and the European Development Fund (which makes grants to the associated states overseas of the EEC). Finally, in recognition of the need for a more systematic coordination of aid efforts, several consultative bodies have been established, the best known of which is perhaps the Development Assistance Committee set up in 1960 to represent member countries of OECD.

The changing pattern of capital exporters and importers

The lenders

For most of the post-war period, the US and UK have supplied between them 80 to 90 per cent of the world's international capital. More recently, other nations have become sizeable foreign investors.

Table 3 indicates the average annual net flow of long-term capital and official donations from the main capital-exporting countries between 1951 and 1964. For the period as a whole, the US supplied 68 per cent of all net exports and the UK 10 per cent, but their shares of the total have been falling: for the US from 78 per cent in the first five years (1951/5) to 59 per cent in 1962/4; for the UK, from 10 per cent to about 8 per cent. Indeed, in 1960/61 France and Germany replaced the UK as the second and third largest net overseas investors. However, most of the new strength of these countries appears to have been in the field of official capital exports: in 1961, for example, both imported more *private* capital than they exported. Here the US is by far the most important creditor; between 1964 and 1966 it accounted for 92·0 per cent of the net private foreign investment of creditor countries. The only other net exporters were the UK (6·0 per cent of the total), Switzerland[2] and Japan (2·0 per cent) (International Monetary Fund, 1968).

Again, it is important to note that these figures refer to *net* capital exports. But one of the features of the last decade has been the increasing number of countries which have emerged as *both* exporters and importers of capital, i.e. where the traffic investment is essentially 'two-way' in character. In 1966, for example, there were at least nine countries which exported (gross) \$100 millions or more of private capital.[3]

Two examples of this 'two-way' traffic in capital are set out in Table 4. At the end of 1966, the US owned long-term private foreign assets worth over \$75 billions; but, at the same time, foreigners owned similar assets in the US worth \$27 billions. The Bank of England has estimated that the value of direct and portfolio assets held overseas came to close on £10 billions in

2. Excluded from total.

3. US, UK, Germany, Netherlands, Canada, Italy, France, Switzerland and Japan.

Table 3 Developed Countries: Average Net Exports of Long-Term Capital and Official Donations (millions of dollars per annum)

	US	*UK*	*Belgium Luxemburg*	*France*	*West Germany*	*Japan*	*Netherlands*	*Switzerland*	*Total*
Private									
1951/5	1280	477	70	−59	30	−18	−38	160	1902
1956/9	2924	595	113	−277	74	−8	−47	243	3617
1960/61	2958	70	−17	−15	−167	59	−14	182	3056
1962/4	878	182	46	289	129	95	42	81 *	1742
1951/61	2183	446	70	−130	10	—	−37	194	2736
1951/64	1903	389	65	−40	36	20	−20	170	2523
Official									
1951/5	2244	−6	−38	171	68	22	45	23	2529
1956/9	2326	375	36	520	708	115	78	33	4191
1960/61	2974	468	47	1043	839	62	98	68	5599
1962/4	3302	415	88	900	395	154	70	3	5327
1951/61	2406	228	4	456	441	63	67	35	3700
1951/64	2598	268	22	551	431	83	68	28	4049
Total									
1951/5	3524	471	32	112	98	4	7	183	4431
1956/9	5250	970	149	243	782	107	31	276	7808
1960/61	5932	538	30	1028	672	121	84	250	8655
1962/4	4180	597	134	1189	524	249	112	84	7069
1951/61	4589	674	74	326	451	63	30	229	6436
1951/64	4501	657	87	511	467	103	48	198	6572

* 1962–3 average only.

Table 4 International Investment Position of the UK and US, 1962 and 1966

	Assets						Liabilities					
	1962		*1966*		*1962–6*		*1962*		*1966*		*1962–6*	
	UK	*US*	*UK*	*US*	*UK*	*US*	*UK*	*US*	*UK*	*US*	*UK*	*US*
	$ million	*$ million*	*$ million*	*$ million*	*percentage increase*		*$ million*	*$ million*	*$ million*	*$ million*	*percentage increase*	
Private investments												
Short term*	(2479)	7293	(5057)	10,670	103·9	46·3	2833	13,344	5164	20,796	89·1	55·8
Long term:												
Direct	(4855)	37,226	(6400)	54,562	31·8	46·6	(2170)	7612	(3185)	9054	46·3	18·9
Portfolio	(3000)	15,506	(3200)	21,003	6·7	35·5	(1050)	12,604	(1025)	17,946	−2·4	42·4
Total long term	(7855)	52,732	(9600)	75,565	22·2	43·3	(3220)	20,216	(4210)	27,000	30·7	33·6
Total private	(10,334)	60,025	(14,657)	86,235	41·8	43·7	(6053)	33,560	(9374)	47,796	57·5	42·4
Official investments												
Short term†	2056	20,333	2158	17,692	5·0	−29·9	3044	12,720	4485	12,593	47·3	−0·1
Long term	709	16,042	983	21,182	38·6	32·0	(2650)		(2536)		−4·3	
Total official	2765	36,375	3141	38,874	13·6	6·9	(5694)	12,720	(7021)	12,593	23·3	−0·1
All investments	(13,099)	96,400	(17,798)	125,109	35·9	29·8	(11·747)	46,280	(16,395)	60,389	40·8	30·5

* Banking and other external claims in domestic and foreign currencies and trade credits.

† Gold and convertible currency reserves; monetary authorities' holdings of convertible currencies; short-term claims and IMF gold tranche position.

N.B. Figures in brackets are precarious estimates and/or known to be incomplete.

Source: Bank of England and US Department of Commerce.

1966; comparable investments by foreigners in the UK in that year amounted to just over £4·2 billions.

Likewise with other countries. Between 1962 and 1966, the estimated gross outflow of direct investment from Germany was $1134 millions and the gross inflow $2825 millions. Italy was similarly placed, with an outflow of $794 millions and an inflow of $1800 millions. By contrast, the Netherlands invested $652 millions abroad and received $393 millions from foreigners: the corresponding figures for Japan were $438 millions and $356 millions (International Monetary Fund, 1968). The proportion of capital transactions *between* developed countries is increasing. In 1965, excluding oil investments, some two-thirds of the direct foreign assets of the main capital-exporting countries were located in the developed countries. This proportion has slightly risen during the 1960s.

Apart from the liberalization of capital movements and the widening territorial horizons of many enterprises, the main reason for this trend seems to lie in the heterogeneity of the 'package deal' so often involved in international business investment. Capital exports are no longer homogeneous or near-homogeneous, as in the last century; more often than not they are accompanied by specialized knowledge and techniques which, like the exports of goods, reflect the particular economic structure of the investing country. Just as it pays a country to specialize in the production of goods with the lowest comparative costs and exchange these for others which it is less suited to supply, so, similarly, it often pays to trade factors of production. Indeed, it is only by an unrestricted flow of capital and knowledge across national boundaries that the world's resources can be most effectively utilized.

Thus it is quite consistent that the UK should wish to invest in oil wells in the Middle East, while welcoming US capital and expertise in its own motor-vehicles and pharmaceutical industries; that the Canadians should encourage British capital to exploit their iron-ore mining and wood-pulp industries, while they themselves set up foreign subsidiaries to manufacture agricultural machinery in France and Germany; that Latin American republics should seek long-term capital from the US and Europe, while exporting large sums of flight capital to North

America. Although the *net* flow of long-term funds from the main capital-exporting countries is now substantial in absolute terms, it amounted to a little less than 1 per cent of their combined gross domestic product and to just under 6 per cent of their combined gross domestic savings in 1960/64.

The borrowers

The capital-importing countries may be classified into four main groups:

1. Advanced industrial countries, such as the US and most of Western Europe, which offer large and developed markets and good opportunities both for business and portfolio capital. Such countries attract the great proportion of entrepreneurial investment in manufacturing industry, and a large proportion of portfolio investment. They are mainly *net exporters of capital* and currently receive very little aid from foreign governments or international agencies.

2. Rapidly expanding countries rich in natural resources, with a high income per head and a substantial industrial sector. Australia, New Zealand, Italy and Canada fall within this category, each of which is a *net importer of capital* and attracts business investment in both manufacturing and in resource exploitation. Such countries also receive a limited amount of portfolio investment and official capital and donations.

3. Low-income countries, well endowed with a specialized range of raw materials such as oil and non-ferrous metals, which attract direct investment by the large international business in resource exploitation, and also some official capital and donations for basic development projects. Venezuela, Brazil, Argentina, Mexico and the Middle East oil states come within this group.

4. Low-income countries, in general unattractive to entrepreneurial investment as they have neither large domestic markets nor important natural resources to offer. These include densely populated and underdeveloped areas such as India, and it is here that aid from official sources is most concentrated.

Groups 1 and 2 may be broadly defined as the *developed countries* and groups 3 and 4 as the *less developed* countries.

So far as the *gross* outflow of private capital from the developed countries is concerned, between 1958 and 1960 group 1 countries received 40 per cent, group 2 countries 36 per cent, and groups 3 and 4 24 per cent between them. For direct investment alone, as has already been pointed out, the developed countries absorbed a considerably larger share.

As regards official donations and loans, the situation is quite different. Of the total donations of nearly $18 billions made between 1951 and 1959, five-sixths went to the less developed countries as did more than two-thirds of the official loans and the net disbursements of the World Bank and IFC. As far as all net capital exports are concerned, the proportion absorbed by the less developed areas, either directly or through financial intermediaries, has increased from 68 per cent in 1951/5 to 70 per cent in 1956/9 and 77 per cent in 1960/61. Put another way, the net flow of funds from capital-exporting countries to the less developed countries more than trebled over this period, whereas the flow to other regions (and to international agencies) rose by a little over 150 per cent.

Looking at the matter from the recipient countries' viewpoint, the developed capital-importing countries received all their capital from private sources in the last decade; in fact, they were net exporters of official capital while being net importers of private capital. For the less developed countries the relative significance of private and official capital largely depends on their stage of development and income levels. In 1959/64, those countries with a *per capita* national income of $350 or more in 1962 received equal proportions of their foreign capital from private and official sources; those with a *per capita* national income of $150 or less received 91 per cent of their receipts from official loans and donations (United Nations, 1966).

Capital flows to less developed countries

Indeed, over the years, the poorer developing countries have come to rely upon official aid even more, while those slightly better off have been financed increasingly by private capital. Thus Latin America, with only one-sixth of the population of all less developed countries, received half of the *private* long-term capital in 1961/4, the same proportion as ten years earlier. Africa and South East Asia, in contrast, with two-thirds of the population, received only 26 per cent and 6 per cent respectively. Of the total capital imports absorbed in 1965 by the less developed countries, 49 per cent originated from the US, 25 per cent from Western Europe, 6 per cent from international institutions and 3 per cent from the Sino-Soviet bloc.

While the impact of foreign investment on the level of individual incomes in less developed countries is, as yet, insignificant – most of the countries in question have not reached the take-off stage in their development and their populations are increasing rapidly – the contribution of non-resident capital to economic resources has steadily increased over recent years. The inflow of long-term capital and donations has risen three times as fast as the export earnings of the recipient countries, with the result that such capital contributed one-sixth of the total foreign exchange receipts of the less developed countries in the early 1960s.

When related to *size of population*, the average flow of capital into less developed countries in the period 1959/64 was \$3·3 per head; in South America it was as high as \$3·9; in South East Asia – the most densely populated area of all – \$2·8. Expressed as a proportion of *gross domestic product* the contribution of foreign capital averaged nearly 3·3 per cent, although there were very wide variations between countries; from over 23 per cent in Puerto Rico to ½ per cent in Morocco. As a percentage of *gross domestic capital formation* the differences were even more noticeable. The average was 21 per cent over the period 1958/64, but the foreign contribution was well above this figure in some cases (e.g. South East Asia 60 per cent, and Latin America 7·9 per cent). Of particular significance is the fact that whereas the proportion of *domestic* savings to gross domestic product has fallen for most less developed countries since 1950, that of *foreign* savings has generally risen. Indeed, it is mainly due to the enlarged flow of foreign capital that these countries have been able to raise or maintain their total supply of savings for economic development.

No less significant, and, in some cases, more easily discernible in its impact on income and growth, has been the contribution of foreign capital to the economies of some of the developed countries. It has been estimated that for the period 1949/64 the inflow of overseas capital to Australia (nine-tenths of which was direct investment) contributed about a tenth of total savings (Commonwealth of Australia, 1965). In Canada, *net* capital imports financed 15 per cent of total imports between 1955 and 1960 – a higher proportion than at any time since before 1930. Foreign-owned enterprises in Norway account for 32 per cent of the net income of all corporations (Stonehill, 1965). In the UK, foreign firms accounted for a quarter of all British exports in 1966 and, on present trends, will be responsible for about the same proportion of UK manufacturing output by 1980. Over these same years, the accumulated US capital stake, as a proportion of Europe's gross national product, rose from 1·2 per cent to 3 per cent. Whatever measure is used, there is no doubt that the contribution of foreign capital in the economic growth of many developed economies has risen markedly in the last decade. We now turn to consider reasons for this.

The role of international business investment

We have seen that, in recent years, over a third of the *net* outflow of capital from capital-exporting countries has comprised private long-term capital investment; when calculated in terms of *gross* capital exports, the proportion rises to about three-fifths. At least three-quarters of *net* private exports, and more than four-fifths of *gross* private exports, took the form of entrepreneurial or business investment. Like donations and loans from the public sector, this has risen markedly in the last decade. Partly, at least, this reflects the built-in growth component of reinvested profits. The value of US (direct) business assets abroad in 1965 amounted to $45 billions, compared with under $12 billions in 1950; those of British overseas companies (excluding oil and insurance) increased by 42 per cent between 1960 and 1965.

The multinational company is a new force in the world economy. It has been estimated that the total foreign sales of such enterprises (both exports and local output) in 1966 were second in value only to the gross national product of the United States and the USSR, and that, if present trends continue, at least one-third of the output of the free world will be supplied by subsidiaries and associates of non-resident companies by the mid 1970s.

The great majority of multinational enterprises are American or British in origin. In 1966, some 56 per cent of the total foreign capital stake of such businesses and 52 per cent of their foreign income was accounted for by American corporations; the respective figures for British companies were 19 per cent and 18 per cent. In the last five years, other countries, notably Japan and Germany, have become quite important overseas investors. Of the 200 largest corporations in 1967, other than those incorporated in the US forty-three were Japanese. Most of these engage in international operations.

The majority of international investments are still owned by a comparatively few firms. Probably three-quarters of the total stake of $85 billion is owned by the leading 500 companies and as much as half by the largest 100. Some of these enterprises derive more of their income from foreign than domestic operations. Of the 109 manufacturing and mining companies with world-wide sales of $1000 million or more in 1966, fifty-five had at least one-quarter of either their assets or sales[4] outside their country of origin (*Management Today*, 1968). Some twenty-three of these companies were European and, in a number of cases, the significance of their foreign operations is overwhelming.[5]

The extent to which European companies have been, for many years now, dependent on external markets for their growth and prosperity is not always appreciated as it might be. Too often, one is too dazzled by the magnitude of US interests abroad to appreciate that the foreign business operations of other countries are, relatively speaking, even more important to their economies. Table 5 ranks countries according to the income earned from direct overseas investment, expressed as a proportion of their gross national product. This shows that, in 1966, apart from the UK and the US, the five countries which were most dependent on their foreign business ventures were all quite small European

4. Including direct exports.

5. Nestlés, for example, sells less than 3 per cent of its total output in Switzerland and the sales of Philips Eindhoven outside Holland are ten times greater than those within (Sampson, 1968).

economies. In most cases, these interests date back well beyond those of American companies, whose major contribution has been only since 1950 or thereabouts. They reflect one thing: the recognition that, due to the limitations of domestic markets, the

Table 5 Income Earned on Foreign Direct Investment as a Percentage of Gross National Product, 1966 (Selected Countries)

	%
Switzerland	2·54
Netherlands	1·55
United Kingdom	1·10
Belgium	0·81
United States	0·76
South Africa	0·58
Norway	0·24
Canada	0·23
Sweden	0·22
Australia	0·19
Italy	0·16
France	0·15
Denmark	0·10
Austria	0·08

Source: IMF Balance of Payments Year Book and *UN Statistical Year Book.*

best way to create companies of any size is to engage in international operations, either by export or the establishment of foreign producing facilities (Economists Advisory Group, 1969).

Why firms invest abroad

The forces making for direct investment abroad are many and varied. Basically, the investing firm is interested in the contribution which such a capital outlay will make to the prosperity of the *whole organization.* In general, it would seem reasonable to assume that the firm will invest abroad as long as the marginal rate of return is greater than could be earned elsewhere (allowing for any differences in risk). It is, however, increasingly unusual for this to be the case, as there are so many ways in which the establishment of a foreign enterprise can and does affect the profitability of the investing company. Exports may be increased or raw materials procured more easily and cheaply; there may be a valuable feedback of technical knowledge; markets may be preserved against competitors, and so on.

The fact that the international business venture has become such a potent force in recent years may be due as much to the growing importance of these factors, as to the profits earned on the capital invested. Thus, in 1965, about two-fifths of the total US capital invested abroad was concentrated in resource industries – e.g. petroleum and mineral extraction – compared with a third before the war. No less than one-quarter of American imports are currently derived from US productive facilities overseas (30 per cent in the case of imports from Canada and Latin America). As the US exhausts more of her indigenous raw materials, the urgency of the need to develop new supplies abroad increases (Lary, 1968). This form of 'international backward integration' also explains many Western European investments in the Middle and Far East and is the modern counterpart of the 'colonial-type' investments of the nineteenth century.

A no less important reason for the migration of business operations abroad has been the desire to expand horizontally or laterally, either to overcome import restrictions of one kind or another or to open up new markets. Not only may it be cheaper for a firm to manufacture in a foreign country than to export to it; fear of competition has also been a powerful inducement. In 1965, manufacturing investments (including petroleum refining) accounted for 39 per cent of all US investments abroad (in advanced industrial nations 48 per cent). Sometimes such investments will lead to an increase in the exports of the investing company and/or country (a quarter of American exports of machinery are currently bought by US subsidiaries abroad); sometimes they lead to a decrease.

Empirical evidence on this subject is mostly impressionistic. According to one survey, over four-fifths of US firms with manufacturing subsidiaries in Canada claimed that their exports had been either raised or unaffected as a result of local production. There is reasonable, though by no means conclusive, evidence that US direct investment abroad has stimulated rather than curtailed exports of US goods and services. Whatever the truth, the desire to penetrate new markets or to protect existing ones is one of the most commonly stated factors influencing foreign investment. Opportunities for this latter type of overseas investment have been very favourable in recent years – particularly in the case of the US, where between 1950 and 1965 the rate of return earned on manufacturing capital at home and the rate of growth in manufacturing output was generally well below that in most other developed industrial countries.

This prospect of higher profits and market growth has also prompted British investment overseas, and latterly German and French as well. Looking at the geographical *distribution* of UK direct overseas investment since the war, we see that between 1952 and 1956 Canada was the main attraction. Then, when the Canadian boom burst, attention was switched to Australia, and since the formation of the EEC the continent of Europe has been the most favoured. Most of this investment has been undertaken for both defensive and aggressive reasons. Unlike US overseas investment, however, it has rarely been productive of higher returns, e.g. for the period 1960/64 the net profits to net assets ratio of UK firms in the major industrial areas worked out at 8·0 per cent, compared with 7·2 per cent at home. Nevertheless, it has often led to very valuable indirect benefits, such as a feedback of technical knowledge (particularly so in the case of US and German investments), and to increased exports.

The increasingly significant role of the multinational enterprise is strikingly illustrated by the fact that, between 1946 and 1967, the investments of US companies in foreign subsidiaries and affiliates increased at twice the rate of the domestic assets of US corporations.[6] The income of UK companies abroad as a proportion of income earned at home rose from under a third in 1950 to over two-fifths in 1966. To the extent that direct investment finances its own growth out of re-invested profits, and the more advanced less developed countries develop their own economies and markets with the aid of official capital, private investment will gradually assume the predominant role, as it is doing in many South American states.

6. In 1966, these same foreign companies produced abroad goods worth four times the value of US exports and earned an income equal to 19·6 per cent of these same exports – compared with 17·2 per cent in 1960.

Modern economic conditions favour the growth of the multinational company, and today most European companies of any size have to look beyond their national boundaries for growth. This has been accelerated by changing international demand and supply conditions. On the demand side, as incomes have expanded and communications have improved, international tastes have become more and more standardized. On the supply side, developments in capital intensive technology and the increasing cost of research and development programmes have reinforced the need for companies to seek new markets to spread costs economically. In part, these needs have been met by exports, but, increasingly, conditions have favoured the replacement of these by the establishment of local producing facilities. Besides transport costs, these include tariff barriers and the formation of regional economic blocs, the importance of adapting to local markets, after-sales servicing and so on. There has been a growing impetus of companies to invest abroad and this has been enhanced by the concentrated structure of competition which exists between international firms. At a national level, no country can afford to adopt an entirely isolationist policy. Small countries invest abroad to secure the markets to enable them to compete with large countries. Large innovating countries, e.g. US, invest to protect existing markets and as a way of promoting new outlets (Economists Advisory Group, 1969).

As might be expected, the *form* of entrepreneurial investment varies according to the local situation and policy of the parent company. In some cases complete ownership is considered desirable; in others, joint participation with local firms. In almost every instance, however, technical and managerial expertise is exported with capital, and disseminated into the economy of the host country. The influence of the international corporation as a pioneer of new products, new techniques and new skills is now spreading across national boundaries with a vengeance. Sometimes knowledge is transmitted by licensing arrangements, which usually involve no financial investment but, where management is important, an equity control is often required. Local manufacturing is preferred to exports, partly on the basis of costs, partly on the basis of offering servicing facilities and adaptations to local market needs.

Attitude of lending countries

In recent years, the international flow of capital has been restricted by both lending and borrowing countries. Up to 1960, the US actively encouraged overseas investment, but since that date, balance of payments difficulties have forced a reappraisal of the effects of such investment and there has been some pressure to reduce the outflow of capital. For similar reasons, the UK has controlled overseas investments for most of the post-war period, although the scope and intensity of control have varied with the balance of payments position.

In addition, there are other longer term considerations which have led some countries to question the desirability of foreign investment. It has been argued, for example, that even if the private rate of return on overseas investment is higher than that at home, the loss of tax revenue, the possible deterioration of the terms of trade, the retardation of growth at home due to a deflection of capital overseas – these and other drawbacks may outweigh any benefits in the form of higher profits and external economies arising from investment.

To what extent this is true it is difficult to say, although recent empirical studies on the costs and benefits of foreign investment would seem to suggest there has been little or no misallocation of resources – except perhaps when viewed from the short-term external position. (Hufbauer and Adler, 1968; Reddaway, Potter and Taylor, 1967–8). Nevertheless, both the US and most European countries have treated foreign investment – particularly security investment – as somewhat of a luxury in the post-war period, the quantity allowed having varied very closely with the balance of payments and the likely effects of such investment on the investing country's economic growth and stability (Kindleberger, 1969).

Views of borrowing countries

Borrowing countries have also regarded the inflow of foreign capital with mixed feelings. Increasing attention is now being given to analysing the repercussions of such investment and, through a variety of policy measures, to align its magnitude and composition to national resource allocation and growth. In the past, the most substantial benefit of foreign investment has been its stimulus to economic development. Direct investment is particularly welcomed as it brings to the recipient country all the elements necessary to create new production units: improved technology, new products and marketing methods, patents and trade-mark rights, managerial expertise and entrepreneurial initiative. By example, and contact with other firms, these benefits percolate to the rest of the economy.

Capital also brings with it access to research activities of the parent company: some years ago, it was estimated that more than a quarter of US research and development was made available to the UK economy through the media of American subsidiaries (Dunning, 1958). Clearly, the impact of such investment will depend on the *direction* of investment and its industrial spread; usually, however, the package-deal type of investment is attracted to growth industries. There are other benefits to the host country, such as the additional supply of capital provided and the taxation levied on the income it creates.

Set against the benefits are the costs of foreign investment – particularly direct investment. These fall broadly into two groups: (a) the servicing of the debt and (b) the fear that national economic, strategic or cultural objectives may in some way be interfered with or thwarted. The latter applies particularly where foreign enterprise controls keys sectors of an economy (Kindleberger, 1969). As with the investing country, the balance of advantage will depend on many factors, such as the type and ownership of capital invested, its character and its industrial distribution. Thus, investment by foreign firms in the exploitation of natural resources for export to the investing country may prove less beneficial to the host country than would investment, if forthcoming, in public works or manufacturing industry. Since, too, the indirect benefits of entrepreneurial investment tend to lessen with the passing of time, while the cost of its servicing tends to increase, a minimum foreign equity stake consistent with the acquisition of these benefits may be thought preferable to a 100 per cent control. In certain circumstances, also, foreign investment may adversely affect domestic savings and cause a deterioration in the host country's terms of trade.

To maximize the benefits and minimize the costs of foreign investment, it may well be that the host country will consider it desirable to integrate and regulate the capital flow not only into a particular project but in the light of its expected contribution to the national development programme as a whole (Meier, 1963). This may require a discriminatory policy designed to attract capital into particular sectors of the economy where it will have the maximum catalytic effect of mobilizing national resources, while restricting the inflow elsewhere, e.g. into luxury industries. To minimize and stabilize the cost of foreign borrowing, while obtaining the maximum technological advantages, thus implies the drawing of distinctions between various types and forms of foreign capital.

Extent of foreign control

More recently, other causes for concern have been voiced and have led to a more cautious attitude being adopted to foreign investment. This is shown particularly among the advanced industrial nations, where a growing proportion of domestic capital is owned by foreigners, and such capital is concentrated in a number of key growth sectors. In Canada, in 1965, non-resident investors owned over half the capital in manufacturing industry and nearly two-thirds of the capital in all industry. In Australia, about one-quarter of all company assets are currently owned by foreign firms, who occupy an important role in thirteen of the twenty-five industrial groups listed as 'large and highly concentrated'. In the UK, where profits of overseas companies account for 12 per cent of all company profits, nine-tenths of the investment is concentrated in the fast expanding trades of motor-cars, oil refining and petro-chemicals, industrial instruments, office machinery, pharmaceuticals, rubber tyres and electrical equipment. In France, the fastest growing industries (telecommunications, petroleum, chemicals and vehicles) are also dominated by foreign firms.

Foreign investment in manufacturing industry is usually directed either to the mass production of consumer goods or to producer goods trades which are highly capitalized and/or usually dependent on research and development for their prosperity. These latter industries are also those which are vital in the implementation of government planning. Hence, the fears which are currently being voiced by many advanced countries that investment planning at a national level is in danger of being jeopardized by industries under foreign control which will not be so amenable to planning and control. Not only this, it is argued that such industries may well operate to the detriment of the economy: that decisions taken by foreign firms may not be in the best interests of the host country.

Several examples of this might be cited. The Canadians for several years have been concerned that the purchasing policy of US parent companies has meant that Canadian subsidiaries have had to buy their parts and components from the US rather than in Canada. Often too, the parent companies control the allocation of markets of their subsidiaries and, in some cases, by refusing to grant export franchises, deprive them of opportunities of seeking new outlets. Indigenous research may be stifled where foreign capital monopolizes the research-based industries. Little effort is made to develop local technical and scientific talent when easy access to the parent company's research facilities is available.[7]

These arguments and others have also been put forward by the less-developed countries, although the policies adopted have usually been more specific than in the advanced countries (Vernon, 1968). Various devices have been adopted to channel investment in the 'right' direction. The Philippines control the remittances of foreign companies according to their 'social productivity' rating; Indonesia levies a special tax on the transfer of dividends; Burma prohibits capital repatriation altogether. In some countries, such as India, efforts are made to limit the foreign participation in domestic businesses to not more than 50 per cent of the equity capital, while others insist that overseas-controlled enterprises employ a certain minimum proportion of local workers (Wells, 1962). Such restrictions as these are understandable and, up to a point, reasonable. But, all too often, the price of political expediency is carelessly paid – and the cost in terms of economic progress is unnecessarily high (Stikker, 1968).

7. In fact, this latter assertion is not true by any means; several US subsidiaries in this country operate sizeable research units.

Conclusion

From what has been written in this chapter, it is clear that the world is entering a new era of international capital movements. These movements are of two distinct, yet complementary, types. First, there is the export of official capital and donations, either transacted directly between countries or through the medium of international lending agencies. Such capital is mainly used to finance the infra-structure of developing economies, preparatory to private investment. Because of this, the capital is absorbed very largely by the underdeveloped areas, and though there are signs that its significance is growing, it still has a long way to go to fulfil the tasks required of it.

The other main kind of capital outflow is entrepreneurial investment. This takes a variety of forms[8] and is motivated primarily by the prospect of private gain. It is in this field, in particular, that both capital-importing and capital-exporting countries are attempting to evaluate the costs and benefits. It is becoming increasingly recognized that the package-deal type of direct investment is not the only (nor always the most desirable) form of business capital import. It is, as has been said, a short cut to development, in that the ingredients for production are 'pre-fabricated'; but it can also be very expensive.[9]

In the nineteenth century, portfolio investment and export of labour and knowledge proceeded concurrently but independently of each other. It is possible that, quite apart from the introduction of new kinds of licensing or technical assistance agreements (Behrman, 1962), something in between direct and security assistance agreements could evolve in the future. Thus, a country may find it cheaper to borrow capital from one source and obtain managerial and technical skill from another. Indeed, as an alternative to direct investment the Economic Commission for Latin America has suggested that new industries in less developed countries should be financed by official loans or grants and that

8. These are very succinctly outlined by Vernon (1968). For an evaluation of joint ventures by potential investors, see National Industrial Conference Board (1966).

9. For example, the average rate of return on direct investment in South America in fields other than public institutions averages 20 per cent. Since the cost of local capital is only 7 per cent, Latin America is in effect paying 13 per cent for knowledge and entrepreneurial services.

their organization, management and operation be contracted out to foreign firms for the first few years. Under this arrangement, the developing country would borrow its capital at a fixed rate of interest and receive the benefits of foreign technical and managerial skills for a once-and-for-all payment. Other possibilities being explored include the formation of a consortia of business investors, in which foreign private capital is associated with local private capital or public official capital; the co-production agreement, under which an entity is owned and managed by a public authority in the host country but receives technical assistance from foreign enterprises (Benoit, 1967), and joint ventures between a foreign company and the government of the developing country (or a development corporation set up by it) in which the former invests up to 49 per cent of the capital for a pre-arranged period, after which time its interests are bought out by the host government (Singer, 1950; Streeten, 1967). Some examples of the kinds of arrangements so far negotiated between non-resident enterprises and governments of less developed countries in resource industries are given in Mikesell (1967).

These are undoubtedly years of experiment in finding new combinations of the international savings/investment process and new means of transmitting skills and knowledge across national boundaries (Gabriel, 1967; Rosenstein-Rodan, 1967). Whatever the *form* of investment, one feels that some selective control of foreign investment will continue to be necessary, both by investing and recipient countries. For the recipient country, this may require a discriminatory tax structure and other devices to promote investment considered most in keeping with national objectives. As far as the investing country is concerned, more research is necessary into the cost/benefit balance of foreign investment – both inwards and outwards. From a private investor's viewpoint, the improvement of investment guarantees and insurance facilities, more fiscal incentives (Lent, 1967; OECD, 1965), and the removal of foreign exchange obstacles would do much to help (Stikker, 1968). Nevertheless, it seems reasonable to suppose that the volume of private investment will continue to rise and that the next ten years will show a greater volume of capital exports than at any time since the decade before the First World War.

References

ADLER, J. H. (ed.) (1967), *Capital Movements and Economic Development*, Macmillan.

ATKIN, J. M. (1968), 'British overseas investment, 1918/31', Ph.D. thesis, University of London.

BEHRMAN, J. N. (1962), 'Foreign investment and the transfer of knowledge and skills', in R. Mikesell (ed.), *US Government and Private Investment Abroad*, University of Oregon Books.

BENOIT, E. (1967), 'East–West business cooperation', *New Rep.*, vol. 156, pp. 21–3.

COMMITTEE ON INVISIBLE EXPORTS (1967), *Britain's Invisible Earnings*, British National Export Council.

COMMONWEALTH OF AUSTRALIA (1965), *Private Overseas Investment in Australia*.

DUNNING, J. H. (1958), *American Investment in British Manufacturing Industry*, Allen & Unwin.

ECONOMISTS ADVISORY GROUP (1969), *The Location of International Offices*, Committee on Invisible Exports.

GABRIEL, P. P. (1967), *The International Transfer of Corporate Skills*, Harvard Graduate School of Business Administration.

HUFBAUER, G. C., and ADLER, F. M. (1968), 'Overseas manufacturing investment and the US balance of payments', *US Treasury Tax Research Policy Document*, no. 1.

KAFKA, A. (1967), 'Economic effects of capital imports', in J. H. Adler (ed.), *Capital Movements and Economic Development*, Macmillan.

KINDLEBERGER, C. P. (1969), *American Business Abroad*, Yale University Press.

LARY, H. B. (1968), *Imports of Manufactures from the Less Developed Countries*, National Bureau of Economic Research and Columbia University Press.

LENT, C. E. (1967), 'Tax incentives for investment in developing countries', *IMF Staff Pap.*, July.

LEWIS, C. (1948), *The United States and Foreign Investment Problems*, Brookings Institution, Washington.

Management Today (1968), 'The march of the multi-nationals', *Management Today*, April, pp. 98–103.

MEIER, G. (1963), *International Trade and Development*, Harper & Row.

MIKESELL, R. (1962), 'US post-war investment abroad: a statistical analysis', in R. Mikesell (ed.), *US Private and Government Investment Abroad*, Oregon University Press.

MIKESELL, R. (1967), 'Healing the breach over foreign resource exploitation', *Col. J. world Bus.*, vol. 2, pp. 25–32.

NATIONAL INDUSTRIAL CONFERENCE BOARD (1966), *Joint Ventures with Foreign Partners*.

OECD (1965), *Fiscal Incentives for Private Investment in Developing Areas*, Paris.

PAZOS, F. (1967), 'The role of international movements of private capital in promoting development', in J. H. Adler (ed.), *Capital Movements and Economic Development*, Macmillan.

REDDAWAY, W. B., POTTER, S. J., and TAYLOR, C. T., (1967–8), 'The effects of UK direct investment overseas; final report', *University of Cambridge, Department of Applied Economics, Occasional Paper*, no. 15.

ROSE, S. (1968), 'The rewarding strategies of multi-nationalism', *Fortune*, 15 September, pp. 100–105, 180–82.

ROSENSTEIN-RODAN, P. (1967), 'Philosophy of international investment in the second half of the twentieth century', in J. H. Adler (ed.), *Capital Movements and Economic Development*, Macmillan.

SAMPSON, A. (1968), *The New Europeans*, Hodder & Stoughton.

SINGER, H. W. (1950), 'The distribution of gains between investing and borrowing countries', *Amer. econ. Rev., Proc.*, vol. 40, pp. 473–85.

STIKKER, D. (1968), *The Role of Private Enterprise in Investment and Promotion of Exports in Developing Countries*, United Nations, New York.

STONEHILL, A. (1965), *Foreign Ownership in Norwegian Enterprises*, Oslo Central Bureau of Statistics.

STREETEN, P. (1967), *New Approaches to Private Overseas Investment for Development*, Institute of Development Studies.

UNITED NATIONS (1949), *International Capital Movements during the Inter-War Period*, New York.

UNITED NATIONS (1953), *International Flow of Private Capital, 1946/52*, UN Department of Economic and Social Affairs, New York.

UNITED NATIONS (1956), *International Flow of Private Capital, 1953/5*, UN Department of Economic and Social Affairs, New York.

UNITED NATIONS (1959), *International Flow of Private Capital, 1956/8*, UN Department of Economic and Social Affairs, New York.

UNITED NATIONS (1961), *International Flow of Long-Term Capital and Official Donations, 1951/9*, UN Department of Economic and Social Affairs, New York.

UNITED NATIONS (1963), *International Flow of Long-Term Capital and Official Donations, 1959/61*, UN Department of Economic and Social Affairs, New York.

UNITED NATIONS (1966), *International Flow of Long-Term Capital and Official Donations, 1961/*5, UN Department of Economic and Social Affairs, New York.

VERNON, R. (1968), 'Conflict and resolution between foreign direct investors and less developed countries', *Pub. Pol.*, vol. 17, pp. 333–51.

WELLS, D. (1962), 'Economic analysis of attitudes to host countries toward direct investment', in R. Mikesell (ed.), *US Private and Government Investment Abroad*, Oregon University Press.

Part Two
The Theory of Foreign Investment

No formal model of international capital movements was developed by the classical economists who, in their doctrine of international trade, assumed the immobility of factors of production. In the inter-war years, Nurkse (Reading 3) and Ohlin (1933) developed theories which tried to explain foreign portfolio investment in terms of interest rate differentials between countries. At the same time, another group of economists, following the lead of Taussig (1927), Viner (1924) Wilson (1931) and White (1933) and stimulated by the difficulties of Germany in making her post-war reparation payments, were concerned with the transfer problem, i.e. the balance of payments adjustment process of capital movements. Professor Metzler's (1942) article summarizes the main issues involved. Examples of more recent thinking are contained in Bloomfield (1950), Borts (1964) and Johnson (1956). The reader is invited to read Carl Iversen's (1936) classic text to get a general perspective of thinking on this subject.

Since the Second World War, economists have been concerned with two main issues of theoretical importance. The first is the effect of the international capital movements on the economic welfare of importing or exporting countries. MacDougall's well-known essay on the impact of inward investment is reproduced as Reading 5. More recently Pitchford (1969) has attempted to incorporate more dynamic factors into this model. An analysis of the effects of foreign investment to the investing country are contained in the essay of Jasay (Reading 4). The writings of Balogh and Streeten (1960), Frankel (1965) and Murphy (1960) should also be consulted. The most recent and most ambitious approach to the subject is that presented in the Pearce and Rowan article (Reading 7). The authors seek to solve the problem by a general equilibrium approach. The reader is also invited to consult Chakravarty (1961), Jones (1967) and Kemp (1969).

The second area of theoretical interest has been that surrounding the determinants of foreign investment. We have already cited some of the more important readings in the introduction, but the approach here has been primarily an extension of the theory of investment appraisal, on the one hand (see Jorgenson and Siebart, 1968), and that of market imperfections on the other (Aliber, 1970; Kindleberger, 1970). Several essays in this volume, notably that of Caves (Reading 11) and Johnson (Reading 18), touch upon this issue.

References

ALIBER, R. Z. (1970), 'A theory of direct foreign investment', in C. P. Kindleberger (ed.), *The International Corporation*, MIT Press.

BALOGH, T., and STREETEN, P. (1960), 'Domestic versus foreign investment', *Bull. Oxf. Inst. Stat.*, vol. 22, pp. 213–14.

BLOOMFIELD, A. (1950), *Capital Imports and the American Balance of Payments*, University of Chicago Press.

BORTS, G. (1964), 'A theory of long-run international capital movements', *J. polit. Econ.*, vol. 72, pp. 341–59.

CHAKRAVARTY, S. (1961), 'A structural study of economic capital movements', *Economia internazionale*, vol. 14, pp. 377–402.

FRANKEL, M. (1965), 'Home versus foreign investment: a case against capital exports', *Kyklos*, vol. 18, pp. 411–32.

IVERSEN, C. (1936), *Aspects of the Theory of International Capital Movements*, Oxford University Press.

JOHNSON, H. G. (1956), 'The transfer problem and exchange stability', *J. polit. Econ.*, vol. 64, pp. 212–25.

JONES, R. W. (1967), 'International capital movements and the theory of tariffs and trade', *Q. J. Econ.*, vol. 81, pp. 1–38.

JORGENSON, D. W., and SIEBART, C. D. (1968), 'A comparison of alternative theories of corporate investment behavior', *Amer. econ. Rev.*, vol. 58, pp. 681–712.

KEMP, M. (1969), *The Pure Theory of International Trade and Investment*, Prentice-Hall.

KINDLEBERGER, C. P. (1970), *The International Corporation*, MIT Press.

METZLER, L. A. (1942), 'The transfer problem reconsidered', *J. polit. Econ.*, vol. 4, pp. 398–414.

MURPHY, J. C. (1960), 'International investment and the national interest', *S. econ. J.*, vol. 27, pp. 11–17.

OHLIN, B. (1933), *Interregional and International Trade*, Harvard University Press, rev. edn 1967.

PITCHFORD, J. D. (1969), 'Foreign Investment and the national advantage in a dynamic context', unpublished research paper, Canberra.

TAUSSIG, F. W. (1927), *International Trade*, Macmillan.

VINER, J. (1924), *Canada's Balance of International Indebtedness, 1880/1913*, Harvard University Press.

WHITE, H. D. (1933), *The French International Accounts, 1880/1913*, Harvard University Press.

WILSON, R. (1931), *Capital Imports and the Terms of Trade*, University of Australia Press.

3 Ragnar Nurkse

Causes and Effects of Capital Movements[1]

Ragnar Nurkse, 'Causes and effects of capital movements', in G. Haberler and R. M. Stern (eds.), *Equilibrium and Growth in the World Economy. Economics Essays by Ragnar Nurkse*, Harvard University Press, 1961, pp. 3–21. First published as 'Uraschen und Wirkungen der Kapitalbewgungen', *Zeitschrift für Nationalökonomie*, vol. 5, 1933, pp. 78–96.

The theory of capital movements has not been treated systematically, so far, in the literature of economics. The reason for this neglect may well be found largely in the fact that the classical doctrine of international trade, the theory of comparative costs, rests on the fundamental assumption that while the factors of production, labor and capital, are freely mobile inside a given country, they are lacking external freedom of mobility.[2] This basic premise of the international immobility of capital seems to have prevented the possibility of a theoretical approach to capital movements, at least from the standpoint of international trade theory.[3] It is significant that whenever the so-called problem of transfers comes up in the orthodox theory of international trade, the discussion is always[4] concerned with indemnity payments between governments and matters of this kind, never with spontaneous, economic money transfers, i.e. with capital movements in the strict sense.[5]

1. Translation by Mrs Ragnar Nurkse.

2. The question of mobility does not arise, of course, with regard to the third factor of production. Land is immovable.

3. Capital theory has not been concerned with the question of capital movements, either.

4. Even F. W. Taussig while giving numerous examples of transfer, confines himself to compulsory payments (America to Germany).

5. We need not be detained here by historical research into the reasons why the classical economists made the assumption of the international immobility of the factors of production the cornerstone of their trade theory. We can agree with Bertil Ohlin (1930, p. 162): 'That classical economists have shown so little concern with this important problem need not be attributed to the fact that international capital movements were less important a hundred years ago than they are today. The root of the matter is more

Secondly, the theory of capital movements undoubtedly suffers from the fact that the transfer problem, which arises in capital movements as well as in indemnity payments, has taken up far too much room at the center of the stage. No attempt has been made to look beyond it, either at the causes of capital movements or at their effects. The discussion has been limited to the immediate process of international transfers, in the belief that practical and theoretical problems could be seen here which actually have turned out to be largely spurious. After the war, the mechanism of transfer naturally attracted more attention than ever on account of the question of reparations. It was generally held that everything there was to observe on the subject of transfer of reparations must also apply automatically to the case of capital movements. This assumption was, to say the least, somewhat premature. Since the causes and effects of capital movement are utterly different from those of reparations and indemnity payments, differences are bound to arise as well with regard to the mechanism of transfers; only a few of these can be mentioned here later. (The general theory of transfers can be assumed to be understood and will not be discussed in this paper.) What it is that divides the causes of capital movements from those of indemnity payments and similar unilateral money transfers is obvious, and needs no explanation. The main difference lies in the fact that the latter are not economically oriented. They move in an opposite direction from that indicated by profit expectation; otherwise the transfer would have taken place earlier, of its own accord. There will be no further reference to reparations and indemnity payments in this paper. We are exclusively concerned with the study of spontaneous, economic and productive capital movements

The immediate cause of profit-oriented capital movements is an interest-rate differential. The main point is to find out how this interest-rate differential can come about. A useful though somewhat superficial view consists in assuming the interest rate to be

likely to be found in the structure of their theory of international trade as a labor theory of value. On the other hand, the study of international trade on the basis of the modern theory of the interdependence of prices (i.e. the reciprocal dependence between cost of factors of production and price of products) must obviously lead to an investigation of this problem.'

the outcome of capital supply and demand. Consequently, a change in the interest rate can be induced either from the supply or from the demand side.

An interest-rate differential, hence a capital movement from A to B, can thus come into being in the following way: country A, for one reason or another, saves more than country B; in other words, the supply of capital rises. Or both interest-rate differential and capital movement in the same direction are caused by a fall in the savings rate in country B, which means a decline in the supply of capital. (The possibility of creating an interest-rate differential by increasing the capital supply in country A artificially through credit creation may be mentioned briefly as a factor on the supply side.) These variations in the savings rate have no problems to offer. Of greater interest are the variations that occur in the demand for capital and produce both interest-rate differentials and capital movements.

To begin with, suppose that a technical discovery or an improvement in methods of production takes place in country B, that B's products become cheaper on this account and that physical output expands. But the value of output will obviously rise only if the elasticity of demand in the relevant sector of the demand curve is greater than one. Industrial profits go up in B, the entrepreneurs strive to increase production, this in turn drives up the cost of the factors of production – including the interest rate – and the result is a capital movement towards B. The more labor saving the discovery in B and the greater the elasticity of demand for B's product, the more extensive the ensuing capital influx. An opposite effect is conceivable: the improvement in technical methods of production may release capital in B and lead to an export of capital from B. But this is not very likely to happen. It can occur only if (a) the invention is a capital-saving one[6] and (b) the elasticity of demand is lower than one. That the first requirement alone is not enough is shown by the fact that even if the discovery is only relatively capital saving, a high elasticity of demand can lead to such substantial extensions in production that surplus capital will be necessary.

In the case we have just considered capital movements were

6. Capital-saving discoveries are relatively unlikely. See Hicks (1932, p. 125).

brought about, in the last analysis, by a change in the technical requirements of production. In the case we shall take up next, the cause of capital movements is a shift in demand for various end-products as the result of a change in consumers' tastes.

For the sake of simplifying the demonstration, a gold standard will be assumed. Further, labor as a factor of production is assumed to have no external mobility. Lastly, we will suppose that the world consists of different 'countries' in the following sense; each country manufactures several kinds of consumer goods and the higher stages in production required for the manufacture of each of these consumer goods are to be found in the same country as the end-product. For the purpose of this example, international trade is assumed to consist of consumer goods alone and no exchange of intermediate products or capital goods takes place among different countries.

A transformation in consumption habits, a widespread change in consumer preferences will be followed by a decline in demand for the products of country A, for instance, and a rise in demand for those of country B. In the former country export prices fall, in the latter they go up. Production in A becomes less profitable and is therefore reduced. Capital will be released or at any rate no new savings capital will be available for investment. The reverse is the case in B: the producers of the consumer goods that the shift in demand has favored make more profits and develop a wider demand for capital in order to extend production. The interest rate goes up.[7] The outcome is a capital movement towards B. A higher proportion of the flow of new savings finds its way into the country whose products are more intensely desired and have consequently risen in price.

It might seem that the rise in demand for B's export goods will not necessarily provoke a rise in their prices. If the industry favored by the shift in demand is subject to the law of increasing returns, that is, if it operates with diminishing costs, prices to all appearances can fall instead of rising. A case of falling costs of

7. More precisely, the demand curve for capital shifts to the right. Either a higher interest rate can be paid on the former capital supply or a greater quantity of capital can be used at the former interest rate. If the capital-supply curve is a horizontal one, the interest rate need not rise at all in the present case, or will rise imperceptibly.

this kind becomes a little more involved under our present assumptions. Let us imagine that country B specializes, among other consumer goods, in the manufacture and export of pencils. Now let us have an increase all over the world in the demand for pencils. Country B shows an export surplus for the time, and gold flows into B. The influx of gold shifts the consumers' monetary-demand curve in B to the right. In the same way, a rise in the monetary cost and supply curves might be expected. The pencil industry's supply curve can display a negative slope: because of the gold influx (because of the greater quantity of money in B), the curve presently shifts upward all along the line so that the rise in demand makes the price of pencils go up instead of down. But this would not be a defensible argument. If an upward shift occurs in the pencil manufacturers' individual monetary-cost curves (on account of the gold influx and of their increased demand for means of production), a falling or negative supply curve cannot be valid for the pencil industry as a whole. In these circumstances it will have to have a positive slope, and there is little cause for surprise if the price of pencils goes up.[8] Nevertheless we reach the same result – rise in price as the result of a general rise in demand – even if the pencil industry shows a falling supply curve in a sense presently to be explained. Supposing that we let the rise in demand for pencils take place in country B alone, it may proceed at the expense of some other product also manufactured in B for which demand will decline. Means of production in the latter industry will be released for expansion of the pencil industry. Because the means of production required for its expansion are placed at the disposal of the pencil industry while costs remain constant, external savings can be achieved that will not be overcompensated by a rise in the cost of the means of production and that produce a negative slope in the corresponding sector of the collective supply curve. Should the rise in demand for B's pencils occur outside country B and happen at the expense of a product not manufactured by B, but rather by country A, the international immobility of labor presumably prevents an adjustment of the real wage rate, which goes up in B. This counteracts the tendency towards external savings

8. Concerning the connection between cost and demand curves see especially Jacob Viner (1931).

and falling costs in the pencil industry, and may convert the pencil industry's supply curve from a falling curve to a rising one. This seems to be a reason for assuming in the theory of foreign trade, at least in the case of international shifts in demand, that supply curves have in general a positive slope.[9]

The price increase of export goods in country B which induces a capital flow towards B will mean an improvement in net terms of trade for this country.[10] It is well known that discussions of the transfer problem have been mainly concerned with the question of whether capital movements in themselves create a change for the better or for the worse in the net terms of trade. The 'orthodox' viewpoint has it that capital transfers bring about a deterioration in the net terms of trade for the paying country and an improvement for the receiving country. We have just seen that the causal connection between capital movements and the net terms of trade can take the opposite direction: an improvement in the terms of trade is the cause of capital imports. Because of this fact, certain difficulties appear in verifying these mutually conflicting transfer theories – a subject to which we will briefly return below.

The immediate effect of this rise in demand for B's product is to create an export surplus in that country, followed by an influx of gold with the function of closing the gap between exports and imports, and of providing the inhabitants of country B with a greater share in the 'world product'. The gold influx is succeeded by certain price movements that remove the discrepancy between exports and imports after a while. At the same time, the increase in demand for B's product calls for a capital movement towards B and this provokes a second gold influx, with the function and effect of inducing a discrepancy between exports and imports in the other direction, of bringing about an import surplus. Capital flows into B in the shape of goods. It is evident both that the first

9. Professor Lionel Robbins has indicated the basis in general theory for the above remarks in a lecture on the theory of costs delivered at the Economic Society in Vienna in April 1933, in which he refers to the impossibility of postulating negatively inclined supply curves without shifts in demand. The latter release the means of production in one place for use where they are needed in another.

10. Variations in the actual rate of exchange (Taussig's 'net barter terms of trade') are measured by the relation between export and import prices.

kind of gold import will not be enough for this purpose and that the two kinds are only to be distinguished one from the other by analysis; they are separable neither practically nor temporally.

Let us consider briefly what effects the increase in demand for its product and the subsequently induced capital imports will have on the general structure of production in the pencil-producing country. Since the land and labor supply remains unchanged in B and only the capital stock is enlarged, it means a transition to more roundabout methods of production in B, to a more capital-intensive structure, while in A, the country whose products have suffered a decline in demand, there follows likewise a shortening of the methods of production. If we observe the pencil industry in particular, we find that it is led by wage increases to replace labor with capital. More capital is used in relation to the other factors of production, the 'average period of production' becomes longer, the 'coefficients of production' have altered in favor of capital – whichever way one wants to put it. It will not be the same, of course, if the shift in demand takes place among consumers in a single country or if, regardless of whether it happens all over the world, the industries affected by the shift in demand, whether favorably or unfavorably, are to be found in the same country. If within each 'country' full freedom of mobility is assumed for the factor of production labor, the industry favored by the shift in demand develops 'horizontally', with no change in the existing coefficients of production. Conversely, the industry that has been prejudiced will shrink 'horizontally' and there is no incentive for a change in its 'average periods of production'.[11] In the latter case, the increase in consumer demand for pencils is met by an extension of production as a whole through intensified application of all the factors of production in approximately the same ratio, with no essential change in methods of production. In the former case, on the other hand, consumer wants are satisfied, thanks mainly

11. The immobility of the third factor of production, land (inside a country as well), can obviously not impair this result and is compensated for by the mobility of the remaining factors of production, which tend to settle where land is cheapest – taking into account all the advantages of situation, quality, etc.

to the increase in output afforded by more roundabout methods of production.[12]

We have considered capital movements as being due to shifts in demand and fluctuations in the price of end-products. Let us now give up the assumption that international trade consists of consumer goods alone. From a mainly 'horizontal' analysis, we move on to a 'vertical' one.

In fact, the world's international trade is made up not only of finished goods ready for consumption but also, and to a far greater extent, of capital goods, 'intermediate products' and 'goods of higher order'.[13] Even if a country specializes in a certain consumer commodity, the principle of comparative costs determines that the goods of higher order required in the capital-intensive production of this commodity are not all manufactured in the same general neighborhood as the end-product. Needless to say, the principle of comparative costs applies to capital goods as well as consumer goods. From the standpoint of average length of the capital-intensive process of production, the geographical distribution of the various districts where each

12. What has been said under the assumption of the external immobility of labor applies inside a country as well, in the case of 'noncompeting groups'.

Further, our assumption of a system under a gold standard is not quite as unrealistic as it may seem at first. Any theoretical discussion which is based on the gold standard is applicable to any country in a domestic sense, even if no international gold standard exists. Ohlin (1924, p. 119) says: 'A discussion on the basis of the gold standard, i.e. of a rigid exchange system, is altogether valid not only for trade between different countries under a gold standard but, with insignificant modifications, for trade between different regions in the same country as well.'

We shall go on making use of both these assumptions. The third is about to be discarded.

13. If capital is viewed as an 'aggregate of intermediate products' (with Böhm-Bawerk *et al.*), any kind of trade in capital goods would have to be considered as a capital movement even if it takes place for ready cash. But the transport of capital goods is not of theoretical interest in itself. When we speak of capital movements, it is evidently a matter of 'capital supply'. That exports of machinery in Britain were prohibited in the time of Ricardo, for instance, did not affect freedom of 'capital' in any way in the sense of 'capital supply'. The concept and terminology of real capital and capital supply are lucidly interpreted in Fritz Machlup (1931, ch. 2).

separate stage in production takes place is accidental and unimportant.[14]

Capital movements that originate in a shift in demand for goods of higher order will now be discussed. With this in mind, let us imagine a closed economy – the world, for instance – divided into three geographical sections of equal size. The first region, which we will call A, specializes in the highest stages of production, i.e. farthest from the consumer (primary production, mining, etc.). In the second region, B, we have a concentration of industries devoted to the 'middle' stages of production, nearer consumption (machinery, semimanufactured products), while the third region, C, is connected with the final stages of production, those nearest to consumption. All consumer goods (the 'real income' of our closed economy, A, B, C) are therefore exclusively produced in C. Out of this flow of consumer goods C retains one-third, shall we say, to pay for its own initial means of production. Two-thirds are handed over to region B, where C's intermediate products come from. B in turn keeps half the consumer goods it receives from C for itself and exchanges the other half for the intermediate products farthest removed from consumption produced by A, which leaves A provided with one-third of the total real income.

Now let us find out what happens when the supply of capital increases in C: when the savings rate goes up – or when inflationary credit creation takes place there. The resulting 'capital surfeit' leads to lengthening of the stages of production that are

14. In practice, a strong correlation probably exists between the length of the roundabout processes of production in time (capital-intensity), and of those in space, the latter being detours in a literal sense, although the connection is meaningless from the standpoint of capital theory in which space is neglected. This correlation would not be hard to explain. As more and more steps in production are fitted into the process of production, it becomes less likely that a single specific region will be the most suitable place for production at all stages. The various stages of production will tend to be more and more widely scattered. On the other hand, it may be chiefly the opportunity for a longer roundabout method of production in space (an opportunity increased through improvements in the transport system and restricted by customs duties), which first allows the adoption of correspondingly longer methods of production in time. This parallel is suggested in certain passages of Eugen Böhm-Bawerk himself. See, for instance, Böhm-Bawerk (1909–12, pp. 131, 133).

found in C, the structure of production in C becomes more capitalistic, which means more intensive and continuous use of capital goods or intermediate products. In consequence, demand rises for the products of country B and this creates an improvement in B's net terms of trade. The increase in the price of products from the lowest levels of production in B extends the price margins between all the levels of production in B, which drives up the interest rate in B. Because the interest rate has gone up in B, part of the newly available capital supply in C, say one-third, finds its way into B in the shape of C's consumer goods. This leads to an extension in the processes of production in B, hence to a rise in demand for country A's products. As formerly in B, the interest rate rises in A and calls for a capital import: the residual third of the newly created capital supply in C is fed into A. And again it happens by means of an increase in the import of consumer goods from C to A, which first enables A to extend its processes of production, since during the transition to more roundabout methods of production A's exports will fall and so fail to provide for the usual amount of consumer goods. But once the transition has been completed, thanks to the capital import from C, A will be in possession of a much larger 'subsistence fund', a greater quantity of intermediate products on their way to be exchanged for C's consumer goods.

We have seen how price movements at different levels of production – and consequently variations in the 'terms of trade' for the regions or countries concerned – furnish the mechanism by means of which an increased flow of savings capital becomes evenly distributed among all the levels of the vertical structure of production, through the medium of interregional capital movements. The mechanism operates in exactly the same way if the increase in the supply of capital in C is due to an extension of credit and not to a rise in the savings rate. But in this case, the increase in the capital supply leads to an extension of the roundabout methods of production which no longer corresponds to an increase in the net subsistence fund.

A time comes inevitably when the means of subsistence ready for consumption are used up before capital goods in the process of production have turned into consumer goods.... The price of consumer goods will (then) rise on the market, while the price of producers' goods will go down (von Mises, 1924, p. 371).

This change in price relations is the cause of a shrinkage in the process of production, a depression.

A further observation should be made in connection with the interrelations between price fluctuations and capital movements which we have been discussing, with the help of our model of the three regions. The question could be raised of why the increase in the capital supply in C does not lead to an immediate export of capital to A and B. It must promptly cause a fall in the interest rate in C, while in the other two regions the interest rate stays at its former level. Both interest-rate differential and capital movements are the direct result, with no need for the roundabout methods of demand and price increases as described above. However, the earlier demonstration is more in keeping with reality because of the fact that a number of 'frictions' and sluggish periods have to be overcome before an interregional capital movement can take place. Capital mobility, whether in a single 'region' or between several 'regions', is never absolute. Among other adverse factors, the risk factor should be mentioned as perhaps the most significant. It may be compared to a threshold, which must be crossed before a capital movement can take place. The risk factor induces a certain amount of 'idling': if the interest-rate differential stays within a certain range, no capital movement takes place. We have a complete analogy here with transportation costs in commodity movements. If a commodity has the same price in two districts, A and B, a decline in the price in A will not lead at once to an export to B. In spite of the price margin, there will be no commodity movement as long as the price margin is less than the cost of transportation from A to B.

Aside from risk, entrepreneurial savings may be mentioned as another serious obstacle to capital mobility. To go back to our model, when the increase in the savings rate in C is due to entrepreneurial savings alone, the outcome is as follows: the entrepreneurs save more and invest the proceeds in their own undertakings, without placing them on the capital market and without reducing their previous demands on the capital market.

This spells a transition to more capital-intensive methods of production and means a greater need for goods of a higher order, which improves the net terms of trade in B as described, makes production more profitable, and drives up the interest rate. Now at last an interest-rate differential occurs, to draw some of the capital out of C's capital market into B.

The risk factor has a similar effect. At first, the increase in the capital supply in C will only make the interest rate in C go down. As long as this is not enough to overcome the risk threshold, new capital will be invested in C itself. Then the demand for B's export goods rises, their prices go up, country B makes more profits, its activity is stimulated and this alone improves conditions for the influx of foreign credit. Now the interest rate goes up in B, which widens the interest-rate differential already produced by the decline in the interest rate in C. The risk period and other 'elements of friction' are overcome and a capital movement from C to B is brought about. The mechanism runs its course essentially according to the earlier model.

From this standpoint, it would be interesting to investigate the variations in price relations between raw materials and finished goods on the world market, and subsequent fluctuations of the net terms of trade of the countries involved, in connection with capital movements to primary-producing countries. The practical difficulty is, that in reality succesive stages in production are not as neatly and distinctly organized, each in a separate region, as our former example would assume. So-called industrial countries export consumers' end-products as well as machinery and other equipment for production. Where so-called primary-producing countries are concerned, products such as timber, rubber, nitrate, tin, etc., should no doubt be classified under higher stages in production than cotton, for instance, or wheat, coffee, etc. There has been no attempt so far to bring ordinary statistical distinctions between 'primary products' and 'finished goods' (besides finished consumer goods, the latter often include equally 'finished tools and machinery'), or between raw foodstuffs and industrial raw materials on one hand, into somewhat closer harmony with the 'vertical' model of the successive stages in production of capital theory. The obstacles to an empirical view are further increased by the fact that retail trade, the nearest step in production to the consumer, is necessarily dispersed. Therefore in a depression, when wholesale prices fall, the well-known phenomenon of the comparative rigidity of retail prices is unable to influence the 'net terms of trade' of any particular region. On the whole, though, it can be said that so-called 'primary-producing countries' specialize on the average in higher stages in production than so-called 'industrial countries' that turn out finished products.

An account of capital movements and the net terms of trade for the period 1921–31 appears in an excellent study of statistical material published by the League of Nations.

Of the years considered . . . [1921 to 1931], 1924, 1925 and 1928 were those during which price relations were most favourable to the countries exporting raw materials . . . and the same years also mark the apex of capital exports from the lending countries. In the years 1926 and 1930–31, on the other hand, the terms of trade of the countries exporting raw materials became unfavourable and the capital supply shrank.

This brief report offers a good example of the main difficulties and dangers in verifying economic theory. The orthodox theory of transfers teaches that capital imports improve the net terms of trade and that capital exports have the opposite effect. The facts that have just been quoted seem to provide splendid empirical 'proof' of this assertion. That the striking correlation between capital movements and variations in the terms of trade can be explained quite differently is evident from the analysis sketched above. From our point of view, the analogy between capital movements and variations in the terms of trade does not lie in the fact that the latter are caused by the former. The two are actually two closely related symptoms of a common cause, which is the extension of credit and the formation of capital savings in the lending countries.

These considerations are evidence for the practical impossibility of verifying transfer theory, the impossibility of establishing empirically whether a capital movement improves or deteriorates the terms of trade of a particular country. If we must speak of a causal connection in cases where capital movements inevitably go hand in hand with an improvement in the terms of trade and where the improvement is the cause of the capital import rather than the other way round, it becomes difficult to determine whether and, if so, in which direction the capital movement in itself exercises an autonomous influence on the terms of trade. When capital movements are caused by an improvement in the terms of trade, it seems hardly possible to find out what proportion of the improvement is caused, on the contrary, by the transfer of capital. And while it has been correctly maintained (Haberler, 1930) that a capital transfer is as likely to induce a deterioration in the terms of trade for the receiving country, we fail to discover how far the terms of trade would otherwise improve if capital transfers had no such influence on trade conditions.

A few of the effects of capital movements will now be briefly discussed from another point of view. The example of three regions in which the successive stages of production are located will no longer be required. For the moment, the possibility of creating inflationary credit will be excluded. The market rate of interest corresponds to the natural rate of interest, everywhere and at all times.

Let us assume that for some reason – various possible causes have already been reviewed – the interest rate in country B goes up in relation to the interest rate in country A. Capital flows from A to B. The interest rate in A rises to a certain extent. The demand for producer goods (intermediate products) declines in A, their prices go down.

At first the capital flow from A to B will consist of newly created capital savings.[15] But if the volume of new savings being

15. A clear distinction should be made here between the two sources of free capital supply. The first consists in actual, new savings that arise from a reduction in consumption spending. The other may be called, with Gustaf Åkerman, 'retained' or 'accumulated' savings, and consists in previously accumulated savings which the saver has refrained from consuming. It is represented by amortization quotas, renewal funds, and reinvestment of circulating capital. According to Dr Åkerman (1923, p. 51): 'They could perhaps be described as savings that have been held on to. Meanwhile, as long as they are reinvested for the saver's benefit, sustained savings also belong to the supply of loanable funds which therefore includes actual savings in part, in part sustained savings. Even in a static society where real savings do not take place, there is a capital market with loanable funds and it will consist of "accumulated", "disentangled savings" alone (*ausgereift*).' The difference can also be expressed as follows: economically speaking, the

channeled into B is inadequate to close the interest-rate differential between A and B, the capital flow will also be fed in part from the volume of 'retained' savings in B. It is inconceivable that the amortization quotas (this shorter term is used to indicate retained savings) will have been impaired as a result of the capital export before all of the new savings have been transferred to B. For the fact that more roundabout methods of production imply diminishing profits, the gap resulting from the migration of part of the amortization quotas will obviously be filled at once by the amount of new savings still remaining in A. This flow of savings still available to A will not be used instead for a lengthening of the roundabout methods of production in A.

If we assume that the interest-rate differential margin[16] is too large to be closed by the export of new savings from A, the amortization quotas themselves will migrate from A to B. The second of the main sources of free capital supply will be tapped. Let us examine the reactions in A. Amortization varies a good deal according to different capital goods. For circulating capital, e.g., the turnover rate, can amount to five a year (i.e. the whole of the capital supply that is tied up in circulating capital becomes available five times in the course of one year). For fixed capital goods, the turnover rate may amount to as little as one-fifth a year if durability of the capital is five years. It is clear that the amount of 'retained' savings that finds its way into B as a result of the interest-rate differential will be drawn mainly from such capital goods as can be more quickly used up or consumed. These capital goods are not replaced and the fixed capital loses its complementary capital goods. Isolated capital goods are generally unprofitable, however. Different kinds of capital goods complement each other but as they have different amortization rates, each is the more dependent on the cooperation of 'circulating' capital goods in proportion to its own durability and comparative lack of mobility, i.e. to the longer time required in order

---

volume of new savings serves to extend the average periods of production, while 'sustained' savings insure the maintenance of existing length of the production period.

16. The circumstance referred to above, that within certain limits the interest-rate difference can be ineffective on account of risk and other factors, does not concern us here.

to release the capital supply. To the extent that sustained savings are involved and become diverted in the process, the mere fact of shifting the capital supply in a geographical sense will result in a certain depreciation (or virtual destruction) of fixed capital.[17]

This form of capital depreciation through capital movements could obviously be avoided if all capital goods had the same amortization rate. Secondly, there would be no loss of capital regardless of unequal amortization rates if the savings rate (the new savings) were adequate to close the interest-rate differential. Here we see the advantages of a progressive economy. In a stationary economy no net new savings occur; hence every one of the causes that call for capital movements will produce capital depreciation at the same time.[18]

There is another form of capital depreciation, not to be confused with the above. If an unforeseen shift in demand occurs, the producers for whose products demand has declined will not be given time or opportunity to wait until the capital that is tied up in their capital goods can be released, and transferred to the industry that has been favored by the shift in demand. Capital depreciation takes place at once, and would do so even if all capital goods had the same amortization rate.

We have not included the general theory of transfers in the range of these observations, if only because the bulk of transfer literature is already swollen to an almost disproportionate extent. At this point, we may be allowed to isolate one particular effect of the process of transfer in capital movements, and no more. To put it briefly, the usual view is that the beginning of a capital movement, the rise in demand for foreign currency pushes the rate of exchange in A down to the export point of gold. Gold flows from A to B and this raises the general price level in B. Commodity imports go up in this country, exports go down, and capital is transferred from A to B in the form of an additional flow of goods. Of what kinds of goods this flow is composed is

17. Depreciation of capital will not be avoided if, in order to keep his durable capital goods active and to preserve their value, the owner is prepared to pay a higher price for use of the cooperating circulating capital. The yield of the corresponding durable capital goods will be reduced, which again causes depreciation. See also Machlup (1932, p. 513).

18. This does not mean that new savings, sufficient only to compensate for existing capital losses, are excluded from a 'static' economy.

not, as a rule, specified: they may be capital goods at a distant stage in production just as well as luxury goods and other end-products for immediate consumption. In the latter case, means of production for the manufacture of capital goods will be released in the importing country. What kinds of good will be imported and, on the other hand, which are the export goods that in whole or in part cease to be exported, is generally assumed to be unascertainable. All depends on the scale of comparative costs.[19]

This reasoning would apply if the transfer of purchasing power that accompanies a capital movement should provoke a general, uniform price rise in debtor country B, or at least if uneven price increases were to follow at random for a variety of goods. But capital imports encourage price increases for a particular class of goods, namely capital goods and intermediate products.[20] Capital movements alter the scale of comparative costs.[21] The capital import in B makes it probable that capital goods and intermediate products (producer goods, in short) will make up most of the additional flow of imports. It is also to be expected that the first goods that B ceases to export will be producer goods, even if a consumer commodity happened to come next

19. Wilhelm Röpke (1928, pp. 25–6) has expressed it in the following way: 'Whether the additional imports attributable to foreign credit are composed mainly of capital goods or consumer goods . . . depends on whether it is more expedient for the extension and renewal of the apparatus of production that means of production should be drawn from foreign or from domestic industries. If means of production such as machinery of all kinds are not imported, and consumer goods are imported, it does not imply that instead of contributing to the extension of the apparatus of production in Germany, foreign credit has become consumer credit in the economic sense.'

20. If total monetary demand is divided among producer goods and consumer goods, the capital import will cause a shift in favor of the former. The price of consumer goods is not affected at first by the capital import. Price margins between the stages in production are reduced only by the rise in price of producer goods. In this connection, see F. A. von Hayek (1931).

21. Producer goods move down on the scale, consumer goods move up to take the place formerly occupied by producer goods. Of course, the nature of the scale may favor the importation of consumer goods and the exportation of producer goods to such an extent that a shift of this kind will not yet influence the composition of imports and exports in terms of goods. What we have is a tendency in the direction that has been indicated.

in the scale of comparative costs before the capital transfer began.[22]

A more familiar approach yields the same result. The capital import in B leads to a decline in the interest rate in B, which brings about certain changes in price relations. Because the various branches of production have average production periods of varying length, i.e. because the proportion of 'capital' in relation to the other factors of production is unequal, consumer goods that require comparatively more capital decline in relative price while goods in the production of which less capital is needed go up in price. These shifts in relative prices of end-products undoubtedly cause a change in the scale of comparative costs. It can also be said, however, that intermediate products in general have a shorter production period behind them than is the case with end-products, and therefore less capital is needed in their manufacture. In this way, we come to the conclusion, also on the supply side;[23] that the new imports following a capital transfer are more likely to consist of producer goods than of end-products ready for consumption, because the scale of comparative costs has altered in favor of the former.

When the interest-rate differential that leads to a capital movement from A to B has not been prompted or followed by a rise in the savings rate,[24] the capital transfer has similar effects on the composition of the additional exports from A. The demand for producer goods declines in A, the price goes down and they are exported in greater quantity.

It is therefore by no means as unlikely as is often assumed in the discussion of transfer problems that the goods that are affected by the rise in monetary demand in the debtor country will be the same as the goods that are released by the decline in demand in the creditor country. This applies especially to inter-

22. The reason why the classical theory of foreign trade contains no reference to variations in the scale of comparative costs as a result of capital movements may be explained by the fact that it rests on the assumption of the international immobility of capital (as well as of the other factors of production).

23. A more detailed account of the circumstances cannot be attempted here.

24. According to whether the interest margin occurs because of a decline in the interest rate in A or a rise in B.

mediate goods in the highest stages in production: the higher the stage, the less specific the producer goods.

But if the rise in the interest rate in B leads to a rise in the savings rate in A and if the resulting additional savings are transferred to B, then the goods that are released in A, that decline in price and are exported, will be consumer goods. There is no change in the interest rate in A. Even so the scale of comparative costs will shift and this time in favor of consumer goods. As against our earlier observations, the likelihood of a case of this kind occurring in practice is remote. It can generally be assumed that the supply of savings does not respond to a change in the interest rate as long as the change keeps within ordinary limits. The response may even take the opposite direction.

The study of transfer effects of this kind in capital movements reveals one of the characteristics by which capital movements differ from movements of other factors of production: labor, for instance. The capital movement alters the material conditions of transfer. The transfer does not happen simply as the result of an unspecified increase in the flow of goods in the direction of the capital movement. Normally, it has a tendency to proceed in the form of specific kinds of goods, specifically in such a way that the confusion between movements of the 'abstract capital' (capital movements proper) and movements of 'capital goods' may be less harmless than appears at first sight.

The connection between movements of capital and movements of capital goods disappears if the interest margin, the means by which the capital movement is released from A to B, is the outcome of a decline in the interest rate in A through an extension of credit. When a capital import is induced in this way, the demand for producer goods rises in B. The demand for the same kind of goods rises in A as well. The price of producer goods will therefore rise in both A and B, in which case the transfer of capital from A to B will not 'release' any goods for additional export to B as was the case in 'normal' capital movements. Increases in the price of producer goods in A and B tend to push each other up and the capital transfer in the shape of goods from A to B takes place according to the old scale of comparative costs. It is no longer possible to determine in advance what goods the import surplus in B will consist of.

The problem of the effects of 'inflationary' capital movements can be examined no further in this paper. It is evident that the part which capital movements play as 'business-cycle carriers' must furnish a chapter in business-cycle research with the task of explaining the spatial propagation of trade cycles and the synchronization of cyclical phases between various countries. A more complete theory of capital movements than has been available so far in the economic literature is an indispensable foundation for the study of the international, or more generally the interlocal, aspects of business cycles.

References

ÅKERMAN, G. (1923), *Realkapital und Kapitalzins*, Centraltryckeriet, Stockholm.

BÖHM-BAWERK, E. (1909–12), *Positive Theorie des Kapitales*, Wagner, Innsbruck, 3rd edn.

HABERLER, G. (1930), 'Transfer und Preisbewegung', *Zeitschrift für Nationalökonomie*, vol. 1, pp. 547–54.

HICKS, J. R. (1932), *The Theory of Wages*, Macmillan.

MACHLUP, F. (1931), *Börsenkredit, Industriekredit und Kapitalbildung*, Springer, Vienna.

MACHLUP, F. (1932), 'Theorie der Kapitalflucht', *Weltwirtschaftliches Archiv*. vol. 36, pp. 512–29.

OHLIN, B. (1924), *Handelns Teori*, Centraltryckeriet, Stockholm.

OHLIN, B. (1930), 'The connection between international trade and international labour and capital movements', *Zeitschrift für Nationalökonomie*, vol. 2, pp. 161–99.

RÖPKE, W. (1928), 'Auslandskredite und Konjunktur', *Schriften des Vereins für Sozialpolitik*, vol. 173, pp. 213–46.

VINER, J. (1931), 'Cost curves and supply curves', *Zeitschrift für Nationalökonomie*, vol. 3, pp. 23–46.

VON HAYEK, F. A. (1931), *Prices and Production*, Routledge & Kegan Paul.

VON MISES, L. (1924), *Theorie des Geldes und des Unlaufsmittel*, Duncker & Humbolt, Munich, 2nd edn.

4 A. E. Jasay

The Social Choice between Home and Overseas Investment[1]

A. E. Jasay, 'The social choice between home and overseas investment', *Economic Journal*, vol. 70, 1960, pp. 105–13.

How much of its accruing saving should a country invest at home and how much, if anything, abroad? The question presumes that the relevant criteria for a country as a whole are not the same as those for individual investors – for if they were, the result of individual choices between home investment and capital export would coincide with the socially optimal investment distribution, and no separate question about national advantage could be asked. On the other hand, differences in the two sets of criteria, the social and the individual, raise issues of public policy including, in private-enterprise economies, government control (subsidy, tax or rationing) of private capital exports, and in State capitalist systems, some rationally based settlement of the competing political claims of domestic development and foreign lending or aid.

The present paper is concerned with a purely formal framework for analysing these issues. The first section examines prevalent arguments about the possible conflict between the individual and the social optimum, the second develops a formal theory of the social optimum allocation, while the third seems to compare the result of private choices with this optimum.

It will be assumed throughout that private investors aim at maximizing profit, while society would seek to maximize national income regardless of its distribution (on the ground that if it has taxing or rationing powers to bring about a certain investment combination, it also has powers to alter, if it wishes to, the domestic income distribution which would result from that

1. For helpful comments on this article, and particularly for eliminating a *non sequitur* from section III, I am indebted to Mr J. Black. Any remaining errors are, of course, my own.

combination). Society will be taken to be 'selfish', i.e. unconcerned about foreign real income except inasmuch as it has repercussions on its own income. It will also be assumed that the degree of domestic factor utilization is the same regardless of the investment pattern (specifically, that employment is kept 'full' whether domestic saving is taken out in the form of domestic capital formation or of a current-account balance of payments surplus).

I

The vulgar type of statement of the conflict between social and private optima in home and overseas investment asserts that while home investment augments the national income by an amount given by the capital–output ratio (some of the increase accruing to home profits and the rest to home wages), overseas investment raises it only by an amount given by the rate of profit abroad (the whole increase accruing to home profits). The equation at the margin of the domestic and the foreign rate of profit involves a loss of national income equal to the share of wages in the extra domestic output which could have been secured by home investment, but was forgone in favour of income from capital exports. More concisely, home investment raises domestic, overseas investment raises foreign real wages.

The fallacy of this argument springs from the double confusion of an average with a marginal *and* of a statistical-historical with a *ceteris paribus* capital–output ratio. The marginal capital–output ratio, in the *ceteris paribus* sense of knowledge and other factor endowments (labour, land) remaining constant, is of course nothing but the reciprocal of the marginal physical productivity of capital. The corresponding capital-to-national income ratio is the reciprocal of the marginal value-productivity of capital. The intellectually more respectable case against capital exports is based on this latter concept.

If factor rewards are equal to marginal value-products, the home and foreign rates of profit will be equal to the marginal value-productivities of capital at home and abroad respectively. Let these be denoted by r_h and r_f. Assuming that production functions are normal so that, with other factors held constant, the marginal value-productivity of capital falls as its stock is increased, r_h will decrease upon home and r_f upon foreign investment. The prima facie equilibrium combination of the two investment flows will be that which keeps r_h and r_f equal.

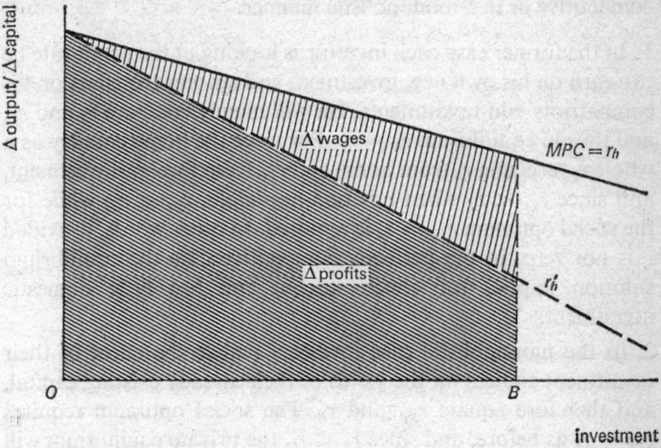

Figure 1

In Figure 1 the y axis measures the marginal value-productivity of capital *MPC* in the home country, and the x axis the addition to its existing capital stock, i.e. investment. An investment of *OB* increases national income by the area under the $MPC = r_h$ curve, of which the shaded area below the corresponding marginal curve r_h' accrues to profits and the dotted area above it to wages. Thus, for home investors taken together, the relevant reward is r_h the marginal rate of profit. Similarly for the foreign profit rate r_f there is a corresponding marginal rate r_f' showing the addition to the total income of investors abroad, while the difference between r_f and r_f' goes to foreign wages.

Part of total profit income abroad, however, accrues to the capital-exporting residents of the home country. If as yet they own none of the capital stock of the foreign country, they receive the profit rate r_f on their new overseas investment. If they already own all the existing capital overseas, they (taken together) merely receive r_f'. If they own some non-negligible share c of the overseas capital stock, their collective reward will accrue at some rate r_{fc}, where $r_f \geqslant r_{fc} \geqslant r'_f$.

There are hence two possible equilibrium solutions depending on whether investors in the home country behave in a perfectly competitive or in a monopolistic manner.

1. In the former case each investor is looking at the profit rate he can earn on his own new investment and ignores the effect on his compatriots' old investments. He will merely compare r_h and r_f, and thus in equilibrium $r_h = r_f$. But since the home country as a whole is receiving r_h from home and r_{fc} from foreign investment, and since $r_{fc} < r_f$ when c is non-negligible, $r_{fc} < r_h$; while for the social optimum $r_{fc} = r_h$ is required. In other words, provided c is not zero, in the perfectly competitive case the equilibrium solution implies too much foreign and too little domestic investment.

2. In the monopolistic case investors realize the effect of their investment choices on the yields of their already existing capital, and therefore equate r_{fc} and r'_h. The social optimum requires $r_{fc} = r_h$ as before, and since $r'_h < r_h$, the private equilibrium will again imply too much foreign and too little domestic investment.

In case 1 the private and social optima will diverge provided c, the proportion of capital in the foreign country owned by residents of the home country, is not negligibly small. In case 2, on the other hand, there will be a divergence even if $c = 0$ to start with, and *a fortiori* if $c > 0$. In both cases interference with private choices, by altering the allocation of a given volume of investment in favour of home investment, will result in a greater increment of national income than could be obtained from the private equilibrium allocation.

This, *in abstracto*, is the intellectual basis of the case against free capital exports. However, in the next section the requirement $r_h = r_{fc}$ will be shown to be a false criterion of the social optimum, and an alternative one will be deduced.

II

Implicit in the above argument is the condition that increases in the capital stock abroad must leave the marginal value-productivity of capital at home unaffected. However, this could strictly be so only in the special case of the closed economy. A closed economy, in turn, does not (and cannot) export capital, so that the question of conflict does not arise. If, on the other hand, the home economy is an open one, the domestic value-productivity of capital will depend in some manner on the capital endowment of the rest of the world.[2] More precisely, the overseas capital stock will itself be a parameter of the function relating the domestic marginal value-productivity of capital to its domestic stock.

One way of augmenting the overseas capital stock is for the home country to export capital. A classic example of the effect on domestic marginal value-productivity is the case of the home country developing, by capital exports, foreign sources of raw materials. The benefit then clearly manifests itself in the home country's terms of trade. But comparative advantage works in more roundabout and subtle ways, too, which may connect mainly manufacturing, and not patently and obviously complementary, countries. The terms-of-trade effect may be disguised, taking the vaguer form of external economies. Long descriptive

2. The above functional dependence also suggests that the marginal value-productivity of capital abroad will in turn move with the capital endowment of the home country; but this will be ignored in the main text for the following reasons:

If the home capital stock grew without the foreign capital growing, the long-run terms of trade would change (normally worsen for the home country). The effect on the marginal value-productivities of capital in two areas of causing capital to be invested in one area rather than another (in our example, at home rather than abroad) can, in principle, be expressed as a change in the terms of trade compared to the terms of trade which would have obtained without the geographical reallocation of investment. *Reducing* foreign and *increasing* home investment by a given amount will imply a given percentage change in the long-run terms of trade between the home country and the rest of the world; and for small ranges, within which supply and demand functions can be treated as iso-elastic, *increasing* foreign and *reducing* home investment by the same given amount will imply the same percentage change of opposite sign in the terms of trade. Now if trade between the home country and the rest of the world absorbs a greater share of the national product of the former than of the latter – or, what comes to the same thing, if the home country is small – the effect will be relatively larger on the home country than on the rest of the world. This, admittedly, implies treating the rest of the world as a homogeneous entity, i.e. one

tracts could be written on this aspect alone; but perhaps it may suffice to remind ourselves at this juncture that 'the division of labour [the scope for gains from trade] depends on the extent of the market'.

At the same time no rigid one-way dependence should be assumed. While increased wealth abroad should, *ceteris paribus*, more often than not raise marginal value-productivity at home,[3] it may in certain circumstances have adverse terms-of-trade effects or result in external diseconomies; perhaps more improbably, beneficial and adverse effects may exactly balance, by accident satisfying the closed-economy condition underlying the argument summarized in section I that the domestic marginal value-productivity of capital is independent of the foreign capital stock. Circumstances may well be allowed to alter cases, but not a formal apparatus designed to cover them all. The apparatus of this section is presented in terms of a positive and perceptible beneficial effect of a growing overseas capital endowment on domestic capital productivity. However, as will be observed, it can, *mutatis mutandis*, be turned to the analysis of other types of case also.

---

country. However, even if the effect of home investment on the rest of the world is of more than second-order importance compared to the effect of foreign investment on the home country, allowance can be made for it. Anticipating matters a little and turning to Figure 2, successively higher foreign profit rate (r_f and r_{fe}) curves can be drawn for successively greater volumes of home investment and the relevant intersections with the home capital productivity curves correspondingly lifted. However, not much would be gained by introducing this refinement in the main analysis. Therefore it is conducted as if there were only one effect, namely, that of the foreign capital stock on home productivity, and no effect of the home capital stock on foreign productivity.

3. In treating this as the more 'likely' or important case, the present article may appear to challenge the notion that the more similar are factor endowments in two countries, the lesser are the potential gains from trade between them. If we express the latter in terms of the value-productivity of capital in the capital-exporting country A, the *MPC* curve in Figure 2 ought therefore to be shifting downwards with increases in the capital stock in B, rather than upwards as it is doing – the presumption being that A is the capital-intensive country and its capital exports are making B capital-intensive, too. However, no such challenge is intended. For it is, of course, known that the gains from trade need only fall as factor ratios become more similar if the production functions in A and B are similar. But even if this

The diagram (Figure 2), is drawn on the assumption that there is OQ of investible resources (annual saving from a full-employment income) to be allocated between home and overseas investment in such a way as to maximize the resulting domestic 'growth' (increment in the home country's national income). MPC_o is the domestic marginal value-productivity of capital *given* the overseas capital stock. If, however, the latter were increased by an amount QE_x, the former would shift upward to MPC_x. This, of course, means that by devoting capital QE_x to foreign rather than domestic investment, the home country could cause the marginal value-productivity of the capital OE_x (remaining for home investment) to rise from MPC_o to MPC_x,[4] and so on for successively larger capital exports until, with the export of all available capital QO, the home marginal productivity reaches OZ. For want of specific information to the contrary, the MPC curves are assumed to be linear and to shift vertically without change of slope upon an increase in the foreign capital stock, their height being some linear function of it.

With the whole available capital allocated to home investment, the increment of national income would (as in section I) be the area under MPC_o from O to Q. With capital exports of QO, some very high value-productivity Z would be reached, but no

were the case (which is improbable wherever natural resources are important and dissimilar), and the gains from trade were becoming smaller as factor ratios in the two countries moved nearer to each other, this would still leave out of account the income effect of *increasing the factor endowment* of B at any given *factor ratio*. Putting it crudely, while the change in B's factor ratio *may* shift B's production pattern from exports to import-substitutes, the increase in its total factor endowment *will* increase its total production and its total domestic absorption of both exportables and imports. There is thus still room for A to gain if B's production of exportables increases more than its domestic demand for them and if its demand for imports increases more than its production of import-substitutes. The weight of historical evidence seems overwhelmingly to be on the side of this being the likelier outcome.

4. Readers will have noted a remote analogy with the optimum-tariff argument, with restriction of home investment (and expansion of overseas investment) standing for the export tax or import duty. The principal difference is that while the optimum-tariff argument relies on movements *along* supply and demand curves, the theory of capital exports developed here derives a somewhat similar effect from movements *of* supply and demand curves.

capital would be left over for home investment to take advantage of it. Neglecting, for the moment, profit income from overseas investment, here is a simple maximum problem: the task is to

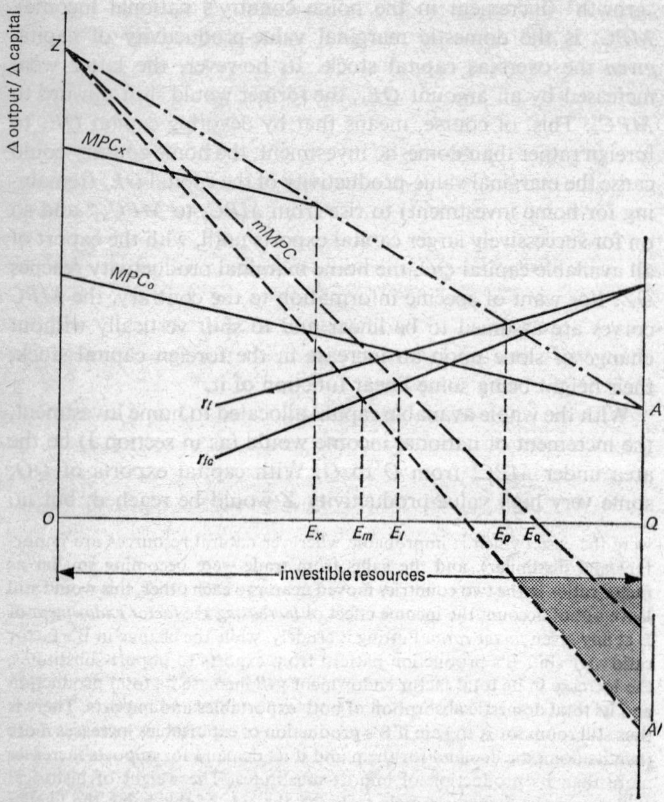

Figure 2

choose an MPC_x curve between MPC_o and Z so as to maximize the area under it, given the condition that the higher the (selected) MPC_x curve, the greater must have been the capital exports needed to reach that height, and therefore the lesser the capital remaining for home investment. The problem is not unlike that of maximizing total revenue: the higher the price, the smaller must have been sales, total revenue reaching its maximum where marginal revenue falls to zero.

'Marginal revenue' in this context is the increase of the area under successively lower *MPC* curves as home investment is 'expanded' and capital exports 'reduced' by moving from left to right in Figure 2. Assuming that this movement (the fall of the share of overseas investment in total investment *OQ*) can proceed in perfectly divisible steps, there will be infinitely many *MPC* curves between *Z* and MPC_o. The locus of their right-hand ends will be the envelope *ZA*. Its corresponding marginal curve is *mMPC* (as it were, the 'marginal' marginal value-productivity of home investment with respect to overseas investment). It bisects every possible *MPC* curve, as the area under it must at every point be identical with the area under the particular *MPC* curve which could be reached by selecting the ratio of home to overseas investment represented by the abscissa of that particular point.

Since *mMPC* reaches zero at E_a, OE_a is the optimum share of home and QE_a that of overseas investment which it would pay the home country to undertake even if it received no direct return on the latter, so that QE_a practically represents foreign *aid* granted; the subscript *a* in E_a is to suggest this.

Now we can introduce the profit rate on overseas investments. It is represented by the curve r_f, which, of course, slopes from right to left, falling as foreign investment increases; r_{fc} and r_f' can be derived from it along the lines of section I. The socially relevant rate is r_{fc}; as drawn, it intersects *mMPC* at E_l, and thus QE_l will be the optimum share of accumulation devoted to foreign *lending*. Not unexpectedly, optimum *lending* (QE_l) is greater than optimum *aid* (QE_a); this confirms the common-sense conclusion that the more willing the receiving country was to service its external indebtedness and/or allow the repatriation of profits from foreign-owned investments, the more foreign capital it would get.

If, however, the capital-importing country were a discriminating monopsonist of capital, it should first refuse to pay interest or profits, since the exporting country should, in its own interest, still be anxious to grant it development aid equal to QE_a.[5] After successful negotiation of the aid, it should liberalize capital imports and guarantee the repatriation of profits, thereby inducing further foreign investment of $E_a E_l$.

III

This formal apparatus can now be applied to adjudicate on the supposed conflict between the social and private optimum allocation. The argument summarized in section I alleged that the private allocation must almost invariably lead to more capital exports than is good for the home economy; the one exception being when, in case 1 (perfect competition among investors), the home country does not as yet own more than a negligible fraction of the overseas capital stock. However, in section II it was shown that the social optimum is satisfied not by $r_h = r_{fc}$ as the prevalent arguments seem to hold, but by $mMPC = r_{fc}$. Will private choice tend to diverge from this equality, and if so, in which direction?

For any point along the x axis (i.e. for any volume of capital exports), r_h is higher than $mMPC$ so long as ZA runs above $mMPC$, i.e. so long as more development overseas could lift the marginal value-productivity of home capital. ZA is the locus of successively lower marginal productivities consistent with successively smaller capital exports; hence it is also the locus of the various possible home profit rates r_h earned by the domestic investor.

Perfectly competitive private investment choice will seek to equate r_h to r_f. The particular r_h (out of the multitude of various possible ones) capable of becoming equal to r_f is that found at

5. There is an even more sinister implication here. If ZA was inelastic enough for $mMPC$ to intersect the x axis between O and Q, refusal of the foreign country to *accept* development aid would involve the home country in a loss (forgone increment) of national income equal to the dotted triangle under the x axis in Figure 2. The foreign country could thus exact an annual tribute from the home country in exchange for its consent to accept development aid, and spend the tribute on arms, palaces or means of princely conveyance; for as long as the tribute demanded fell short of the amount represented by the triangle, the home country would still be better off than if investment equal to the base of the triangle failed to take place in the foreign country.

the intersection of ZA and r_f. Clearly, $ZA = r_f$ need not coincide with $mMPC = r_{fc}$. There *may* therefore be a conflict between social and private choice. However, it is difficult to detect any obvious tendency to divergence one way or the other; for while $ZA > mMPC$ suggests that private capital exports will be too small, $r_f > r_{fc}$ suggests that they will be too large. Any divergence either way between the competitive private (QE_p) and the social (QE_l) optimum can result only from a net balance of these two offsetting biases.

If, on the other hand, the choice between home and foreign investment were made by a monopolist who owned all the already existing home and foreign investments, his aim would be to equate the marginal addition to his home and to his foreign profits. The latter is shown by the area under the r_{fc} curve, and thus coincides with the socially relevant criterion. The former, however, diverges from what is relevant for society. For society the return from home investment is the area under *mMPC*; but this area includes *both* the profits of new investment *and* the amount by which the new investment reduced profits on old investments and increases real wages.

For the monopolist (though not for society, which includes wage-earners) the transfer of this amount from profits to wages is a loss which he deducts from the total area under *mMPC* to arrive at the net addition to his total home profits. This addition is represented by the ZA' curve in Figure 2, the area under which is, at every abscissa, equal to the *rectangle* under the particular *MPC* curve consistent with the proportion between home and foreign investment shown by the abscissa in question. The difference between *mMPC* and ZA' is that the former shows the change of the whole area under a shifting *MPC* curve, while the latter shows the change of the area of the rectangle under the same shifting *MPC* curve. Since *MPC* slopes downward, the area of a rectangle under it is everywhere smaller than the whole area under it; therefore ZA' must everywhere lie below *mMPC*. This, in turn, means that ZA' must intersect with r_{fc} further to the left (at E_m) than *mMPC* (at E_l), so that a perfect monopolist would, to maximize profit, invest less at home and more abroad than is required to maximize total national income.

Fortunately, this is a too fanciful case to warrant concern; for while it could be true, particularly in the case of direct overseas investment, which is often the preserve of a few larger firms, that capital is being exported from a country by a monopolist or quasi-monopolist, it is most unlikely that the home country's capital stock should also be largely owned by the same monopolist.

Save this last contingency, one can draw a relatively complacent conclusion in favour of letting private investment decisions take their course. A conflict between private and social investment optima is entirely possible; what appears impossible is to *establish the presumption of a general bias* for private overseas investment to be either too large or too small. Nor can therefore a general recommendation be made for public policy in this regard. If there is a case for stimulation or obstruction of overseas investment it can only be established by a quantitative study of the specific instance on hand – a study which, even if feasible, is bound to be exceedingly complicated and full of sources of potential error.

5 G. D. A. MacDougall

The Benefits and Costs of Private Investment from Abroad: A Theoretical Approach[1]

G. D. A. MacDougall, 'The benefits and costs of private investment from abroad: a theoretical approach', *Economic Record*, vol. 36, 1960, pp. 13–35. Reprinted in *Bulletin of the Oxford University Institute of Statistics*, vol. 22, 1960, pp. 189–211.

I

The benefits and costs of private investment from abroad are a matter of considerable importance for Australia. This paper suggests one possible method of analysing some general aspects of the problem. It is mainly theoretical and does not attempt to reach clear-cut practical conclusions. This would require much more factual analysis and consideration of many other aspects. Some of these were discussed by Professor Arndt (1957), an article which also deals with many of the points analysed below.

The analysis is for the most part static and thereby ignores certain dynamic considerations that may be important. It attempts to assess the difference made to the real income of Australia at a given moment of time by the presence of more or less foreign-owned private capital in the country, on the assumption that the economic forces involved have had time to work themselves out (the analysis is thus a long run one). For ease of exposition this is done by starting with a given situation and then considering the effects of an increase in the foreign-owned capital stock; the analysis could equally be applied to a reduction. The moment of time may be thought of as a number of years ahead, in which case we are considering the effects on Australian income at that time of a greater or smaller inflow of capital in the intervening period.

We shall consider only relatively small changes in the stock of

1. This article was written while the author was Visiting Professor of Economics and Finance at the Australian National University. I am grateful to several economists, including Professor T. W. Swan, Mr H. P. Brown and Dr W. E. G. Salter, for discussing these matters with me, and especially indebted to Dr I. F. Pearce for his help.

foreign capital. This simplifies the analysis and seems legitimate provided one is not looking too far ahead. For differences in capital inflow are then unlikely to make a large proportionate difference to the foreign capital stock or, *a fortiori*, to the total stock. It will be suggested later that, in real terms, the foreign private capital stock in Australia may have increased since the war by perhaps 6 per cent per annum on average. If this rate were increased or diminished by, say, one-half, it would make a difference of only around 15 per cent in the foreign capital stock in five years' time, and a much smaller percentage difference in the total stock – say $1\frac{1}{2}$ per cent if we make a rough guess that the foreign-owned stock is of the order of one-tenth of the total;[2] certainly the great bulk of the capital is still owned by Australians.

We start with drastic assumptions. The main ones, which will be relaxed as the analysis proceeds, are:

1. The government maintains 'full employment without over-employment' or, more generally, a constant degree of employment of Australian resources.

2. No taxation.

3. The size of the labour force is independent of the stock of foreign capital.

4. The stock of Australian-owned capital is independent of the stock of foreign capital.

5. No external economies.

6. Constant returns to scale.

7. Perfect competition.

8. More or less investment from abroad has no effect on the terms of trade.

2. This is only an illustrative order of magnitude based on various 'back-of-the-envelope' calculations. For the sake of exposition it will be used on several occasions but the general arguments would be unaffected if the true figure were substantially higher, say one-fifth, and true *a fortiori* if it were less than one-tenth.

It is hard to say whether the ratio of the *flow* of new foreign investment to total new investment since the war has been greater than the ratio of the *stocks*. The ratio of the flows has been quite high in certain sectors such as manufacturing.

9. It creates no difficulties for the balance of payments which can be adjusted smoothly, and without cost, as required.

10. The increase in foreign capital considered does not require changes in Australian policy that themselves may involve a loss to Australia.

II

The line *GK* in Figure 1 relates the physical capital stock in Australia to the physical marginal product of capital, given the amount of other factors of production, which we shall call 'labour'. Initially, the capital stock is *AC*, of which *AB* is owned by Australians and *BC* by non-Australians (called 'foreigners' hereafter). Since, on our assumptions, profits per unit of capital equal the marginal product of capital, total profits are *FEBA* on Australian capital and *EDCB* on foreign capital. Output is *GDCA* so that labour gets *GDF*.[3]

Now suppose a small increase in foreign capital from *BC* to *BL*. Foreign profits become *IKLB*. The new foreign capital earns *JKLC* and the 'old' foreign capital loses *EDJI* because the marginal product of capital, and hence the profit rate, have fallen. Total foreign profits are almost certain to rise on balance because, for reasons to be given shortly, the 'elasticity of demand for foreign capital' (as we shall call the percentage increase in the stock of foreign capital associated with a 1 per cent fall in its marginal product) almost certainly exceeds unity.

Australian capitalists lose *FEIH*. Labour gains *FDKH*. Australia as a whole thus gains *EDKI*. Since *DKJ* is relatively small, Australia's gain is approximately *EDJI* which is the loss of income on the 'old' foreign capital. Australia does not, as is sometimes thought, gain the whole of *FDJH*, i.e. the whole of the increase in real wages resulting from labour's higher marginal productivity, but only a proportion corresponding to the ratio of

3. This assumes that labour could not produce any output in the absence of capital. If it could, such output should be added to the amounts shown for both total output (*GDCA*) and total real wages (*GDF*). Since the subsequent argument would be unaffected, we have retained our assumption for simplicity of exposition and to avoid the use of mathematics other than geometry. See also footnotes 9, 10 and 12.

foreign to total capital; the great bulk of labour's gain is merely a redistribution from Australian capitalists.

[Here, incidentally, we have one argument for restriction of foreign investment by the investing countries – which we shall call 'Britain'. Assuming no risk differential, British investors, if

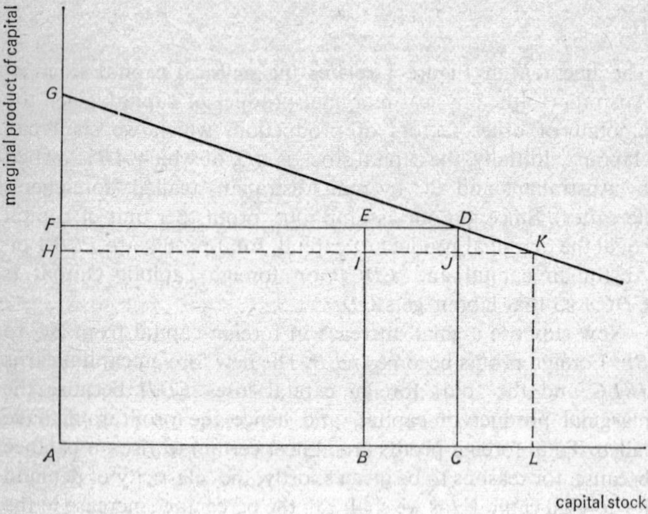

Figure 1

left to their own devices, equate the returns on home and foreign investments. But, while the marginal *national* (British) product on investment in Britain equals the private return, it falls short of this on investment in Australia to the extent of the reduction in profits on existing British investments there – *EDJI* in the diagram.[4] This loss of profits goes to Australian labour whereas the corresponding loss when there is more investment in Britain goes to British labour. If there is a difference in risk on investments in the two places – in either direction – the conclusion is

4. If 'Britain' is only one of a number of foreign countries with capital in Australia, and invests an additional *CL* there, the loss on her existing investments will, of course, be less than *EDJI*; part of Australia's gain will be at the expense of the other foreign countries.

unaffected provided British investors correctly evaluate the difference.]

Australia's gain (and Britain's loss) from more foreign investment in Australia is, however, unlikely to be at all large on our present assumptions. If total capital is of the order of ten times foreign capital, the 'elasticity of demand' for foreign capital will be about ten times that for total capital (i.e. ten times the elasticity of the curve *GK* at *D*);[5] and this latter elasticity is itself likely to be considerable because the substitutability of capital for labour is probably fairly high in Australia. The 'elasticity of demand' for foreign capital is thus likely to be high, so that *EDJI* will be small in relation to *JKLC*. In other words the great bulk of the extra output (approximately *JKLC*) will go to foreign capitalists; Australia's share will be small.

III

Now remove assumption 2 and allow for taxation. Suppose the rate of tax on foreign profits is t. This often approaches one-half where all profits are distributed and we shall, for simplicity, use this fraction as an illustrative order of magnitude, though it should be borne in mind that it is on the high side.[6] Australia now gains, in addition to *EDJI*, the tax on the net increase in foreign profits and this is likely to be a considerably more important gain. Put in another way, Australia now gains $t(JKLC)$ plus, it is true, only $(1-t)$ $(EDJI)$ instead of *EDJI*, but this a relatively small matter.

Taxation is not shown in the diagram to avoid complicating it. The case where the extra foreign capital is induced by lowering the tax rate will be considered in section XI; it is ruled out at present by assumption 10.

[We now have a much more important argument for restriction

5. If a 1 per cent change in the marginal product of capital is associated with a change of x per cent in total capital, it will be associated with a change of $10x$ per cent in foreign capital if Australian-owned capital is constant.

6. If there is a tax on profits of 7s. 6d. in the £ plus a withholding tax of 15 per cent on dividends, the total rate of tax will be 47 per cent. In fact, something approaching this rate seems to be fairly common although some foreign profits are charged substantially less for various reasons; and if profits are undistributed the rate is also, of course, lower.

of investment by 'Britain'. Double taxation agreements are complicated things, but for our present purpose it is probably legitimate to assume that the British Treasury gets only the excess (if any) of the British rate of tax over the Australian rate, after the Australian Treasury has levied its tax in full. Now, if the British tax rate is the higher, British investors (ignoring differences in risk) equate the returns after the *British* rate of tax on investments in the two places, which means that they also equate the *gross* returns (before tax). But, while the marginal *national* (British) product is the gross return on investment in Britain (since Britain gets the tax), it is the net return, after Australian tax, on investment in Australia,[7] and this may be little more than half as great. If the Australian tax rate is the higher, the difference between the marginal national products equals tax at the British rate; the marginal national (British) product on investment in Australia may still be only about half that on investment in Britain.[8] These asides about 'Britain' do not, of course, constitute a full analysis of the pros and cons of investment abroad from the point of view of investing countries.]

IV

Next remove assumption 3 and allow the size of the Australian labour force to be dependent on the amount of foreign capital. It is not unreasonable to suppose that immigration policy (and the supply of would-be immigrants) will be related in some way

7. For simplicity of exposition we ignore here the reduction in profits on existing British investments in Australia discussed in the last section.

8. Let r_a and r_b be the gross returns in Australia and Britain and t_a and t_b the rates of tax.

If $t_b > t_a$, British investors will make

$r_b(1-t_b) = r_a\{1-t_a-(t_b-t_a)\} = r_a(1-t_b)$.

i.e. $r_b = r_a = r$ (say).

The marginal national (British) product is r on investment in Britain but $r(1-t_a)$ on investment in Australia, the ratio of the latter to the former being $(1-t_a)$.

If $t_a > t_b$, British investors will make

$r_b(1-t_b) = r_a(1-t_a)$.

The marginal national (British) product is then r_b on investment in Britain but $r_a(1-t_a) = r_b(1-t_b)$ on investment in Australia, the ratio being $(1-t_b)$ which is still not much over one-half for many taxpayers.

to the level of Australian incomes and these will be affected by the amount of foreign capital.

The gains from additional foreign capital so far described – there are more to come in later sections – will raise income per head if the labour force is not increased. It will thus be possible, if desired and if practicable, to increase population to some extent without reducing income per head below the 'initial' level, by which we mean the level it would have attained in the absence of the extra foreign capital. (This could still, of course, be consistent with a rise in income per head over time.) It is impossible to say how immigration policy might in practice be related to levels of income and thus, indirectly, to foreign investment, but some highly simplified illustrations may be helpful.

Suppose that the extra foreign capital increased total capital by 1 per cent (which would mean a 10 per cent increase in foreign capital if this were one-tenth of the total). If then the labour force were allowed to increase by 1 per cent there would, on our present assumptions, be an increase of 1 per cent in total output, total profits and total wages above the initial level; the wage rate would be reduced again to the initial level, the profit rate restored to the initial level. Assuming no taxation, and no change in the number of Australian capitalists, the average Australian worker (including the extra immigrants) and the average Australian capitalist would then be as well off as initially, i.e. as they would have been had there been no increase in foreign capital and no consequential increase in the labour force.

The new position is shown in Figure 2. (This is the same as Figure 1 apart from the addition of the lines *GN*, *DN*, *NK*.) *CL* is 1 per cent *AC*. The 1 per cent addition to the labour force has shifted the line relating the marginal product of capital to the capital stock from *GK* to *GN*. Compared with the initial position, total output is up 1 per cent, from *GDCA* to *GNLA*; the wage bill is up 1 per cent, from *GDF* to *GNF*; total profits are up 1 per cent, from *FDCA* to *FNLA*.[9] Australian profits are *FEBA*, the same as

9. If labour could produce some output with no capital (see footnote 3), this output would be increased by 1 per cent as a result of the increase in labour. The wage bill and total output would still be up by 1 per cent.

It will be noticed that the new marginal product of capital curve goes through *G*, as the old one did. This is obviously necessary for geometric

they were initially. Foreign profits are *ENLB*, higher than they were initially in proportion to the rise in foreign capital.

If we allow for taxation the outcome will depend on fiscal policy. Since we are merely giving an illustration let us make the simple, though admittedly unrealistic, assumption that only

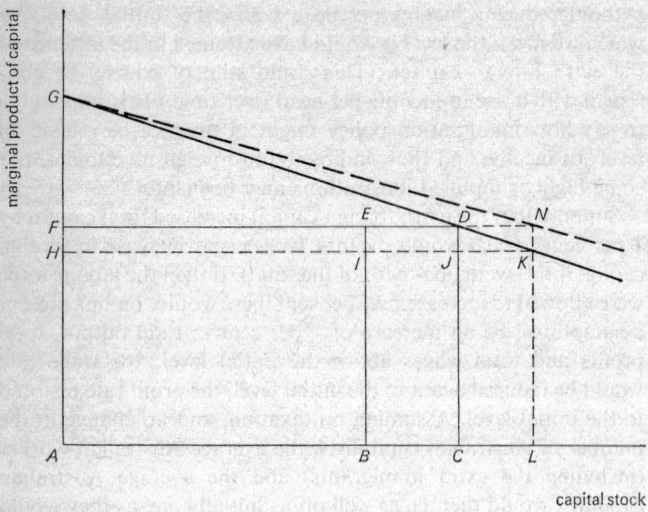

Figure 2

profits are taxed and that the resulting revenue is used wholly to finance social services for workers. Since tax revenue from profits (Australian and foreign) will be 1 per cent higher than it was initially, social services per worker will then be maintained at the initial level, as will profits after tax per Australian capitalist.

If the criterion for immigration were that it should vary with foreign investment in such a way that variations in the latter should not affect the standard of living of workers or the average

---

reasons, if straight lines are used as in the diagram, to make the area under the curve increase by 1 per cent; and it can be shown mathematically that it is generally true, given our assumption of constant returns to scale. (With some production functions, the marginal product curve will be asymptotic to the vertical axis.)

income of Australian capitalists, it would then be possible, given our present assumptions, to increase the labour force (compared with what it would otherwise have been) in the same proportion as the higher foreign investment increased total capital, i.e. by 1 per cent in our example.

This would, however, reduce average income per head. Population would be up by 1 per cent (we assume that Australian capitalists are also workers and that the labour force is a constant fraction of the population). But total income accruing to Australia would be up by less than 1 per cent since total labour income would be up by 1 per cent while total Australian profits were constant. This would be true whether we assumed (a) no taxation or (b) taxation of profits to finance social services with the latter counted as part of labour income and profits reckoned after tax. More generally, Australian income per head would be down whatever the nature of fiscal policy (provided that, as we are at present assuming, the tax rate on foreign profits is unchanged) because output would be up by 1 per cent and foreign profits after tax by more than 1 per cent so that Australian income would rise by less than 1 per cent, i.e. by less than population was increased.

If the criterion for immigration were that variations in foreign investment should not affect total income per head (and it may be worth repeating that this would not preclude a rising income per head over time), it would not then be possible to increase population by as much as 1 per cent. But some smaller increase would be possible since, if there were none, income per head would be raised by the extra foreign capital.

Numerous other immigration policies are conceivable that would allow population to vary with investment from abroad. The policy actually chosen will depend on the relative importance attached to growth of population and of income per head; views on the distribution of income; fiscal policy; the supply of would-be immigrants; and so on. The question remains, however, whether more immigration resulting from more foreign capital would bring a gain of income to Australia *additional* to the gains already described in sections II and III.

While this is highly likely it is not absolutely certain. For, though the extra labour would raise output in Australia, it would also raise the marginal product of capital and so foreign profits after tax, and possibly by as much as, or more than, it raised output; there would then be no further increase in total Australian income (including the income of the extra immigrants) or even a reduction of earlier gains.

To illustrate the possibility, consider the case depicted in Figure 2. Compared with the position after the increase in foreign capital but before the increase in labour (with output *GKLA*), the increase in labour raises output by *GNK* but it also increases foreign profits, after tax, by $(1-t)ENKI$, and this could conceivably be as great as, or greater than, *GNK*.[10]

That an increase in Australian income is in fact very probable can conveniently be shown with the aid of a further diagram. The line *SV* in Figure 3 shows the marginal product of *labour* corresponding to different amounts of labour, with the total capital stock fixed at the level reached *after* the increase in foreign capital. *OP* is the labour force initially. If it is now increased a little (by immigration) to *OU*, output goes up by *WVUP* (ignoring the small triangle *QVW*). The wage bill goes up from *RQPO* to *TVUO*, i.e. by *WVUP* minus *RQWT*. Total profits go up by *RQWT*, Australian profits by $(1-c)RQWT$ – shown as *RXYT* – and foreigners' profits by $c(RQWT)$ – shown as *XQWY* – where c is the ratio of foreign to total capital. Foreigners' profits after tax go up by $c(1-t)(RQWT)$, i.e. by $(1-t)XQWY$. Total Australian income thus changes by *WVUP* minus $(1-t)XQWY$, i.e. by *WVUP* minus $c(1-t)RQWT$, so that it will increase if $WVUP/RQWT > c(1-t)$.

Now $WVUP/RQWT$ is the 'elasticity of demand for labour' (as we shall call the elasticity of the amount of labour with respect to its marginal product, which equals the wage rate, i.e. of the line *SV* at *Q*).[11] If we call this elasticity e, the condition becomes $e > c(1-t)$. Now e is likely to be considerable, because the substitutability of labour for capital is probably fairly high

10. If labour could produce some output with no capital, the increase in output would be greater than *GNK*, but it might still be less than $(1-t)ENKI$. (See also footnote 9.)

11. If L is the quantity of labour and M its marginal product,

$$\frac{WVUP}{RQWT} = -\frac{M\Delta L}{L\Delta M} \text{ approximately.}$$

and almost certainly greater than $c(1-t)$, which is of the order of $\frac{1}{10}\times\frac{1}{2}=\frac{1}{20}$. (An elasticity as low as $\frac{1}{20}$ would mean that, to employ 1 per cent more workers – say forty thousand – with a given capital stock, but allowing all the time necessary for long-run adjustments, the real wage rate would have to fall by nearly one-fifth).

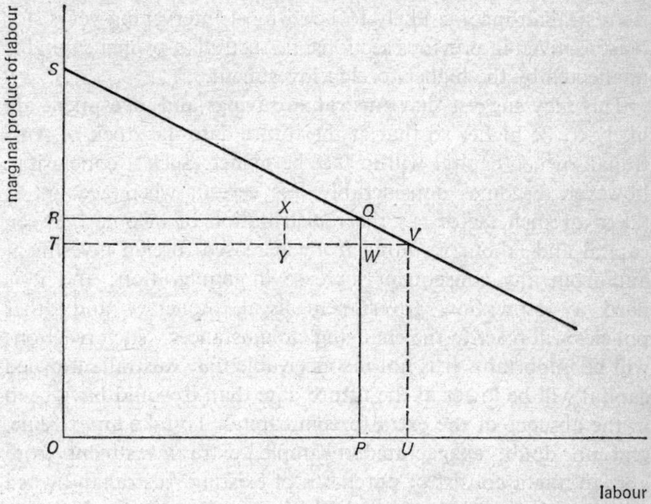

Figure 3

An increase in labour with capital constant is thus most likely to increase total Australian income. If extra immigration is allowed as a result of extra foreign investment it is thus most likely, on balance, to raise total Australian income beyond the level resulting from the gains described in sections II and III.

(It will be noticed that we have not relied in this section – as is sometimes done – on fixed technical coefficients, i.e. a fixed ratio of capital to labour, to show that more foreign capital will allow a larger labour force to be employed. The assumption of flexibility seems more realistic, especially as we are concerned with the long run and with the economy as a whole. The possible applicability of the analysis to 'dual' economies in underdeveloped countries will be briefly touched on in section XII.)

V

Now remove assumption 4 that the stock of Australian-owned capital is independent of the amount of foreign capital. The higher the stock of foreign capital at some future date, the higher must the inflow be between now and then and the higher is the stock likely to be at most intervening dates. The higher therefore is Australian income likely to be in most intervening years, for reasons given in previous sections, if Australian-owned capital is unaffected by the higher foreign investment.

This may suggest that Australian savings and investment are likely to be higher so that at the future date the stock of Australian-owned capital will in fact be higher. Such a conclusion, however, becomes considerably less certain when account is taken of such factors as the redistribution of income between capital and labour resulting from increased foreign investment and from any consequent increase in immigration; and it is hard to know how government fiscal, monetary and other policies will react to the changing circumstances – such reactions will be important. It is not inconceivable that Australian-owned capital will be lower at the future date than it would have been in the absence of the extra foreign capital. To take an extreme, and no doubt exaggerated, example, extra investment from abroad might consist of purchases of existing Australian-owned assets, and the proceeds might be spent on extra foreign consumption goods, of a type not obtainable at home, whose importation was previously prohibited but is now allowed following the improvement in the balance of payments; the extra foreign-owned capital would then be fully offset by a reduction in Australian-owned capital.

The actual outcome is hard to predict. If, as is perhaps most likely, Australian-owned capital is increased, it can easily be seen, using the same type of diagrammatic analysis as before, that there will be a further increase in Australian income, over and above the increases described earlier, equal to the profits on the extra Australian capital plus the reduction in foreign profits, after tax, resulting from the lower profit rate. (The reduction in profits on the 'old' Australian capital will be a gain to Australian labour.) If this higher income leads to more immigration there will be a still further increase in total Australian income for reasons given earlier.

If Australian capital is reduced, Australian income will be less than it would have been (i.e. the gain for other reasons will be diminished) by the profits on the Australian capital not created plus the increase in foreign profits, after tax, resulting from the higher profit rate; and if immigration is in consequence reduced there will be a further reduction in total Australian income.

If Australia is prodigal enough to allow the extra foreign capital to be fully offset by a reduction in Australian-owned capital (compared with what it would otherwise have been), then Australian income at the future date will, on our present assumptions, actually be lower than it would have been had the extra foreign capital not come in. For, assuming no change in immigration policy, total labour, total capital and total output will be the same as they would have been, but of this output foreigners will get an extra amount equal to the profits, after tax, on their extra capital; if, in the circumstances, immigration were reduced, there would be a further reduction in Australian income.

VI

Now remove assumption 5 and allow for possible external economies from extra foreign investment in Australia, i.e. economies external to the foreign firms investing the extra capital. If the value added to output by this capital exceeds the profits, before tax, earned on it, the difference will be the value of such external economies. These will very probably bring a further gain to Australia.

We shall still assume that there are no external economies *of scale* resulting from the growth of the Australian economy generally; such economies will be considered in the next section. We shall be concerned at present only with external economies of foreign investment resulting from other factors such as (a) the breaking of bottlenecks (probably much less important now than it may have been in the early post-war years) and (b) the introduction of 'know-how' by foreign firms.

Such know-how is presumably becoming less important as Australian technical and administrative knowledge broadens. It is perhaps hardly worth mentioning that it can bring an additional gain to Australia only if it gets outside the foreign firms. This may happen where, for example, the latter train workers who are later employed by Australian firms or where the superior techniques they bring to the country are somehow passed on to locally owned businesses which are both made aware of them and forced to adopt them if they are to survive foreign competition. If any gain accrues to Australia from this 'know-how', it does not necessarily mean that it might not have been preferable to buy or hire it without importing the capital.

While these external economies seem likely to bring an extra gain to Australia, they might conceivably reduce the gains mentioned earlier. The extra gain (which may be negative) will be equal to (a) the resulting change in the wage bill plus (b) the resulting change in profits of Australian capitalists plus (c) the tax on the resulting change in profits on the 'old' foreign capital. If the benefit of the external economies spreads to both capital and labour – and this seems *a priori* the most likely outcome – (a), (b) and (c) will all be positive and there must be a further gain to Australia. There must also be a further gain so long as labour benefits, even if capital loses; for, since the external economies will presumably increase output, labour's gain must exceed capital's loss, and only part of the latter is borne by Australia. There will still be a further gain even if labour does not benefit at all, provided there is no absolute reduction in the wage bill. But if there is an absolute reduction, Australia *may* lose.

Such a reduction might occur if, for example, the presence of extra foreign firms spread knowledge of production methods that enabled other firms to produce the same output with their existing capital but with less labour while the marginal product of labour at full employment was reduced. There would then, as a result of the external economies, be a higher total output in Australia but a lower wage bill. Profits would go up more than the wage bill fell. This would, however, presuppose an improvement in techniques rather heavily biased towards labour saving as opposed to capital saving.

The possibility is illustrated in Figure 4.[12] The external

12. It is assumed that capital could produce no output if there were no labour. This is analogous to the assumption mentioned in footnote 3.

economies shift the marginal product of labour curve from the full to the dotted line. Output is up by $E-C-B$, which is positive. The wage bill is down by $A+B$. Profits are up by $E+A-C$.

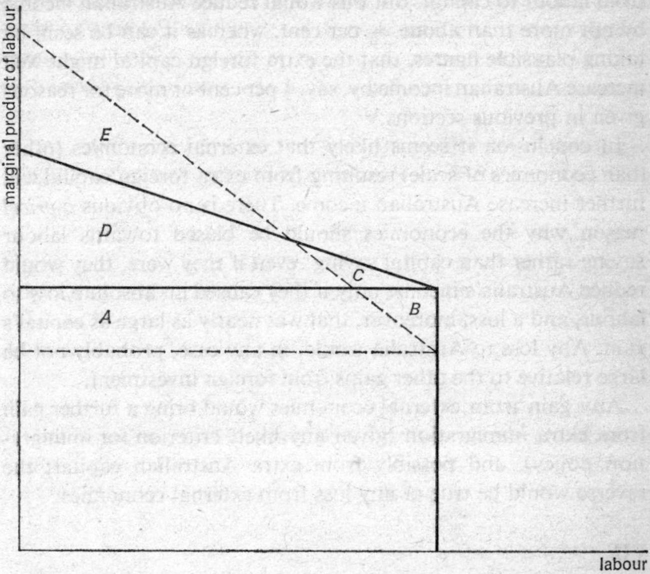

Figure 4

Australia would, however, lose only if labour's loss was nearly as large as capital's gain. For she would get the great bulk of the latter, either in profits or in taxes, actually $1-c(1-t)$ of capital's gain where, as before, c is the ratio of foreign to total capital and t the rate of tax on profits. Taking c and t as the order of $\frac{1}{10}$ and $\frac{1}{2}$, Australia would gain about $\frac{19}{20}$ of the increase in profits. She would thus lose only if labour's loss were more than about $\frac{19}{20}$ of capital's gain, i.e. only if the redistributive effect of the external economies were large compared with the gain in output.

Australia's loss could not, at worst, be more than about $\frac{1}{20}$ of labour's loss. While it cannot be proved that this would necessarily be small relative to the gains from foreign investment described above, it seems likely that it would be. It is hard to believe that an increase in foreign capital equal to, say, 1 per cent of total capital could change production methods sufficiently to redistribute more than say 1 per cent of the national income from labour to capital. But this would reduce Australian income by not more than about $\frac{1}{20}$ per cent, whereas it can be seen, by taking plausible figures, that the extra foreign capital might well increase Australian income by, say, $\frac{1}{2}$ per cent or more for reasons given in previous sections.[13]

In conclusion it seems likely that external economies (other than economies of scale) resulting from extra foreign capital will further increase Australian income. There is no obvious *a priori* reason why the economies should be biased towards labour saving rather than capital saving; even if they were, they would reduce Australia's income only if they caused an absolute loss to labour, and a loss, moreover, that was nearly as large as capital's gain. Any loss to Australia would, in any case, probably not be large relative to the other gains from foreign investment.

Any gain from external economies would bring a further gain from extra immigration (given any likely criterion for immigration policy), and possibly from extra Australian capital; the reverse would be true of any loss from external economies.

VII

Now remove assumption 6 and allow for the possibility of economies of scale in the sense that, if labour and capital were both increased by 1 per cent, output would increase by more than 1 per cent, whether the extra capital were foreign or Australian. The economies of scale considered here do not, therefore, include any external economies resulting from the presence of more foreign, as distinct from Australian, capital; these latter economies could arise even if there were no increase in total capital or in labour, the extra foreign capital being offset by a reduction in Australian capital.

13. Of course, if the external economies benefited foreign more than Australian capitalists in relation to their respective capitals, Australia's loss could be greater; but this would be inconsistent with our present assumption of perfect competition which means that the profit rate is the same for Australian and foreign capital.

Economies of scale could be external to firms or internal; the latter type would be possible only under imperfect competition, about which more will be said in the next section. The economies could be biased in a labour-saving or in a capital-saving direction as in the case of the external economies described in the last section. They seem likely, however, to bring a further gain to Australia when foreign capital is increased. There could conceivably be a loss for reasons similar to those discussed in the last section, but this seems intuitively to be even more improbable, since a mere increase in scale seems less likely to cause drastic changes in methods of production than the presence of additional foreign capital, where the quantity of extra capital is the same in both cases.

Gains from economies of scale will, of course allow further gains from extra immigration (and possibly from extra Australian capital), and conversely for losses.

VIII

So far we have assumed perfect competition. It might be argued that this was a reasonable assumption on the ground that, according to some post-war studies, it corresponds fairly closely to reality in the long run, or at least more closely than many pre-war theories implied. If, on the other hand, we remove assumption 7 and allow for imperfect competition, the analysis becomes much more complex and it is not easy to make useful generalizations about the modifications required in our previous analysis.

Assume first that the same 'normal' rate of profits is earned everywhere. Wages plus 'normal' profits will then exhaust the total output but the reward per unit of capital or labour will be the marginal *revenue* product, which is the marginal *physical* product (assuming the firm expands) *less* this product multiplied by the reciprocal of the elasticity of demand facing the firm (where this elasticity is defined so as to be positive).[14] The *ratio* of the wage rate to the profit rate will still, however, equal the ratio of the marginal *physical* products of labour and capital.

If, now, growth took place wholly through multiplication of

14. We assume a perfectly elastic supply of labour and of capital to the firm. Units of each product are defined so as to make their prices unity. The demand curve for each firm will be tangential to its average cost curve.

identical firms, and assuming no external economies, a given proportionate increase in both capital and labour would result in the same proportionate increase in the number of firms and in total output. There would thus be constant returns to scale for the economy as a whole. (The latent internal economies of scale implicit in our assumptions – according to a well-known theorem in the theory of the firm – would not be exploited.) It is intuitively plausible that each factor would then receive its marginal (national) *physical* product, even though it received less than what the marginal physical product would have been had individual firms expanded; a proof is given in the footnote.[15] On these assumptions, therefore, the preceding analysis applies. It would also seem to be a reasonable approximation even though firms are not identical, provided the new ones were representative.

If, at the other extreme, growth took place wholly within existing firms, each growing in the same proportion, the latent internal economies of scale would be exploited and capital and labour would get less than their marginal physical products. Extra foreign capital would then probably bring a gain to Australia as a result of the internal economies; for the profits it earned would be less than the extra output it created, the differ-

15. Let the production function of each of n firms be $y = f(k, l)$, where y is output, k capital and l labour. Let Y, K, L be corresponding totals for the economy, π the profit rate and w the wage rate. Suppose an increase in total capital sufficient to allow for an extra firm producing the same output as each old one and for the maintenance of the output of each old one. Part of the extra capital will go into the new firm and part into the old firms to compensate for the labour withdrawn for use in the new one.

The increase in total output of the new firm which equals that of each old one, i.e.

$$\Delta Y = y. \quad \mathbf{1}$$

Rewards to the factors exhaust output in each firm, i.e.

$$y = k\pi + lw. \quad \mathbf{2}$$

The increase in total capital is the capital in the new firm plus the increase in all the old ones, i.e.

$$\Delta K = (k+\Delta k)+n\Delta k. \quad \mathbf{3}$$

There is no change in the output of the old firms, i.e.

$$\Delta k\frac{\partial y}{\partial k}+\Delta l\frac{\partial y}{\partial l} = 0. \quad \mathbf{4}$$

The ratio of the profit rate to the wage rate equals the ratio of the marginal

ence going to existing factors. This gain, however, is merely that resulting from economies of scale and already allowed for in the previous section.

On the above assumptions, therefore, imperfect competition does not seem to require much, if any, modification of our previous analysis. The assumptions are, of course, unrealistic. For example, in so far as the foreign capital creates new firms, these may, to get a foothold in the market, have to charge prices lower than those ruling for similar existing products that are in no way superior, simply because buyers are conservative in their habits. The new firms, if they used the same techniques, would then make a lower rate of profit than that earned elsewhere – there would no longer be the same 'normal' rate everywhere – and there would be a gain to Australia additional to those already considered. The same might be true in so far as growth was within existing firms, for extra foreign capital would probably be concentrated on a small proportion of such firms, especially those in which foreign capital was already invested.

On the other hand, the growth of foreign firms might put them in a monopolistic position in which they could exploit Australian buyers, and this might involve a loss to Australia. (Foreign investment need not, of course, foster monopoly. On the contrary,

---

physical products of capital and labour (assuming firms were to expand), i.e.

$$\frac{\partial y/\partial k}{\partial y/\partial l} = \frac{\pi}{w}. \qquad \textbf{5}$$

From **4** and **5**,

$$\pi\Delta k + w\Delta l = 0. \qquad \textbf{6}$$

From **1**, **2** and **3**,

$$\frac{\Delta Y}{\Delta K} = \frac{k\pi + lw}{k + (n+1)\Delta k}.$$

substituting from **6**

$$\frac{\Delta Y}{\Delta K} = \pi\left[\frac{k\pi + lw}{k\pi - (n+1)w\Delta l}\right].$$

Now $-n\Delta l$ is the labour in the new firm (being the sum of the transfers from the old firms) and therefore also the labour in each old firm in the new situation. In the old situation their labour (l) was $-\Delta l$ greater. Therefore $-(n+1)\Delta l = l$.

Hence $\Delta Y/\Delta K = \pi$, i.e. the profit rate equals the marginal national physical product of capital. Similarly for labour.

it may break down local monopolies and, by accelerating the growth of the economy and so of the Australian market, widen the scope for competition by increasing the number of firms of reasonable size possible within existing industries.)

Endless further examples could be elaborated, but this would be pointless. The present method of analysis is admittedly unsatisfactory for dealing with imperfect competition and a better method might substantially modify our earlier results. On the other hand, we have seen that, on certain assumptions, the perfect competition analysis gives a reasonable first approximation and that the removal of these assumptions leads to modifications that do not all work in the same direction and may partly cancel each other out.

IX

Now remove assumption 8 and allow for possible effects of investment from abroad on the terms of trade. We still assume in this section that the balance of payments can be adjusted smoothly as required, so that international reserves are held constant without economic or social cost by, among other things, variations in exchange rates or in Australia's cost level relative to cost levels abroad with fixed exchange rates.

Let us start by also assuming, as is quite common in the analysis of such problems, (a) that trade barriers are not raised and lowered to correct tendencies to international deficit and surplus respectively; (b) that an improvement in the balance of payments requires a worsening in the terms of trade, and conversely. On these assumptions, which will be critically reviewed later, extra foreign investment may affect the terms of trade in three main ways.

First, the transfer of the profits abroad will tend to require a worsening in the terms of trade to generate the necessary surplus in the other items of the balance of payments.

Secondly, the terms of trade may be affected by the increase in output and income in Australia resulting from the extra foreign investment, and by any consequent changes abroad (output abroad might, for example, be less than it would otherwise have been because there is now less capital for investment there). The outcome will depend on such factors as the pattern of changes, at home and abroad, in supply of, and demand for, different types of goods (especially export-type, import-type and other). This raises very large questions that cannot be discussed here, but it seems that the terms of trade might tend to be either worsened or improved.

Thirdly, the movements of capital across the exchanges will affect the terms of trade. An inflow will tend to improve them, by creating a tendency to surplus in the balance of payments (which, on our present assumptions, has to be corrected), provided the capital does not reflect entirely additional imports of capital goods and remembering that the government is assumed to maintain a constant degree of employment (otherwise we should have to allow for the inflationary effects of complementary Australian investment and the like). Similarly, the terms of trade will tend to worsen if and when the foreign capital flows out again. (This may happen even with direct investment if, for example, depreciation allowances are repatriated or if foreign assets are sold to Australians.)

It is hard to say whether, on balance, these various forces will improve or worsen the terms of trade. Fortunately, however, this does not matter too much, since any change is unlikely to be very large – once more for three main reasons.

First, it is rather widely believed that the terms of trade are to all intents and purposes a *datum* for Australia. The supply of imports must certainly be highly elastic since imports are such a small fraction of consumption of similar goods abroad; and, while one cannot be so confident about the elasticity of demand for exports, this too seems likely to be high, in the long run we are here considering, especially when account is taken of competition between wool and synthetic fibres.

Secondly, even if the terms of trade are not a *datum*, deficits or surpluses may in practice be prevented, in part at least, by a raising or lowering of trade barriers which limits any worsening or improvement in the terms of trade.

Thirdly, even if trade barriers are not varied in this way, tendencies to imbalance may be largely corrected by other measures so that only small changes in the terms of trade are required. Dr I. F. Pearce (1961) has argued that, assuming 'full employment' is maintained at home and abroad, a country's balance of payments deficit, for example, can usually be removed in large part by (a) a cut in expenditure at home approximately equal to the deficit, together with a corresponding increase in other countries (which will be necessary to maintain full employment there as their surplus vanishes); (b) a reduction, by exchange depreciation or otherwise, in the prices of non-traded goods at home relative to the prices of *both imports and exports*, and conversely abroad. These, in his view, are the important changes in relative prices necessary to restore balance. They will help to do so by stimulating production, and discouraging consumption, of both import-type and export-type goods at home, and conversely abroad. Any change in the ratio of import to export prices is, by contrast, likely to be relatively small. (He also reaches the somewhat surprising conclusion that any change in the terms of trade is equally likely to be in either direction; but whether this is a valid generalization and whether it applies to Australia are questions that cannot be pursued here.)

For all these reasons any gain or loss through changes in the terms of trade resulting from extra investment from abroad seems unlikely to be large. If there is a loss it is most unlikely to offset the gains already mentioned (this could, I think, be shown by an analysis broadly similar to one developed in another context – see MacDougall, 1957, app. XIIF); nor does it seem likely to be as important as the losses that could arise for reasons given in the next section.

X

We now remove assumption 9 and allow for the balance of payments problems that may arise if Australia runs into substantial deficit. If exchange rates are fixed, reserves inadequate and emergency overseas borrowing impracticable or undesirable, there will probably have to be (a) deflationary measures that will interrupt growth and cause unemployment of resources – we are here removing assumption 1 – except in so far as the deficit can be removed by eliminating excess demand; and possibly (b) intensified import restrictions that may cause shortages, disrupt production and investment plans, create rigidities in the economy and involve more than optimum protection (this may also happen if tariffs are raised). If the currency is devalued there will be social problems and a weakening of trust in the Australian pound. Moreover, devaluation may not quickly remove the deficit because, though trade may be quite highly responsive to relative price changes in the long run, it is much less so in the short run; deflationary measures and restrictions may thus have to be maintained for some time. Nor would freely fluctuating exchange rates solve the problem; and they have various disadvantages of their own (MacDougall, 1954; 1957, pp. 335–42 and 383–7).

The question is whether extra investment from abroad might contribute to these troubles. The analysis required is quite different from that of possible effects on the terms of trade.

Let us assume for the moment that there are no large and rapid fluctuations in the flow of new investment. If then, with a given flow, the Australian balance of payments tends to improve over the years ahead with fixed exchange rates, an increase in foreign investment will not cause trouble by swelling the profits that have to be remitted across the exchanges, provided the increase is not too large. If, on the other hand, the balance tends to worsen with a given flow of investment, recurring crises will in any case be likely. Extra foreign investment would not necessarily then aggravate them; it might alleviate them. The higher payments of profits abroad might be offset, or more than offset, by the higher capital inflow and by favourable effects on the balance of payments resulting from the extra production; for this might be what is sometimes called 'import saving' or 'export creating'.[16] Extra foreign investment might, however, aggravate the problem, especially if it were 'import creating' or 'export discouraging'.

16. The correct meaning of these much-abused terms varies with the context. Here we are really combining them and postulating that, apart from the capital inflow and the additional profits payable abroad, the extra investment is 'balance-of-payments-improving', given fixed exchange rates. To determine whether this was likely, we should have to assess (a) any effects on Australia's price level relative to price levels abroad and (b) any 'structural' effects on her trade (see next paragraph); these would comprise the effects of faster growth generally (whether financed by foreign or Australian capital) and of any special twist given by the foreign capital to the pattern of development. As is well-known, such an assessment is difficult, not least because the indirect effects can be so important.

There could then be more serious and more frequent crises and the resulting losses would have to be debited against the gains from extra foreign investment described earlier.

One convenient method of assessing the future trend of the balance of payments, given fixed exchange rates, is to consider first the likely course of the Australian price level relative to price levels abroad (i.e. the comparative rates of inflation, if any), and secondly any 'structural' changes that might affect the balance of payments even if price levels at home and abroad moved in line. It is possible to be pessimistic or optimistic on both counts. No judgement is attempted here but, if one were only moderately optimistic, it would not seem that a continuation of something like the post-war rate of growth of private foreign investment in Australia during, say, the decade ahead would obviously cause trouble.

An uncritical interpretation of the crude figures may exaggerate the past rate of growth. They suggest that between mid-1947 and mid-1958 the value of direct foreign investments outstanding rose by an average of 15 per cent a year.[17] A more careful examination substantially alters the picture. First, the crude figures include undistributed profits of subsidiaries only since 1947; if those accumulated earlier were added, the rate of growth might be reduced to perhaps 13 per cent a year. Secondly, and much more important, it seems that a large part of the increase merely reflects the fall in the value of money (both between 1947 and 1958 and before 1947; for the fixed assets existing at mid-1947 were all installed before that date). A very rough (but complicated) calculation, based on a method used in another context,[18] suggests that the rate of increase of direct investments, in real terms, may have been only about 6 per cent per annum. While not much significance can be attached to this result, a check on its plausibility is that, in money terms, income on foreign investments in Australia (excluding public authority interest) rose from about 1·1 per cent to about 1·3 per cent of the

17. Including undistributed profits of subsidiaries since mid-1947. Calculated from tables 5, 6, 8, 9 of *Annual Bulletin of Oversea Investment, 1957–8*.

18. MacDougall (1957, pp. 534–5). There is no space to describe the calculations for Australia and little need since the result is purely illustrative.

gross national product during the same period.[19] This is not inconsistent with investments outstanding rising by 6 per cent a year in real terms and the real national product by, say, 4–5 per cent.

If, in future, foreign, investments grew at 6 per cent per annum in real terms (one can admittedly make more startling extrapolations by taking US and UK investments separately) (Arndt, 1957, p. 258), the growth of income on them would not obviously be embarrassingly rapid in relation to the growth of trade; for, with the real national product growing by, say, 5 per cent a year, trade may well tend to grow by, say, 4 per cent in real terms (there may be reasons why it will grow more slowly than the national product but the difference is unlikely to be very great). Since profits on foreign investments in Australia are still quite a small fraction of trade in goods and services, imports would not have to rise so very much more slowly than exports to cover the growing income payable abroad, even if we ignore the growing support to the balance of payments that would result from the rising inflow of new capital.[20]

If we now remove the assumption of no large fluctuations in this inflow, there is the possibility that these might help to cause crises, especially if a sharp reduction in the net inflow (allowing for withdrawals of foreign capital) coincided with a worsening in the balance of payments for other reasons. The higher the average flow over a period of years the more serious is this danger likely to be and this is a further cost of more rather than less investment from abroad. (The *extra* danger would, however, be diminished or removed if more investment resulted in an improved balance of payments, and a building up of reserves, either automatically or through deliberate policy.)

It is not obvious that the inflow of private capital will become a dangerously high fraction of the balance of payments in the foreseeable future. It has averaged only about 10 per cent of payments

19. Calculated from papers on *National Income and Expenditure*; adjusted for annual fluctuations. The figures are not quite comparable with those given earlier.

20. The relationships between growth of trade, foreign investment and income on it could be further elaborated, but this seems unnecessary for our present purpose.

on current account in recent years (including undistributed profits)[21] and we have seen that it will not grow so very much faster than trade if the post-war trend continues. Nevertheless, the net inflow can contract sharply – it fell by over two-thirds between 1951–2 and 1952–3 and might even become negative – and a loss of even, say, 7–10 per cent in foreign exchange receipts can be embarrassing when reserves are low, especially if other receipts are falling at the same time.

Direct investment may be less dangerous in this respect than portfolio investment in Australian companies, since the latter is probably more volatile. (It also brings little, if any, know-how, one of the main gains from direct investment; and, though the rate of return on it may appear lower, this becomes less certain if allowance is made, as with direct investments, for the undistributed profits being set aside for the benefit of shareholders.)

XI

Finally let us remove assumption 10, that the increase in foreign capital considered does not require changes in Australian policy that themselves may involve a loss. The previous analysis would require no consequent modification if we were considering the effects of changing conditions abroad, say, a fall in the rate of profit there that encouraged the flow of capital to Australia. But if, say, the government were considering whether to provide more information abroad about investment opportunities in Australia, the cost of so doing would have to be debited before striking a balance. Attempts to attract foreign capital by firmer guarantees on freedom to repatriate might increase the danger of future balance of payments difficulties. Higher protection, designed to encourage investment in Australia by foreign producers thereby prevented from exporting direct, might mean sacrificing some of the benefits of the international division of labour; there might also, of course, be further well-known benefits from higher protection, but some of these have already been allowed for in this paper.

Conversely, measures that might reduce capital inflow, such as insistence on a minimum Australian participation in the equity of subsidiaries of foreign firms or the outlawing of restrictions on

21. The balancing item is excluded; see R. J. Cameron (1957, pp. 263–4).

exporting by such subsidiaries (Arndt and Sherk, 1959), might bring other economic or political benefits.

The only case we shall consider in any detail is where investment from abroad is encouraged by a reduction in tax rates on foreign profits, whether or not this applies equally to domestic profits. (The analysis will, of course, apply in reverse to higher tax rates.) If rates are reduced, the gain from taxation will be smaller than that described in section III. There could even be a reduction in tax revenue from foreign profits.

It can easily be shown that this will be avoided if

$$\frac{1/\eta_d+1/\eta_s}{1+1/\eta_s} \leqslant t,$$

where t is the tax rate as before and η_d and η_s the elasticities of demand[22] for, and supply of, foreign capital; they measure the relationship between changes in the *stock* of foreign capital in Australia and in the profit rate, before tax in the case of demand, after tax in that of supply. If we took the tax rate as one-half, this would reduce to

$$\eta_s \geqslant \frac{1}{1-2/\eta_d}.$$

If, for example, η_d, were infinite, 10, 4 or 2, η_s would have to be not less than 1, $1\frac{1}{4}$, 2 or ∞. We have seen that η_d is probably high, so that a fall in tax revenue might be avoided if the elasticity of supply of foreign capital were not less than, say, some figure between 1 and 2.

It might be thought that this was highly probable since foreign capital in Australia is such a tiny fraction of foreign capital abroad. But the market is very imperfect; only a very small fraction of all foreign capitalists are interested in investment in Australia. An elasticity of supply of, for example, $1\frac{1}{2}$ would mean that, if the rate of profit, after tax, on foreign capital were, say, 9 per cent rather than 8 per cent, this would in the long run make a difference of nearly one-fifth, or perhaps £250 million or more, in the amount of foreign capital in Australia. Whether this is likely it is very hard to say.

It certainly seems possible that, if investment from abroad were

22. Defined so as to be positive.

encouraged by tax remission, there would be no gain to Australia from increased tax revenue, at least if we confine our attention to the stage of the analysis reached in section III. The reduction in tax rates might still be worth while, for the other consequences might be favourable to Australian income on balance (and might possibly convert a tax loss into a tax gain). But it should be remembered that any gains from higher immigration, and possibly more Australian capital, would now be substantially smaller than in our previous analysis, because they there depended considerably on the rise in Australian income resulting from higher tax revenue from foreign profits.

XII

The main conclusions of this analysis are fairly straightforward and obvious. The most important direct gains to Australia from more rather than less private investment from abroad seem likely to come through higher tax revenue from foreign profits (at least if the higher investment is not induced by lower tax rates), through economies of scale and through external economies generally, especially where Australian-owned firms acquire 'know-how' or are forced by foreign competition to adopt more efficient methods.

These gains may permit higher immigration, which will further increase Australian income, if immigration policies are related in some way to the standard of living. They may also lead to higher domestically financed investment, which will later increase Australian income still further, but this is problematical and depends considerably on government policy; if domestically financed investment were allowed to fall when more foreign capital came in, Australian income could actually be lower at some future date than it otherwise would have been.

The effects of extra foreign investment on the terms of trade, which might be favourable or unfavourable, are unlikely to be large. The effects on the balance of payments could be more important. They could be favourable, but the danger of future balance of payments crises might be increased; for there are inevitably fluctuations in the net inflow of private capital and part at least of the foreigners' profits have to be transferred across the exchanges.

These are some of the results obtained by applying rather conventional tools of economic analysis. The assumptions used are still highly simplified even after those listed at the beginning of the article have been removed. For example, allowance is made for only two factors of production. No distinction is made between fixed interest and equity investment. No explicit account is taken of government-owned capital or of government borrowing from abroad; throughout most of the paper these are implicitly assumed to be independent of changes in private investment from abroad. The analysis, as was emphasized at the outset, is mainly static. Even if it were made more dynamic it would still fail to take account of considerations not allowed for in most economic theories and about which the economic historian, for example, might have more useful things to say. Many aspects of the problem are left uncovered, such as the relative merits of government borrowing and private investment from abroad, and little is said about short-run implications. No attempt is made to assess the political costs and benefits.

The analysis will not apply to countries other than Australia without modification, but such modification may sometimes be possible. In many underdeveloped countries, for example, there may be heavy unemployment of labour, or under-employment where the marginal product is far less than the wage rate, and marginal product, of labour in the organised sector, or perhaps even zero. The foregoing analysis might then perhaps be adapted by considering the organized sector and assuming employment in it to be as great as was feasible at a given real wage rate; more investment from abroad would then make possible more 'immigration' from the unorganized sector just as, in section IV, we allowed for the possibility that it might permit more immigration into Australia from overseas.

Despite its many limitations it is hoped that the analysis in this paper may be of some relevance, at least to Australia, and that it may provoke others to correct and improve it and to explore other aspects of the problem.

References

ARNDT, H. W. (1957), 'Overseas borrowing – the new model', *Econ. Rec.*, vol. 33, pp. 247–61.

ARNDT, H. W., and SHERK, D. R. (1959), 'Export franchises of Australian companies with overseas affiliations', *Econ. Rec.*, vol. 35, pp. 239–42.
CAMERON, R. J. (1957), 'Comment', *Econ. Rec.*, vol. 33, pp. 261–4.
MACDOUGALL, G. D. A. (1954), 'Flexible exchange rates', *West. Bank Rev.*, August, pp. 1–3.
MACDOUGALL, G. D. A. (1957), *The World Dollar Problem*, Macmillan.
PEARCE, I. F. (1961), 'The problem of the balance of payments', *Int. econ. Rev.*, vol. 2, pp. 1–28.

6 Murray C. Kemp

The Benefits and Costs of Private Investment from Abroad: Comment

Murray C. Kemp, 'The benefits and costs of private investment from abroad: comment', *Economic Record*, vol. 38, 1962, pp. 108–10.

Sir Donald MacDougall (1960) has shown that capital imports may stop short of the point at which the borrowing country receives zero marginal net benefit. In particular, this possibility will be realized if capital imports are unimpeded, if perfect competition prevails, if returns to scale are constant, if external economies and taxation are absent, and if the terms of trade are independent of capital movements (MacDougall, 1960, section II).

Suppose that MacDougall's conditions are satisfied. Should the borrowing country proceed to *encourage*, perhaps by subsidy, capital imports? That, at first encounter, would appear to be an obvious implication of his analysis. I shall argue, however, that a self-seeking borrowing country should tax all earnings of foreign-owned capital and, by implication, *curb* the capital inflow. Such a tax is the counterpart, on capital account, of the more familiar optimal tariff.

Suppose that each country produces a single commodity and that that commodity is the same in each country.[1] Suppose, further, that the lending country possesses a physically homogeneous capital stock consisting, say, of machines of a versatile kind.[2] Part of this stock is invested abroad, the balance at home. It is desired to compare, from the viewpoint of the *borrowing* country, the free market and optimal foreign investments.

Production in each country is carried on with the aid of machines, and certain other factors of production, the latter all

1. If all commodities are traded and if the terms of trade are constant, one may proceed as though there were a single commodity.

2. A justification of this assumption is offered in Kemp (1962).

in inelastic supply. It follows that the production function of the lending country may be written as

$$f_1(K_1 - K),$$

where K_1 is the lending country's total stock of capital and K is the amount of capital sent abroad; and that the production function of the borrowing country may be written as

$$_2(K_2 + K),$$

where K_2 is the borrowing country's owned stock of capital.

In competitive equilibrium, without artificial curb on (or encouragement of) capital movements, the world's stock of capital is so distributed between the two countries that the marginal return on investment is the same in both countries, that is, that

$$f'_1 = pf'_2,$$

where p is the lending country's terms of trade and primes denote derivatives. Total foreign earnings are Kf'_2.

Suppose now that the government of the borrowing country seeks to maximize that country's income by imposing a tax, at an *ad valorem* rate of $100t_2$ per cent, on the earnings of foreign capital. (Temporarily agnostic concerning the sign of t_2, we concede that the tax may turn out to be a subsidy.)

Foreign earnings net of tax are $K(1-t_2)f'_2$ and the net income of the borrowing country is

$$f_2 - K(1-t_2)f'_2.$$

The problem then is to maximize this expression with respect to t_2, subject to the revised marginal condition

$$f'_1 = p(1-t_2)f'_2.$$

The maximizing t_2 is readily found to be

$$t_2 = \frac{-\mu_1\,\varepsilon_1}{1-\mu_1\,\varepsilon_1},$$

where $\mu_1 = \dfrac{K}{K_1 - K}$

is the ratio of the lending country's foreign investments to its domestic investments,

and $\varepsilon_1 = (K_1 - K)\frac{f_1''}{f_1'}$

is the elasticity of the marginal product of capital curve in the lending country (that is, the reciprocal of the elasticity of demand for capital in that country).

Since $\mu_1 \geqslant 0$ and $\varepsilon_1 < 0$, $t_1 \geqslant 0$; that is, in an investment optimum foreign earnings are *taxed*, not subsidized. In the limiting case in which the lending country contributes only marginally to the capital of the borrowing country, $\mu_1 = 0$ and the optimal tax is zero.

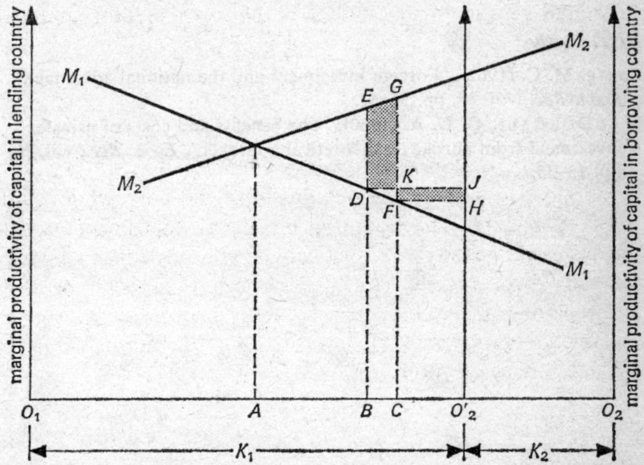

Figure 1

The same conclusion may be reached diagramatically. In Figure 1 the world's capital stock is measured along the horizontal axis. The curve of the marginal product of capital in the lending country is $M_1 M_1$; the corresponding curve in the borrowing country, referred to the origin O_2, is $M_2 M_2$. In competitive equilibrium, with no taxation of foreign earnings, the lending country invests AO_2' abroad. If, however, a tax t_2 is imposed, foreign investment shrinks to BO_2' and a gap $DE(= t_2 f_2')$

is opened between the two marginal products. Suppose now that t_2 is increased very slightly, to (t_2+dt_2), so that foreign investment is reduced further, to CO'_2, and the gap widens, to FG. Evidently net foreign earnings fall, from $BDJO'_2$ to $CFHO'_2$. The income of the borrowing country, on the other hand, is subject to two conflicting pressures: it increases by $FKJH$ $(= Kf''_1\,dk)$, but decreases by $DEGK$ $(= -t_2 f'_2\,dK)$. In an optimum, these two pressures balance,

$$t_2 f'_2 = -Kf''_1,$$

that is by easy steps,

$$t_2 = \frac{-\mu_1\,\varepsilon_1}{1-\mu_1\,\varepsilon_1}.$$

References

KEMP, M. C. (1962), 'Foreign investment and the national advantage', *Econ. Rec.*, vol. 38, pp. 56–62.

MACDOUGALL, G. D. A. (1960), 'The benefits and costs of private investment from abroad: a theoretical approach', *Econ. Rec.*, vol. 36, pp. 13–35.

7 Ivor F. Pearce and David C. Rowan

A Framework for Research into the Real Effects of International Capital Movements

Ivor F. Pearce and David C. Rowan, 'A framework for research into the real effects of international capital movements', in T. Bagiotti (ed.), *Essays in Honour of Marco Fanno*, Cedam, Padova, 1966, pp. 505–35.

Introduction

No more appropriate place could be found for a review of some of the problems of international capital movements than within the covers of a book of essays in honour of Professor Marco Fanno. Reflecting upon the very considerable contributions of Professor Fanno in this field and at the same time upon those issues which currently generate the most interest and excitement an old truth makes itself felt with added force. New problems are simply old problems in disguise. Indeed in reviewing the literature of economics nothing is more curiously disturbing than the way in which the same basic question seems to change in character with each relatively trivial development in the context in which it is discussed; a reflection perhaps of the partial nature of much of the analysis. Thus, we note that whenever a capital transfer is involuntary, being due to a deficit on the balance of trade, attention has traditionally been focused upon consumer demand and our efforts directed towards finding what price (terms of trade) adjustments are necessary to correct the capital loss. In this case we say we have a balance of payments problem. On the other hand, in the essentially similar circumstance where the object is to create a *surplus* on the balance of trade so as to be able to make capital payments against an aid programme, or against reparations, it has been more usual to talk of the 'transfer problem'. Here the centre of interest has been in employment effects or how to raise the money. Only in connection with the 'real burden' of the transfer have we, almost casually, inquired into its effect upon the real terms of trade.

More recently we have sought to discover in what circumstances international private lending is desirable either from the point of view of the lending or the borrowing country. In this case it is common practice to ignore the terms of trade effect completely and to point only to the fact that investment reduces the rate of interest, causing the social and private rates of return to diverge. This is in spite of extensive independent inquiries into the effect of differing rates of growth (capital accumulation) upon the real terms of trade between two countries. It is seldom explicitly recognized that the act of lending abroad is an act which *ipso facto* causes the borrowing country to grow faster than it otherwise would. By the same token the lending country grows less fast than it otherwise would.

In fact all of these problems are basically the same in that some temporary or continuous capital transfer is involved with the same fundamental consequences. The price, expenditure and commodity output levels required to sustain any given transfer of capital in one time period are identical, if full employment is to be maintained, whether the transfer is a loan, repayment of debt or simply that required to balance current international payments. Any differences which arise do so only because of the secondary effects implied by the original transfer.

A once-for-all payment of a capital sum, if it is to be anything more than a simple handing over of gold or foreign exchange reserves, demands certain relative price and production changes according to the manner of expenditure of the amount transferred. But these changes are only temporary. The situation reverts to normal at the end of the time period. If, on the other hand, the capital transfer is a steady flow per unit of time, the new relative price and production patterns are maintained as long as the capital flow persists. A model similar to that below which implicitly treats these 'impact effects' of overseas investment permanent or temporary has already been published by one of the present authors (Pearce, 1961), the problem in essence being the same as that involved in improving the balance of trade. We shall take it for granted, therefore, that the impact effects of any real transfer are understood.

In many cases, however, a transfer of capital is undertaken for reasons which in themselves imply secondary consequences, for example, when the transfer is due to an act of foreign investment. If the capital movement is simply the repayment of a loan there is no particular reason to suppose that in consequence the real capital stock of the receiving country will thereby be augmented. We do not normally, therefore, consider any secondary effects. A real trade surplus is established to sustain the flow of repayments and that is the end of the matter. But where the payments represent transfers of money specifically for investment abroad, the secondary effects clearly cannot be ignored. They must be assumed to become more important and long lasting than the impact effect itself. Indeed an act of investment will create permanently:

1. An increase in real capital stock abroad and hence an increase in total production abroad.

2. A continuous flow of interest payments on the debt.

The actual transfer of the capital sum has, as previously explained, no more than a transient effect which is adequately described in the model (Pearce, 1961) already referred to.

The purpose of the present paper is to develop a model, essentially the same as that in Pearce (1961), but extended so as to yield information on the consequences of 1 and 2 above. The very general applicability of the model should be noted. In fact 1 is equivalent to a rate of capital accumulation per time period equal to the capital transfer and 2 is again a continuous flow of capital transfer no different from that treated in Pearce (1961). In what follows we shall deal with the two simultaneously but it should be understood that all that is needed to examine problems of growth is straightforward separation of the two elements of the investment analysis.

To fix our ideas we state the particular case. Suppose that we have two countries one of which can be thought of as the 'home' country and the other as the 'rest of the world'. The home country is supposed to invest a certain sum of money abroad once and for all. The transient impact of the actual transfer of the loan will be ignored. On the other hand, the permanent effects 1 and 2 above will alter total consumption, the terms of trade, and other relative prices, as well as the patterns of production and factor prices, and in particular the rate of interest. It is these permanent effects with which we are to be concerned.

The individual investor in the home country will see only the rate of return he earns on capital lent. He will make judgements about the desirability of his investment accordingly. But the welfare of the home country, and indeed of the foreign country, will be affected not only by the returns but also by changes in the terms of trade. Furthermore, changes in the foreign interest rate affect home welfare since part of the home country's income is earned by foreign investment. We shall develop our model so as to be able to examine in a completely general way the nature and degree of the difference between the private return to the investor and the social return to the country as a whole.

This is of course a problem which has already been investigated by a number of writers so that reasons should be given for turning to it again. These are:

1. That as recently as 1963 attention has once more been drawn to the issue by certain passages in the second report of the United Kingdom National Economic Development Council (1963, pp. 36–9) which suggest a proper interest on the part of those concerned with the formulation of economic policy.

2. That it is clear that the authors of the NEDC report are far from satisfied that the last word has been said. This is a view shared by most academic economists who have written on the subject, including, or course, the present contributors.

The NEDC report argues that although the private rates of return on direct investment at home and abroad appear to be the same, there are many reasons quite apart from the effect of taxation why the social rate on overseas lending may differ from the private. In particular the possible influence on the terms of trade is cited. It concludes, however, that it does not seem possible to make any useful generalizations at present. It is hoped that the following pages represent a first step towards the desired end.

In particular it is claimed that two contributions of some value have been made. Both arise from the fact that the model is developed essentially as a general equilibrium model in the fullest sense of this term, that is, it is in the Walrasian rather than the Marshallian tradition. First it is clear that within such a framework it is impossible not to include explicitly the effects of international lending on the terms of trade. Failure to do this is one of the weaknesses of earlier treatments, which, as previously indicated tend to ignore or remark only in passing upon the possibility. This is true of the work of Jasay (1960), and it is true of a more recent study by Paul B. Simpson (1962). It is also the case that, in his paper analysing the effect of foreign investment in the capital receiving country, Sir Donald MacDougall (1960) proceeds in the main on the straightforward assumption of invariant terms of trade. Finally we find the same approach in the most recent work of Professor Murray Kemp (1964). By contrast the results below force the present writers to conclude that to ignore the terms of trade is not only undesirable but amounts almost to a logical contradiction.[1]

The second contribution claimed by the authors is much more important and bears more upon the general discussion with which this paper began. It is becoming increasingly clear that the classical qualitative approach to economic theory is of strictly limited value. In the present problem for example, from the purely qualitative point of view, the work carried out simply confirms our suspicion that anything can happen. No further progress can be made without quantitative studies. But quantitative studies in turn await the development of models of the *right type*. The words 'right type' here call for some explanation.

Unfortunately a great deal of received theory, particularly in the field of international trade, is developed in terms of concepts which are applicable only to the problem in question. It is common practice for example to analyse the gains from overseas investment by drawing a single falling marginal product of capital curve for each of two countries without any explanation of what such a curve means in general equilibrium terms. This

1. In an unpublished paper on this question (written in collaboration with Dr J. H. Dunning and submitted to the NEDC), one of the present authors followed the practice of assuming invariant terms of trade. The present paper arose largely from his dissatisfaction with the earlier formulation and his growing belief that this assumption, though convenient, removed most of the interest from the analysis. Cf. J. H. Dunning and D. C. Rowan (1964).

may be satisfactory for qualitative work, but there is no hope whatever of measuring the slope of such a curve so as to obtain quantitative results except by observing the actual effects of overseas lending itself, which is impracticable. What is needed is an analysis in terms of elasticities of demand and supply, properly defined independently of the problem under review, which can be measured by general methods not necessarily connected with the question to be put. Quantitative answers can then be worked out by substituting estimates of the various parameters into previously prepared formulae.

The model described below is a model of the right kind in this sense. Although it is set out in terms of three commodities and three factors of production primarily for the purpose of qualitative inquiry, it is nevertheless immediately generalizable into as many countries and commodities as desired. It could be used as the basis for an econometric study which, whilst it would be a large undertaking with many difficulties, is now possible in principle. Such a study might yield unexpected dividends. Our model represents also an invitation to econometricians to concentrate more attention upon measurement of the basic elasticities of supply and demand common to all economic problems by whatever means are available, rather than upon the setting up of specific models to answer specific questions. Once the values of the basic parameters are known all else follows by the methods of this paper. We turn now to the analysis.

The marginal social return on overseas investment

The measurement of social return on investment involves difficulties over and above those normally associated with the calculation of return on capital, for we have to assess the welfare significance of the consequent change in the pattern of prices and production as well as the direct return. Nevertheless this is simply accomplished in principle by a method due to Professor J. E. Meade (1955, section 2). To decide whether a given marginal investment is socially desirable, we value the change in total consumption of all commodities (including investment goods) at the original prices.

Apart from its intuitive appeal this procedure may be rationalized as follows. Let X_i be consumption of the ith commodity including items of capital and let p_i be prices. Now welfare, W, is a function of total consumption so that

$$W = W(X_i, \ldots, X_n)$$

and hence $$dW = \sum \frac{\partial W}{\partial X_i} dX_i \qquad \mathbf{1}$$

as a first approximation.

But competition will ensure that the marginal £1 spent on each commodity adds the same to welfare whether the item is a consumer or producer's good. In other words

$$\lambda = \frac{1}{p_i} \frac{\partial W}{\partial X_i} \quad \text{for all } i,$$

where λ represents the welfare derived from each last £1 spent. Thus from **1** the total change in welfare deriving from any marginal act of investment (or any policy whatever) is given by

$$dW = \lambda \sum p_i \, dX_i$$

or, measuring the welfare change in terms of money by dividing by λ,

$$\frac{1}{\lambda} dW = \sum p_i \, dX_i. \qquad \mathbf{2}$$

$\sum p_i \, dX_i$ is, of course, the total value of the change in consumption which it was claimed above measures the welfare gain. This must be greater than the interest on the amount to be invested if the policy is to improve welfare.[2]

For present purposes it is more convenient to rewrite this criterion in another form. To this end we define Y as total *money* expenditure, K_f as the total amount of money invested abroad and S_i as home production of the ith good. And total expenditure on all commodities must equal the total value of consumption so that

$$Y = \sum p_i \, X_i. \qquad \mathbf{3}$$

2. The reader will note that, as **1** is written as a differential, an approximation is involved equivalent to taking the first term in a Taylor Series. It would be more correct of course to say that, if $\sum p_i \, dX_i$ is greater than the interest on the amount of money to be invested, then there exists some finite sum of money which, if invested, would increase welfare.

Similarly total expenditure for the country as a whole must equal total income derived from production plus the income from overseas investment. (It is assumed throughout the balance of payments is identically balanced and that full employment prevails both before and after any change. Thus savings equals investment and total expenditure equals total income.) If S_i is the home production of the *i*th commodity, then

$$Y \equiv \sum p_i S_i + r' K_f \qquad \mathbf{4}$$

where r' is the money rate of interest abroad. *Primes will be used throughout to indicate* 'belonging to the foreign country'.

From **3** and **4** we obtain

$$\sum p_i \, dX_i + \sum X_i \, dp_i = \sum p_i \, dS_i + \sum S_i \, dp_i + r' dK_f + K_f \, dr'. \qquad \mathbf{5}$$

Now in a general way, so long as full employment of given resources is maintained at all times, $\sum p_i \, dS_i$ must be zero in the region of competitive equilibrium; for each factor of production earns the same marginal revenue product in every use. The shifting of factors from use i to use j yields a negative $p_i \, dS_i$ equal in magnitude to the positive $p_j \, dS_j$.[3]

Thus we have from **5**

$$\sum p_i \, dX_i = \sum (S_i - X_i) \, dp_i + r' dK_f + K_f \, dr'. \qquad \mathbf{6}$$

For all non-traded commodities $S_i - X_i$ is zero as supply equals consumption. Otherwise $S_i - X_i$ is exports or imports according to whether it is positive or negative. We write these quantities exported or imported in l. c. symbols, e.g. x_i, to derive a perfectly

3. An exception to this rule would occur if domestic production functions were affected by the act of investment. This 'technical transference effect' (Dunning and Rowan, 1964) might occur for example if association with a foreign firm led to increased 'know how'. For present purposes however we assume zero TTE. In an earlier paper submitted to the NEDC, Dunning and Rowan (1964) defined 'technical transference effects' to consist in the upward shift of domestic production functions resulting from overseas investment. Some empirical evidence concerning these effects was presented. This was derived from Dr Dunning's work. From a purely formal point of view incorporation of such effects into the present model would present no problems. However, since we have no theory to explain the nature of the shift in the domestic production functions which would result, there seems little point in adding any further complication to the analysis.

general formula for a money measure of the welfare change coming about as the result of any kind of policy whatever. Specifically we assume the policy to be overseas lending and, to be exact, write the *rate* of change of welfare rather than a finite change as follows

$$\frac{dW}{dK_f} = \sum x_i \frac{dp_i}{dK_f} + r' + K_f \frac{dr'}{dK_f}. \qquad \mathbf{7}$$

All that is necessary now is to set up a model which expresses the rates of change of price dp_i/dK_f and dr'/dK_f in terms of fundamental elasticities whose magnitude and sign we hope to determine and substitute in **7**. Before proceeding to this however we may use **7** as a peg for one or two comments upon earlier work.

Term one in **7** gives the terms of trade effect by weighting the price changes by import and export quanta. Terms three and four together measure the marginal rate of return on the increment of capital invested as compared to the average return r' which is the concern of the individual lender.

In the literature, as previously indicated, it has been usual to assume that term one is small relative to the others. But unless there is some reason for supposing that the percentage rates of change of commodity prices are very small relative to the percentage rate of change of the rate of interest, the truth must be quite the contrary. At least this is so in the United Kingdom where annual exports are of the same order of size as overseas capital holdings. Moreover, there is a logical inconsistency involved in concentrating attention upon dr'/dK_f to the exclusion of dp_i/dK_f for we shall show that, for constant return to scale, zero price changes imply zero rate of interest changes in which case the point of the discussion is lost. Indeed no proof of this is really needed for it follows at once from the fact that factor prices, of which the rate of interest is one, determine commodity prices uniquely for small changes.

This is not the only weakness of received theory on the subject. The common practice has been to adjust the second and third terms of **7** for taxation and to write

$$\frac{dW}{dK_f} = \left(r' + K_f \frac{dr'}{dK_f}\right)(1 - t_f), \qquad \mathbf{8}$$

where t_f is the foreign rate of tax on profits. The next step is to define t_d as the domestic tax rate on profits and hence, on the assumption that double tax relief prevails, to identify $r'(1-t_d)$ with the net private rate of return. It is then suggested that, provided K_f is significant,[4] provided t_d and t_f are not very different, and given dr'/dK_f is negative then

$$r'(1-t_d) > \left(r'+K_f\frac{dr'}{dK_f}\right)(1-t_f). \qquad 9$$

Thus it is claimed that, from a social point of view, free competition leads to overlending.

But it should be noted that even this limited argument, which ignores the terms of trade, rests upon the unproven assertion that dr'/dK_f is always negative. In most texts (e.g. Kemp, 1964) it is taken for granted that there exists a production function for 'output' as a whole, subject to diminishing returns to capital. This is in contradiction with the results obtained by 'growth' theorists who have developed multisectoral models suggesting that an increase in capital stock need not reduce the rate of interest. Indeed, it is intuitively obvious that an increase in output and income might well raise the demand for capital goods by an amount greater than the value of the increased stock which caused it if there is a change in the relative outputs of the different sectors. We shall show below that, where there are three or more commodities involved it cannot be proved that dr'/dK_f must always be negative (Appendices I and III, pages 188 and 190). The aggregate notion of diminishing marginal productivity of capital is not satisfactory, although of course, in any single sector of the economy, marginal productivity of every factor diminishes when other inputs remain constant.

In the remainder of this paper we set up two models which permit us to inquire into the nature of, and connection between, the various elements of **7**. The first is a simple two-country, two-commodity, two-factor system developed for purposes of exposition only. The second is a more realistic model including non-traded commodities by means of which we explore the possibility of qualitative results. The way in which the more

4. Cf. A. E. Jasay (1960). As we shall see later the concept of 'significance' requires interpretation.

general model can be extended as the basis for econometric inquiry is briefly commented on.

The expositional model – two goods and two factors

The reader is reminded that the two countries of the model may be thought of as the home country and the rest of the world and that the policy under review is the lending of capital by the home country to the rest of the world. Factors of production are capital and labour, the total country endowment of each being K and L respectively. An increase in K_f i.e. lending abroad, means a corresponding increase in the total stock of capital K' of the rest of the world. The following points also are worth repeating.

1. The approach is one of long-run comparative statics. Hence the problem of the capital transfer, arising out of the direct, once for all investment, is ignored.

2. The knowledge of technique, that is the production functions, both at 'home' and in the 'rest of the world' are assumed to be unaffected by overseas investment.

3. Tariffs and transport costs are ignored.

4. Full employment is assumed to rule in both countries both before and after the investment.

5. The labour supply in both countries is invariant.

In each country there are two demand and supply functions. These are as:

$$\left.\begin{aligned} S_1 &= S_1(K, L, p_1, p_2) \\ S_2 &= S_2(K, L, p_1, p_2) \end{aligned}\right\} \begin{matrix}\text{supply}\\ \text{functions}\end{matrix} \left\{\begin{aligned} S_1' &= S_1'(K', L', p_1, p_2) \\ S_2' &= S_2'(K', L', p_1, p_2) \end{aligned}\right\},$$

$$\left.\begin{aligned} X_1 &= X_1(Y, p_1, p_2) \\ X_2 &= X(Y, p_1, p_2) \end{aligned}\right\} \begin{matrix}\text{demand}\\ \text{functions}\end{matrix} \left\{\begin{aligned} X_1' &= X_1'(Y', p_1, p_2) \\ X_2' &= X_2'(Y', p_1, p_2) \end{aligned}\right\}. \qquad 10$$

We take X_1 as the 'home' exportable, X_2 as the 'rest of the world's' exportable. Primes, which will be used throughout, denote that the parameter or variable concerned refers to the 'rest of the world'. Supply functions written as above may not be entirely familiar so that some explanation must be given. We assume that, in both countries, the underlying production functions are homogeneous of degree one in capital and labour; that is:

$$S_1 = \Phi\,(K_1, L_1)$$

is homogeneous of degree one where K_1 and L_1 denote the quantities of capital and labour utilized in the production of good 1. More generally for the *i*th good,

$$S_i = \Phi_i\,(K_i, L_i) \quad (i = 1, 2, \ldots, n). \qquad \mathbf{11}$$

Now it is well known that with constant returns to scale and for any given total factor endowment of K and L, K_i and L_i are determined by the commodity prices ruling (the p_i). Hence, by substitution in **11** we can write,

$$S_i = S_i\,(p_1, p_2, K, L) \quad (i = 1, 2, \ldots, n), \qquad \mathbf{12}$$

which gives the supply of the *i*th commodity as a function of the overall factor endowment and commodity prices.

The definition **12** however, gives rise to an important but unfamiliar parameter which will appear frequently below, namely,

$$\frac{\partial S_i}{\partial K}, \qquad \mathbf{13}$$

that is, the change in the supply of the *i*th good due to an increase in the *total* capital endowment *prices being held constant*. It should be noted that this is *not* the marginal product of capital except in the impossibly, simple case where only one commodity is produced. On the other hand, it is clear that, in all models involving growth or change in capital stock for any reason, the new parameter must be as crucial as the ordinary supply elasticity. The character of $\partial S_i/\partial K$ will be investigated later.

Our aim is to find an expression, in terms of the parameters of the demand and supply functions, for:

$$\frac{dW}{dK_f} = \sum x_i \frac{dp_i}{dK'} + r' + K_f \frac{dr'}{dK'}, \qquad \mathbf{14}$$

where dK' ($\equiv dK_f$) is the increase in the 'rest of the world's' capital stock resulting from 'home' direct investment overseas.

It is convenient to think of this problem as having two elements:

1. We need to obtain an expression for each dp_i/dK' – the changes in the terms of trade.

2. We need an expression for dr'/dK' which, as we know, is a function of every dp_i/dK'.

For simplicity we begin with 2.

Evaluating dr'/dK'

Our model is one of long-run equilibrium. As a result we assume that profits are continuously maximized. From this it follows that the marginal value product of capital in each use must be equal.

Hence $$r' = p_1 \frac{\partial S'_1}{\partial K'_1} = p_2 \frac{\partial S'_2}{\partial K'_2}. \qquad 15$$

The partials $\partial S'_i/\partial K'_i$, it should be noted, are derived from the production functions (not the supply functions) and the suffixes are used to indicate this fact. Any increase in capital, K', must be allocated between industries 1 and 2.

Hence $$\frac{dK'_1}{dK'} + \frac{dK'_2}{dK'} = 1. \qquad 16$$

Thus using **15** we may write

$$r' = p_1 \frac{\partial S'_1}{\partial K'_1}\frac{dK'_1}{dK'} + p_2 \frac{\partial S'_2}{\partial K'_2}\frac{dK'_2}{dK'}. \qquad 17$$

We now wish to obtain an expression for r' in terms of the supply functions rather than the production functions. To do this we recognize that, by definition of $\partial S'_i/\partial K'$,

$$p_i \frac{\partial S'_i}{\partial K'} = p_i \frac{\partial S'_i}{\partial K'_i}\frac{dK'_i}{dK'} + p_i \frac{\partial S'_i}{\partial L'_i}\frac{dL'_i}{dK'}, \qquad 18$$

in the special case in which the dK'_1/dK' and dK'_2/dK' are chosen so that p_1 and p_2 are unchanged.

Thus, remembering that the sum of all dL'_i/dK' is zero for L' constant,

$$r' = p_1 \frac{\partial S'_1}{\partial K'} + p_2 \frac{\partial S^2}{\partial K'} \qquad 19$$

is a special case of **17**. It should be noted that the restriction implied by the word 'special case' does *not* mean that **19** is true only for restricted values of p and K. On the contrary **19** is an identity. It does mean, however, that **19** holds only for the partial derivatives $\partial S'/\partial K'$ and not for arbitrary total derivatives, which is no more than we should expect.

We may now evaluate dr'/dK' by the following method.

1. Without loss of generality we take dp_2/dK' to be zero: that is, we use commodity 2 as a *numéraire*.

2. L' – the labour force in the 'rest of the world' is taken as constant.

We then differentiate **19** totally with respect to K' remembering that p_2 is invariant by assumption. This operation calls for some rather tedious use of received production theory so that the working has been relegated to Appendix I (page 188). The result is very simple. In fact, it is shown that in a two-good world with commodity two as *numéraire*

$$\frac{dr'}{dK'} = \frac{dp_1}{dK'}\frac{\partial S_1'}{\partial K'}, \qquad \mathbf{20}$$

so that solving for dr'/dK' entails two operations:[5]

1. Solving the model for dp_1/dK' – the change in the terms of trade.

2. Deriving a value for $\partial S_1'/\partial K'$ from the production relations.

Since the second of these operations is considerably the simpler we shall begin with that.

Obtaining the value $\partial S_1'/\partial K'$

The production relations in the 'rest of the world' may be written as:

$$\begin{aligned} K' &= a_{11}\, S_1' + a_{12}\, S_1', \\ L' &= a_{21}\, S_1' + a_{22}\, S_1', \end{aligned} \qquad \mathbf{21}$$

5. This, of course, is not necessary. The system could be solved directly for dr'/dK'. Our aim, however, is to bring out as fully as possible, the role of dp_1/dK'.

where K', L' denote overall factor endowment

and $a_{11} \equiv \frac{K_1'}{S_1'}$, $a_{21} \equiv \frac{L_1'}{S_1'}$, etc.

In this formulation the a_{ij} are unit input/output ratios. Indeed **21** is no more than the column sums of an ordinary Leontief input/output system. Production functions are homogeneous of degree one in the K_i, L_i, so that the a_{ij} is uniquely determined by p_1 and p_2. Clearly, since L' and K' are given, we can solve **21** for each S_1' in terms of factor endowments and the a_{ij} to give the supply functions of **10**. These can be differentiated with respect to K' – prices being held constant – to obtain $\partial S_1'/\partial K'$. The necessary operations are carried out in Appendix I, the solution for $\partial S_1'/\partial K'$ being

$$\frac{\partial S_1'}{\partial K'} = \frac{a_{22}}{a_{11}\,a_{22} - a_{21}\,a_{12}} = \frac{a_{22}}{J} \qquad \textbf{22}$$

where J (assumed $\neq 0$) is the determinant of the unit input/output coefficients. Now a_{22} is necessarily positive. J, however, may be negative or positive.

Evidently the sign of J depends upon the relative factor intensities of production. (This interpretation is, of course, acceptable only in the two-good, two-factor model, for, where the number of factors exceeds two, no meaning can be assigned to the concept of factor intensities.)

By definition of J we have:

$J > 0$, S_1' is the capital-intensive output.
$J < 0$, S_1' is the labour-intensive output.

The case $J = 0$ leaves $\partial S_1'/\partial K'$ undefined but this can arise only as a result of an almost impossible coincidence. It implies first that there is some factor price ratio at which labour and capital are most profitably used in the same proportion in both commodities one and two. This is possible, of course, but $\partial S_1/\partial K'$ zero requires the further coincidence that the factor endowment ratio K'/L' should be this very same proportion. Such a coincidence leads furthermore to infinite supply elasticities which, with minimal transport costs induce complete specialization contrary to the assumptions of the model. We assume therefore $J \neq 0$.

The meaning of the results obtained so far may perhaps be better understood by noticing that the argument leading to **22** implies also that

$$\frac{\partial S_2'}{\partial K'} = -\frac{a_{21}}{J} \qquad \textbf{23}$$

and hence $$p_1\frac{\partial S_1}{\partial K'}+p_2\frac{\partial S_2'}{\partial K'} = \frac{p_1 a_{22}-p_2 a_{21}}{J}. \qquad \textbf{24}$$

Both sides of **24** must necessarily be positive whatever the sign of J since both must be equal to the rate of interest r' by **19**. Since both *a*s and *p*s are positive it follows that $\partial S_1'/\partial K'$ and $\partial S_2'/\partial K'$ must be of opposite sign; that is, an increase in capital endowment prices constant entails the reduction in supply of one commodity and an increase in the supply of the other. In fact the good whose output is reduced is always the labour intensive good. This is illustrated geometrically in Figure 1.

ABCD is the familiar Edgeworth 'box' and *AEC* the 'contract' curve (Stolper and Samuelson, 1941–2). E is the initial point of equilibrium. *AB* measures L' and *BC* measures K'. The increment in capital dK' defines a new 'box' *ABFG*. Since, by assumption, p_1/p_2 is invariant, the ratios of K_i'/L_i' in each case are similarly invariant, being functions of p_1/p_2. The new point of equilibrium is therefore formed by constructing, from F, a line parallel to *CE*. This cuts *AE* at E'. E' is therefore the new equilibrium point at which the ratios of K_i'/L_i' in each case are unaltered and their weighted average equals the factor endowment ratio, K'/L'.

Clearly E' lies to the left of E. Less capital and labour are used in producing good 1. Hence its output has fallen. Equally clearly good 1 is the labour-intensive good. Hence, if commodity prices are to remain unchanged, output of the labour-intensive good must contract, although total expenditure has increased.

Demand cannot be satisfied unless good 1 is an inferior good; in general, therefore, p_1/p_2 cannot remain unchanged. It follows that an increment in K will change the terms of trade.

We now deduce from **22** and **20** that, if $J \neq 0$,

$$\frac{dr'}{dK'} = \frac{a_{22}}{J}\frac{dp_1}{dK'}. \qquad \textbf{25}$$

This confirms that if there is a change in the terms of trade there must be a change in the rate of interest and vice versa.

In the next section we turn to the task of evaluating dp_1/dK' the change in the terms of trade.

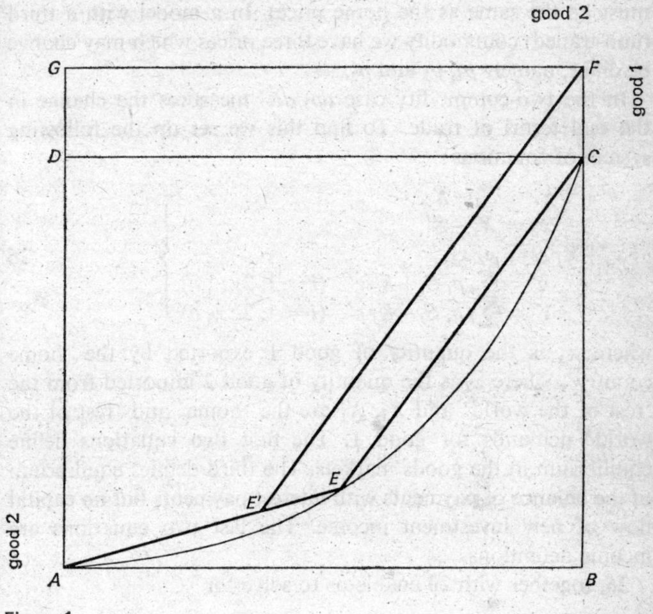

Figure 1

Evaluation of dp_1/dK'

At this point the reader should perhaps be reminded that we have been assuming throughout that the price of commodity two does not change, i.e. that commodity two is taken as *numéraire*. This is, of course, not an expedient but a necessary device arising from the fact that proportionate changes in all factor and commodity prices leave the real economic situation unchanged. Thus there are an infinity of solutions in terms of absolute prices which are all equivalent. In order to get a unique solution we have to work in relative prices. The most convenient way to do this is to assume that one price remains constant throughout, although it should be understood that whichever way we choose to work the answer remains the same. For convenience also we measure prices in the foreign country in units of the home currency. Thus in the two-commodity model we have only one price p_1 (the foreign price of traded goods must be the same as the home price). In a model with a third (non-traded) commodity we have three prices which may change or differ, namely p_1, p_3 and p_3'.

In the two-commodity case dp_1/dK' measures the change in the real terms of trade. To find this we set up the following system of equations:

$$\left.\begin{aligned} x_1 &= S_1 - X_1, \\ x_2 &= X_2' - S_1', \\ p_1 x_1 + K_f r' &= p_2 x_2, \\ Y &= \textstyle\sum_i p_i S_i + K_f r' \quad (i = 1, 2, \ldots, n), \\ Y' &= \textstyle\sum_i p_i S_i - K_f r' \quad (i = 1, 2, \ldots, n), \end{aligned}\right\} \qquad \mathbf{26}$$

where x_1 is the quantity of good 1 exported by the 'home country', where x_2 is the quantity of good 2 imported from the 'rest of the world' and X_1, X_1' are the 'home' and 'rest of the world' demands for good 1. The first two equations define equilibrium in the goods markets. The third defines equilibrium of the balance of payments with interest payments but no capital flow of new investment income. The last two equations are income definitions.

26, together with **20** enable us to solve for

$$\frac{dp_1}{dK'}, \frac{dx_1}{dK'}, \frac{dx_2}{dK'}, \frac{dY}{dK'}, \frac{dY}{dK'}, \frac{dr}{dK'},$$

the six unknowns of the system.

We proceed by differentiating **26** with respect to K' in the light of the functional relations and assumptions set out, solving the resulting equations appropriately. The actual operations are carried out in Appendix III see equation **27**, page 191. Here we merely state the result. To do this in a convenient form we introduce the following notation:

$\sigma_{ij} = \dfrac{\partial X_i}{\partial p_j} + X_j \dfrac{\partial X_i}{\partial Y}$ = the compensated demand partial derivative with respect to price, i.e. the Slutsky substitution term.

$S_{ij} = \frac{\partial S_i}{\partial p_i}$ = the supply response of the ith commodity with respect to the jth price.

$R_{ij} = \sigma_{ij} - S_{ij}$.

From received theory of demand and supply we know that $\sigma_{ii} < 0$ and $S_{ii} > 0$ hence $R_{ii} < 0$.

Making use of this notation we find the following expression for the change in the terms of trade:

$$\frac{dp_1}{dK'} = \frac{\partial S_1'/\partial K' + K_f(\partial X_1'/\partial Y' - \partial X_1/\partial Y)dr'/dK' - r'\partial X_1/\partial Y}{R_{11} + R_{11} + (\partial X_1/\partial Y - \partial X_1'/\partial Y')x_1}, \quad \mathbf{28}$$

where $\frac{\partial S_1'}{\partial K'} = \frac{a_{22}}{J}$ when $J \neq 0$ as shown above.

Qualitative conclusions can be drawn from this result. Consider first the denominator of **28**. In this expression both R_{11} and R'_{11} (from **27**, page 191) must be negative. Hence unless the home country's marginal propensity to spend on good 1 considerably exceeds that of the rest of the world, the denominator will certainly be negative. Furthermore, as one of the present writers has already argued elsewhere, the smaller is R_{11} the greater the likelihood that $\partial X_1/\partial Y - \partial X_1'/\partial Y$ is smaller still (Pearce, 1961); for less substitution possibilities mean high complementarity, i.e. fixed proportions, and fixed proportions suggest some technical reason why the proportion should be the same in both countries. If this is accepted then the sign of the denominator is determined.

The sign of the numerator is, on the contrary, uncertain, for a_{22}/J can be negative (if $J < 0$) or positive (if $J > 0$).

Let us proceed on the assumption that $\partial X_1'/\partial Y' - \partial X_1/\partial Y$ is small. Then the numerator reduces approximately to:

$$\frac{\partial S_1'}{\partial K'} - r'\frac{\partial X_1}{\partial Y}.$$

Suppose J is negative. Then since r' and $\partial X_1/\partial Y$ are positive, the numerator is negative. It follows then that $\partial p_1/\partial K'$ is positive. The terms of trade improve.

This result is in complete accordance with our earlier intuitive argument for, as we have already shown, output of the capital-intensive good (in the rest of the world) must be expanded. With $J < 0$, this is good 2. Hence the price of good 2 must be expected to fall relatively to good 1; the terms of trade must improve.

When J is positive the sign of the numerator is less easy to determine. It is shown in Appendix II (page 190), however, that where $\partial S_1'/\partial K'$ is positive the numerator will also be positive provided

$$p_1 \frac{\partial X_1}{\partial Y} < 1.$$

Since this condition must be met unless good 2 is inferior, we can assume it to hold. Hence if $J > 0$ so is the numerator. It follows that $J > 0$ entails a deterioration in the terms of trade. This again accords with our earlier argument.

In short: $J < 0$ implies $\frac{dp_1}{dK'} > 0$,

$J > 0$ implies $\frac{dp_1}{dK'} < 0$.

It is, of course, always possible for dp_1/dK' to be zero, if either R_{11} or R'_{11} or both are very large. This may occur if price elasticities of demand are high or if price elasticities of supply are high or both. It should be noted however that very high elasticities of supply imply $J \to 0$ with consequences which should be carefully considered. Zero dp_1/dK' may also occur exceptionally with small R if the assumptions of Appendix II and the preceding paragraph regarding the sign and magnitude of $p_1(\partial X_1/\partial Y)$ are relaxed (cf. Appendix II).

As a footnote readers are reminded that this discussion in terms of factor-intensities is relevant only in the two-factor case. The concept of factor-intensity cannot be generalized. In later sections of this paper, where a more general model is developed, it is therefore dropped.

The value of dr'/dK'

We have now shown (**25**) that

$$\frac{dr'}{dK'} = \frac{a_{22}}{J} \frac{dp_1}{dK'}$$

provided $J \neq 0$ and, since $J < 0$ implies $dp_1/dK' > 0$ and conversely (see previous section), the sign of dr'/dK' is independent of the sign of dp_1/dK'. r' usually falls as the result of overseas investment. The reader is warned, however, that this result does not readily generalize to the case where some commodities are excluded from trade (cf. Appendix III).

An expression for the magnitude of dr'/dK' is obtained by substituting **28** into **25** thus,

$$\frac{dr'}{dK'} = \frac{(a_{22}/J)(\partial S_1'/\partial K' - r'\partial X_1/\partial Y)}{R_{11}+R_{11}'+x_1 K_f(a_{22}/J)(\partial X_1/\partial Y - \partial X_1'/\partial Y')}. \quad \textbf{29}$$

The argument above implies that whatever the sign of J the numerator will necessarily be positive. And provided

$$\frac{\partial X_1}{\partial Y} - \frac{\partial X_1'}{\partial Y'}$$

is relatively small the denominator will be negative. Hence dr'/dK' is normally negative as indicated. The money rate of profit falls as the result of investment overseas *provided overseas investment changes the terms of trade*. [But note that $dr'/dK' \to 0$ as $(R_{11}+R_{11}') \to \infty$.] We are now in a position to evaluate the marginal social product of investment overseas, which was the principal object of the inquiry.

The marginal social and private products

In the second section it was shown that, leaving aside tax complications, the marginal social product of unit investment is given, remembering that p_2 does not change, by

$$\frac{dW}{dK_f} = x_1 \frac{dp_1}{dK_1} + r' + K_f \frac{dr'}{dK_f}. \quad [7]$$

Hence on substituting **7** becomes:

$$\frac{dW}{dK_f} = x_1 \frac{dp_1}{dK'} + r' + K_f \frac{dp_1}{dK'} \frac{a_{22}}{J}. \quad \textbf{30}$$

The marginal private product is, under competitive conditions, simply

$$r'. \quad \textbf{31}$$

Hence the excess of the marginal social product over the marginal private product is:

$$E = \left(x_1 + K_f \frac{a_{22}}{J}\right) \frac{dp_1}{dK'}. \quad \textbf{32}$$

When $J > 0$, $dp_1/dK' < 0$. Hence **32** will be negative and the marginal social product must be *less* than the private.

When $J < 0$ on the other hand $dp_1/dK' > 0$ and the sign of **32** depends upon the sign of the expression in brackets on the right-hand side of **32**. The sign of this expression cannot be established *a priori* for the absolute value of J could be very small. This is clear when it is recalled that $\|J\|$, read modulus J, reflects in part the extent to which the factor/output ratios differ in the production of goods 1,2. As these ratios approach each other so that both approach the overall ratio K'/L', $\|J\|$ approaches zero and $\|a_{22}/J\|$ approaches infinity. Hence, even if K_f is very small in relation to x_1 (the export quantum), it is still far from certain that the expression in the brackets in **32** will be dominated by x_1. Conversely even if K_f is very large in relation to x_1, the latter may dominate the expression if J itself is not small. It is K_f times its 'weight' (a_{22}/J) rather than the size of K_f alone which is the determinant of the 'significance' of K_f.

It is also clear from **32** that the marginal private and social products may coincide if $dp_1/dK' > 0$. This will occur when

$$x_1 - K_f \frac{a_{22}}{\|J\|} = 0$$

which is certainly not impossible. Equally, even if the terms of trade improve, **32** may still be negative provided

$$K_f \frac{a_{22}}{\|J\|}$$

is large enough.

We end this account of the two-good model by reminding ourselves of the relation between it and earlier work. In our notation much of this seems to proceed as follows. First, only one good is assumed to be produced overseas.

Hence $r' = p_1 \dfrac{\partial S_1'}{\partial K_1}$

which, since the whole capital endowment is always employed in the production of good 1 is the same as saying

$$r' = p_1 \frac{\partial S_1'}{\partial K_1'}.$$

Or, since the terms of trade are held constant, the 'real' marginal product of capital is

$$\frac{r'}{p_1} = \frac{\partial S_1'}{\partial K'}.$$

Finally $\dfrac{dr'}{dK'} = p_1 \dfrac{\partial(\partial S'/\partial K')}{\partial K'}$

is taken, with p_1 and p_2 invariant, to be negative on the argument that $\partial S'/K'$ is now a function of K'/L' only. This is clearly a highly restrictive condition and one which it would be most improper to use as the basis for any kind of policy decision.

Before proceeding to the more complicated and realistic model which follows, it may be helpful to draw together the main conclusions to be derived from our expository model. These are:

1. Neglecting tax complications, the marginal and average rates of return on investment overseas can differ if and only if investment changes the terms of trade; or some other price where it is included in the model (see the next section).

2. Hence arguments which take the terms of trade to be invariant involve a logical contradiction.

3. The direction in which the terms of trade change is determined by the relative factor intensities ruling overseas.

4. Where the terms of trade deteriorate ($J > 0$), the marginal private product will exceed the marginal social product.

5. Where the terms of trade improve ($J < 0$), the marginal private product may be less, equal to, or greater than, the marginal social product.

These conclusions must not be regarded as having general applicability. They are stated simply because they suggest that it would be worthwhile to attempt to test their validity in the more general case. We now turn to this.

A model including non-traded goods

A more general model which permits each country to produce a non-traded good (X_3 and X_3') introduces two new prices p_3 and p_3'. Apart from this complication, everything is in all essentials similar to the two-good version introduced for expositional purposes. All manipulation of the model is carried out in Appendix III (page 190), the results only being set out below. In the more general case we have:

$$\frac{dr'}{dK'} = \frac{\partial S_1'}{\partial K'}\frac{dp_1}{dK'} + \frac{\partial S_3'}{\partial K'}\frac{dp_3'}{dK'}, \qquad [59]$$

where dp_2/dK' is taken to be zero as before. (See Appendix I, page 188.) Solving for the dp_1/dK' gives:

$$\frac{dp_1}{dK'} = \frac{\Sigma_{13}' + K_f(dr'/dK')(\Phi_{13}' - \Phi_{13}) - r'\Phi_{13}}{\Psi_{13} + \Psi_{13}' + x_1(\Phi_{13} - \Phi_{13}')} \qquad [58]$$

and

$$\frac{dp_3'}{dK'} = \left[\frac{\partial S_3'/\partial K' + K_f(dr'/dK')\partial X_3'/\partial Y'}{R_{33}'}\right] -$$

$$-\frac{(R_{31}' - x_1\,\partial X_3'/\partial Y')\{\Sigma_{13}' - K_f(dr'/dK')(\Phi_{13} - \Phi_{13}') - r'\Phi_{13}\}}{R_{33}'\{\Psi_{13} + \Psi_{13}' + x_1(\Phi_{13} - \Phi_{13}')\}} \qquad [60]$$

where $\Psi_{13} = \dfrac{1}{R_{33}}\begin{vmatrix} R_{11} & R_{13} \\ R_{31} & R_{33} \end{vmatrix}$

$$\Phi_{13} = \frac{1}{R_{33}}\begin{vmatrix} \dfrac{\partial X_1}{\partial Y} & R_{13} \\ \dfrac{\partial X_3}{\partial Y} & R_{33} \end{vmatrix}$$

$$\Sigma_{13}' = \frac{\partial S_1'}{\partial K} - \frac{R_{13}}{R_{33}'}\frac{\partial S_3'}{\partial K'},$$

and $\partial S_i'/\partial K' = J^{ii}/J$, where J^{ii} is the minor of J, the determinant of technical coefficients a_{ij}, formed by leaving out the ith row and column.

The usefulness of the new parameters Ψ_{13} and Φ_{13} etc. is clear on comparison of **59** with the corresponding 2-good result. Here the terms in R_{11} and R_{11}' are replaced by weighted averages of the R and, along the same lines, the term $\partial S_1'/\partial K'$ is replaced by a weighted average of supply partials. The behaviour of these terms is discussed in Appendix III. Apart from Σ_{13}' they present little difficulty and have properties analogous to their two-good counterparts. Σ'_{13} is, however, sufficiently awkward to render it impossible to reach any qualitative conclusions. This is not altogether surprising for the $\partial S'_i/\partial K'$ are now the ratios of the determinant J (now of third order) and its minors. For example

$$\frac{\partial S'_1}{\partial K'} = \frac{J^{11}}{J} J \neq 0. \qquad \textbf{33}$$

Attaching a sign to J does not now permit us to deduce the sign of **33** since J^{11} can be negative or positive whatever the sign of J whereas, in the two-good case, J^{11} is simply a single number of positive sign.

Summary of conclusions

Our primary object has been to inquire whether or not we can agree with Professor Murray Kemp (1964, p. 193) and others that, 'under competitive conditions capital-rich countries tie up too great a proportion of their resources in foreign ventures', in other words, that the private rate of return is always greater than the social rate.

The work above makes it clear that we cannot so agree. It is, or course, true that in general either too much or too little will be invested, but there are no reasonable economic assumptions upon which we can be sure that we know which way the difference will go. All that can be said is that competition will not necessarily be in the best interest of the lending country.

This agnostic conclusion holds equally, even with the highly restrictive assumption that all goods enter into trade and even if we suppose that it is always the capital rich country which invests abroad.

The main reason for the difference in the results obtained in this paper and elsewhere lies in the proof above that the effect of lending on the terms of trade cannot be ignored. There is no reason to suppose that this effect is negligible compared with changes in the rate of interest. Indeed, quite the contrary is true.

Despite this we would urge that the model above should not be regarded simply as an exercise in destructive analysis. We have in fact produced a formula which tells us all that we could wish to know entirely in terms of properly defined price elasticities of demand, elasticities of supply and elasticities of supply with respect to factor endowment changes. In addition we have shown how the third of these classes of parameters can be computed in terms of familiar Leontief input/output coefficients. Other elasticities can be calculated by traditional methods or by any other means which might be devised. Thus, to develop quantitative results, it is not necessary to institute econometric enquiries into the investment problem itself which might be difficult. All that is necessary is to estimate the basic parameters which are common to *all* economic problems.

Engineers who build bridges calculate their strength by using information previously obtained on the strength of the materials used and not by loading the completed structure until it falls down. It is time that economists adopted similar methods.

Appendix I: the derivation of dr'/dK'

1. It is shown in the text that we may write:

$$r' = \sum_i p_i \frac{\partial S_i}{\partial K'}. \qquad 34$$

We now wish to prove that:

$$\frac{dr'}{dK'} = \sum_i \frac{\partial S_i}{\partial K'} \frac{dp_i}{dK'}. \qquad 35$$

2. From **34** it is evident that:

$$\frac{dr'}{dK'} = \sum_i \frac{\partial S_i}{\partial K'} \frac{dp_i}{dK'} + \sum_i p_i \frac{d(\partial S_i/\partial K')}{dK'}. \qquad 36$$

Hence to prove **35** it is only necessary to show that

$$\sum p_i \frac{d(\partial S_i/\partial K')}{dK'} = 0. \qquad 37$$

3. Now all the supply functions, S_i, are homogeneous of degree zero in the p_i. Hence

$$\sum_i p_i \frac{\partial S_j}{\partial p_i} = 0. \qquad 38$$

From the theory of supply $\partial S_i/\partial p_j = \partial S_j/\partial p_i$ so that:

$$\sum_i p_i \frac{\partial S_i}{\partial p_j} = 0. \qquad 39$$

4. Now **37** written in full is

$$\sum_j \sum_i p_i \frac{\partial^2 S_i}{\partial K' \partial p_j} \frac{dp_j}{dK'} + \sum_i p_i \frac{\partial^2 S_i}{\partial K' \partial K'}. \qquad \textbf{40}$$

5. Differentiating **39** with respect to K' yields

$$\sum_i p_i \frac{\partial^2 S_i}{\partial K' \partial p_j} = 0 \quad \text{so that} \quad \sum_j \sum_i p_i \frac{\partial^2 S_i}{\partial K' \partial p_j} \frac{dp_j}{dK'} = 0, \qquad \textbf{41}$$

whence to prove **36** we now need to show only that $\partial^2 S_i/\partial K'\partial K'$ is also identically zero. This is simply proved as follows.

6. Our production functions are subject to constant returns to scale. Hence,

$$K_j = \sum_i S_i a_{ji} \qquad (j = 1, 2, \ldots, n), \qquad \textbf{42}$$

where K_j is total endowment of the jth factor and a_{ji} is the input of the jth factor required to produce a unit of the ith output. Hence, solving for S_i yields:

$$S_i = \frac{|a_{11}, \ldots, K_j, \ldots, a_{nn}|}{J}, \qquad \textbf{43}$$

where J is the determinant of unit input coefficients (the a_{ij}) and $|a_{11}, \ldots, K_j, \ldots, a_{nn}|$ is the same determinant with the vector of factor endowment substituted for the ith column.

7. Now the a_{ij} are functions of prices alone. Hence $\partial S_i/\partial K_j$ is a function of prices alone.

$$\text{In fact} \quad \frac{\partial S_i}{\partial K'_j} = \frac{J_{ij}}{J}, \qquad \textbf{44}$$

where J_{ij} is the minor of J formed by eliminating the jth row and the ith column. Hence,

$$\frac{\partial^2 S_i}{\partial K' \partial K'} = 0, \qquad \textbf{45}$$

and **34** is established.

Appendix II: the sign of $\partial S'_1/\partial K' - r'\partial X_1/\partial Y$ when $\partial S'_1/\partial K' > 0$

1. We already know that

$$r' = p_1 \frac{\partial S_1}{\partial K'} + p_2 \frac{\partial S'_2}{\partial K'}, \qquad \textbf{46}$$

so that, to show that

$$\frac{\partial S_1'}{\partial K'} - r' \frac{\partial X_1}{\partial Y} > 0 \quad \text{if} \quad \frac{\partial S_1'}{\partial K'} > 0,$$

we need to prove that:

$$\frac{\partial S_1'}{\partial K'} - \left(p_1 \frac{\partial S_1'}{\partial K'} \frac{\partial X_1}{\partial Y} + p_2 \frac{\partial S_2'}{\partial K'} \frac{\partial X_1}{\partial Y}\right) > 0 \qquad \textbf{47}$$

if $\frac{\partial S_1'}{\partial K'} > 0$.

2. Now **47** may be written

$$\frac{\partial S_1'}{\partial K'}\left(1 - p_1 \frac{\partial X_1}{\partial Y'}\right) - p_2 \frac{\partial S_2'}{\partial K'} \frac{\partial X_1}{\partial Y} > 0. \qquad \textbf{48}$$

Clearly the first term is greater than zero if

$$p_1 \frac{\partial X_1}{\partial Y} < 1,$$

which we can assume.

3. We have already proved that if $\partial S_1'/\partial K' > 0$ then $\partial S_2'/\partial K' < 0$.

Hence, the second term is positive if $\partial S_1'/\partial K' > 0$.
Hence, the whole expression is positive.
Hence, **47** is established.

4. This proposition is, of course, applicable only to the two-good case.

Appendix III: solution of the two-factor model

1. From **26** we have:

$$\left.\begin{aligned} x_1 &= S_1 - X_1, \\ x_2 &= X_1' - S_1', \\ p_1 x_1 &= p_2 x_2 - K_f r', \\ Y &= \sum p_i S_i + K_f r' \quad (i = 1, 2), \\ Y' &= \sum p_i S_i - K_f r' \quad (i = 1, 2), \end{aligned}\right\}. \qquad \textbf{[26]}$$

2. Differentiating with respect to K', remembering that home supply is independent of the foreign factor endowment, i.e. that $\partial S_1/\partial K'$ and $\partial S_2/\partial K' = 0$ and p_2 is constant, yields:

$$\begin{bmatrix} R_{11}-X_1\dfrac{\partial X_1}{\partial Y} & 1 & 0 & \dfrac{\partial X_1}{\partial Y} & 0 \\ R'_{11}-X'_1\dfrac{\partial X'_1}{\partial Y'} & -1 & 0 & 0 & \dfrac{\partial X'_1}{\partial Y'} \\ x_1 & p_1 & -p_2 & 0 & 0 \\ X_1+x_1 & 0 & 0 & -1 & 0 \\ X'_1-x_1 & 0 & 0 & 0 & -1 \end{bmatrix} \begin{bmatrix} \dfrac{dp_1}{dK'} \\ \dfrac{dx_1}{dK'} \\ \dfrac{dx_2}{dK'} \\ \dfrac{dY}{dK'} \\ \dfrac{dY'}{dK'} \end{bmatrix} = \begin{bmatrix} 0 \\ \dfrac{\partial S'_1}{\partial K'} \\ -\left(K_f\dfrac{dr'}{dK'}+r'\right) \\ -\left(K_f\dfrac{dr'}{dK'}+r'\right) \\ K_f\dfrac{dr'}{dK'} \end{bmatrix}, \tag{27}$$

where $R_{11} = \sigma_{11}-S_{11}$.

3. We can then solve **27** for dp_1/dK'. And this solution can be substituted into **25** to give dr'/dK'.

4. The solution obtained for dp_1/dK' is:

$$\frac{dp_1}{dK'} = \frac{\partial S'_1/\partial K'+K_f(dr'/dK')(\partial X'_1/\partial Y'-\partial X_1/\partial Y)-r'\partial X_1/\partial Y}{R_{11}+R'_{11}+x_1(\partial X_1/\partial Y-\partial X'_1/\partial Y')}, \qquad 49$$

provided $J \neq 0$.

5. This result can now be substituted into **25** to yield **29**.

6. The solution of the three-good model proceeds along essentially similar lines. In place of **26** we have:

$$\begin{aligned} x_1 &= S_1-X_1, \\ x_1 &= X'_1-S'_1, \\ 0 &= X_3-S_3, \\ 0 &= S'_3-X'_3, \\ p_1 x_1 &= p_2 x_2-K_f r', \\ Y &= \textstyle\sum_i p_i S_i+K_f r' \quad (i=1,2,3), \\ Y' &= \textstyle\sum_i p_i S_i-K_f r' \quad (i=1,2,3). \end{aligned} \qquad 50$$

7. Differentiation with respect to K' using as before,

$$\frac{\partial S_1}{\partial K'} = \frac{\partial S_2}{\partial K'} = \frac{\partial S_3}{\partial K'} = 0 \qquad \textbf{51}$$

yields:

$$\begin{bmatrix} R_{11}-X_1\frac{\partial X_1}{\partial Y} & R_{13}-X_3\frac{\partial X_1}{\partial Y} & 0 & 1 & 0 & \frac{\partial X_1}{\partial Y} & 0 \\ R_{31}-X_1\frac{\partial X_3}{\partial Y} & R_{33}-X_3\frac{\partial X_3}{\partial Y} & 0 & 0 & 0 & \frac{\partial X_3}{\partial Y} & 0 \\ R'_{11}-X'_1\frac{\partial X'_1}{\partial Y'} & 0 & R'_{13}-X'_3\frac{\partial X'_3}{\partial Y'} & -1 & 0 & 0 & \frac{\partial X'_1}{\partial Y'} \\ R'_{31}-X'_1\frac{\partial X'_3}{\partial Y'} & 0 & R'_{33}-X'_3\frac{\partial X'_3}{\partial Y'} & 0 & 0 & 0 & \frac{\partial X'_3}{\partial Y'} \\ x_1 & 0 & 0 & p_1-p_2 & 0 & 0 & \\ X_1+x_1 & X_3 & 0 & 0 & 0 & -1 & 0 \\ X'_1-x_1 & 0 & X'_3 & 0 & 0 & 0 & -1 \end{bmatrix}$$

$$\begin{bmatrix} \frac{dp_1}{dK} \\ \frac{dp_3}{dK} \\ \frac{dp'_3}{dK} \\ \frac{dx_1}{dK'} \\ \frac{dx_2}{dK'} \\ \frac{dY}{dK'} \\ \frac{dY'}{dK'} \end{bmatrix} = \begin{bmatrix} 0 \\ 0 \\ \frac{\partial S'_1}{\partial K'} \\ \frac{\partial S'_3}{\partial K'} \\ -\left(K_f\frac{dr'}{dK'}+r'\right) \\ -\left(K_f\frac{dr'}{dK'}+r'\right) \\ K_f\frac{dr'}{dK'} \end{bmatrix} \qquad \textbf{52}$$

which we write in matrix form, $Ax = y$.

$$\left.\begin{aligned}\Psi_{13} &= \frac{1}{R_{33}}\begin{vmatrix} R_{11} & R_{13} \\ R_{31} & R_{33} \end{vmatrix} \\ \Phi_{13} &= \frac{1}{R_{33}}\begin{vmatrix} \frac{\partial X_1}{\partial Y} & R_{13} \\ \frac{\partial X_3}{\partial Y} & R_{33} \end{vmatrix}.\end{aligned}\right\} \quad 53$$

Making use of these we may write the value of the determinant $|A|$ as:

$$|A| = -p_2\, R_{33}\, R'_{33}\{\Psi_{13}+\Psi'_{33}+x_1\,(\Phi_{13}-\Phi'_{33})\}. \quad 54$$

This can be compared with the result for the two-good model which is:

$$p_2\left[R_{11}+R'_{11}+x_1\left(\frac{\partial X_1}{\partial Y}-\frac{\partial X'_1}{\partial Y}\right)\right]. \quad 55$$

We now need to evaluate the determinant $|A_{11}|$ to obtain

$$\frac{dp_1}{dK'} = \left|\frac{A_{11}}{A}\right|$$

where $A_{11} = |A|$ with the first column replaced by the vector on the right-hand side of **52**.

8. Manipulation yields the result:

$$A_{11} = -p_2\, R_{33}\, R'_{33}\left[\Sigma'_{13} + K_f\frac{dr'_1}{dK'}(\Phi_{13}-\Phi_{13}-r'\Phi_{13}\right] \quad 56$$

$$\text{where} \quad \Sigma'_{13} = \left(\frac{\partial S'_1}{\partial K'}-\frac{R_{13}}{R'_{33}}\frac{\partial S_3}{\partial K'}\right). \quad 57$$

$$\text{Whence,} \quad \frac{dp_1}{dK'} = \frac{\Sigma'_{13} + K_f\,(dr'/dK')\,(\Phi'_{13}-\Phi_{13})-r'\Phi_{13}}{\Psi_{13}+\Psi'_{13}+x_1(\Phi_{13}-\Phi'_{13})}. \quad 58$$

9. So far the Ψ and Φ have been introduced as definitions designated to simplify the notation. Readers however should be made aware that:

(a) Ψ has properties similar to the familiar income compensated partial derivatives with respect to price of the demand function. It behaves therefore not unlike the R.

(b) Φ is a weighted sum of the partial derivatives of demand with respect to income. In the absence of complementarity it possesses all the properties of a simple income partial.

(c) Σ' is, analogously, a weighted average of the partials of the two overseas supply functions with respect to K'.

These parameters, though unfamiliar, are therefore not hard to interpret. Furthermore, it has been shown elsewhere (Pearce, 1964, ch. 4), that many, indeed almost all, of the results of international trade theory based upon a two-commodity model generalize readily if the parameter R is replaced by Ψ and the parameter $\partial X/\partial Y$ by Φ. This contention is well supported by a comparison of our own two-good result with **58** as below:

$$\frac{dp_1}{dK'} = \frac{\partial S_1'/\partial K' + K_f(dr'/dK')(\partial X_1'/\partial Y' - \partial X_1/\partial Y) - r'\partial X_1'/\partial Y}{R_{11} + R_{11} + x_1(\partial X_1/\partial Y - \partial X_1'/\partial Y')}. \qquad [49]$$

$$\frac{dp_1}{dK'} = \frac{\Sigma_{13}' + K_f(dr'/dK')(\Phi_{13}' - \Phi_{13}) - r'\Phi_{13}}{\Psi_{13} + \Psi_{13}' + x_1(\Phi_{13} - \Phi_{13}')}. \qquad \mathbf{58}$$

A fuller account of the properties and surprising usefulness of the new parameters is given in Pearce (1964, ch. 4).

10. All the arguments of the main paper regarding sign readily generalize to **58**. Just as R_{11} and R_{11}' must be negative so must Ψ_{13} and Ψ_{13}'. If we choose units so that, in the initial equilibrium, all prices are equal to unity, Φ_{13} and Φ_{13}' are positive in the same way as ordinary income partials and are $\leqslant$ unity provided there is no complementarity in demand. Finally Σ_{13}' is simply a weighted sum of the two partials of the supply functions namely $\partial S_1'/\partial K'$ and $\partial S_3'/\partial K'$. The sign of this expression depends, as we have already shown, upon the ratios of the factor inputs: that is, upon the value of J and its minors where J is now:

$$J = \begin{vmatrix} a_{11} & a_{21} & a_{31} \\ a_{12} & a_{22} & a_{32} \\ a_{13} & a_{23} & a_{33} \end{vmatrix} \quad J \neq 0.$$

The sign of dp_1/dK' is therefore, as before, uncertain. The real terms of trade may either worsen or improve. Very strong assumptions are now necessary to impose a sign on dp_1/dK'.

11. We now proceed to find dr'/dK' for the general case. From **35** we already know that:

$$\frac{dr'}{dK'}=\frac{dp_1}{dK'}\frac{\partial S_1'}{\partial K'}+\frac{dp_3'}{dK'}\frac{\partial S}{\partial K'} \qquad \mathbf{59}$$

(with dp_2 zero).

To find dr'/dK' we must therefore solve the system for dp_3'/dK', the change in the price of the rest of the world's non-traded goods.

12. It is worth noting that, unlike the two-good case, $dr'/dK' \neq 0$ does not now entail $dp_1/dK' \neq 0$ since $dp_1/dK' = 0$ does not entail $dp_3'/dK' = 0$.

13. Solving for dp_3'/dK' is rather more tedious. The result is:

$$\frac{dp_3'}{dK'}=\frac{\partial S_3'/\partial K'+K_f(dr'/dK')\partial X_3'/\partial Y'}{R_{33}'}-$$

$$-\frac{(R_{31}'-x_1\,\partial X_3'/\partial Y')[\Sigma_{13}'-K_f(dr'/dK')(\Phi_{13}-\Phi_{13}')-r'\Phi_{13}]}{R_{33}'\,\Psi_{13}+\Psi_{13}'+x_1(\Phi_{13}-\Phi_{13}')]}. \qquad \mathbf{60}$$

14. This may be written:

$$\frac{dp_3'}{dK'}=\left(\frac{\partial S_3'}{\partial K'}+K_f\frac{dr'}{dK}\frac{\partial X_3'}{dY}\right)\frac{1}{R_{33}'}-\frac{dp_1}{dK'}\left\{R_{31}'-x_1\frac{\partial X_3'}{\partial Y'}\right\}\frac{1}{R_{33}'}$$

$$=\frac{1}{R_{33}'}\left[\left(\frac{\partial S_3'}{\partial K'}+K_f\frac{dr'}{dK'}\frac{\partial X_3'}{\partial Y'}\right)-\frac{dp_1}{dK'}\left(R_{31}'-x_1\frac{\partial X_3'}{\partial Y'}\right)\right]. \qquad \mathbf{61}$$

15. Since we cannot determine the sign of dp_1/dK' it follows that we cannot determine the sign of dp_3'/dK'. Equally it is now clear that invariant terms of trade imply $dp_3'/dK' \neq$ zero.

16. It is not worthwhile even for the sake of completing the formal exercise to write out the solution for dr'/dK'. The resulting expression is cumbersome and unsuited to qualitative analysis. Its sign cannot be determined without econometric investigation. The interested reader may easily set out for himself the formula by substituting from **58** and **60** into **59**.

17. Some comment might be made, however, upon the probability of a negative dr'/dK since this has been previously referred

to. Consider the simple special case in which $K_f = 0$. The reader may easily satisfy himself that in such a case

$$\frac{dr'}{dK'} = \frac{\Sigma'_{13} - r'\Phi_{13})\{\Sigma_{13} + (x_1/R'_{33})\partial S_3/\partial K'\}}{\Psi_{13} + \Psi'_{13} + x_1(\Phi_{13} - \Phi'_{13})} + \frac{(\partial S_3/\partial K')^2}{R'_{33}}.$$

We might then attempt to show that the signs of the bracketed expressions are dominated by the sign of Σ'_{13} and argue that since $(\Sigma'_{13})^2$ is positive and the denominator is almost certainly negative (following the argument of pages 179–82), then term one is negative. Term two is certainly negative, soon these assumptions the whole is negative. But the assumptions are very strong. Following the methods of Appendix II, using the fact that

$$r' = \sum_i p_i \frac{\partial S_i}{\partial K'},$$

it is possible to show a presumption that $\Sigma'_{13} - r'\Phi_{13}$ is of the same sign as Σ'_{13}, but even this depends on the assumption that the ratio of marginal propensities to consume commodities one and three is approximately equal to the ratio $p_1 R_{31}/p_3 R_{33}$. Moreover, no similar argument can be applied to

$$\Sigma'_{13} + \frac{x_1}{R'_{33}} \frac{\partial S_3}{\partial K'}.$$

Indeed, there is nothing to prevent Σ'_{13} being quite small or even zero. Clearly in such a case nothing can be said about the sign of term one and hence dr'/dK'. It should be noted that unlike the two-good case we are now unable to say whether $\partial S'_1/\partial K'$ and $\partial S'_3/\partial K'$ are of the same or different sign. Finally, we remark that even if the sign of dr'/dK' could be established we should still be no closer to any qualitative conclusion regarding the relative magnitudes of private and social return since the signs of the crucial price changes are still unknown.

In short, in the three-good case, qualitative analysis breaks down. For any general conclusion, quantitative econometric inquiry is essential.

References

DUNNING, J. H., and ROWAN, D. C. (1964), 'The rate of return on British private investment overseas', unpublished.

JASAY, A. E. (1960), 'The social choice between home and overseas investment', *Econ. J.*, vol. 70, pp. 105–13.

KEMP, M. C. (1964), *The Pure Theory of International Trade*, Prentice-Hall.

MACDOUGALL, G. D. A. (1960), 'The benefits and costs of private investment abroad: a theoretical approach', *Econ. Rec.*, vol. 36, pp. 13–35.

MEADE, J. E. (1955), *Trade and Welfare – Mathematical Supplement*, Oxford University Press.

NATIONAL ECONOMIC DEVELOPMENT COUNCIL (1963), *Conditions Favourable to Faster Growth*, HMSO.

PEARCE, I. F. (1961), 'The problem of the balance of payments', *Int. econ. Rev.*, vol. 2, pp. 1–28.

PEARCE, I. F. (1964), *A Contribution to Demand Analysis*, Oxford University Press.

SIMPSON, P. B. (1962), 'US private and government investment abroad', in R. Mikesell (ed.), *Foreign Investment and National Economic Advantage: A Theoretical Analysis*, Oregon University Press.

STOLPER, W. F., and SAMUELSON, P. A. (1941–2), 'Protection and real wages', *Rev. econ. Stud.*, vol. 9, pp. 67–8.

Part Three
Foreign Portfolio Capital and International Capital Markets

This Part contains just two contributions. The first is concerned with some of the principles underlying the choice of investment portfolios, when securities are denominated in foreign currencies. This is really an extension of optimal portfolio analysis as developed by Markowitz (1959) and others. Professor Grubel's contribution (Reading 8) focuses on the main variables likely to affect the flow of private capital across national boundaries, when no management or control is envisaged.

Professor Cooper's essay (Reading 9) is concerned with the implications of recent trends in the international capital market and particularly the growth of new forms of international securities e.g. the Euro-dollar and Euro-bond. He points to the resurgence in the flow of private capital abroad, both as a result of new institutional arrangements and the operations of multinational companies, and analyses the effects of these dealings on international rates of interest.

Reference

MARKOWITZ, H. (1959), *Portfolio Selection: Efficient Diversification of Investments*, Wiley.

8 Herbert G. Grubel

Internationally Diversified Portfolios: Welfare Gains and Capital Flows

H. G. Grubel, 'Internationally diversified portfolios: welfare gains and capital flows', *American Economic Review*, vol. 58, 1968, pp. 1299–1314.

The models of portfolio balance developed by Markowitz (1959) and Tobin (1958) explain the real world phenomenon of diversified asset holdings elegantly and properly. The models have been criticized, extended and empirically tested; by now their basic content has become economic orthodoxy. Strangely, however, the analysis has not yet been applied explicitly to the explanation of long-term asset holdings that include claims denominated in foreign currency.[1]

The present paper fills this gap and yields some interesting results. First, the international diversification of portfolios is the source of an entirely new kind of world welfare gains from international economic relations, different from both the traditional 'gains from trade' and increased productivity flowing from the migration of the factors of production. This specific theoretical proposition is illustrated with some calculations based on empirical data drawing on *ex post* realized rates of return from investment in eleven major stock markets of the world.

Second, the theoretical model shows that international capital movements are a function not only of interest rate differentials but also of rates of growth in total asset holdings in two countries. As a result, capital may flow between countries when interest rate differentials are zero or negative and may not flow when a positive interest differential exists. Third, the analysis has some important policy implications in a growing world where monetary and fiscal policies are mixed to achieve internal and external balance.

1. The importance of the real world phenomenon is exemplified by the recent report in the *Wall Street Journal* (1967).

The static model

Consider a world consisting of two countries, A and B, each with independent monetary and fiscal authorities and initially economically isolated from each other. Populations, income and wealth are constant through time. There are only three forms of holding wealth: real assets, money and bonds. The latter are issued by the government to provide investors with an interest-bearing instrument that allows bridging individuals' periods of net savings and dissavings over their lifetimes. In addition, the quantity of bonds in the market and the interest rate they fetch are regulated by the government in such a manner as to maintain full employment. For example, if there is unemployment, the government purchases bonds, paying for them with newly issued money. As a result of the increased money holdings and the lower yield of bonds, real assets are relatively more attractive than money and bonds, and individuals try to adjust their portfolio imbalance through the purchase of more real assets, which has the desired upward effect on employment.

Assume that initially domestic portfolio balance exists at interest rates on bonds of R_A and R_B, and variances and covariances of returns of σ_A^2, σ_B^2, $\sigma_{A,B}$, where the subscripts A and B refer to the two countries and are measured from the point of view of country A. That is R_B, σ_B^2, and $\sigma_{A,B}$ include an adjustment for exchange risk stemming from past variations in some shadow price of foreign exchange. Furthermore, assume for analytical convenience that when economic relations between the two countries are opened up only bonds and consumer goods can be exchanged so that the opening of trade does not affect the return and variance from holding real assets and money. Consequently, attention can be focused on the changes in bond holdings resulting from the opening of trade.

Before trade the expected rate of return $E(R_A)$ and risk $V(R_A)$ on the 'average' investor's bond portfolio in country A and B are:

$$E(R_A) = R_A, \quad (1)$$
$$V(R_A) = \sigma_A^2, \quad (2)$$
$$E(R_B) = R_B, \quad (3)$$
$$V(R_B) = \sigma_B^2. \quad (4)$$

After diversification a portfolio containing bonds of both countries A and B has the following expected rate of return:

$$E(R_{A,\,B}) = P_A\,R_A + P_B\,R_B. \qquad 5$$

Where P_A and P_B are the proportions of bonds of country A and B respectively held in the average portfolio of country A, P_A plus P_B must sum to one and neither may be negative. The variance of the diversified portfolio is

$$V(R_{A,\,B}) = P_A^2\,\sigma_A^2 + 2P_A\,P_B\,\sigma_{A,\,B} + P_B^2\,\sigma_B^2. \qquad 6$$

As the two equations show, investors have the opportunity to choose from a whole range of combinations of expected rates of return and variance by picking the appropriate sizes of P_A and P_B. Which specific combinations of risk and return they choose depends on their personal preferences, as has been demonstrated by Markowitz (1959) and Tobin (1958).

While the exact diversification is not important for the present purposes of analysis, it is useful to demonstrate with the help of a numerical example that diversification results in portfolios superior to one-asset portfolios of either kind of bonds.[2] Assume that $R_A = R_B = 5$ per cent. Therefore, before trade,

$$E(R_A) = E(R_B) = 5.$$

Diversification of the nature $P_A = P_B = 0{\cdot}5$ yields an expected rate of return:

$$E(R_{A,\,B}) = E(R_{B,\,A}) = 5. \qquad 7$$

Assume that the variances of expected returns on country A and B's properly adjusted for exchange rate fluctuations are

$$\sigma_A^2 = \sigma_B^2 = 10,$$

with a correlation between the two rates of return of $r = 0{\cdot}3$. The variances on undiversified portfolios are

$$V(R_A) = V(R_B) = 10$$

but the variance on the portfolio containing both assets is

$$V(R_{A,\,B}) = 6{\cdot}5. \qquad 8$$

2. The discussion of circumstances under which diversification does not take place, i.e. investors are risk lovers, domination of assets, perfect correlation of returns, etc., go beyond the scope of this paper and it is assumed that investors and assets in both countries meet the necessary requirements for diversification to take place.

Thus, holding both assets does not change the expected rate of return but does reduce the riskiness of the portfolio as compared with the one-asset portfolio. By similar calculations and data it can be shown that the exchange of financial assets can lead to higher expected rates of return with equal risks and other combinations of returns and risks, all of which are superior to those from undiversified portfolios and, therefore, make the holders of wealth better off than they were without the opportunity for international diversification. The same principles apply to the residents of country A and country B.

The quantity of foreign bonds demanded by the residents of country A and country B after the opening of trade in this model depends on five primary factors. First, the size of total wealth assets held by the public: since the variables P_A and P_B represent proportions, the absolute size of bond holdings is greater the greater the stock to which these proportions are applied.

Second, the size of the interest rate differential: given the variances and covariance of the two-asset returns for any risk avoider, the trade-off between return and risk is more favorable the greater the foreign interest rate and, therefore, the more of the foreign assets will be held in the portfolio. Third, the size of the risk differential: for a given earnings differential and covariance of returns, the foreign asset is more attractive the smaller the risk attached to it, given the riskiness of the domestic asset.

Fourth, the degree of correlation of returns on domestic and foreign assets: as can be seen from equation **6** the variance of a diversified portfolio is smaller the smaller the correlation of returns. Thus, given the earnings differential and variance of each asset independently, diversification reduces portfolio variance more and, therefore, is more desirable the smaller the covariance. Fifth, the tastes of the public: the combination of risk and return actually chosen from among the combinations made possible by diversification depends on wealth holders' preferences with respect to risk and return and current *v.* future consumption.

Given the magnitudes of the five determinants of the demand for foreign bonds, the opening up of economic relations between the two countries is assumed to lead to a mutual exchange of bonds by the private wealth holders. Only if tastes, returns, variances and relative sizes of total wealth holdings are equal are the demands generated by each country equal. In the following analysis the empirically most relevant and theoretically most interesting assumption is made that the potential demand for foreign bonds by the residents of country A exceeds that by the residents of country B. The real effects of such a net excess demand are analysed first, under the assumption of rigidly pegged exchange rates, and second, under the assumption of perfectly flexible exchange rates.

First, at pegged rates country A's excess demand for bonds tends to depress its exchange rate and official sales of B's currency are required to keep it stable. We assume that the government of A obtains this foreign exchange from the government of B in return for its official IOUs.

When international relations are opened, the private residents of A sell off some of the bonds issued by their own government and acquire those of country B. Some of A's bonds thus offered are purchased by residents of country B, but under the present assumption of an excess demand for bonds by country A, that government must purchase some of its old obligations to maintain aggregate portfolio balance and full employment. At the same time B's government issues a net supply of new bonds to the residents of A.

All of these changes in the balance sheets of governments and private wealth holders are completed a certain time after opening of international relations. The length of the adjustment depends on institutional arrangements in the bond markets and is not important for the present analysis. In the new equilibrium the excess demand for foreign exchange ceases and along with it the need for official intervention.[3] The excess demand by country A's residents has caused the government of A to be indebted to the government of B rather than to its own citizens. B's government finds its obligation to A's private citizens matched by claims on A's government.

3. The lower the risk or higher the return on bond holdings in both countries, the more likely an increase in the total demand for assets. Under these circumstances, savings will increase causing a fall in the interest rate and requiring changes in employment policy. We neglect these effects by assuming that they are likely to be small. On the same grounds we disregard balance of payments and income problems arising from net interest payments.

At no time between the two points of asset equilibrium did the exchange rate move and since full employment in both countries has been maintained there have been no income or price effects on the balance of trade and no real resources transferred between the two countries. The new pattern of asset holdings involves a net transfer of resources only if the interest rate on the official IOUs issued by government A and held by government B is different from that paid on the bonds issued by government B and held by the public in A, assuming equal liquidity and other service yields on each type and assuming equal taxation rates.

Second, under flexible exchange rates the net demand for B's bonds causes a lowering of A's exchange rate, the appearance of a balance of trade surplus for A, which persists until real resources equal in value to A's excess demand for bonds is realized. Then the exchange rate returns to its previous level under the present assumptions of a static world.

Assuming that neither government changes the quantity of its bonds outstanding, the net demand for B's bonds from the residents of A tends to raise the prices and lower the yields on B's bonds, inducing the residents of B to substitute real assets transferred from A for these bonds in their portfolios. There is a tendency for the return on real capital to fall in B and rise in A, reducing what *ceteris paribus* would have been the net excess demand for bonds in A. However, given the other determinants of this demand, total asset holdings and tastes, there is no necessity for this net asset demand to be moved to zero.

As long as the interest rate paid by country B on the bonds held by the residents of A is equal to the marginal productivity of the resources transferred to B, the real income in both countries is the same as before the opening of international relations, except for the welfare gains accruing to the wealth holders from the diversification of their portfolios.

The model just presented gives rise to the possibility that real capital flows away from the country with the higher to the one with lower physical productivity of capital. Such an event occurs if the size of total asset portfolios in country A is greater than that in country B so that even at the initial interest rate differential in favor of A a net demand for B's bonds is created. Under flexible exchange rates these conditions result in a transfer of real resources to country B through the process described in the preceding paragraphs.

It is clear that the welfare gains accruing to wealth holders through international diversification of their portfolios are different in nature from those known from the traditional literature in international economics, i.e. the Ricardo–Heckscher–Ohlin gains from trade and the classical gains from factors moving to higher productivity employment.

Some empirical estimates of potential gains from diversification

In order to demonstrate the range of possible gains to American investors from international diversification of their portfolios, information on rates of return from portfolio-investment in common stock market averages of eleven major countries (see Table 1) was collected, covering the period from January 1959 to December 1966.[4] For each of these eleven markets the following monthly observations were obtained: indexes of common share prices (P), dividend yields on the shares in the index (Y) expressed as per cent per year, and the dollar exchange rate (X), defined as the price of one dollar. Subscripts 0 and 1 used below refer to the beginning and end of each monthly investment period; the share price index and exchange rate at the end of the current month is considered to be the price at which the next month's investment is made.

The monthly rates of return were calculated on the basis of the following considerations. The dollar price of one foreign stock market index unit is $PE_0 = P_0/X_0$. The dollar value of the investment at the end of the first month (VE_1), is equal to the foreign currency value of dividends received $DP_1 = P_0\,Y_0/12$ plus the foreign currency value of one unit of the index at the end of the month (P_1) converted to dollars at the exchange rate (X_1), i.e.

$$VE_1 = \frac{(P_0\,Y_0)/12 + P_1}{x_1}. \qquad 9$$

4. January 1959 was chosen as a starting point because in December 1958 European currencies became convertible *de jure*. Common stocks rather than bonds were analysed because of the greater variance around the average returns and across countries found in the former. The theoretical analysis can easily be modified to account for foreign stock purchases.

Table 1 Rates of Return and Standard Deviation from Investing in Foreign Capital Market Averages 1959–66

	% per annum (*1*)	*Value of $100 at end of period* (2)	*Standard deviation* (*3*)	*Correlation* (*R*) *with USA* (*4*)
USA	7·54	178·92	47·26	1·0000
Canada	5·95	158·82	41·19	0·7025*
United Kingdom	9·59	208·00	65·28	0·2414*
West Germany	7·32	175·95	94·69	0·3008*
France	4·27	139·69	49·60	0·1938*
Italy	8·12	186·74	103·33	0·1465
Belgium	1·09	109·02	37·56	0·1080
Netherlands	5·14	149·33	86·34	0·2107*
Japan	16·54	340·21	92·52	0·1149
Australia	9·44	205·75	34·87	0·0585
South Africa	8·47	191·60	61·92	−0·1620

* Statistically significant at the 5 per cent level.

Note: For computational methods see text.

Sources: The share price index for the United States is Moody's industrial average of common stocks from *Moody's Industrial Manual*, June 1967. The share price index for Canada is the industrial series from the *Toronto Stock Exchange Supplement Booklet*, no. 2, the Toronto Stock Exchange, 15 January 1966.

The share price indices for the United Kingdom, West Germany, France, Italy, Belgium and the Netherlands are from the industrial series of the *Allgemeines stat. Bull.*, European Economic Communities, various issues. The share price indices for Japan and Australia are industrial series from *Int. Fin. Stat.*, International Monetary Fund, various issues. The price index for South Africa is a gold mining shares index from the *Quart. Bull.*, South Africa Reserve Bank, various issues.

The industrial dividend yields for the United States are from *Moody's Industrial Manual*, June 1967. The dividend yield on industrials series for the United Kingdom, West Germany, France, Italy and the Netherlands are from *Allgemeines stat. Bull.*, European Economic Communities, various issues; for Belgium, from personal correspondence with the Credietbank; for Japan, from *Orient Econ.*, various issues; for Australia, from personal correspondence with the Reserve Bank of Australia; for Canada, from one published by Moss Lawson and adapted to the Toronto Stock Exchange Industrial Index, from personal correspondence with the Toronto Stock Exchange.

The dividend yield on gold mining shares series for South Africa is from personal correspondence with the South Africa Reserve Bank.

The exchange rates for all countries are taken from *Int. Fin. Stat.*, International Monetary Fund, various issues.

The problem then becomes to find the solution value for r_1 in the equation

$$VE_1 = PE_0(1+r)^{\frac{1}{12}} \qquad \mathbf{10}$$

which after some manipulation and substitution becomes

$$r_1 = \left[\left(\frac{Y_0}{12}+\frac{P_1}{P_0}\right)\left(\frac{X_0}{X_1}\right)\right]^{12} - 1. \qquad \mathbf{11}$$

A matrix of correlation among the eleven countries' monthly returns was computed and the variances and covariances were used in the subsequent calculations. Average rates of return were computed by taking the geometric mean of ninety-five monthly rates:[5]

$$R = \left[\prod_{i=1}^{95}(1+r_i)\right]^{\frac{1}{12}} - 1. \qquad \mathbf{12}$$

This formula, thus, computes the annual rate of return from capital gains due to common stock price and exchange rate changes, under the assumption that dividends are reinvested each month in fractional shares at current prices and that interest is compounded annually. No adjustments were made for withholding taxes on income or transactions costs. It should also be noted that exchange rate variations are assumed to be the only risks attached to foreign investment. Risks on foreign investment stemming from war, confiscation and exchange restrictions could not be quantified and were disregarded. Consequently the variances used in the subsequent calculations understate foreign risk and the estimates of gains from diversification are biased upward.

The empirical calculations are unrealistic in one other important respect. Due to indivisibilities, transactions costs and limited portfolio sizes, it is virtually impossible for anyone to hold portfolios containing all of the shares making up the indices used in the calculations. Because the portfolio variance decreases

5. Taking the simple arithmetic mean of the monthly rates vastly overstates the value of the capital gains between the beginning and the end of the period plus the value of the dividends. For a discussion of the biases inherent in the calculation of indices and averages see Fisher (1966).

with the number of individual stocks held, the underestimate of variance available to investors implicit in the calculation procedure is smaller the more diversified portfolios are in the real world. In general, the bias may not be too large in view of the availability of mutual funds in most of the foreign markets, though more empirical information on the investment patterns, transactions costs, etc., of these funds is needed.

In Table 1, column (1) shows average rates of return calculated in the manner just discussed while column (2) shows the capital value in December of 1966 of $100 invested in January of 1959. Columns (3) and (4) report the standard deviation of monthly returns and the correlation of these fluctuations with those of Moody's industrial average of common stocks. As can be seen, the US yield has been the sixth lowest, but the riskiness of the investment as measured by variance has been the fourth lowest.

Given these historic rates of return and interdependencies of the national stock markets, it is possible to compute rates of return and variances of portfolios which would have accrued to investors who had purchased foreign assets in various combinations. The most interesting of these combinations are those which for any given variance maximize the return. Portfolios which have these characteristics and are attainable with the available set of assets can be found through methods of quadratic programming, for which standard computer algorithms are available.[6]

Table 2 presents the results of two different calculations for efficient sets of internationally diversified portfolios. Part A is based on rates of return and variances of the eleven industrialized countries mentioned before, while part B is restricted to the data of the eight countries of the Atlantic Community. The eight portfolios shown for each case are so-called corner portfolios, i.e. those at which further reduction in variance can be achieved only through the inclusion or omission of additional assets. The rates of returns and standard deviations for the corner portfolios are shown in the last two rows of parts A and B of Table 2 and are

6. The program used is available in SHARE program under the code RSQPE4. It has been developed by the RAND Corporation. Finding the efficient set for eleven assets required 124 seconds on the IBM 7040. For the eight assets the time requirement was sixty-five seconds.

Table 2 Efficient Internationally Diversified Portfolios

	Percentage of portfolio invested in country portfolio number							
Country:	*1*	*2*	*3*	*4*	*5*	*6*	*7*	*8*
A. Eleven industrial countries								
United States						12·3	12·8	12·5
Canada							14·0	15·9
United Kingdom		2·4	6·3	11·9	12·0	10·7	8·4	7·6
West Germany								
France								2·7
Italy					0·2	1·7	1·7	1·5
Belgium								
Netherlands								
Japan	100·0	97·6	74·9	32·1	30·8	17·0	8·5	7·0
Australia			18·9	42·6	43·1	42·6	39·0	37·3
South Africa				13·4	13·8	15·7	15·6	15·4
Portfolio Return	16·54	16·37	14·76	11·61	11·50	10·25	9·15	8·84
Portfolio s.d.	92·62	90·55	71·02	37·12	36·26	27·37	22·82	22·09
B. Atlantic Community countries								
United States			26·6	42·9	35·7	32·1	29·5	16·4
Canada					21·3	24·9	27·3	25·4
United Kingdom	100·0	90·8	63·4	43·3	31·0	26·0	22·4	8·5
West Germany				4·7	5·0	4·3	3·6	
France						6·8	11·1	12·9
Italy		9·2	9·9	9·2	7·1	5·8	5·0	1·3
Belgium								34·4
Netherlands							1·1	1·2
Portfolio Return	9·59	9·45	8·90	8·47	7·87	7·48	7·20	4·65
Portfolio s.d.	65·28	60·63	46·67	39·76	34·49	32·23	30·96	25·10

Note: For computational method see text.
Sources: Same as Table 1.

plotted in Figure 1.[7] Other attainable combinations of return and standard deviations can be found by interpolation between corner portfolios, as is done by the lines drawn between the points in Figure 1.

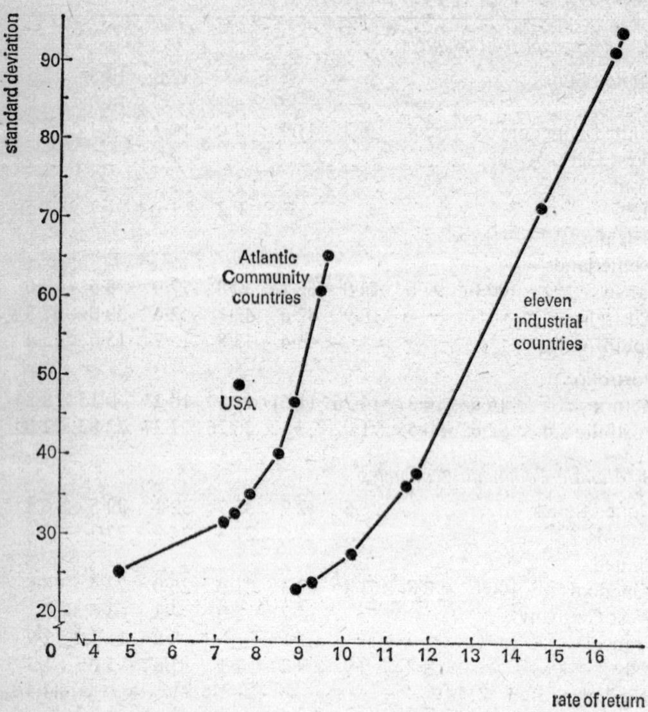

Figure 1 Efficient portfolios

As can be seen, diversification among the assets from the eleven countries in general would have permitted investors to attain higher rates of return or lower variance of their portfolios than they could have by purchasing a portfolio consisting of

7. In the plotting of the data it was more efficient to use standard deviations rather than variances. Throughout this section the two terms are used interchangeably since this leaves substantive conclusions unaffected but facilitates exposition.

Moody's industrial average of common stocks. Which combination of assets given investors would in fact have chosen cannot be known since it depends on their individual marginal rate of substitution between risk and return. It can be said unambiguously, however, that if an investor had wanted to maintain the same variability in return found in the New York investment, international diversification would have permitted him to earn 12·6 per cent as against 7·5 per cent, a gain of 68·0 per cent in the annual rate of return. When the opportunities for investment in Japan, South Africa and Australia are excluded from consideration, the opportunity for gains from diversification are reduced considerably, as can be seen from part B of Table 2 and the appropriate efficiency frontier in Figure 1. However, the increase in return attainable at the New York variance is from 7·5 per cent to 8·9 per cent, a gain of 18·7 per cent. As can be seen from Table 2, part B, column 3, such a portfolio would consist of the following approximate investments: 26·6 per cent in New York, 63·4 per cent in London and 9·9 per cent in Italy.

Analogous calculations can be carried out to demonstrate the reduction in variance attainable by investing in internationally diversified portfolios with the same expected rate of return as that from investment in New York alone. Such calculations are not shown here; rough estimates can be made by inspection of Figure 1.

In general, the preceding analysis and calculations suggest that recent experience with foreign investment returns would have given rise to substantial gains in welfare to wealth holders. If past experiences are considered to be indicative of future developments, then these data suggest that future international diversification of portfolios is profitable and that more of it will take place.[8]

8. The validity of this statement depends on the interpretation of the results. One could argue that US investors are in equilibrium and that the measures of risk used in the calculations represent an underestimate, which if properly accounted for would show little advantage to be gained from diversification. On the other hand, one could also argue that the calculations show the existence of a disequilibrium, that in fact US investors are in the process of making stock adjustments which are taking time to accomplish. See pages 217–19 and footnote 10 for more comments on this possibility.

The dynamic model

Some interesting conclusions from the model of internationally diversified portfolios result from the assumption that assets in both countries are growing through time. To simplify the analysis it is assumed that growth occurs in perfect balance, i.e. that income and assets in various forms grow at the same rate r_a and r_b for countries A and B respectively, and that exchange rates are pegged rigidly. If $Q^0_{A,B}$ and $Q^0_{B,A}$ are the initial stocks of foreign assets in static equilibrium in countries A and B respectively, then the gross flows ($\dot{Q}^t$) at any point in time t are

$$\dot{Q}^t_{A,B} = r_a e^{r_a t} Q^0_{A,B} \qquad 13$$

$$\dot{Q}^t_{B,A} = r_b e^{r_b t} Q^0_{B,A} \qquad 14$$

and the net flow from A to B ($\dot{N}^t_{A,B}$) is

$$\dot{N}^t_{A,B} = r_a e^{r_a t} Q^0_{A,B} - r_b e^{r_b t} Q^0_{B,A}. \qquad 15$$

Thus, it can be seen that the net flows of bonds between the two countries is a function of the growth rates and the size of the initial stocks in both countries. It is recalled that the initial stocks are determined primarily by the relative sizes of the two countries' wealth holdings and the existing interest rate differential.

Because of these determinants of bond flows, we have the following interesting possibilities. First, *gross* capital flows can occur between countries even if interest rates differentials are zero at all times. This is true whenever initial stocks of foreign bonds and growth rates are positive. Second, net capital flows into the low interest country (assumed to be country A) can take place when first, $r_a > r_b$ and $Q^0_{A,B} = Q^0_{B,A}$, second, $Q^0_{A,B} > Q^0_{B,A}$ and $r_a = r_b$; third, $r_a > r_b$ and $Q^0_{A,B} > Q^0_{B,A}$; fourth, $r_a < r_b$ and $Q^0_{A,B} > Q^0_{B,A}$. In the last two cases, however, the net flow to country A occurs only if the growth effect outweighs the stock effect or vice versa.

Under the assumed system of fixed exchanges rates there are no equilibrating forces set into motion by *net* bond flows as long as the government of the country selling the private bonds is willing to accept the other country's official IOUs in the manner described on pages 202–7. In the long run, however, these stocks of official IOUs can become very large and it is doubtful that any governments are willing to accumulate them indefinitely. Pressures for a real transfer of resources will be generated and these will bring into being equilibrating forces.

The nature of these forces can be discerned most readily in the world of perfectly flexible exchange rates, where the net demand for bonds by residents of country A results in the transfer of real resources to country B through the generation of a trade surplus for A. This transfer has two effects. First, the rate of real economic growth in B increases while that in A decreases. Second, the marginal productivity of capital falls in B and rises in A. Both the real growth and interest rate effects tend to reduce the gross demand for bonds in A and raise the gross demand for bonds in B. The effects persist until gross bond flows have become equalized. However, such equality does not necessarily occur when the interest rate differential is zero. The differential can be either positive or negative and gross flows can remain equal as long as the products of growth rates times stocks of foreign assets are equal for both countries.

Interest elasticity of capital flows

In this part special attention is given to the role of interest rates in the preceding models, primarily because of some interesting policy conclusions following from the analysis.

In the static model after stock equilibrium has been established, bonds cease to flow between the two countries. However, the potential for flows in response to interest rate changes is always present. Thus, if for some domestic policy purpose country A decides to lower its interest rate, foreigners will decrease their holdings of country A's bonds and domestic wealth holders will increase their holdings of foreign bonds. The result is a net demand for bonds by country A which leads to a transfer of IOUs to the government of B or to the transfer of real resources in the manner discussed above. However, it is important to note that in this static model the flow of capital following the interest rate change is a once-and-for-all stock adjustment, which is accomplished within a certain time period, the length of which depends on institutional characteristics of the bond market.

In the dynamic version of the model the change in the interest rate differential calls forth the equivalent of a stock adjustment flow which is superimposed on the flow due to portfolio growth. The duration of this stock-adjustment flow component depends on the institutional characteristics of the bond market, as in the static model. After completion of the stock adjustment flow, the regular transfer of bonds continues to grow at the same rate as before, but the level is different. These points can also be made with the help of the accompanying Figure 2.

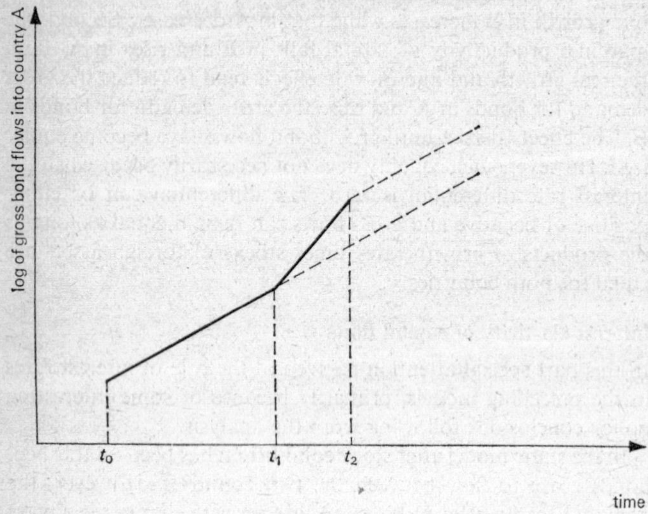

Figure 2

On the horizontal axis we plot time, on the vertical axis the log of gross capital flows from B to A. The line segment $t_0 t_1$ has a slope r_a, equal to the rate of growth of wealth portfolios in country A. At period t_1, country A lowers its interest rate and the growth rate of foreign bond holdings in A increases, as is shown by the steeper slope of the line segment $t_1 t_2$. After the completion of the stock-adjustment process, the rate of growth in foreign bond holdings returns to its old level r_a but the *level* of bond holdings is raised at any given moment in time by the vertical distance between the solid and broken growth lines as a result of the increased rate differential.

Some implications of the model

First, the classical theory of factor movements considers rates of return alone as the determinants of international capital flows. In its basic form, therefore, it cannot explain the real world phenomenon of simultaneous European investments in the United States and US investments in Europe. Direct investment of this nature has been explained as resulting from the cost conditions in oligopolistic industries (Grubel, 1967). The present model provides an additional explanation that is especially applicable to the purchase of foreign bonds and other non-control conferring assets.

Second, the present model suggests that the empirical measurement of the interest elasticity of international capital movements can be improved by the inclusion of independent variables representing the growth in total asset portfolios and by studying gross flows of capital from each country. Consider, for example, the interest rate differential is zero, gross flows are positive and large but net flows are zero. In our model it is possible that an increase in the rate of economic growth of one country causes the rise of that country's gross purchases of foreign assets and causes the appearance of a net flow even though the interest rate differential remained at zero.[9] A measurement of the interest elasticity of net flows would yield nonsensical results, but the measurement of gross flows and inclusion of total portfolio growth can explain the phenomenon.

Third, the model leads to the hypothesis that the large scale US investments in Europe during the last decade are part of a stock adjustment phenomenon that started when European currencies became convertible *de jure* in 1958 after having been convertible *de facto* a few years earlier. If this hypothesis is correct, then there may eventually take place a slowdown in the rate of US capital outflows to Western Europe.[10] However, because of the proportionately larger size of US portfolios, normal growth in both continents leads to the expectation of a continued net demand for European assets. If this is so, European governments

9. Harry G. Johnson (1966) has suggested a similar dependence of international capital flows on rates of economic growth.

10. This point has also been made by J. Tobin (1966, p. 168).

must either be willing to accept more of the US government's IOUs or permit a greater trade surplus to occur if the free convertibility of the major Western currencies is to be maintained. Equalization of interest rates will be insufficient to equalize gross flows, because of the different sizes of total asset holdings in Europe and the United States.

Fourth, the portfolio model suggests that a once-and-for-all change in international interest rate differentials leads to only a once-and-for-all stock adjustment, after which gross flows return to their old levels. This implication of the portfolio model leads to an empirically important extension of the arguments over the proper mix of monetary and fiscal policy for the achievement of internal and external balance.

In Mundell's (1962) formulation of this argument, the domestic interest rate is set at such a level as to attract a quantity of foreign capital sufficient to fill the current account gap in international payments while fiscal policy is set at a level of restrictiveness sufficient to attain domestic full employment. Our model suggests that at the international interest rate differential initially chosen, there will be a stock-adjustment flow of a size that cannot be sustained beyond the attainment of the new stock equilibrium. If the external deficit on current account persists beyond this point of new stock equilibrium, then the interest rate differential has to be raised again to finance the deficit in the next period and so on until it is eliminated by some other policies. If foreign wealth holders run into diminishing returns to international diversification, then the subsequent increments to the interest differential have to be increasingly larger.[11]

Fifth, the model can be used to explain holding of foreign short-term assets as well as bonds, corporate securities and direct investment. Continuous and growing international diversification demand for short-term assets has some interesting implications for US balance of payments 'deficits' under the liquidity definition. Even if the growing exchange of short-term assets between the United States and the rest of the world is perfectly balanced, the United States would show a continuous and growing balance of payments deficit since the foreign holdings of

11. I have proved the existence of such diminishing returns to diversification in the traditional quadratic utility function (Grubel, 1966, p. 20).

short-term dollar assets are considered to be a potential claim on US reserves which the balance of payments statistics are designed to reflect. Yet, the model presented suggests that these potential liabilities are counterbalanced by US holdings of foreign short-term assets and that the foreign asset demand is normal and permanent because of the continued welfare gains from holding internationally diversified portfolios. The model thus strengthens the arguments made against the use of the liquidity concept and in favor of the official-reserve-transactions concept.[12]

References

FISHER, L. (1966), 'Some new stock market indexes', *J. Bus.*, vol. 39, pp. 191–225.

GRUBEL, H. G. (1966), *Forward Exchange, Speculation and the International Flow of Capital*, Stanford University Press.

GRUBEL, H. G. (1967), 'Intra-industry specialization and the pattern of trade', *Canad. J. Econ.*, vol. 33, pp. 374–88.

JOHNSON, H. G. (1966), 'Some aspects of the theory of economic policy in a world of capital mobility', in T. Bagiotti (ed.), *Essays in Honour of Marco Fanno*, Cedam, Padova.

MARKOWITZ, H. (1959), *Portfolio Selection: Efficient Diversification of Investments*, Wiley.

MUNDELL, R. A. (1962), 'The appropriate use of monetary and fiscal policy for internal and external stability', *IMF Staff Pap.*, 9 March, pp. 70–77.

REVIEW COMMITTEE FOR BALANCE OF PAYMENTS STATISTICS (1965), *The Balance of Payments Statistics of the United States: Review and Appraisal*, Bureau of the Budget.

TOBIN, J. (1958), 'Liquidity preference as behaviour towards risk', *Rev. econ. Stud.*, vol. 25, pp. 65–86.

TOBIN, J. (1966), *National Economic Policy*, Yale University Press.

Wall Street Journal (1967), 'European investors step up their purchases of American corporate securities', *Wall St J.*, 12 October.

12. These issues have been analysed in Review Committee for Balance of Payments Statistics (1965).

9 Richard N. Cooper

Towards an International Capital Market?

Richard N. Cooper, 'Towards an international capital market?', in C. P. Kindleberger and A. Shonfield (eds.), *North American and Western European Economic Policies*, Macmillan, 1971, pp. 192–208.

Introductory

This paper discusses the growth and development of the international capital market during the past decade, considers whether it can be said that a genuine international capital market now exists, and discusses the advantages and disadvantages of one integrated capital market transcending national economies. 'Capital markets' involve the mobilization of savings by those who want or are willing to accept financial claims, for investment (or consumption) by others who are willing to accept financial liabilities or share their equity. Capital markets are usually distinguished from 'money markets' by the maturity of the claims that are traded there, the capital market referring to transactions in claims with maturities in excess (definitionally) of one year, and usually in excess of five years, although any clear distinction between the two must be arbitrary, for these markets may be, and typically are, closely related. Medium-term bank lending, for example, involves maturities in excess of one year but ordinarily does not give rise to marketable securities.

Several geographically distinct capital markets can be said to be integrated – that is, effectively one market – to the extent that a significant number of savers do not distinguish among claims on the basis of the geographical location of the borrower. In the international context, this means that a significant number of savers do not distinguish among borrowers on the basis of nationality. This failure to distinguish must include, of course, both the willingness to accept claims on foreigners and the ability to do so, the latter implying an absence of balance of payments and other restrictions against foreign investment.

The extent to which there can be said to be an Atlantic capital market, encompassing Canada, the United States and many or most of the countries of Western Europe, can be approached empirically from two angles. We can ask about the absolute and relative volume of long-term financial transactions crossing national boundaries and about the nationality and other characteristics of the borrowers and lenders. Or we can apply the economically more meaningful test of the extent to which bond yields and share prices have been brought into harmony. One market implies one price for identical goods or claims, and similar prices for similar goods or claims. A genuine Atlantic capital market would therefore imply similar interest rates or yields for financial claims of similar risk and liquidity. The next two sections of this paper offer some sketchy evidence on both of these approaches. Following this evidence, I will draw some implications for economic policy of the tendency towards one market and offer an assessment of the advantages and disadvantages at the present time of a unified capital market spanning national boundaries.

The size and growth of international capital movements

The rapid growth in foreign bond flotations during the decade of the 1960s has been a source of universal astonishment. From barely more than $200 million in 1958 (close to $400 million if the United Kingdom is included), foreign bond issues in Europe grew to over $4·7 billion in 1968, a compound growth rate of nearly 30 per cent a year. The growth is far less dramatic, but still dramatic, if the United States market is included: total foreign bond issues on both sides of the Atlantic rose from $1·5 billion in 1958 to $6·3 billion in 1968,[1] a fourfold increase (Table 1). A distinction may be drawn between foreign bonds issued in national markets, denominated in the national currency of the market in which it is floated, and 'international' bond issues, which are denominated in a currency (usually United States dollars but also German marks, two or more currencies, and units of account) different from that of the country (or countries)

1. It might be noted in passing that recent levels compare favourably in absolute magnitude to the average annual $2·0 billion in foreign bonds issued in Europe and the United States during 1924–8, the alleged heyday of the international capital market.

in which it is floated.[2] International issues grew from negligible amounts in the early 1960s to $3·5 billion in 1968.

The overwhelming bulk of the long-term foreign borrowing in the United States is by Canadians, although Japan, Israel, the World Bank and (before the imposition of the interest equalization tax in 1963) several European countries have also been

Table 1 Foreign Bond Issues,* 1958–68 ($ million)

	Foreign issues on domestic markets		*International*	
	United States	*European*†	*issues*†	*Total*
1958	1138	302	82	1522
1959	802	337	31	1170
1960	636	393	29	1058
1961	558	559	79	1196
1962	1185	430	—	1615
1963	1414	426	119	1958
1964	1191	263	838	2293
1965	1532	264‡	1192	2989
1966	1317	550‡	1155	3021
1967	1619§	404‡	2002	4025
1968	1576§	1185‡	3517	6278

* Including private placements and convertible bonds.

† Foreign bonds issued in Germany after imposition of the 25 per cent coupon tax on German bonds in March 1964 are treated as international issues, since they are exempt from the tax.

‡ Including the Canadian market.

§ Excludes portion purchased by foreigners.

Sources: 1958–66: OECD (1968, p. 717); 1967–8: US Department of Commerce (1967–8) and Morgan Guaranty Trust Company, *World Financial Markets.*

important borrowers. United States corporations and their subsidiaries have been the single most important group of borrowers in European markets, accounting for nearly half of all new issues (many of them convertible bonds) in 1968. Non-American corporations accounted for nearly a quarter of the borrowing, and

2. Foreign bonds denominated in German marks are considered 'international' bonds after March 1964, even when floated on the German market, since they were exempt from the coupon tax levied on interest payments to foreign holders of German bonds and hence had lower yields than German bonds floated on the domestic market.

governmental bodies and international institutions for the remainder. Characterizing the lenders is more difficult, since it is not known who ultimately purchases these bonds. In the United States, insurance companies and pension funds provide a steady source of demand for new bond issues. In the European market, individuals and family trusts are relatively more important (leading to correspondingly higher selling costs for the 'retail' market). It has been estimated for the mid-1960s that about half the purchases of foreign bonds issued in Europe were by banks and trusts in Switzerland, acting on behalf of customers from all over the world; another 20 per cent of the funds came from other continental European countries (Williams, 1967, p. 61).

Over three-quarters of the international bond issues, narrowly defined, were denominated in United States dollars, and therefore over two-thirds of total foreign bond issues outside the United States were so denominated. Like a language, a currency is useful in proportion to the number of people who use it. By using a common currency, the market is widened and the potential liquidity of financial claims is increased – potential since this liquidity depends on the development of secondary markets where securities are bought and sold after issue and before maturity, and secondary markets in Europe have developed more slowly than the new issues market. During 1968 and 1969 use of the German mark became more prominent, as the German monetary authorities deliberately maintained low interest rates and took other steps to encourage the export of capital, making DM-denominated bonds less costly to borrowers than dollar-denominated ones.[3]

Foreign and international bond issues have grown rapidly relative to the total activity on the various national capital markets, as well as in absolute volume. Comparable measures are difficult to obtain, but on the basis of total net new bond issues on the eight major European capital markets plus the United States, as computed by the OECD, the share of foreign and international bond issues rose from 5 per cent in 1960 to 11 per cent in 1965 and to an estimated 14 per cent in 1968.[4]

3. Expectations of a future revaluation of the mark also helped lower coupon rates on DM-denominated bonds.

4. OECD (1968, *statistical annex*, pp. 122–3) and the sources there cited.

Equity shares comprise another part of the capital market. Here one must turn to the secondary market for relevant information, since it is far more important, relative to new issues, than is the case for bonds. Until 1967 and 1968, net movements of funds between countries on account of purchases of stocks (excluding direct investment, aimed at management control) was rather small. Americans added very little to their holdings of foreign stocks during the 1960s, while the British engaged in large-scale net liquidation of their foreign share holdings. Net foreign purchases of American stocks rose sharply after the mid-1960s, however, from $200 million in 1963 to nearly $2·3 billion in 1968, with purchases from Europe and Canada accounting for the bulk of them. Mutual funds spread rapidly in the late 1960s, especially in Germany and Italy, and many of these specialized in the purchase of foreign – mainly American – stocks.

From the viewpoint of the integration of capital markets, however, it is *gross* rather than net transactions that count. These have been substantial, even when net transactions were small. In 1968, for instance, foreigners bought $13·1 billion in American stocks and sold $10·8 billion, over six times the levels of 1960; American purchases of foreign stocks (except for dealers, generally subject to the interest equalization tax of 15 per cent) amounted to $1·6 billion in 1968, while sales came to $1·2 billion, both over double the levels of 1960. These sums are of course small relative to the total gross value of stock sales ($125 billion on the New York Stock Exchange alone in 1968). But here, as elsewhere in economics, it is the marginal buyer that counts. The question, therefore, is whether international transactions in stocks and bonds were sufficiently large at the margin to influence or even to govern prices in the various national markets.

Before turning to an examination of the evidence on that point, two other important dimensions of international capital movements should be mentioned, for while they are not strictly part of 'capital markets' as defined here, both short-term capital movements and direct investments provide potential indirect linkages between capital markets to the extent that there is some substitutability between short- and long-term financial claims, on the one hand, and between long-term financial claims and real assets, on the other. Capital markets could be fully integrated in the economically meaningful sense of price equalization for claims of similar quality even with no movement of long-term portfolio capital between countries, for instance, provided that money and capital markets were tightly linked within each country and that national money markets were closely linked internationally.

National money markets are linked these days primarily through Euro-dollars, a market in short-term dollar claims located in London and other European financial centres. Where national exchange regulations permit the outward movement of short-term funds, those with such funds to invest will compare their earning opportunities at home with those in Euro-dollar deposits, and will shift funds accordingly. Even where regulations limit the outward movement of funds, credit-worthy borrowers will draw funds from the Euro-dollar market when rates there are more attractive than in their home markets. In this way national money markets tend to be tied together.

The Euro-dollar market has grown to substantial proportions. At an estimated $25 billion of total liabilities by the end of 1968, excluding inter-bank deposits, the Euro-dollar market was roughly equivalent in size to the total money supply in Italy, Japan or the United Kingdom, and was substantially exceeded only by the money supplies in France and the United States. It has shown surprising responsiveness, moreover, to new demands placed on it. Switches of borrowers or lenders between the Euro-dollar market and domestic markets can therefore exert a powerful influence on domestic monetary conditions, and for many countries could in principle largely undercut monetary policy as an instrument of economic stabilization. This extreme has not yet been reached, in part because a switch between dollars and local currencies requires either that the switching party take on an exchange risk or that he insure against it, e.g. by selling forward the currency he has purchased. The presence of exchange risk serves to insulate national money markets from one another even when all the technical facilities for one integrated market are present.

Direct investment abroad can also provide a link between capital markets. Recent work on the motivation for direct investment has rightly emphasized the exploitation of quasi-monopoly powers arising from patents or other unique technological or managerial advantages. Many direct investors borrow in local markets, both to establish credit lines and to hedge against exchange risks, and this practice suggests that direct investment is not primarily in response to national differences in long-term bond yields. Nevertheless, direct investment does usually involve the transfer of funds from one country to another, and since the early 1960s such transfers have taken place on a substantial scale.

United States takeovers of European firms bid up the price of existing assets, and takeovers for cash shift funds from the United States capital market to the capital or money markets of Europe. Investments in new plant and equipment are more ambiguous in their effects, since any flow of funds from the parent company is accompanied by an increased demand for funds that may more than offset it, depending on the extent of local borrowing and the size of multiplier effects. But many international corporations, with access to two or more national capital markets, are influenced in their source of funds by relative costs and hence tend to bring borrowing conditions in national markets into closer harmony. Direct investment also plays a role in bringing national money markets together, as corporations with temporarily idle funds place them where the yield–risk combination is most attractive or fill short-term cash needs by borrowing in the money market where costs are lowest. Indeed, international corporations have been among the major participants both in the Euro-dollar market and in the Euro-bond market.

In passing, it is of interest that both the Euro-dollar market and the international bond market were encouraged by the imposition of national controls that inhibited the most advantageously situated national market from serving an international role. In 1957 the British commercial banks were circumscribed in their ability to lend sterling outside the United Kingdom, but were left free to carry on in other currencies, so began to accept deposits and lend in dollars. In 1963 the interest equalization tax effectively closed the New York bond market to a large class of foreign borrowers and thereby generated a demand for issues in Europe, a demand that was greatly augmented two years later by the voluntary limitations placed on United States financing of direct investment abroad.

Interest rates and asset prices

The flow of funds across national boundaries unquestionably increased sharply during the 1960s, both absolutely and relative to internal financial transactions. Identifiable international money and capital markets appeared. But were these developments sufficient to integrate the national financial markets in the sense of bringing together prices of similar financial assets? A unified market requires a single price for the same commodity prevailing everywhere at each point in time. When this condition is not met, markets are to that extent fragmented.

It is difficult to test empirically the extent to which we have achieved integrated money and capital markets among the major industrial countries, since assets in different countries continue to be different in one important respect: they are denominated in different currencies. The possibility of changes in exchange rates among the currencies introduces an element of risk which, from the viewpoint of a resident of any particular country, is not present when all assets are denominated in a single currency. The assets also differ in other, less important respects. A comparison of interest rates on high-quality short-term assets and on long-term government bonds none the less reveals a marked tendency towards convergence following the move to currency convertibility by the major European countries in late 1958. Table 2 shows that the dispersion around the mean of short-term interest rates for eight countries declined substantially after 1958. The decline in dispersion was less marked for long-term bond rates, but except for 1966 the dispersion declined steadily relative to the mean bond yield, suggesting some convergence in the long-term capital market as well. The sharp increase in bond-rate dispersion in 1966 is attributable solely to a 2 percentage point increase in German bond rates, to 8·4 per cent, in a period in which the German State and local authorities were borrowing at an exceptionally heavy rate and the Bundes-bank tightened credit to dampen total spending. The increase in absolute and relative dispersion of short-term rates in 1968 is attributable to a combination of high rates in Britain and France, reflecting doubts about the exchange rates of their respective currencies, combined with an exceptionally low rate in Germany designed both to stimulate capital outflow and to promote domestic capital spending in the aftermath of the recession generated by excessively tight monetary conditions in 1966.

Table 2 International Convergence of Interest Rates,* 1958–68

	Short-term†			*Government bonds*‡		
	Mean	*Standard deviation*	*Coefficient of variation*§	*Mean*	*Standard deviation*	*Coefficient of variation*§
1958	2·86	1·22	0·43	4·48	0·94	0·21
1960	3·37	1·21	0·36	4·66	0·93	0·20
1962	2·96	0·95	0·32	4·80	0·89	0·19
1964	3·66	0·74	0·20	5·36	0·93	0·17
1966	4·80	0·83	0·17	5·89	1·13	0·19
1968	4·74	1·75	0·37	5·97	0·81	0·14

* Average rate for June of indicated year.

† Unweighted mean and standard deviation of three-month Treasury bill or call-money rates for Belgium, Canada, France, Germany (West), Netherlands, Switzerland, United Kingdom and United States.

‡ With maturity in excess of twelve years, for countries listed in preceding footnote plus Italy and Sweden.

§ Standard deviation divided by mean.

Source: Underlying data from *International Financial Statistics.*

In addition to coming closer together over time, interest rates showed a greater tendency to move together through time from 1962 to 1967 than before, indicating a greater influence of one market on another (Figure 1). This tendency was reversed in late 1967 and 1968, when a series of exchange crises disturbed interest-rate relationships and induced several countries to impose tight controls on capital movements.

Equity prices are more difficult to compare for European firms publish too little financial information to compute price–earnings ratios and other measures of performance from the perspective of the shareholder. This fact not only makes analysis difficult, but it also inhibits the effective integration of the markets for equities. Indices of share prices do show some sympathetic movement from country to country (Figure 2). The movement

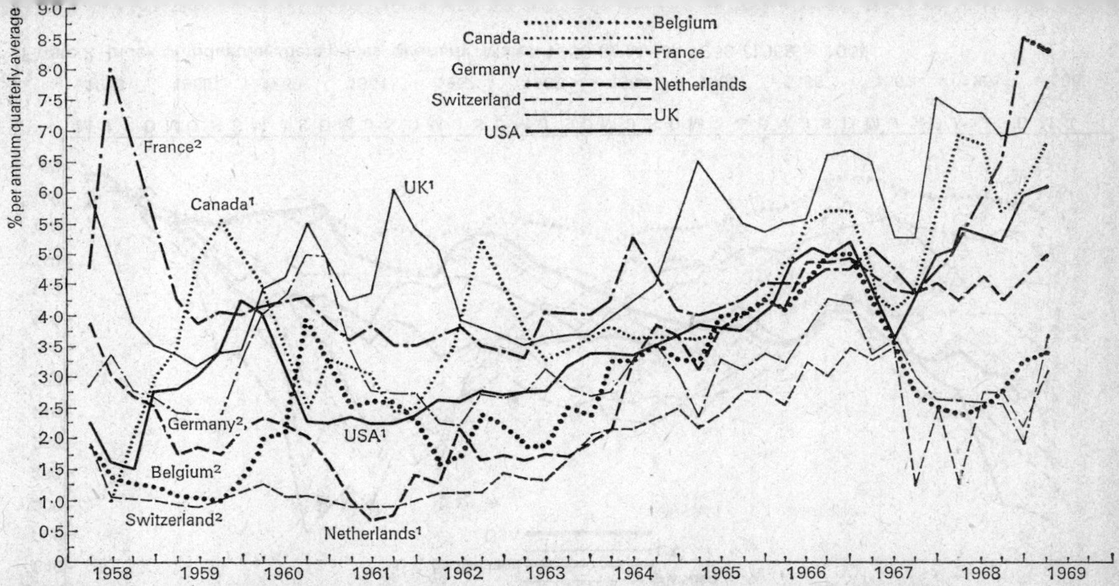

Figure 1 Short-term rates for the United States, the United Kingdom, Canada, France, Germany, Belgium, the Netherlands and Switzerland, 1958–69.

1. Average tender rate for three-month Treasury bills.
2. Average of daily or weekly call-money rates.

Source: IMF, *International Financial Statistics*

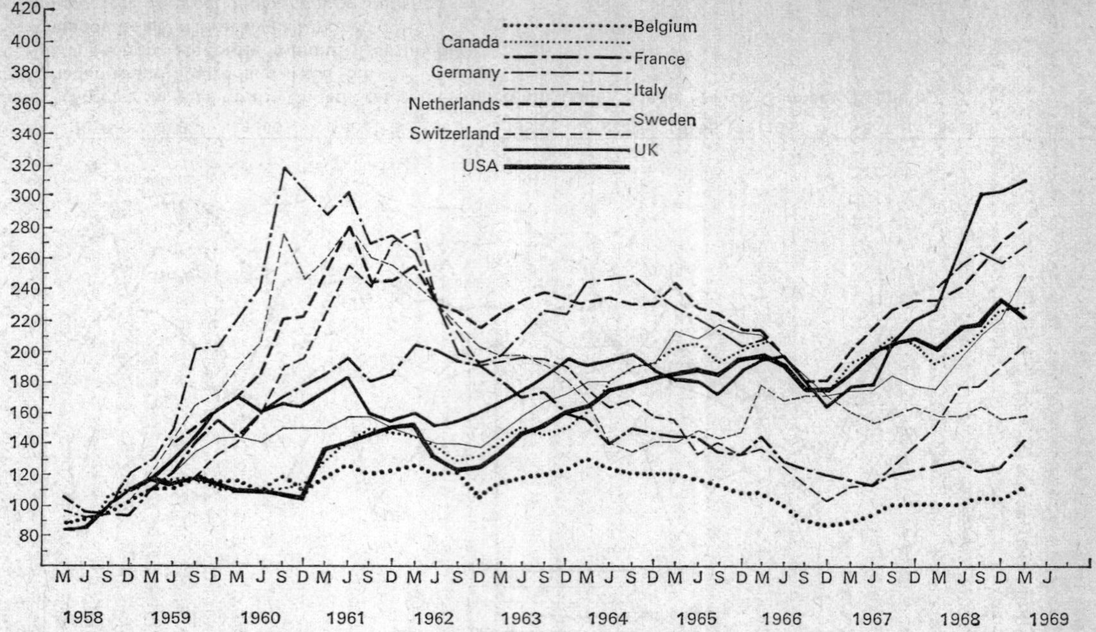

Figure 2 Index of industrial share prices, quarterly, March 1958 to March 1969 (1958 = 100)

may reflect broadly sympathetic movements in national economic conditions rather than direct buying and selling links between equity markets, although the universal drop in equity prices in 1966, in the face of sharply divergent national economic developments, suggests more direct links. Expected or actual changes in exchange rates will also influence equity prices; currency overvaluation will weaken profit performance in manufacturing, while devaluation will improve it. Currency revaluation may have played a role in the fall in German and Dutch equity prices in 1961; on the other hand, Canadian equity prices closely paralleled those of the United States during 1961–3 (indeed, throughout the 1960s), despite the Canadian devaluation of 1961–2.

The challenge of and response to financial integration

All this evidence points to the conclusion that there has been some integration of money and capital markets during the past decade, but that there is still a substantial way to go before we can speak of unified markets. Even the integration that has taken place so far, however, has important implications for the economies involved. The integration of financial markets limits the scope for the autonomous pursuit of national policy. This is most obviously the case for monetary policy, but it is also true for taxation and regulation of business and for exchange-rate policy.

Consider monetary policy first. In a world of high capital mobility under fixed exchange rates, a tightening of monetary conditions, e.g. through open-market sales by the central bank or through higher bank reserve requirements, will serve less to dampen domestic spending than to attract an inflow of funds from abroad. Similarly, an attempt to ease domestic monetary conditions to stimulate spending will instead simply stimulate an outflow of funds. Financial integration thus poses a profound threat to the traditional reliance on monetary policy for stabilization of the domestic economy. The effectiveness of monetary policy for this purpose is greatly reduced by high capital mobility across national boundaries, for the rest of the world in effect becomes a residual source of demand for excess domestic liquidity and a residual source of supply of funds.

By the same token, however, monetary policy becomes very

effective as an instrument for influencing a country's short-run international payments position. A slight tightening of domestic credit will attract funds from abroad and thus may be used to finance a payments deficit. Monetary policy used for this purpose will be more effective in the short run than it will in the long, partly because some of the initial inflow of funds in response to tighter monetary conditions will represent stock adjustment of a once-for-all character, partly because, in the absence of perfect capital mobility, higher interest charges on outstanding short-term indebtedness must be set against whatever continuing inflows there are.

An additional implication of increased capital mobility is that fiscal policy will become more effective at influencing domestic demand. The monetarist claim, that the impact on aggregate demand of 'pure' fiscal action – changes in the government budget position with no accommodating change in the money supply – will be largely if not wholly offset by interest-induced changes in investment demand, ceases to apply in a world of high capital mobility. In the limiting case of perfect capital mobility, an increase in government spending can be financed by bond sales at unchanged interest rates by all but the largest countries, without intervention by the monetary authorities, for funds from abroad will produce the required increase in the monetary supply. Thus while the effectiveness of monetary policy in stabilizing the economy will decline with increased capital mobility, generating a need for alternative stabilization measures, the effectiveness of fiscal policy at influencing aggregate demand will increase.

The weakening of monetary policy for stabilization purposes nevertheless poses a serious problem for governments, since it is usually the most flexible instrument of policy at hand and for institutional reasons it is also more insulated from short-run political considerations. Not surprisingly, governments are loath to give up their reliance on monetary policy – indeed, it is not clear either that they should or that they can, politically speaking – and they have therefore taken a number of steps to counteract the integrating tendencies evident in money and capital markets. These actions in turn make more difficult any analysis of the degree to which money and capital markets have become unified:

the potential unification may be far greater than that actually observed, as summarized by the data in the preceding sections, because of deliberate countervailing steps to reduce the integrating pressures in the interests of preserving some degree of national autonomy in the exercise of monetary policy.

Government response to the greater interdependence between national capital markets has been widespread. These responses have often been taken under the guise of balance of payments' policies, but that is merely the other side of the coin. Special measures to restrain capital outflows serve to protect the balance of payments in periods in which for domestic reasons the monetary authorities desire to maintain a greater degree of monetary ease than prevails abroad. That these measures are not governed principally by balance of payments considerations is indicated by the fact that countries in payments surplus have also taken steps to insulate their economies from high international capital mobility, even though balance of payments pressures were not so acute as for countries in deficit.

The devices used are well known. Virtually all countries restrict foreign access to their domestic capital markets, usually on the grounds that unlimited access by foreigners could create undue disruption of imperfectly developed national capital markets. Britain and the United States, however, restrict access on balance of payments grounds, in the case of the United States through an 'interest equalization tax' on United States purchases of European and certain other issues, which is to say that the authorities in those countries would not like to be obliged to maintain interest rates at the levels required to limit foreign borrowing. Both countries also limit purchases by their residents of outstanding foreign securities. The interest equalization tax applies in the United States, and Britain in effect imposes a tax by requiring British residents wanting to invest abroad to buy foreign currency at a premium but to sell a portion of receipts from liquidation of foreign assets to the authorities at the official exchange rate. These and other countries also limit the amount of short-term investment that can be undertaken abroad.

High capital mobility can be as frustrating to countries wanting to tighten domestic monetary conditions as to those wanting to ease them. At various times France, Germany, the Netherlands and Switzerland have all prohibited interest payments on deposits by foreigners, to inhibit an inflow of short-term funds. Special reserve requirements have been imposed on foreigners' deposits with the same aim. Since 1964 Germany has imposed special withholding taxes on interest paid to foreign holders of domestic bonds, a kind of negative interest equalization tax. (Foreign bonds floated in Germany are exempt from this tax, so they command lower nominal yields and therefore draw funds largely from outside Germany.) Both Germany and Italy, and to a lesser extent the Netherlands and Switzerland, have encouraged their banks to channel short-term funds abroad through directives or attractive forward swap arrangements, thereby regaining some control over domestic monetary conditions. But the technique will work only so long as domestic non-bank borrowers do not have direct access to foreign sources of funds, a condition that has eroded over time.

International transactions in equities do not escape the national restraints. The taxes imposed by Britain and the United States apply to equities as well as to bonds. Several countries limit purchases of foreign equities by their residents to those quoted on the national stock exchange, which in turn are restricted. In the late 1960s the growth of mutual funds in Europe provided a closer link between equity markets, especially in Germany and Italy, for they permitted residents to purchase balanced and diversified packages of foreign securities of which they had little direct knowledge. In 1969, however, the Italian Government limited sharply the activities of these mutual funds, despite the fact that Italy was running a large payments surplus at the time, because they were drawing equity away from prospective domestic issuers at a time when the Italian authorities wanted to stimulate domestic investment.

In sum, national authorities do not yet seem ready to accept the limitations imposed on their own freedom to influence domestic financial conditions by an integrated capital market spanning national boundaries.

High international mobility of capital also imposes limits on national autonomy in matters of taxation and business regulation, although these limitations are both less obvious and far less evident than is true for monetary policy. There is little question, however, that one of the principal attractions of foreign bonds to investors is that income on them can be more easily concealed from the domestic tax authorities. Foreign bond issues registered on the London market, unlike domestic issues, are not subject to British withholding tax (where tax treaties eliminate British withholding on domestic issues, they also provide for exchange of information between taxing authorities); but they are not generally subject to withholding tax by the United States or by any other country either. High international capital mobility under these circumstances will erode the ability of international authorities to tax interest income except in those countries where the tradition of voluntary tax compliance is strong, for prospective bond-holders can readily invest in international bonds to escape taxation.

High capital mobility also weakens national regulation of securities markets and corporate financial activity. In early 1969 a Swiss company subverted a Swiss requirement that existing stockholders be given preference on new stock issues, for example, by establishing a financial subsidiary in the Netherlands Antilles to raise desired funds through a convertible bond issue. This kind of escape from regulation through migration was a familiar phenomenon in the United States around the turn of the century, where business regulation by the constitutent states was gradually eroded as the railroad and the telegraph transformed local markets into a national one. Those states most aggressive in the competition for business location set a tone for lax business regulation, and as a result regulatory responsibilities were gradually taken over by the Federal Government.

Pressures for supranational action in the field of business regulation and taxation have not yet reached an advanced stage, but the beginnings of such pressure can be seen both in the desire for increased intergovernmental consultation on such matters and in the attempts, largely so far by the United States, to tax 'foreign' income and to extend its national regulations beyond national boundaries. The Revenue Act of 1962 levied United States taxes on the income of United States-owned corporations operating from tax-haven countries; and the Kennedy Administration had asked for a much broader extension of the United

States tax than that finally passed by Congress. Similarly, in 1965 the Securities and Exchange Commission instructed a number of foreign (mostly Canadian) companies to submit information reports because their securities were being traded in the over-the-counter market in the United States. The foreign companies regarded this as an unwarranted intrusion into their business affairs and they were supported by their governments; but the SEC was merely carrying out its Congressional mandate to protect American investors from possible exploitation by unscrupulous corporate management. The problem of national jurisdiction arose because securities markets transcend national boundaries.

A third area in which high international mobility of capital has important implications is exchange-rate policy. A technically well-developed international money market, among other things, facilitates the movement of funds into or out of different currencies in anticipation of exchange rate changes, so the volume of currency speculation is greatly enlarged during periods of uncertainty about exchange parities. The presence of exchange risk might be expected to inhibit the development of an international capital market.[5] When foreign loans are involved, either the borrower or the lender (or both) runs an exchange risk. If the borrower's home currency is devalued, the burden of a foreign-currency debt will be increased in terms of his own currency. (Whether the real burden on the borrower is increased by devaluation depends on a host of other factors as well, such as whether devaluation raises the profitability of his local investment.) Nevertheless, financial integration may proceed rapidly when exchange risk is perceived to be low. The subsequent emergence of exchange-rate uncertainty will induce many lenders to insure against parity changes either by borrowing or by selling forward. As the volume of outstanding international indebtedness

5. Canadians floated fixed-interest bonds in New York (in United States dollars) on a large scale during the 1950s, when the Canadian dollar was on a floating rate. But expectations (and Canadian monetary policy) kept the Canadian dollar close to parity with the United States dollar. Moreover, Canadian borrowing in New York increased sharply in the 1960s, after Canada switched to a fixed exchange rate. How much of the dramatic increase in foreign borrowing was due to factors other than the change in exchange-rate regime is difficult to say.

increases, the volume of hedging activity in periods of uncertainty will also increase, resulting in corresponding pressure on national reserves. These large and sudden movements of funds in turn may force reserve-short countries into unnecessary parity changes or, on the contrary, delay needed changes because of the reduction in national wealth (in the form of loss of reserves) implied by a change in exchange rate when there is a large but temporary short (for devaluation) or long (for revaluation) foreign position in the currency.

The advantages and disadvantages of an international capital market

Turning now from the analytical and empirical to the normative side, we may ask whether such financial integration as has taken place is a good thing or a bad thing. Or to cast the question into policy terms, are the defensive reactions by governments desirable or undesirable? These questions cannot be answered sensibly without a point of comparison. What are the alternatives? On the standard competitive model, a reduction of artificial barriers to capital movements, whether by reducing ignorance or by removing policy restrictions, will lead to a more efficient use of the world's scarce resources and hence would generally be regarded as desirable. The economic theorist's presumption in favour of free markets is applicable to capital as well as to goods and services. Under competitive conditions, capital will seek higher rates of return, moving from regions of relative abundance to regions of relative scarcity. Total output will rise. In addition, free movement of funds permits individuals and institutions to diversify their risks, and this too is desirable to the extent that individuals deem high risks to be undesirable. Thus there is a diversification as well as an efficiency argument for international capital mobility.

An assessment of the desirability of international capital mobility becomes more complicated when competitive conditions are not fulfilled, for example, because of the presence of import tariffs or income taxes. International capital movements may either mitigate or aggravate the efficiency losses arising from the tariffs, depending on whether the tariffs raise the return to capital more in capital-poor countries than in capital-rich ones. Similarly, different national tax rates may either foster or inhibit the efficient allocation of capital among countries. Tax treaties strive for tax neutrality in the location of capital. But lower tax rates combined with tax deferral or other tax-avoidance devices presumably contribute to better allocation when they draw American capital to Belgium than when they draw French or Italian capital to Switzerland, perhaps to be re-lent to the United States.

Arguments based on allocative efficiency assume that economies have adjusted fully to prevailing conditions. In particular, they assume that balance of payments equilibrium is assured, so that real capital movements correspond to non-compensatory private and official movements of funds across boundaries, and they also assume that the various domestic economies respond quickly and properly to changes in the pattern and level of demand. Neither condition is met in practice. The failure of balance of payments adjustment to take place promptly and appropriately, in the short or even medium run, may lead to no more than opposing movements of private and official capital. In this case the increased mobility of capital implies a need for additional international liquidity. But it may instead lead to the imposition of restrictions on other transactions, introducing resource misallocations or aggravating those already present; or it may lead to unwanted unemployment or inflation, the former entailing obvious resource costs and the latter involving costs of a more subtle sort. Although international capital movements are not ordinarily the source of unwanted deflation or inflation, they may inhibit the prompt correction of excessive deflationary or inflationary tendencies by constraining the use of monetary policy. Fiscal policy can in principle fill the breach left by monetary policy for stabilizing the domestic economy, though not without occasional help from changes in exchange rates if balance of payments equilibrium is also to be maintained. But if for political or other reasons fiscal policy is not in fact readily available for this role, the costs of international capital mobility are correspondingly higher. The United States during the period 1960–64 perhaps offers the clearest, and certainly the most costly, case in which high capital mobility inhibited the use of monetary policy to stimulate a sluggish economy in a period in which fiscal policy could not be brought rapidly into play.

Finally, the increased international mobility of capital will affect the distribution of income. Real capital movements will raise the marginal product of labour in capital-importing countries and will lower the marginal product of labour (relative to what it would otherwise have been, except where the foreign investment has come entirely from increased savings) in capital-exporting countries. Under competitive conditions, labour will be made relatively better off in the former countries, capital better off in the latter. Even imperfect adjustment of real to financial capital flows will produce these effects, although to a lesser degree. In principle, of course, we can separate efficiency from equity, allow flows to take place on principles of efficiency and correct for equity through the tax system. In practice, we have found great difficulty in incentive-free taxes, so a clear separation between the two considerations is not possible. Furthermore, redistributional taxation cannot be laid with impunity on internationally mobile factors, for they can escape taxation through migration or through evasion permitted by high mobility. Redistributive taxation relies on fragmented factor markets to be effective.

A second distributional effect of high capital mobility arises during the transition to a fully integrated capital market. Only the best known (and generally largest) firms and banks can borrow in the major international markets and by shopping around such firms can lower the total cost of their borrowed funds – not least because of the lower international bond rates occasioned by tax evasion. Thus the growing international capital market may foster the concentration of industry. (A countervailing tendency, at least during the transitional phase to full integration, is the invasion of national markets by new foreign competitors.)

How does one weigh these conflicting considerations in assessing the pros and cons of an evolution towards an Atlantic capital market? I conclude that such an evolution is desirable, provided we can coordinate monetary policies effectively among countries and obtain more active fiscal policies within countries, and provided we can assure that real capital movements correspond closely to net financial flows. An international capital market is no substitute for changes in exchange-rate parities and in fact its presence greatly aggravates the currency speculation that can take place in anticipation of changes in parities. It thus suggests the need for smaller and more continuous changes in exchange rates, which in turn may reduce somewhat the high mobility of capital. If balance of payments equilibrium is not assured through coordinated monetary policies and provision made for more frequent changes in exchange rates, however, high capital mobility will exert pressures for trade controls and/or unwanted domestic inflation or deflation. Under these circumstances high international mobility of capital may well leave us with a third- or fourth-best world and governments may be wise in the meantime to restrict international flows in the interests of attaining at least a second-best one.

References

OECD (1968), *Capital Markets Study: III. Functioning of Capital Markets*, Paris.

US Department of Commerce (1967–8), *Survey of Current Business.*

Williams, D. (1967), 'Foreign currency issues in European security markets', *IMF Staff Pap.*, May.

Part Four
Direct Investment and the Theory of Industrial Organization

We have referred to a major current explanation of foreign direct investment being in terms of the theory of market structures. The implications of this territorial diversification of productive activities on this theory and that of industrial organization are explored in the essays of Professors Penrose (Reading 10) and Caves (Reading 11).

The essay of Professor Penrose is a natural extension of her own work on the theory of the growth of the firm. This was one of the first contributions on the subject and it has stood the test of time well. She illustrates her argument from the experiences of foreign firms in Australia.

The contribution of Professor Caves is a very recent one and indicates the work which has been done on the subject since Mrs Penrose's article. Caves draws substantially on the work of the empiricists working in the field and produces his own version of the determinants of direct investment in terms of its impact on industrial structure. This is an important addition to the literature and one which further helps us to explain the characteristics of foreign operations of enterprises.

A good deal of other work has recently been completed or is in the process of being completed, on the effects of foreign investment on market structure – mostly of recipient countries (Rosenbluth, 1970; Steuer *et al.*, 1970). Stephen Hymer (1960) has been particularly prolific in this field with his theoretical contributions. The results of empirical research are contained in a variety of country and/or industry studies. The extra-territorial application of US anti-trust legislation to the operation of the foreign subsidiaries of

American companies and the consequential conflict of interest with the objectives of host countries have also attracted some interest. The issues are well explained in a publication of the Department of Trade and Industry (1971). This is clearly another area where a lot of research is likely to be done in the future.

References

DEPARTMENT OF TRADE AND INDUSTRY (1971), *Report of International Conference on Monopolies, Mergers and Restrictive Practices*, HMSO.

HYMER, S. H. (1960), 'The international operations of national firms: a study of direct investment', unpublished Ph.D. dissertation, MIT.

ROSENBLUTH, G. (1970), 'The relation between foreign control and concentration in Canadian industry', *Canad. J. Econ.*, vol. 3, pp. 14–30.

STEUER, M. D., *et al.* (1970), 'The economic effects of inward investment in the United Kingdom: a preliminary report', unpublished Government document.

10 Edith Tilton Penrose

Foreign Investment and the Growth of the Firm[1]

Edith Tilton Penrose, 'Foreign investment and the growth of the firm', *Economic Journal*, vol. 66, 1956, pp. 220–35.

Such is the desire for an accelerated rate of capital formation in most of the less industrialized countries today, that fears about the ultimate problem of servicing foreign capital invested in the country are often pushed, rather uneasily, into the background, while inducements are held out to attract such capital, in particular to attract private direct investment. In Australia, however, a recent event has emphasized once again the controversial aspect of foreign investment when the investment takes the form of the successful establishment of a foreign subsidiary enterprise in which the ordinary capital, or common stock, is largely held abroad. Most successful firms grow, and if a firm grows by virtue of its own earnings, that is to say, if the rate of new investment in the firm does not exceed the rate of earnings on its past investment, then the foreign equity in the firm grows without any net import of new foreign exchange, i.e. foreign investment in the firm is increasing while there may be a net outflow of foreign funds.

Thus, a relatively small initial dollar investment, for example, may establish a firm whose earnings are sufficient to permit extensive expansion through ploughed-back profits, each increment of expansion increasing the foreign liabilities of the country. It is therefore likely that dividend remittances, when they become an important proportion of profits, will be enormously high in

1. I want to acknowledge here the criticism of the staff of the Economics Department of the Australian National University, and, in particular, that of Professor T. W. Swan, who saved me from some serious errors in the latter part of the paper. I am also indebted to Professor Fritz Machlup and to Professor E. F. Penrose for much helpful criticism, and to the John Simon Guggenheim Memorial Foundation for granting me a Fellowship for research in Australia.

relation to the original dollar investment, although not necessarily high in relation to the total foreign investment in the firm. This paper is concerned with the economic implications of this form of foreign investment for the economic policies of some of the less industrialized countries today.

We shall consider first the particular case of General Motors-Holden's Ltd in Australia; secondly, the general question whether it makes any difference if foreign investment takes place through the expansion of existing foreign-controlled firms rather than in some other form; and finally what solutions, if any, there are to the problems raised.

General Motors–Holden's in Australia

With the publication of its Annual Report for 1954, General Motors–Holden's Ltd, the Australian wholly owned subsidiary of General Motors Corporation in the United States, raised a hornet's nest of controversy about its corporate ears and became more firmly than ever committed to the necessity of convincing the Australian public that 'What's good for General Motors is good for the country'. The storm arose over the revelation that: (a) GMH made a profit A£9,830,000 after taxes in 1953–4, which is variously portrayed as 560 per cent on ordinary capital (the ordinary capital representing in this case the original dollar investment of GMH), 39 per cent on shareholders' funds (net worth), 24 per cent on funds employed or 14 per cent on sales, depending on how the speaker feels about the size of the profit; and (b) that a dividend was declared to the parent company of A£4,550,000, which again is 260 per cent on ordinary capital, 18 per cent on shareholders' funds or 11 per cent on funds employed.[2] The dividend declared is about 8 per cent of the dollar export receipts in the Australian balance of payments for 1954–5.[3]

Newspaper stories and editorials critical of the profit (the highest ever declared by a firm in Australia) and of the dividend payment were followed by an attack by Dr H. V. Evatt, Leader of

2. The par value of the ordinary shares is A£1,750,000; there are in addition A£561,600 of preference shares owned by Australians. The net worth of the company (or shareholders' funds) is A£25 million; total funds employed are A£41 million.

3. There is a 15 per cent tax on dividends and hence the actual dollar remittance was less by this amount.

the Labor Party (the Government Opposition) on the GMH 'Colossus', and letters pro and con appeared in the correspondence columns of the Sydney and Melbourne Press. Economists immediately began debating the issues raised for the Australian economy and H. W. Arndt, Professor of Economics of Canberra University College, stated on the air 'As far as policy towards future overseas investment in this country is concerned, the Holden case may induce some caution in giving indiscriminate encouragement'. He suggested that Australia might do well to 'concentrate less on attracting American capital and more on hiring American technical and managerial know-how'.

The background of the General Motors situation is as follows: the firm began in Australia in 1926 with chassis-assembly plants in various States and in 1931 bought out the Australian-owned Holden's Motor Body Builders Ltd with an issue of preference shares. Until 1945 the combined firm was engaged in building bodies and assembling imported chassis units, but in that year began planning the manufacture in Australia of the Holden car. This car appeared in 1948 and has steadily gained a larger and larger share of the automobile market in Australia.[4] All Australian produced, it is the cheapest and most popular car in its class (medium weight – by Australian standards – and in the middle price range). GMH has been unable to produce enough cars to meet demand at existing prices and the waiting list was announced as being equal to twelve months production. In 1953–4 the retail price of the car was reduced by A£84, or 7 per cent. Further reductions in price would only intensify the shortage and put profits in the hands of 'grey-market' dealers. (It is alleged that at present prices many people buy new Holdens and immediately resell them at A£100 profit.)

Along with the release of the Annual Report, expansion plans were announced involving a 50 per cent increase in production of the Holden (from the present 65,000 a year to 100,000), expansion of the household and commercial refrigeration business and entry into the production of central-heating units and other household appliances. The planned expansion is estimated

4. From 1953 to 1954, however, the Holden share of the market actually declined from 36·5 to 35·1 per cent as a result of the inability of the company to keep up with the demand in an expanding market.

to cost A£21,622,000, bringing the company's post-war expenditure on new plants and facilities to A£47,750,000 and the funds employed in the business to more than A£61 million. (The total assets of the largest firm in Australia, a firm which comprehends the entire steel industry, were A£76·4 million in 1954.)

GMH has successfully established a completely Australian automobile,[5] thus reducing import requirements for automobiles and promoting efficient industrialization. In other words, it has done 'just what the doctor ordered'; for the promotion of industrial development by 'import replacement' through efficient home production is established national policy. But if the post-war rate of expansion continues for long GMH will not only be far more important in the automobile market than all other producers combined,[6] but will also be reaching out into more and more industries. This continued expansion will not involve any further import of dollars; on the contrary, it will be accompanied by an ever-increasing stream of dollar dividends paid out as the equity increases on which the dividends are paid. Taking the ten-year period 1945–54, total profit of GMH was about 10 per cent on sales and 27 per cent on the average capital over the period, but 72·4 per cent of the profit was retained in the business.[7] And there is little reason for believing that either smaller increments of expansion or lower earning rates are going to mark the reasonably foreseeable future.

At first sight it might seem that the problem is basically one of monopolistic profits; the task, accordingly, being to increase the

5. As the saying goes, 'Australian except for the key' – which is made in Wisconsin.

6. The three largest producers are GMH, Ford and British Motors Corporation. Since 1949 the GMH share of the market has risen from 23 to 35½ per cent, that of Ford from 14 to 21 per cent, while that of BMC has fallen from 31 to 20 per cent. Thus the 'Big Three' have 76 per cent of the market and Ford and GMH together have risen from 37 to 54 per cent. Of these only GMH publishes a balance sheet in Australia; nothing is known about the profits of the other two.

7. Consequently, the actual dividends paid out have not until this year been appreciable, only some 7·4 per cent on the average capital employed in the ten years. But this, of course, means that the equity upon which profits are expected to be earned and eventually realized in significant amounts is so much the greater. From now on it may be expected that the GMH dividend will remain high.

amount of effective competition in the automobile industry. In general, and in spite of the periodic pronouncements of the Labor Party against 'monopolies', neither the Australian Government nor the Australian public tend to be much concerned about monopoly as such. There is a very high degree of 'concentration' in the economy – the largest seventy-five firms owning nearly 45 per cent of the total fixed assets in manufacturing.[8] The steel industry and the glass industry are each in the hands of a single firm, 70 per cent of the paper industry in the hands of another, 50 per cent of the rubber industry is in the hands of still another and so on for many important industries. For one firm to gain a dominant position in the automobile industry would not be contrary to the general development of the structure of industry in Australia and would not be expected to raise many eyebrows, especially since the industry is already highly concentrated. In addition, efficiency in meeting market demand seems to be the chief reason for the predominance of GMH – it is hard to trace the failure of competition to reduce its profits to any significant monopolistic practices on the part of GMH itself. Other companies have not produced a car as popular as the Holden (Ford is the only company significantly close to GMH in the market). The tariff on cars not wholly manufactured in Australia is of some importance, but not so much as is generally assumed. To encourage manufacturing in Australia there is a duty on automobile parts of around A£87 on a car equivalent to the Holden when imported from Britain already assembled and A£38 on a vehicle to be assembled in Australia. Since automobiles other than the Holden are assembled in Australia partly from imported and partly from domestically manufactured parts, the duty naturally raises their cost, depending on the extent to which parts are imported.[9] Import restrictions imposed for balance of pay-

8. This figure is subject to a fair margin of error because some of the largest companies in Australia are subsidiaries of foreign firms and do not publish balance sheets. Hence we have no information about their fixed assets. The figure was obtained by taking the largest manufacturing firms listed on the stock exchanges and comparing their fixed assets net of depreciation (because the gross figure is not usually available) with the net fixed assets in manufacturing as given by the Commonwealth Statistician.

9. However, several companies are well forward with plans to produce in Australia.

ments purposes are much more important and at present are very severe.

One simple and obvious step to take would seem to be a reduction in the tariff and of import restrictions. But this might have two unwanted effects. First, it is very probable that it would hurt other local manufacturers of component parts more than it would GMH. There is a large scope for the reduction of the price of the Holden in the face of competition and there is strong reason to believe that while GMH would stand up well to increased competition, especially after the new expansion program is well under way, the others would not. In view of the government's attitude towards the motor-car industry up to the present, it seems unlikely that it would be prepared at this point to risk a discouragement of further local manufacture. Second, and even more compelling from the government's point of view, is the possible effect on the balance of payments. Any increase in imports is considered highly undesirable under present circumstances. Because of a current deterioration in the balance of payments, import restrictions have recently been severely increased. Since it is not at all certain that increased competition from imports would in fact go far to reduce GMH profits but might involve a partial destruction of the rest of the automobile manufacturing industry, a reduction of the tariff, or of restrictions, might have little effect on GMH and merely cause a further deterioration in the balance of payments.

Nevertheless, the tariff is one of the factors in the situation and a fullscale inquiry into the state of the automobile industry, which has been scheduled by the Tariff Board for some time, is now in process. It is possible that tariff revision may to some extent increase competition and reduce the monopolistic element in the GMH profit rate. But competition in this sense will not eliminate the fundamental difficulty – the continued profitable expansion of the firm – unless it eliminates the differentials in expected profit rates which are the very basis for international direct investment.[10]

Various other approaches to the GMH problem have been offered. A favorite of some of the financial commentators is the

10. See the next section for discussion of this point.

suggestion that GMH should forthwith accept Australian equity capital. Even apart from the fact that this implies a repatriation of capital for which special permission is required from the government, the proposal is highly impractical if it is expected to be on more than a token scale designed primarily for its psychological effect. To reduce significantly the foreign-exchange payments if profits and dividends near the present scale are continued, the Australian-held proportion of the total equity in the company would have to be substantial. Let us assume that the parent company would have no objection to 49 per cent of the equity being transferred to Australian hands. Given the present net worth of the company, this might involve a diversion of Australian investable funds to GMH of something like A£90 million. The total investment funds raised in Australia on the capital market by Australian companies and semi-government authorities was not over A£200 million in 1954. Clearly it would take many years before a transfer of funds, including the repatriation of the capital, on this scale could be absorbed by the Australian economy without serious complications.

Finally, it is possible for the government to limit the remittance of dividends either by direct limitation of the amount that can be exported or by very heavy progressive taxation. Some of the problems raised by this are discussed below; it is sufficient at this point to note that in order to attract foreign capital the government has made it more or less clear that this type of action would not be taken; hence it would inevitably be viewed as a repudiation of previously incurred obligations and would create bad feeling all around. As is suggested below, once a foreign firm is established, it is not, from an economic point of view, desirable to limit its growth or to buy it out at its market value, in whole or in part, although from a political point of view a case can be made for acquiring it.

Let us now examine the problem in more general terms. It will be argued that the growth of foreign investment through the reinvestment of retained earnings by firms is subject to different influences from those determining the inflow of foreign investment from other sources. Once a foreign firm is established its continued growth is an increase in foreign investment, but an increase which is more appropriately analysed in the light of a theory of the growth of firms rather than a theory of foreign investment. The issues raised for the receiving economy will then be discussed.

The growth of the firm

In the absence of markedly unfavorable environmental conditions, there is a strong tendency for a business enterprise possessing extensive and versatile internal managerial resources continually to expand, not only in its existing fields but also into new products and new markets as opportunity offers. The expansion is not usually a continuous straight-line process; rather it fluctuates with external conditions and may be retarded by internal difficulties. But for the successful firms over the long haul – and there always are such firms – there seems to be no reason to assume that the progress cannot continue indefinitely or at least for any relevant future. The 'productive opportunity' which invites expansion is not exclusively an external one. It is largely determined by the internal resources of the firm: the products the firm can successfully produce, the new areas in which it can successfully set up plants, the innovations it can successfully launch, the very ideas of its executives and the opportunities they see, depend as much on the kind of experience, managerial ability and technological know-how already existing within the firm as they do upon external opportunities open to all.[11]

Direct foreign investment – and by this I mean the ownership and operation of business organizations in a foreign country[12] – can, in its origin, be of several types. Here we are interested only in direct investment in manufacturing activity which takes the form of the establishment of branches or subsidiaries in foreign countries. In the realm of manufacturing this kind of investment is probably more effective in expanding productivity and promoting industrial efficiency than any other kind of foreign invest-

11. For a fuller, though still incomplete, discussion of the theory of the growth of the firm upon which part of the argument in this paper is based see Penrose (1955).

12. This begs the question of what constitutes ownership or, more precisely, a controlling interest. For the purposes of this paper we need not worry about the kind of precise definition necessary for statistical analyses.

ment.[13] Its advantages derive largely from the fact that behind the new foreign firm are the resources and experience of the parent concern, including not only managerial and technical personnel but also that indefinable advantage in its internal operations which an efficient going concern usually has over a new one. Consequently the receiving country, in addition to foreign capital, foreign technicians and management, also obtains an unlimited drawing account, as it were, on the intangible resources of the investing company. The establishment of foreign subsidiaries or branches is, for the parent company, not essentially different from the establishment of subsidiaries or branches in its own country. To be sure, greater allowance for risk must be made and greater profits are expected if the venture succeeds according to plan. But the new expansion is still part of the process of growth of the parent company.

Once established, however, a new subsidiary has a life of its own and its growth will continue in response to the development of its own internal resources and the opportunities presented in its new environment. This means, in the first instance, expansion in the production of the products contemplated when the subsidiary was originally established, an expansion which may well continue for a considerable period if, as is usually the case, the firm is introducing a new product or was established in an industry with the prospect of rapid growth. In time, however, the possibilities of expanding in other fields will appear attractive, either because expansion in the original lines at the same rates as before is no longer profitable, because new market opportunities have appeared or because the firm has itself developed, or can draw on the parent company for productive services suitable for other types of products (e.g., by-products, innovations related in production or consumption to the original product, a market standing facilitating the sale of other products, etc.). One of the notable characteristics of the growth of large modern corporations is the extent to which they change the

13. By the emphasis on manufacturing I want to exclude from consideration the development of public utilities, railroads and similar industries basic to manufacturing through intergovernmental loans or through international financial intermediaries. Obviously such investment may be equally effective in promoting development.

range and nature of the product they produce as they grow. They introduce entirely new products, they improve and alter existing products, they enter into a wide range of industries, continually adding to their product lines. In other words, firms are not limited to their original fields; they tend to branch out in many directions. The extent to which this process of diversification can continue depends upon the flexibility of management and upon the resources of the firm – no clear limit is as yet discernible, even in the largest United States corporations. GMH in Australia illustrates the principle: even if the profitability of automobile production declines as competition develops, GMH can in principle, and very likely will in practice, continue to expand by going into other activities where a higher rate of return is still available. As noted above, the firm is already making provision for expanding production into a wide range of fields. In short, so long as there are openings in industry in which the firm expects a rate of return on investment sufficient to justify entering it, there is nothing in principle to limit its continued expansion. And if foreign firms have any advantage in management, technology, capital or other resources, foreign firms may be expected to grow somewhat faster than domestic firms, even in the absence of any exorbitant degree of monopoly power. This conclusion is reinforced by the fact that foreign firms tend to enter the newer, and therefore faster-growing and more profitable, industries.

On the whole, foreign subsidiaries have, for a variety of reasons, a greater degree of independence of the parent than have domestic subsidiaries. Where they are in a distant country the distance itself tends to restrict the mobility of personnel; where the subsidiaries operate in a radically different political, economic and social environment more weight is often given to the judgement of their executives, who are likely to possess an understanding of conditions that is not easily available to the parent company; where foreign subsidiaries are concerned, the area over which a close coordination of policy is considered necessary is often smaller than it is with respect to domestic subsidiaries operating in a more closely connected national market. For these and similar reasons, a foreign subsidiary, once it is established, is, with important exceptions, more appropriately treated in many ways as a separate firm. The most important of these exceptions relates to finance.

Foreign subsidiaries can obtain additional capital from their parent companies or, like local firms, from the local capital market. If funds for expansion are obtained from local equity sources the firm will represent foreign investment to a progressively smaller degree as it grows and the problems discussed in this paper will not arise.[14] But a preference for expansion through retained earnings is becoming increasingly characteristic of the modern corporation and of particular interest from the point of view of foreign investment is the situation, especially favored by American firms, in which the parent company holds all, or nearly all, of the equity and permits the subsidiary to expand with its own earnings.

Internally financed foreign investment

The preference of American firms for nearly complete ownership of their foreign subsidiaries contrasts sharply with British practice.[15] Several reasons for the contrast have been put forward by businessmen and economists – on the part of the Americans, a desire for freedom from interference from minority stockholders, a desire to avoid shareholder criticism of a ruthless dividend limitation in the early stages of growth even when profits are high, a desire to avoid precise intercompany book-keeping (such as charging part of the overhead of the parent concern to the subsidiary, charging it for managerial and technical advice, service and 'know-how'), a desire for secrecy;[16] and on the part of the British, an appreciation of the political importance of a

14. There are a variety of ways in which foreign concerns can cooperate with local firms and financial interests in establishing and developing manufacturing activity and without creating the kind of problem typified by the GMH case. See, for example, the methods discussed in United Nations (1955, pp. 85–6).

15. It has been estimated that on the average American companies hold 85 per cent and British companies 40 per cent of the ordinary shares of their subsidiaries in Australia.

16. Foreign subsidiaries in Australia, for example, do not have to publish balance sheets unless they are 'public companies' (some shares being publicly held); GMH issued preference shares in order to acquire the Holden company and for this reason has to publish a balance sheet.

shared ownership. Whatever the reasons may be, the preference is clear. The result is that virtually the entire growth of most American-owned subsidiaries is properly classed as a growth in foreign investment. And a very large proportion of the total increment in United States investment abroad in recent years has taken the form of re-investment of retained earnings of such subsidiaries.[17]

Because of the potentialities for expansion inherent in the modern corporation with its extensive techniques of decentralized management, its emphasis on developing new markets, on innovations and on research, and its power to generate internal funds for expansion, there are several reasons for believing that the flow of direct foreign investment when it is the result of the growth of foreign firms through retained earnings will proceed at a faster rate, in larger amounts and for a longer period than was characteristic of direct investment of the past. Furthermore, a decision by the parent firm to embark on a new foreign venture is taken under substantially different circumstances from those surrounding a decision to permit an already existing (and profitable) venture to expand.

Although it is true that foreign investment is undertaken because a rate of return on capital that is higher than alternative rates obtainable elsewhere is expected (although not necessarily in the short run), it should not be forgotten that a very considerable input of the managerial and technical resources of the investing firm may be required to ascertain what foreign opportunities exist and how they may best be taken advantage of. Indeed, the

17. 'Between 1946 and 1951, for example, no less than three-quarters of all United States new direct foreign investment in manufacturing industry was the result of the ploughing back of profits earned in foreign branches and subsidiaries' (United Nations, 1955, p. 84). According to a very interesting paper on the contribution of overseas companies to Australian post-war industrial development presented to the 1955 meeting of the Australian and New Zealand Association for the Advancement of Science by D. M. Hocking, which was based upon figures developed by the Australian Department of National Development, direct investment in secondary industry in Australia from the United States increased by A£80·1 million between 1945 and 1953. The U S Department of Commerce (1954) estimates that the undistributed profits of Australian subsidiaries of United States firms amounted to A£65·2 million in the period from January 1946 to December 1953.

original investment of many a foreign firm has been little more than an exploratory venture which can be classed essentially as part of the cost of discovering whether or not investment is desirable. The cost of investigation, together with the cost of planning, organizing and actually establishing the new firm must, other things being equal, obviously limit the number and extent of such ventures undertaken. When, however, a profitable foreign subsidiary presents a request that it be permitted to retain some or all of its profits for further investment, the case is different. The parent firm is presented with a program for expansion which has already been evaluated by the management of the subsidiary. It has to consider this program, to be sure, and it may modify it, but the exploratory work has already been done, and been done by men who know local conditions and (presumably) are trusted and responsible officials of the firm. In other words, an interested group in the firm itself presents a case and makes a plea. The degree of uncertainty surrounding such investment, and the cost of making it, is surely much lower than that associated with a new venture, and the investment, therefore, much easier to make.

Secondly, the very operations of the subsidiary in the foreign country, its knowledge of the market and of the conditions of production, the experience gained by its officials and the position it may have established for itself with its own customers and in the country generally all tend to create new opportunities for further investment, opportunities that did not exist at the time the firm was established. These, since they are new opportunities for the growth of the foreign firm, are by definition, new opportunities for the growth of foreign investment.

Finally, there is the fact that it is often easier not to go into an activity than it is to abandon it once it has been firmly established. In the modern corporate world, maintaining an established position often requires net new investment to keep up with the innovation of products, production techniques and marketing methods of competitors. Thus new investment may be required indefinitely to enable the foreign subsidiary even to maintain its position in the foreign market. And here enters, in a sense, a non-economic factor. More is involved in a going concern than an investment of funds. An organization has been created, men and women have vested interests in the concern, a publicly recognized entity exists. It seems highly probable, and the suggestion has been confirmed in various conversations with businessmen, that there will be a strong tendency for the parent company to take its 'cut' of the profits and to permit the subsidiary to retain a part long after a comparison of rates of return on capital would attract new investments in the absence of the existing subsidiaries.[18] In other words, even if increasing investment reduces, or even eliminates, the original differential between foreign and domestic rates of return on capital, foreign investment will still increase because foreign-owned firms will continue to grow through their own earnings. There is very little information available to enable us to evaluate the importance of this aspect of the matter. But from what we do know of the general processes of growth of business firms, there seems no good reason for expecting that the growth of the successful foreign firms will cease at any time, and the only important question relating to the growth of foreign investment is whether finance will be obtained from retained earnings or whether the parent company will gradually permit a dilution of the equity with domestically raised capital.

In effect, the profitable operation of foreign companies means, in the first place, that there are likely to be more funds available for foreign investment than there would otherwise have been and, in the second place, that the opportunities for foreign investment are enlarged. More funds are likely to be available because of the general bias in favor of permitting a successful subsidiary to retain some of its earnings for expansion and because of the reduction in uncertainty and risk associated with foreign investment of this kind in comparison with the launching of entirely new ventures. New opportunities are created in the same way in which any growing and aggressive firm creates its own opportunities; it just happens that opportunities for expansion created by foreign firms are at the same time new opportunities for foreign investment.

Such are the reasons for expecting that the flow of foreign investment will increase at a more rapid rate and continue longer

18. This is particularly true if capital repatriation is not permitted and the foreign firm has no alternative but to continue to invest to protect its existing investment.

when it depends on the expansion of existing firms than it would if it depended on fresh imports of capital for new firms. And I suggest that the increasing importance of direct foreign investment in manufacturing in recent years is partly explained by these factors – some investment that would not otherwise have been made is being made for the reasons outlined above. It is direct investment, but of a much less speculative and risky kind than is usually assumed.

The balance of payments problem

Such investment, though ardently desired by the less industrialized countries, is not accepted without misgivings. The misgivings relate to two potential difficulties: the political implication of foreign control and the economic problem of paying for the investment. Both are greatest in the case of direct investment; here we are concerned only with the economic problem. There can be little doubt that in order to provide the means of paying for foreign investment, an economy may, in the absence of expanding exports, be faced with the difficult task of inducing an unpalatable reduction in domestic consumption and investment.

This task may be especially difficult when incomes are expanding rapidly in response to a high rate of investment pursuant to government industrial development and full-employment policies. Under such circumstances, with consumption and investment at high levels, import demand is likely to be very high, not only for consumers' goods, but especially for capital goods. The problem of maintaining economic stability – sustained full employment without inflation – becomes crucial and is particularly difficult in countries whose export proceeds are subject to wide and unpredictable fluctuations from season to season. The goal of governments is to keep inflationary pressures under some sort of control without precipitating deflation, or if deflation threatens, to counteract the recession quickly and thus prevent depression. In pursuance of this goal there is often little hesitation in applying direct exchange and import restrictions or in using Central Bank credit to maintain financial liquidity in order to ensure that unfavorable movements of the foreign balance do not interfere with domestic policy. Yet the foreign balance is likely to be a continual source of trouble because of an excessive demand for imports consequent upon the difficulty of controlling 'excess demand' within the economy without creating unacceptable unemployment. At the same time depreciation as a remedy is looked on with great suspicion, to be used only rarely and *in extremis*.

Such policies have several effects on the problem under discussion. High levels of activity mean high business profits, which not only attract foreign firms but also furnish an easy source of funds for the expansion of already established firms. In a raw-material-exporting economy, where industrial development does not contribute substantially to exports, large amounts of foreign lending may well be necessary to sustain the development program unless demand for the country's raw-material exports is also expanding rapidly. The high levels of activity attract the foreign investment required in the form of direct private investment and, particularly, after foreign firms have become well established, in the form of the growth of foreign firms through retained earnings. We have already shown that direct private investment will tend to grow rapidly and without practical limits as foreign firms grow. So long as these firms retain the greater part of their earnings for re-investment, the effect on the balance of payments of servicing the investment is masked, for the re-investment of profits is equivalent to an import of foreign funds. In not exercising their right to export their profits, the firms leave foreign exchange available to the country that would otherwise have gone into dividend remittances.[19] The effect is similar to the familiar process by which old loans are serviced partly out of the proceeds of new ones. No problem is apparent until the new lending stops. When profits are not paid out it is as if new loans were being made, but when this new 'lending' slows down and dividends are paid on the existing investment the country may find that some difficult readjustments in the economy are required. It has been traditionally held that loans with fixed

19. We are not, of course, taking into account here the effect on the demand for imports (or supply of exports) of the investment which is itself the alternative to the building up of cash balances for the purpose of paying dividends. This is part of the whole question of how industrialization in a primarily raw-material-exporting country affects the demand for imported goods – a question we cannot explore in this paper.

interest payments are likely to be more of a burden on the economy than equity investment, because in the former case the payments have to be made at the same rate in periods of depressed economic activity, while in the latter dividend payments fall when profits are low. This appraisal of the two forms of investment must be revised if, as seems likely, the more severe depressions can be prevented by appropriate internal government policy.

When the readjustments in the economy required to service foreign investment are difficult to make they create what is called a 'balance of payments problem'. And they will be the more difficult to make the greater the pressure of domestic demand on imports and the larger the foreign payments required. Rapidly developing economies attempting to maintain consistently high levels of employment will have continually to struggle to control excess domestic demand. Under the circumstances assumed in this paper, dividend remittances from direct private investment will tend to involve larger transfers of foreign funds than would have been the case if only loans had been received. Consequently a real 'balance of payments problem' in this sense may arise. But it is, in essence, a 'technical' problem, a problem of how best to reduce domestic consumption and investment – whether to use import restrictions, tariffs, exchange rates, taxation, monetary policy or some combination of these, and how to mitigate, if desired, the effects on the distribution of income and on the direction of domestic investment. However, in so far as foreign investment goes into industries producing for the domestic market, total dividend payments are likely to move slowly upward without much fluctuation. If export proceeds fluctuate widely from season to season the dividend payments may cause severe strains on the country's reserves from time to time. In so far as foreign investment takes place in export industries, the profits, and hence the dividends, of foreign firms are more likely to fluctuate with export proceeds and less likely to cause temporary strains. Economic authorities have an understandable reluctance to force far-reaching economic adjustment because of temporary difficulties. In the absence of sufficient flexibility in exchange rates the only alternative lies in the creation of adequate international reserves to maintain service on investment in periods when export proceeds are low.

Australia is an excellent illustration. Exports are only a little influenced by its industrial development.[20] Import demand is continually straining the country's foreign resources. Foreign investment, in particular direct dollar investment through the growth of American firms, is increasing rapidly. The balance of payments problem that this investment may create is masked so long as substantial proportions of the profits of foreign firms are retained. But as the total profits of foreign firms grow and the firms become more solidly established, the tendency to pay out a goodly portion of their profits to the parent companies will increase, particularly if foreign firms become nervous about the balance of payments position. It is highly probable that in time this portion paid out of a growing total will become large enough to make an appreciable contribution to the already existing difficulties of keeping the demand for foreign exchange within bounds, for the profit of the foreign firms, and the firms themselves, will continue to grow so long as the efforts of the government to maintain domestic incomes at a full-employment level are successful. The adjustments required, together with the foreign payments made, are indeed a 'cost' to the economy and the basic question is whether the foreign investment is worth the cost. Is there anything in the nature of the type of foreign investment considered here – the growth of foreign firms – that makes the high cost of this investment 'too high'?

Cost versus benefits

In principle, the growth of foreign indebtedness, like the growth of domestic indebtedness, need not be of particular concern in a growing economy, providing that the net income out of which the indebtedness can be serviced also grows correspondingly. If the increments of investment involved in the growth of foreign firms are of such high productivity that domestic real income is raised to an extent equal to, or greater than, the return on the investment to the owners of the capital, it will pay the economy to accept them. There may be 'technical' problems associated with

20. However, we should not overlook the fact that industrialization may have *reduced* exports by diverting exportable products to domestic consumption and by attracting factors of production away from the export industries.

the remittance of dividends, but in principle if the increase in the economy's productivity is not less than the cost, it will pay the economy to make the required adjustments, provided that the same increase in productivity could not have been obtained at a cheaper price.

There are two types of benefits realized from foreign investment: additional supplies of capital, on the one hand and, on the other, new techniques of production and management, entrepreneurial skill, new products, new ideas. We have suggested that loan capital is in general cheaper than equity capital, but that probably less foreign investment would take place if loans alone were relied on. But it is primarily in the second category of benefits that the special advantages of direct investment lie. The benefits of direct foreign investment, when it takes the form of the establishment of new foreign firms, the introduction of new technology and the provision of experienced managerial and technical services can hardly be exaggerated.[21] In addition, the development of subsidiary industries and the improved productivity of other resources which the entry of a progressive foreign firm into a major industry may stimulate is of great importance in increasing the total productivity of the economy. The importance of the opportunities afforded for training not only the domestic labor supply but also domestic managerial and technical personnel is attested to by the lengths to which many countries go in insisting that foreign firms make special efforts in these directions. If the benefits of direct investment can be obtained in some cheaper way it will, of course, pay to do so. The intrinsic difficulties of controlling direct private investment once it gets established, the problem of paying for it, together with the political fear of foreign 'exploitation' and domination, have led many countries to explore ways of hiring foreign management and technical personnel and purchasing access to foreign technology (United Nations, 1955, pp. 85–7). Such efforts have met with considerable success in some of the Latin American countries, but from an economic point of view it seems doubtful

21. For a survey of the enormous contributions made to the Australian economy by foreign firms see D. M. Hocking (1955, p. 2). John H. Dunning (1955) has discussed a significant aspect of the importance of the contribution of American firms to the British economy.

that they would obtain for the country the full set of advantages which are brought in by new foreign firms, although this will vary appreciably between industries. Nevertheless, a great deal can be gained in these ways which benefits the economy. Furthermore, it must be conceded that from a political point of view there is much to be said for this approach.

Even if a great many of the advantages of foreign investment can be obtained by these cheaper methods, it is still true that so long as still more capital and still further 'intangible' benefits can be acquired by permitting the establishment of foreign firms whose contribution to the domestic product is greater than the cost of the investment, it will pay the economy to accept them. And so long as this condition holds true for further increments of expansion of foreign firms, it will pay the economy to permit the indefinite expansion of these firms.[22] If a point is reached where it does not hold true, i.e. where the profits of the foreign firms contain a strong element of private monopoly gain, the situation is changed and the increase in foreign liabilities may be, to the extent of this gain, a net loss to the economy. This brings us up against the moot question whether the monopoly elements almost inevitably associated with the position of the very large firms are almost necessary conditions for further research, innovation and progress, as has been powerfully argued by many, Schumpeter in particular. In some cases this may be true; in others it plainly is not true. In any event, this is the element in the growth of foreign firms that will cause the increments of foreign investment it represents to take place at 'too high' a cost to the economy, and it is this element, consequently, that receiving countries should pay especial attention to. It is obvious that this particular type of foreign investment is more likely than most others to contain an appreciable amount of unproductive monopoly profit.

Now all of this bears on the proposition, so often put forward, that there is some gain to the economy if arrangements are made after a point to buy out the foreign investor. It is probably true that the contributions of direct foreign investment are of greatest importance in the early stages of the growth of the foreign firms

22. This is, of course, apart from the political question of whether large and powerful firms – foreign or domestic – should be countenanced.

and of industrial development. It seems very likely that as the firm grows the point is reached where the specifically foreign contribution to the operation of the firm becomes less important in relation to the contribution of the locally recruited staff who have grown up with and have been trained in the firm. But if the firm is still paying its way – if the contribution to the productivity of the economy is greater than the return to the owners – it will not be to the domestic economy's advantage to divert scarce domestic capital to replace the foreign capital so long as there are opportunities for the profitable use of domestic capital. On the other hand, if the firm is making monopoly profits it would even less pay the economy to buy the firm at its market value, which would inevitably include the capitalization of prospective monopoly profits. If there is no other way of eliminating the monopoly profit, then the purchase of the firm at a price which did not reflect prospective monopoly profits may be the only economic solution to the problem – this is usually referred to as 'expropriation'.

Thus it is clear that if it is economic to accept direct private foreign investment at all and to permit the establishment of foreign firms, that is to say, if the benefits of foreign investment cannot be obtained in cheaper ways (perhaps over a longer period of time), then it is desirable to permit the continued growth of foreign firms so long as they pay their way.[23] Furthermore, once they are established, under no circumstances does it pay to buy them out at their market value if domestic capital can be more profitably used elsewhere.

The fact still remains, however, that if extensive amounts of direct foreign investment are obtained, the balance of payments problem of the type discussed earlier may require adjustments which create awkward difficulties for many established government policies. If, therefore, there is not a reasonably large gain

23. It has been implicitly assumed in this entire argument, of course, that industrialization itself is, in the long run, a profitable use of the country's resources or rather that the rate of industrial development implied in the investment program is not excessive. If this is not true and if real income would be increased if more resources were devoted to the raw-material-exporting industries and less to domestic industry, then further foreign investment, just as further domestic investment, in industry will be unprofitable to the economy as a whole.

to be had from direct foreign investment, the country may well consider that the investment is not worth the cost of the adjustments required to pay for it. Furthermore, the political repercussions of policies designed to restrict domestic expenditure when it is realized that the restrictions are partly for the sake of paying foreign 'capitalists', may make such adjustments virtually impossible. By calling the balance of payments problem a 'technical' one I do not mean to minimize its difficulties. Policies designed to force the rate of industrialization, coupled with the potentialities for almost indefinite growth inherent in the modern corporation, the modern trend for increasing reliance on internal financing of expansion and the preference, particularly of United States firms, for nearly complete ownership of foreign subsidiaries, raises the possibility that much larger amounts of direct foreign investment may take place in a much shorter period of time when political conditions are favorable than was generally the case in the past. When and if the foreign payments become significant, the countries accepting the investment must also be willing to accept the adjustments in domestic consumption and investment required to service it. One suspects that for some countries there may be a basic incompatibility between the economic objectives of fostering very rapid industrial development and at the same time promoting domestic full employment at all times regardless of the state of the foreign balance, and the acceptance of an unlimited, unknown and uncontrollable foreign liability.

References

DUNNING, J. H. (1955), 'United States manufacturing subsidiaries and Britain's trade balance', *District Bank Rev.*, September, pp. 20–30.

HOCKING, D. M. (1955), 'New products, new skills follow overseas capital', *Austral. finan. Rev.*, 29 September, p. 2.

PENROSE, E. T. (1955), 'Limits to the growth and size of firms', *Amer. econ. Rev., Pap. Proc.*, vol. 45, pp. 531–43.

UNITED NATIONS (1955), *Processes and Problems of Industrialization in Underdeveloped Countries*, Department of Economic and Social Affairs, New York.

US DEPARTMENT OF COMMERCE (1954), *Survey of Current Business.*

11 Richard E. Caves

International Corporations: The Industrial Economics of Foreign Investment[1]

Richard E. Caves, 'International corporations: the industrial economics of foreign investment', *Economica*, vol. 38, 1971, pp. 1–27.

As trade follows the flag, so does applied economics follow the newspapers. Urgent issues of public policy have in the past decade or so called forth a great deal of new factual evidence on the international corporation, as the chief conduit for foreign direct investment.[2] It has been studied as a channel for the international transfer of technology, as a business organization serving more than one national sovereign master and as a force influencing the international financial flows recorded in a country's balance of payments. Yet relatively little emphasis has fallen on what might seem the two principal economic features of direct investment by the international corporation: (a) it ordinarily effects a net transfer of real capital from one country to another; and (b) it represents entry into a national industry by a firm established in a foreign market. This neglect is unfortunate, because recognition of these features lets one bring to bear on the causes and consequences of direct investment two important bodies of economic analysis – the pure theory of international trade and the conceptual structure and evidence of market behaviour reposing in the field of industrial organization.

1. An earlier version of this paper was prepared as the Royer Lectures, University of California, Berkeley, December 1969. Valuable comments were received from Professors J. S. Bain, M. Brunt, H. G. Johnson and R. W. Jones, as well as members of seminar audiences at the University of York, Catholic University of Louvain, and Graduate Institute of International Studies, Geneva.

2. Some of the principal sources of empirical evidence are Barlow and Wender (1955), Behrman (1969), Brash (1966), Dunning (1958), Reddaway, Potter and Taylor (1967–8), Safarian (1966), Stonehill (1965) and US Department of Commerce (1960).

Briefly, the argument of this paper is that foreign direct investment occurs mainly in industries characterized by certain market structures in both the 'lending' (or home) and 'borrowing' (or host) countries. In the parlance of industrial organization, oligopoly with product differentiation normally prevails where corporations make 'horizontal' investments to produce abroad the same lines of goods as they produce in the home market. Oligopoly, not necessarily differentiated, in the home market is typical in industries which undertake 'vertical' direct investments to produce abroad a raw material or other input to their production process at home. Direct investment tends to involve market conduct that extends the recognition of mutual market dependence – the essence of oligopoly – beyond national boundaries. Likewise it tends broadly to equalize the rate of return on (equity) capital throughout a given industry in all countries where production actually takes place. This common profit rate may well exceed a 'normal' or competitive one, however, since persistent oligopoly – national or worldwide – is marked by barriers to entry of new firms and, perforce, to the inflow of capital; direct investment thus does not necessarily tend to equalize rates of return in any country as between industries.

With the character and allocative consequences of foreign direct investment identified within the industry, we can proceed to a simple general-equilibrium model that develops the consequences of high international coupled with low inter-industry mobility of capital.

Direct investment as market behaviour

Direct investment tends to occur only in certain of its possible institutional forms and within only a few of the many industries found in the developed countries. This section seeks to identify and explain the prevalence of these special features. Its empirical aim is to explain the relative importance among industries of the outstanding stock of international corporations or foreign subsidiaries (or of their shares of assets or markets), and not the short-term flow (either across industries or over time). And I shall be concerned with traits intrinsic to the industry and not those that might accidentally mark the firms belonging to it.

Foreign direct investment and the international corporation

Direct investment and the international corporation do not overlap completely although they are often identified with each other. Direct investment can occur without a single corporation carrying on business in more than one country and without any net international flow of capital having occurred – although not without a net flow of equity capital. As defined for purposes of international investment statistics, direct investment requires merely the control of an enterprise located in one country by persons who are not its citizens. A company could thus be foreign-controlled because its founders or subsequent native owners chose to sell a controlling portion of its equity capital to citizens of another country. Although a few firms are controlled abroad without the existence of a specific foreign corporate parent, they are rare birds and seem to be growing proportionally rarer over time; nearly all new direct investments involve a foreign corporate parent.

An economist setting out to explain differences in the net flows of direct investment among the industrial countries would naturally turn to the hypothesis that they move from countries well endowed to those poorly endowed with equity capital. Certainly this hypothesis is often assumed to hold, as when importers of equity capital such as Canada engage in national self-flagellation for an alleged lack of home-bred willingness to bear commercial risks (Aitken, 1961, pp. 119–21). Yet a superficial review of the evidence hardly uncovers compelling support: capital seems to flow toward high-profit countries (or industries, at least), but the countries which export large flows are not obviously low-profit areas. One should not prejudge a test of the capital-abundance hypothesis before it has been performed, but reference to the role of the international corporation would at least render its failure unsurprising. Its investments transmit equity capital, entrepreneurship, and technological or other productive knowledge in an industry-specific package. The influence of national endowments of equity capital need not dominate or even significantly influence its actions.

The prevalent forms of direct investment are restricted not just to transactions of the international corporations, but further to certain kinds of diversification of its activities. A firm's expansion into a new, geographically segregated production facility can take any of three forms: horizontal extension (producing the same goods elsewhere), vertical extension (adding a stage in the production process that comes earlier or later than the firm's principal processing activity) or conglomerate diversification. The overwhelming portion (by value) of direct investments involves either horizontal expansion to produce the same or a similar line of goods abroad or vertical integration backwards into the production of raw material (An important numerical proportion of foreign subsidiaries or branches takes the form of sales agencies, representing a vertical integration forward; the capital invested in them is small, however, and they will be neglected here as compromising adjuncts to their parents' export sales activities unless they undertake production and become 'horizontal'.) Product diversification across national boundaries is almost unknown (Barlow and Wender, 1955, p. 159), however, and there is some evidence that the industries and firms most active in conglomerate mergers in the United States are not among the most prominent foreign investors.

The international corporation's plans to make horizontal and vertical investments abroad are directly comparable to business decisions opting for familiar forms of domestic expansion. Horizontal integration amounts to the acquisition of multiple plants by a firm operating in an industry with submarkets that are regionally segmented, as by heavy transportation costs. From the viewpoint of rivals in the invaded submarket, horizontal direct investment amounts to a market entry by an established firm. Vertical foreign investments afford an exact analogy to 'backwards' vertical integration in the home market. As seen by competing sellers at the processing stage where the entry takes place, it amounts to removal of part of the former open market for the output of this stage; that is, competing independent suppliers of raw materials will expect that the firm now served by its own subsidiary will be less likely than before to undertake or expand purchases from them in response to a given concession from the going market price. Thus the analogy of each type of foreign direct investment to firms' manoeuvres in a domestic market offers potential assistance both for explaining why the manoeuvres are undertaken and establishing their consequences for performance in the market. I now turn to the former problem; the effects of direct investment on market equilibria are discussed below on pages 278–85.

Horizontal foreign investments

Why corporations undertake horizontal investments abroad to produce the same general line of goods as they produce at home has been explained in several ways. Hymer and others have suggested the importance of some unique asset of the firm – a patented invention or a differentiated product – on which it can earn maximum profits in foreign markets only through foreign production (Hymer, 1960). Several empirical studies have pointed to the influence of tariffs excluding exports from foreign markets.[3] Behrman and others have pushed the notion (not entirely free of circularity) that the corporations which invest abroad are those with international decision horizons.[4] Each of these propositions may have some explanatory power. I wish to focus on the first while taking account of the second and third.

For the possession of some special asset to lead the firm to invest abroad, two conditions must be satisfied. First, the asset must partake of the character of a public good within the firm, such as knowledge fundamental to the production of a profitably saleable commodity. Any advantage embodied in knowledge, information or technique that yields a positive return over direct costs in the market where it is first proven can potentially do the same in other markets without need to incur again the sunk costs associated with its initial discovery.[5] Knowledge would seem to be the prototypical asset displaying the character of a public good proprietary to the firm, but it is not the only one. The essential feature of an asset conducive to foreign investment is not that its opportunity cost should be zero, but that it should be low relative to the return attainable via foreign investment. The significance of this qualification will become clear below. Second, the return

3. Barlow and Wender (1955, p. 116), Brash (1966, ch. 3) and Eastman and Stykolt (1967). For statistical evidence of the influence of the height of the foreign tariff see Thomas O. Horst (1969).

4. For example Barlow and Wender (1955, ch. 2). For a survey of these and other hypotheses, see C. P. Kindleberger (1969, ch. 1).

5. This idea is explored by H. G. Johnson (1970, ch. 2).

attainable on a firm's special asset in a foreign market must depend at least somewhat on local production.

The necessary character of these two properties becomes clear when we recognize that the native entrepreneur always enjoys an advantage over a foreign rival from his general accumulation of knowledge about economic, social, legal and cultural conditions in his home market and country. The foreign enterprise must pay dearly for what the native either has acquired at no cost to the firm (because it was part of the entrepreneur's general education) or can acquire more cheaply (because, as it were, the native knows where to look) (Eastman and Stykolt, 1967, p. 80). Thus the firm investing abroad must not only enjoy enough of an information advantage in its special asset to offset the information disadvantage of its alien status; it must also find production abroad preferable to any other means of extracting this rent from a foreign market, such as exporting or licensing an established native producer. The net advantage could of course swing to direct investment on account of the unattractiveness of the alternatives, but the general *positive* reason favouring the service to a market by local production is some complementarity between such production and the rents attainable from local sales.

These requirements, taken together, point to a particular trait of market structures – product differentiation – as one necessary characteristic of industries in which substantial direct investment occurs. A 'differentiated product' is a collection of functionally similar goods produced by competing sellers, but with each seller's product distinguishable from its rivals by minor physical variations, 'brand name' and subjective distinctions created by advertising, or differences in the ancillary terms and conditions of sale (Chamberlin, 1933, ch. 4). Differentiation is inherent in many products because of the number of minor options available in their physical design and fabrication, or because they are subject to taste diversity inherent in 'style'; but to some extent it is a (wasting) capital asset created by the firm through advertising outlays. Its principal consequences for market behaviour are to render the cross-elasticities of demand between rival sellers less than infinite and to open the possibility of rivalry among sellers occurring through advertising and product variation.

In the nature of differentiation, a successful (rent-yielding) product variety is protected from exact imitation by trade marks, high costs of physical imitation or both. Because of varying success in differentiation, firms in such a market will generally not earn the same rate of profit on tangible assets and the excess profits will be at least partly immune from competitive pressure. Here is the link to the basis for direct investment: the successful firm producing a differentiated product controls knowledge about serving the market that can be transferred to other national markets for this product at little or no cost. This is clearly so for the patented good or the product embodying a particularly apt bundle of traits.[6] The proposition probably holds even for differentiation created through advertising; not only does the advertising to some extent spill across national boundaries,[7] but also successful differentiation through advertising is normally accompanied by some accumulation of unique knowledge about marketing the product and adapting it to users' tastes.

Differentiation does not encompass all forms of rent-yielding knowledge available to the firm, but – and this helps greatly to explain why differentiation and direct investment occur in the same industries – it probably does include most forms for which local production *per se* increases the rents yielded by a market. For instance, knowledge in the form of process patents or unique managerial skills in the securing of inputs (e.g. finance) or the organizing of production creates neither differentiation nor any complementarity between local production and rents per unit of sales. Transferable knowledge about how to serve a market (and differentiate a product) probably accounts for most of the advantages which Servan-Schreiber (1968) describes as the organizational skill of American corporations in *The American Challenge*. Pure organizational skill would explain the successful foreign

6. Various studies have noted the tendency of the international corporation to keep its basic research activities at its home location, on account of scale economies, and undertake research in its foreign subsidiaries mainly to adapt its products to local conditions. See Brash (1966, ch. 6) and Safarian (1966, pp. 183–6).

7. Eastman and Stykolt (1967, p. 89) correctly argue that advertising rates may well capture the value of these spillovers for the advertising media; none the less, a positive influence of advertising outlays on profitability has been reported by W. S. Comanor and T. A. Wilson (1969).

investments by American management consulting firms, but not by American manufacturing firms; an enterprise blessed with managerial excess capacity and organizational skills not related to a particular product market would tend to prefer conglomerate expansion at home, since alien status always imposes some penalty on managerial effectiveness.

To conclude this line of analysis, consider explicitly the determinants of the choice which the firm makes among serving a foreign market by export, licensing or direct investment.[8] The choice between production at home and abroad (own or licensed) will of course be affected by national comparative advantage (absolute advantage to the firm) as well as by transport costs and tariffs.[9] The balance of net delivered costs of imported and locally produced goods in a foreign market is not always decisive, however. Survey evidence shows that firms very frequently test a foreign market by exports but then switch to local production through a subsidiary, for better adaptation of the product to the local market or the superior quality (or lower cost) of ancillary service that can be provided. Note that these advantages of local production hold for producer as well as consumer goods; although the heights of differentiation are found in the latter, they are not necessarily absent in the former and the marketing advantages of having production facilities at hand may be particularly great for producer goods. The exporter's disadvantage may lie solely in the fact that his foreign customers feel that a source of supply which must cross oceans and national boundaries is inherently more risky than one at home and for that reason should be avoided. American firms have reported substantially increased foreign sales solely for this reason when they shift to local production (Behrman, 1969, p. 3).

The alternative of licensing a foreign producer[10] can match the profitability of direct investment only in certain cases, namely where the rent-yielding advantage of the parent firm lies in some one-shot innovation of technique or product (Johnson, 1968),

8. For a formal model exploring the choice between exporting and production abroad, see Horst (1969, ch. 1).

9. The empirical evidence is particularly convincing on the influence of tariffs; see the sources cited in footnote 3.

10. On licensing, see Brewster (1958, ch. 7) and Mikesell (1962, ch. 5).

such as a new method for making plate glass or the secret ingredient of a successful soft drink. Only in these cases can the information on which the parent's advantage rests be easily transferred intact to the foreign firm. In other cases, either the information cannot be transferred independently of the entrepreneurial manpower or uncertainty about the value of the knowledge in the foreign market will preclude agreement on the terms of a licensing agreement that will capture the full expected value of the surplus available to the licensor.[11] Finally, the relatively high fixed costs of securing the information necessary to undertake a foreign investment predispose the small firm to settle for licensing. Research on the use of licensing by American firms shows that it is employed by relatively small companies; conversely, the prevalence of large firms among those with direct investments abroad has often been noted.[12]

Empirical research on the inter-industry determinants of foreign investment has not yet provided a full test of the hypothesis ventured here about the role of product differentiation, but casual inspection of several sets of data does seem to support it. For the United States a high rank correlation seems to exist between the extent of product differentiation[13] and the proportion

11. Information might not be fully transferable where the knowledge consists of entrepreneurial skill in serving a differential market; a profit-maximizing licensing agreement might not be feasible where the process of product innovation requires continuous market testing, and the value imputed to one innovation depends on how it is combined with others.

12. U S Senate (1967a, p. 198). The choice between licensing and direct investment can also be influenced by a number of factors less central to the concerns of this paper. As Giorgio Basevi and others have suggested, opting for direct investment implies that the parent firm adds a capital asset to its portfolio denominated in foreign currency, while licensing gives rise only to a claim on the yield of such an asset. Exchange-rate expectations and considerations of portfolio balance thus may influence the choice.

13. The assumption that products or industries can be ranked in terms of the extent of product differentiation is a controversial one and the issue cannot receive full consideration here. In the absence of empirical information on the divergence between price elasticities facing the firm and its industry, one must resort to ranking industries by various traits of the product and its conditions of sale and use. Rankings by these various traits need not coincide and there is no obvious formal method of weighting the various traits in order to consolidate the rankings. My view is that economists who have studied the market behaviour attributable to product

of firms in an industry having foreign subsidiaries. If we calculate the portion of the larger firms in various American industries having foreign subsidiaries, the list is headed by automobiles, other consumer durables, scientific instruments, chemicals and and rubber. At the bottom come primary metals, leather, lumber, paper and textiles. The same pattern emerges if we examine countries that are important gross importers of capital, such as Canada or the United Kingdom, and calculate the portion of production in various industries accounted for by subsidiaries of foreign firms (Barlow and Wender, 1955, p. 41; Brecher and Reisman, 1957, p. 105; Dunning, 1958, table 2, p. 58). A formal statistical analysis has been provided for Canada by Eastman and Stykolt, whose results I would interpret as showing that the portion of foreign ownership in a sample of industries is significantly related to product differentiation and other sources of advantage to the multiplant firm.[14]

Of course, differentiation may not be the only industrial attribute explaining the incidence of direct investment. It has been noted, for instance, that the research intensity of American industries (measured by expenditures on research and development as a percentage of sales) is positively related to the relative importance of sales by American subsidiaries in Western Europe (measured by the ratio of subsidiary sales to American exports to non-affiliated companies); this relation does not hold except for Western Europe (Gruber, Mehta and Vernon, 1967). Also, research and development expenditures on new products have been found related to the outflow of new direct investment from the United States.[15] Once one recognizes that the bulk of indus-

---

differentiation in various industries would agree in general on these rankings and their aggregation.

14. Eastman and Stykolt (1967, ch. 4). Their own interpretation is rather different, primarily because they view multiplant development as a consequence of firms' struggles against the disadvantages of owning plants of suboptimal scale and thus do not recognize the direct connection noted above between differentiation and the advantages of local production to serve the market. Their measure of differentiation fails to emerge as a statistically significant determinant of foreign investment, but it is highly collinear with their proxy for advantages to the multiplant firm (which is significant).

15. Evidence on this point is summarized in Robert Lacroix (1970, ch. 2).

trial research expenditure is on new products and product development, it becomes probable that these results for all practical purposes coincide with the line of analysis advanced previously. The current *flow* of direct investment should then occur predominantly in industries where a high current rate of research expenditure in knowledge creation adds rapidly to their stock of exportable knowledge and biases the choice among means of exporting this knowledge towards direct investment. Formal research expenditures are not the only means of building differentiation, however, and the industrial pattern of the flow of direct investment thus need not (and does not) coincide with the pattern of the accumulated stock.

The relation of differentiation to the influence of tariffs on foreign investment also calls for comment. The impact of tariffs is shown not only by direct survey evidence cited above, but also by the data revealing that subsidiaries in the import-competing manufacturing sectors of such countries as Australia and Canada often report higher production costs than those incurred by their parents at home.[16] Will tariffs cause the establishment of foreign subsidiaries in industries where differentiation is absent? Where potential rents exist for companies making direct investments abroad, tariffs are likely to increase those rents at the same time as they cut the profitability of exporting, and thus encourage the inflow of direct investment. By contrast, a tariff protecting a purely competitive industry with unimpeded entry of domestic capital would foster no direct investment; a foreign entrepreneur contemplating entry could expect only transient windfall profits to stack against the innate disadvantages of being a foreign entrepreneur.[17]

But what if barriers to entry are present and excess profits can and do prevail in the long run? The case of long-run excess profits in a foreign market, associated with oligopoly protected by entry barriers, does provide a definite theoretical exception

16. This should be due to the tariff, since the same surveys indicate that the subsidiaries tend to be profitable relative to their parents. Brash (1966, ch. 7) and Safarian (1966, pp. 201–3).

17. Countries such as Canada and Australia offer pervasive tariff protection to their manufacturing sectors, yet direct investment in such protected but undifferentiated industries as textiles and steel is uncommon.

to the preceding argument for the necessary role of product differentiation. Consider the following plausible circumstances for a large firm located in an undifferentiated oligopoly market. It might enjoy excess profits and a flow of internal funds greater than the amount needed to support a profit-maximizing rate of expansion in its home market. It might possess managerial excess capacity which, combined with its stock of technological and production knowledge, assure that it could establish a plant abroad at no serious disadvantage in long-run average unit costs relative to local firms of efficient scale. In this case foreign investment could clearly occur without differentiation and without any specific complementarity between local production and the profitability of foreign sales. The rate of return attainable through foreign investment to its excess liquidity, technological knowledge and under-utilized managerial resources might exceed what it could earn *either* through pooling these resources for conglomerate diversification in the domestic market *or* through the piecemeal disposal of these assets at home or abroad. The role of seller concentration and entry barriers is thus marked as important for explaining the distribution of foreign direct investment, and these factors will be considered directly on pages 278–85.

Vertical direct investments

Foreign investment in a vertically related stage of production invites analysis in terms of the theoretical determinants of optimal vertical integration. A glance at the prevalent types of vertical investments quickly shows, however, that they represent a particular type – preparation of raw-material inputs – and thus call for a less general analysis. No gain arises from the physical integration of processes when, say, a steel company establishes an iron-ore mine, since the technology at the two stages of production has nothing in common. The corporation may integrate backwards to produce raw materials in less-developed countries where they might otherwise not be forthcoming, due to shortages of local social overhead capital and entrepreneurship; but this line of argument fails to explain extensive vertical direct investments in countries like Canada and Norway which seem well endowed with railroads and local entrepreneurs.

The motives for vertical investments among the industrial

countries seem to turn heavily on the avoidance of oligopolistic uncertainty and the erection of barriers to the entry of new rivals – as in the case of domestic markets (de Chazeau and Kahn, 1959, ch. 3; Penrose, 1968, pp. 46–50, 253–9). In the absence of technological complementarity, such investments would not be expected in a competitive raw-materials industry, unless due to some special difference between the raw-materials producers and the subsequent processors in time horizons, discount rates and the like. Where both the buyers and sellers of the raw material are few in number, where the profitability of investments by both buyer and seller depends heavily on the prices expected to prevail over a long period of time, where these investments are large in absolute size and where the raw material has neither alternative uses nor substitutes in its sole use, much uncertainty can be eliminated through common ownership of the two vertically related stages. In the case of established arm's-length buyers and sellers, the long-term contract offers an alternative to vertical integration. At the time when a natural resource is first developed, however, these arrangements are not necessarily alternatives, since the processing firm making a direct investment in resource-based production may well reach such a contractual relationship with the natural-resource owner.

Another motive for vertical integration besides risk-avoidance arises when the processing industry is populated by relatively few sellers. By controlling their input sources, the existing firms may raise substantial barriers to the entry of new competitors. If the resource is not a ubiquitous one, and known supply sources are tied up through vertical integration, a new entrant to the processing industry must endure the extra costs and uncertainties of finding and developing his own source of raw materials. The going firms can enjoy higher than competitive profit rates without attracting new rivals.[18]

Both sets of motives point to the same determinants of the incidence of vertical direct investments among industries. High seller concentration would seem critical at the production stage

18. See Joe S. Bain (1956). The same motives can operate to explain forward integration by a manufacturer into distribution. For several reasons, however, this seems a less fruitful way to erect barriers to entry, and strong elements of bilateral oligopoly and uncertainty are seldom present.

from which the foreign investment is initiated. It directly generates uncertainty in the market for the raw material. It is also necessary to motivate the *firm* to take actions aiming to raise entry barriers to the *industry*. Furthermore, for the processing firm to undertake a foreign investment involving an enormous financial commitment, in the face of the prevailing influence of lenders' risk on the capital markets, it must initially be of large absolute size. Besides size and concentration in the processing industry, other predictors of vertical direct investment emerge from the other factors tending to increase market uncertainty: the minimum scale and durability of the resource investment and the existence of alternative uses.

The statistical evidence on foreign investment does not lend itself readily to testing these predictions beyond the recital of examples, though these instances do seem to provide considerable support. One additional implication – that vertical direct investment will comprise a greater portion of the total direct outflow from a country with a smaller domestic resource base – has been confirmed by a comparison of the United States and the United Kingdom (Krainer, 1967).

Direct investment and market behaviour

The total impact of foreign investment within the industry depends both on the forces which induce decisions to establish foreign subsidiaries and the consequences these subsidiaries have for market behaviour and resource allocation. This section pursues these effects to the level of the industry, national and international, and the following section employs international-trade models to extend them into general equilibrium. The discussion will be confined largely to horizontal investments.

The preceding section adduced two features that should characterize any industry in which substantial horizontal direct investment occurs: product differentiation and oligopoly. The latter emerged only indirectly and thus needs some supplemental explanation. It was established that the fixed information costs associated with planning a direct investment bias large firms towards preferring this method of extracting rents from a foreign market. Also, the theory of the multiplant firm and the likelihood of scale economies in national sales promotion (for differentiated products) suggest that a firm would not invest abroad while profitable opportunities remained for the exploitation of scale economies in production or sales in the home market. For these reasons a firm that invests abroad will be relatively large and face relatively few competitors at home, since the same structural forces probably determine the sizes of its rivals.[19]

These traits combine to nominate differentiated oligopoly as the most likely market environment for direct investment. This and other concepts drawn from the field of industrial organization can serve to predict and explain the industrial consequences of direct investment. In particular, it seems fruitful to consider a model of a national industry which, when blown up to the level of a 'world industry', would capture the chief characteristics of differentiated oligopoly with direct investment. This is the national oligopoly with regional submarkets, found commonly in national product markets where transport costs or the need to adapt output to local demand characteristics call for decentralized production, and barriers to entry constrict the number of sellers. Examples in the United States are the petroleum refining and brewery industries, which contain both national ('international') and regional ('national') sellers. Horizontal direct investment becomes the equivalent of entry into a regional submarket by a firm established in at least one other submarket.

The barriers to entry into a national market by an international firm can readily be compared with those identified for new domestic entrants in these same markets (Bain, 1956; Hines, 1957). Indeed, the international firm holds advantages against each of

19. The affinity of direct investment for industries of oligopolistic market structure has been documented extensively. In the United Kingdom, Dunning (1958, pp. 155–7) found that two-thirds of the subsidiaries covered in his survey operated in markets of tight-knit oligopoly. Also, a significant relation has been found between the level of seller concentration (portion of sales accounted for by the five largest firms) and foreign participation for a sample of 277 manufacturing industries. This holds for American subsidiaries as well as all foreign-owned firms and examination of a subsample suggests that the foreign presence typically consists of two or more firms rather than a single subsidiary. See M. D. Steuer *et al.* (1970, ch. 4). Rosenbluth reports similar findings for Canada, but shows that the association between foreign ownership and concentration can be viewed as resulting solely from the excess of the absolute size of foreign firms over domestic firms. See G. Rosenbluth (1970) and Wheelwright (1963).

the major sources of entry barriers. If scale economies are significant but prevail at only one stage of fabrication, the foreign firm may be able to carry out that process at a single location and transplant only the others ('assembly operations') to its subsidiary. Thus, foreign subsidiaries are typically less integrated vertically than the domestic firms with which they compete, and the manufacturing operations of subsidiaries less integrated than home production by the parent enterprise.[20] Product-differentiation barriers are, on the argument of the preceding section, definitionally offset by the rent-yielding attributes of the firm that has established itself in a differentiated market abroad. Finally, important among the sources of 'absolute cost' barriers are high capital charges imposed by the market for finance when a large absolute volume of funds is sought. The foreign entrant is able to tap earnings retained abroad and having relatively low opportunity cost, as well as to enjoy a good credit rating. Formally, the international firm can buy factors of production either in the host or the home country, and thus enjoys the intrinsic advantage over the domestic firm that comes from the opportunity to trade at either of two different sets of factor prices.[21]

Against the advantage that the foreign firm enjoys in hurdling conventional barriers weigh disadvantages created by national boundaries. As was mentioned above, the entrant must incur additional costs of gathering information that are fixed in the sense

20. Some data are available on subsidiaries' relative shares of value-added and cost of materials, and can be used to assess their degree of vertical integration, although caution is required. Brecher and Reisman (1957, table 29, p. 107) show that the share of cost of materials is slightly higher in Canadian subsidiaries of American companies than in their domestic competitors. Although the difference is small, it seems indicative; if the subsidiaries' productivity were higher than their competitors', they would tend to report a large value-added share (smaller cost-of-materials share) than their competitors even if the physical degrees of vertical integration were the same. Another study, T. R. Gates and F. Linden (1961), finds the cost-of-materials share in European subsidiaries higher than in their American parents which strongly suggests less vertical integration in overseas operations than at home; the conclusion which the authors draw, however, is that the cost of material inputs relative to labour is higher in Europe.

21. Evidence of the influence of factor prices abroad on subsidiaries' behaviour can be found in two recent studies: G. L. Reuber and F. Roseman (1969) and G. V. G. Stevens (1969).

that they do not vary proportionally with the amount of resources that the firm might stake abroad. A second barrier reposes in the additional risks of investment in a foreign rather than in a home market. In part, this extra risk in the obverse of the high cost of information about foreign markets: where information costs more, one will settle for less of it and, as a result, put up with more uncertainty. But extra risks for foreign investors are also associated with exchange-rate changes, political actions by a foreign government that serves one's competitor but not oneself, and the like. Noting that foreign subsidiaries retain and plough back a much larger portion of their earnings than do domestic firms, Barlow and Wender have hypothesized that firms tend to view profits realized from risky foreign ventures as 'gambler's earnings' and plough them back in the subsidiary even when no export of funds originating in the home market would take place in their absence.[22]

These differences between barriers to entry by the new domestic and the established international firm contribute in several ways to explaining patterns of foreign investment and business performance. All of them help to explain the prevalence of large firms as foreign investors – even the greater risk of foreign investment, since the large firm may be able to pool the risks of several subsidiaries abroad while the small firm can contemplate establishing only one (Shearer, 1964) and (Steuer, 1969, pp. 33–6). The preference of small American firms for investing in closer and more familiar countries such as Canada is thus easily explained. Finally, the greater risk of foreign investment rationalizes the survey evidence showing that a significant minority of firms insist on a higher expected rate of return before approving a foreign-investment project than they would on a comparable domestic investment, and that those who succeed earn more than their competitors in the host country.[23]

22. Barlow and Wender (1955, pp. 164–7). For evidence on high rates of profit retention by subsidiaries, see e.g. Brash (1966, ch. 4). Risk-avoidance regarding the exchange rate is demonstrated by the tendency of subsidiaries to undertake substantial local borrowing, helping to balance their local-currency claims and liabilities. See Mikesell (1962, pp. 95–8).

23. The greater profitability of going foreign subsidiaries probably reflects as well the common practice of transferring the implicit rents from the use of trade marks, technical know-how and the like in the form of profits rather

This analysis of entry barriers also suggests some traits of market structures in industries containing a significant population of foreign subsidiaries. The existence of scale economies makes it likely that a firm producing and selling in numerous submarkets will hold a larger share in the average market than the typical competing firm operating in a single market. A seller is unlikely to expand production in a second region while scale economies remain to be exploited in the first. The more important are scale economies, relative to the size of regional markets, the less often will a seller produce in more than one region, and the more likely is a firm expanding into a new region to pick the one with the largest market.[24] Where the existence of local production facilities gives the firm a competitive edge in marketing its product, multi-regional production may be carried to a greater extent than would minimize costs of production for the industry, and oligopolistic firms which are in active 'product rivalry' – if not price competition – with one another will tend to make parallel moves in extending production to new regions.

Whatever the market structure that results from the influence of direct investment, it can be argued that entry by a foreign subsidiary is likely to produce more active rivalrous behaviour and improvement in market performance than would a domestic entry at the same initial scale. The subsidiary tends to enjoy advantages in unit cost and profitability that stem from the same factors which lower the entry barriers that it faces.[25] Furthermore, as a newcomer it has not settled into the sort of stable pattern of oligopolistic interdependence or mutual accommodation that will normally evolve among a market's long-term tenants. In any case, its experience with such patterns of accommodation

---

than service charges. For evidence on the superior profit performance of subsidiaries over domestic firms, see Brash (1966, ch. 10), Dunning (1969, pp. 130–33) and Safarian (1969, chs. 6, 7).

24. These conclusions are drawn from the Sylos–Bain model, which also identifies a high elasticity of demand as a factor favouring direct investment. For an account see F. Modigliani (1958).

25. A possible source of these advantages in profitability beyond those already mentioned arises if the subsidiary improves the performance of local suppliers from whom it buys and the local distribution channels through which it sells, widening its profit margin in the short run and raising the pay-out for it of greater penetration of the market.

derives from another market in which the game may be played quite differently. Hence its pricing and product strategies are likely to stir up established conduct patterns and increase the amount of independent (as opposed to interdependent) behaviour. The 'gambler's earnings' hypothesis implies that the subsidiary playing for a big win may shun safe conformity in the interests of limited joint maximization of industry profits; but one must also note that the innate riskiness of direct investment could be taken to predict a cautious course that abjures independent action.

These influences of direct investment on market structure and conduct are too diverse to yield any summary prediction about what patterns are most likely to prevail in an industry that has received a heavy inflow of direct investment. We can, however, note one particular model said to fit a number of Canadian industries (Eastman and Stykolt, 1967; English, 1964, esp. ch. 4). It assumes an import-competing differentiated oligopoly receiving significant tariff protection and affected by scale economies that are significant relative to the size of the national market. The selection and maintenance of an industry price is easily effected by taking the world (external) price plus the tariff. If this price would allow more than a competitive profit rate to producers whose plants are large enough to exhaust plant scale economics, both domestic and foreign firms of sub-optimal size tend to populate the industry. Differentiation causes each seller to be confronted with a downward-sloping demand curve. This fact discourages price warfare to drive our rivals (and permit the predator to expand to efficient scale), as does the fact that rivals which are subsidiaries have potential access to the 'deep pockets' of their parents. Entry will continue through the establishment of foreign subsidiaries until the rate of return that a new entrant expects falls short of his target, which would equal the (higher than competitive) rate of profit earned by this industry in countries where its international firms are domiciled.[26]

26. This analysis abstracts from differences that are to be expected among the rates of return on tangible assets earned by firms in a differentiated industry. It also assumes that, these differences apart, the 'limit price' that bears a critical relation to entry in the Sylos–Bain model can be translated into a 'limit rate of return'.

Empirical evidence strongly supports the relevance of this model, confirming both the phenomenon of pricing up to the tariff and a strong dependence of the proportion of plants of sub-optimal size on the size of the national market.[27] This result seems impossible to explain without reference to product differentiation.

As a general proposition, the difficulty of predicting the effects of foreign direct investment on market structure is seen in the suggestion that entry by foreign firms may actually raise seller concentration in the host-country market. Mergers might be induced among the domestic firms, pressed by new competition, leaving the total number of firms smaller than before. This possibility cannot be denied,[28] but its significance is somewhat obscure. If the mergers involve economies, why is the stimulus of a foreign entrant needed? If not, then they probably signal retreat from the market before a rival capable of higher productivity and (possibly but not necessarily) may coincide with an improvement in the industry's productivity and market performance.

It is tempting to proceed to market models that embody mutual dependence recognized among oligopolists in a 'world industry'. Tacit understandings may commit firms to refrain from investing in each other's main national markets, and breakdowns of such understandings may be marked by reciprocal invasions of the home territories (Edwards, 1960). The tightness of oligopoly in national markets may influence the extent to which domestic firms take account of the threat of foreign entry and select their price and product strategies in the spirit of a 'limit price' that

27. Eastman and Stykolt (1967, chs. 1, 3). The same dependence of plant size on national market size is revealed in figures given by Bain which tend to show that median plant size (measured by employment) in manufacturing industries varies strongly with the size of the domestic market. See J. S. Bain (1966, p. 39).

28. There is no fully satisfactory evidence on this or the contrary hypothesis. Rosenbluth (1970, p. 28) reports no association between changes in seller concentration and in foreign control for Canadian industries over the period 1954–64. Steuer *et al.* (1970, ch. 4) found a significant negative association between the *level* of foreign participation in UK industries in 1963 and the absolute change in concentration 1958–63, which casts doubt on the hypothesis stated in the text; but they were without a measure of the *change* in foreign participation over this period.

will just fail to tempt foreign entry. Such theorizing quickly dwindles into taxonomy, however, and the available empirical evidence is insufficient to reveal what shape an effective array of the possibilities would take.

Most models of direct investment in a 'world industry' seem to predict an important tendency for direct investment to equalize rates of return on equity capital in a given industry in all countries where production occurs. This consequence does not depend on the absence of tariffs and other impediments to trade,[29] and, indeed, the hope of import-competing domestic producers that a tariff will raise their profit rates proves illusory in the long run unless that rate lies below what 'sector-specific' capital earns in the capital-exporting countries. This does not mean, however, that direct investment tends to establish a *competitive* rate of return to capital in each industry where it occurs. Because of the oligopoly and entry barriers (and neglecting the effect of differentiation on the variance of firms' profit rates), each industry's common rate of return is likely to lie above a competitive rate to a degree that reflects barriers to entry into the world industry and the attained degree of mutual dependence recognized within it. This hypothesized outcome will receive further theoretical analysis in the next section.

The international corporation in general equilibrium

The impact of sector-specific capital

The analysis to this stage has been concerned with micro behaviour and allocative results at the level of the firm and the industry. Certain features of the industrial structures resulting from direct investment can be built into a simple general equilibrium model.[30] I shall concentrate on the sector-specificity of direct investment, conspiring with entry barriers to equate rates of return between countries in a given industry but not between industries in a

29. As it does in the conventional Heckscher–Ohlin model giving rise to factor-price equalization.

30. And certain others readily cannot – product differentiation and the rent-yielding advantages of the firm undertaking direct investment. No empirical test or defence of the hypothesis of sector-specific capital is offered here beyond suggesting that its theoretical significance is worth exploring.

given country. This invokes the concept of the 'specific factor of production', long familiar in trade theory, and allows use to be made of recent theoretical work on specific factors in a simple general-equilibrium model (Jones, 1971). In the spirit of the Heckscher–Ohlin model, assume two countries, X and Y, capable of producing two products, A and B. Each country is endowed with a labour supply, L_x and L_y, that is homogeneous and perfectly mobile between industries but does not move across national boundaries. Symmetrically, stocks of capital K_a and K_b are potentially mobile across national boundaries but specific to the two respective industries. If the usual assumptions about production functions and trade barriers necessary to produce factor-price equalization were satisfied in this model, but capital were not mobile internationally, equilization would, of course, not occur. Rendering *one* type of sector-specific capital perfectly mobile does cause equalization, however, if both countries remain incompletely specialized. If K_a moves freely between countries, its return is equalized directly. Competitive factor and product markets assure that this also equates the marginal products of labour in both countries' A industries and in their B industries as well. With the marginal product of labour the same in both B industries, the marginal product, and thus the rent, of K_b must be the same in both countries. Three international price links suffice to equate the rewards to three factors. If both K_a and K_b were internationally mobile, a redundant fourth link would be created and one country could be expected to specialize completely and contain none of the stock of one type of capital.

One disturbance that can be explored in this three-factor model is the effect of an exogenous transfer of capital (say K_a) from Y to X. I do not now assume all conditions necessary for factor-price equalization, but wish instead to explore the effect of this disturbance on national factor prices and the incentive for international capital transfers. Jones has shown that an increase in the endowment of one specific factor, holding product prices constant, raises the wage of L_x as the increase in X's production of A draws L_x from B. The marginal product of K_a falls as that of L_x rises, lowering the rent to K_a. But the rent to K_b must also fall, and indeed will fall more than that of K_a if the initial share of wages in total costs for the B industry exceeds that of wages in total costs for the A industry. Symmetrical adjustments will take place in Y. Thus the exogenous flow of K_a to X lowers the rent to K_b in X and raises it in Y. Whatever the mobility of K_b, the incentive for its movement from X to Y is increased and one has an explanation of why direct investment tends to be cross-hauled between countries. If product differentiation were allowed among firms in the A industry, it is also clear that an exogenous flow of K_a to X would tend to induce a reverse flow of K_a initiated by producers resident in X.

This three-factor model also generates some conclusions about the effects of tariffs on income distribution and welfare. In the absence of capital transfers, imposing a tariff on imports of A to X will raise the rent to K_a and lower that to K_b. In contrast to the Stolper–Samuelson conclusion for the two-factor case, the change in the real wage of L_x can be either positive or negative. As L_x is transferred to the A industry, its marginal product falls in A, the domestic price of which has been raised by the tariff, and rises in the production of B, the relative price of which has fallen; the effect on the real wage is indeterminate. If we allow K_a to flow into X in response to this rise in its rent, however, the increase in its marginal product in X's A industry is restricted. An inflow sufficient to keep its marginal product from rising more than proportionally to the tariff-induced increase in A's price would keep the marginal product of L_x from falling in the A industry. (I neglect any product and factor-price changes induced in Y.) With labour's marginal product rising in B and constant in A, its real wage increases. We may have here an explanation, in contrast to the Stolper–Samuelson theorem, of why labour in countries like Canada and Australia seems willing to support tariff protection for capital-intensive manufacturing industries.[31]

Finally, this three-factor model can be related to the welfare conclusions concerning the taxation of trade and capital flows that have been worked out for the two-factor case (Jones, 1967). If each country produces only a single good, then a nation facing an imperfectly elastic foreign supply of (demand for) capital will benefit from imposing a tax on capital flows, analogous to the

31. Sector-specific (and immobile) natural resources could be assumed in place of K_b.

‘optimum tariff’ on trade. With incomplete specialization, however, either the optimum tariff or the optimum tax on capital (but not both) may be negative. Suppose that *X* imports capital from *Y* (not sector-specific, for the moment) and that *Y*’s import-competing industry (*B*) is relatively capital-intensive. Then *X* may benefit from subsidizing capital imports. Such a subsidy drives up the rent to capital in *Y* and the total cost of foreign borrowing to *X*, but it also raises the price in *Y* of the capital-intensive *B* good, which is *X*’s export. *X*’s terms of trade thus improve and this improvement can offset the loss in higher capital costs if *X*’s burden of international indebtedness is small enough relative to *X*’s receipts from export sales. This possibility will remain if we again assume capital to be sector-specific. The condition necessary to make the optimal tax on a flow of one type of capital negative will become more stringent, however. The relation (in *Y*) between relative factor and product prices, essential to the result, survives but is weakened.

Interrelation of trade flows and capital movements

Some additional general relations between trade and foreign investment can be uncovered if we switch to a different trade model involving more extensive descriptive assumptions and capable of generating results that have been suggested by Burenstam-Linder, Drèze and Vernon. I shall sketch briefly the assumptions which in common underlie their work and indicate some predictions they imply about direct investment.[32]

The descriptive assumptions are the following:

1. The countries which enjoy higher average incomes *per capita* are those endowed with relatively more capital (in all its forms) per head.

2. Consumers’ taste patterns can be described as consisting of certain wants or needs, each of which can be served by a variety of different goods. Consumers largely agree on a ranking of all goods produced in terms of their desirability for satisfying any given want, with the ranking running down from the most

32. A somewhat similar analysis, but concentrating on trade flows, appears in Harry Johnson’s (1968) Wicksell Lectures.

desirable and costly.[33] These rankings are similar among the various industrialized countries. When real income per head is growing, consumers raise their standards of living through trading up to more strongly preferred goods.

3. The long-term rise in standards of living tends to bias the search for new consumer goods toward those which will be highly ranked and thus consumed initially by high-income countries and groups. (Some discoveries of course will tend to truncate these rankings by rendering obsolete goods that cost more to produce but rate lower in consumer preferences.) The search for new producer goods is biased in just the same way toward innovations which initially are chosen by entrepreneurs facing high costs of labour relative to capital. This results from the long-term rise in the value of labour-time, the counterpart of increasing real income per head.

In addition, I assume that the determinants and consequences of direct investment operate as suggested in the preceding analysis. One conclusion was that firms selling in a differentiated market would establish their quasi-rent-yielding assets in the native economy of the entrepreneur before venturing abroad. This requires no assumption beyond the information-cost advantage of a native in establishing an asset in the form of market-oriented knowledge. Burenstam-Linder's (1961, pp. 87–123) proposition that a commodity must first be sold in an extensive domestic market before it can be exported thus gains credence for some industries. He also suggests that exports of manufactured goods will be destined disproportionately to other countries at similar levels of income *per capita*, a proposition that also follows for differentiated goods if we make the second assumption listed above about consumers' taste patterns. Drèze (1960) offers the related proposition that a small industrial country will tend to find its comparative advantage lying in undifferentiated manufactures, because scale economies in sales promotion put the differentiated producer in the small market at a capital-cost disadvantage in product design and the attainment of marketing experience. This hypothesis gains empirical support from Belgium's trade pattern but holds less obviously for the other small

33. This description draws upon J. S. Duesenberry (1949, ch. 2).

industrial countries. Furthermore, it is a decidedly partial proposition, in that would-be exporters of differentiated goods compete in the sense of comparative advantage not against foreign sellers of similar products but against other domestic industries which would employ the same stock of factors of production.

Finally, Vernon has suggested that product innovations are likely to be discovered and initially produced in high-income countries, then diffused to others through trade, foreign investment and imitation (Vernon, 1966; Wells, 1969). The third assumption stated above explains the predominant origin of discovery in wealthy countries. The contact needed in the early stages between the producer and his market and suppliers and the presumed price-inelasticity of demand for a 'novelty' call for the initial location of production in the high-income country whatever long-run comparative advantage may indicate. Initial exploitation of foreign markets will be through export; but costs eventually tell and production spreads abroad if cost minimization so indicates. If the innovation represents a new product variety, especially a patentable one, the diffusion of production abroad is likely to be through direct investment. If the innovation is primarily one of producer goods or production technology, licensing or imitation is probable.

These propositions, primarily about trade patterns, can also be made to yield predictions about the international structure of foreign direct investment, in particular about a country's balance of international direct investment: the ratio of the book value of enterprise capital abroad controlled by its citizens to the value of capital within its borders controlled by foreigners. The deductions depend primarily on recalling the influence of comparative cost (absolute cost to the producer) on the choice between serving a foreign market by export and by direct investment, and on noting that the international mobility of capital tends to remove its influence as a determinant of national patterns of comparative advantage. Thus, the country with high efficiency wages will tend to be a relatively small importer of direct investment. Whether it is a large net exporter of equity capital, however, will depend on the sorts of commodities it exports. If its comparative advantage lies in undifferentiated manufactures or natural resource-intensive goods, it will show little tendency to export direct investment, even though it might be a net capital exporter through portfolio investments abroad. High efficiency wages may be due to a nation's role as an innovator, causing its exchange rate (and thereby its money cost level, relative to costs in other countries) to be elevated by a significant volume of 'technological gap' exports. Apart from the tendency for some direct investment to occur ultimately as the manufacture of new products is diffused, such a country will also tend to be an exporter of direct investment from other industries. This is because the elevation of efficiency wages biases the choice of other producers of differentiated goods (besides the innovators) towards production abroad rather than exports.

Large size of a country's domestic market, other things equal, will favour inflows of direct investment because the foreign firm contemplating an investment will not be deterred by problems of securing an efficient level of output; against this, however, cuts a 'composition effect', in that the absolute capital requirements of efficient scale (for marketing) in a large country will be onerous to foreign firms if they are based in smaller markets. Finally, the countries with a relatively cosmopolitan culture will tend to swap direct investments with each other. So will countries at similar levels of income *per capita*, by expansion of Burenstam-Linder's argument.

These predictions are capable of a certain amount of superficial testing by example. Several of them help to explain the position of the United States as a large net exporter of direct investment, and that of Britain as a large gross importer and exporter. For other countries, however, the various criteria tend to cut against one another. As has been noted before, it often seems necessary to involve political and cultural factors in explaining bilateral patterns of foreign investment (Chakravarty, 1961).

Some welfare implications

The remainder of this paper considers selected welfare implications of the preceding analysis, particularly for the character of welfare gains from direct investment and their distribution between the lending and borrowing countries. I shall not discuss the numerous popular and political concerns about foreign investment which have received attention elsewhere (Brecher and Reisman, 1957, ch. 8; Kindleberger, 1969).

In the absence of externalities and market imperfections, the case for free movement of direct investment as a means of maximizing world welfare is simply the case for allowing any factor or product to flow towards locations where it has the greatest excess of marginal value over marginal cost. Theoretical attention has recently focused on the more complex question of national welfare, and the theory of bilateral monopoly has been employed to identify the general interest of both lending and borrowing country in restricting capital flows when the influence of their volume on the price received or paid can be perceived. The second-best aspects of the taxation of capital flows have been explored at both the general-equilibrium and micro levels, as well as the strategic situation arising from the discordant interests of the lending and borrowing countries.[34] I have argued in the preceding sections that the bulk of direct investment can be characterized in ways somewhat different from the general assumptions commonly employed in recent theoretical work. Do the differences alter the results of this theoretical analysis or make them more specific?

The interpretation of the international corporation as an exporter of sector-specific capital in an oligopolistic market clearly conflicts with the assumption of independent, competitive supply and demand curves for international capital transactions at the national level. To the extent that capital-exporting firms in a national industry recognize their impact on their industry's rate of return from foreign investments, the lending country's interest in monopolistic restriction of capital outflows is looked after privately; a nationally optimal level of capital exports would be achieved if sellers in each industry sent abroad the amount that would maximize their private joint profits, in the absence of complementarity or substitutability among the various industry outputs in the foreign market. Thus the exception in the United States' anti-trust laws allowing collusion in export sales through joint selling agencies is rational from a nationalistic viewpoint (US Senate, 1967a, p. 153). It is an interesting confirmation of

34. See Corden (1967), Hamada (1966), Jones (1967), Kemp (1966) and earlier references cited in these papers.

the role of differentiated oligopoly in foreign trade and investment, however, that such agencies in fact are rare and persist only in export industries characterized by small firms producing a homogeneous product such as paper, phosphate or carbon black (US Senate, 1967b, pp. 34–46). One would expect price-fixing agreements and joint selling agencies to be either not feasible or else unnecessary vehicles for collusion in industries of tight-knit differentiated oligopoly.

What of the interests of the borrowing countries? Even if they face a supply of foreign equity capital already restricted through collusion among foreign corporations, further monopolistic restriction will nevertheless raise their welfare if the supply of direct investment is, in effect, less than perfectly elastic (i.e. the rate of return can be pushed down). But the analysis of differentiated oligopoly raises the possibility that this inelasticity may be lacking. If the firms dominating a 'world industry' would all experience the same net revenue per unit of sales in any subsidiaries they established in this borrowing country, and if they all adhered to 'limit pricing' through insistence on a common target rate of return, then they would confront the borrowing country with a perfectly elastic supply curve of capital. The chances of this outcome should not be exaggerated, however, because the failure of the first of these necessary conditions to hold is quite likely in a differentiated industry.[35] Given some dispersion in the profit rates which foreign international corporations can earn in a borrowing country's markets, its most satisfactory instrument for capturing some of the gains from foreign investments might be an excess profits tax on rates of return beyond what is deemed to be the 'limit' rate.

Given these doubts about the extent of gains available to the borrowing country, other sources of potential gains to it, and empirical evidence of their importance, merit examination. The three main possibilities are corporation income taxes, benefits from manpower training and uncaptured productivity spillovers.

35. Some evidence that Britain's *aggregate* supply of foreign investment is less than perfectly elastic appears in Reddaway's finding that post-tax rates of return on UK direct investments are lower in those countries imposing relatively high corporation taxes. Cf. Reddaway, Potter and Taylor (1967–8, pp. 219–20).

Analysis of the corporation income tax, generally applied to the net incomes of domestic firms and foreign subsidiaries alike, has shown that, if borrowing and lending countries applied the same (marginal) rate, general neutrality would exist between home and foreign investments for the lender and between subsidiary and domestic production for the borrower (Krause and Dam, 1964, ch. 4). Actual rates do show a tendency to cluster just under 50 per cent, so that this neutrality is rather nearly attained in practice. This depends, of course, upon some convention whereby either the borrower or the lender, but not both, apply the common tax rate to the net incomes of foreign subsidiaries. The well-established practice is that the borrower gets first crack, with subsidiaries' tax liabilities to the host government credited against tax liability on the same profits to the home government. This tax flow guarantees a substantial source of real benefits from foreign investment to the borrower. As Hamada has shown, it also offers the virtue of avoiding the 'prisoner's dilemma' game situation likely to result from any other convention. Differential tax rates on the net incomes of domestic and foreign-owned corporations, or on corporate income from domestic and foreign sources, appear quite uncommon, so that tax-induced distortions in the international allocation of equity capital are likely to be minor (apart from distortions that may result from the existence of the corporate income tax itself). The virtues of this situation lie not only in its contribution to world welfare but also in the unedifying nature of the alternative: to the extent that capital is sector-specific, a different tax rate in every industry would be optimal from a national viewpoint.

Apart from tax revenues, benefits to the borrower from direct investment depend on the inability of the foreign subsidiary to capture the full social product resulting from the capital, managerial skills and technological knowledge that it transplants to the host country. Two sources of leakage command particular interest, manpower training and productivity gains to domestic firms induced by the subsidary's market behaviour.

Benefits from labour training will *not* redound to the host economy if the following conditions hold: (a) workers invest in their own training up to the point where its marginal costs to them equal the present discounted value of its marginal benefits;

(b) corporations provide training to the extent that maximizes their profits. The survey evidence on foreign subsidiaries is rather various but does suggest that they operate with some frequency in environments where these assumptions may fail to hold. The scale of labour-training programmes that are undertaken is sometimes very extensive, especially in countries such as Brazil and Mexico where the alternative opportunities for labour to acquire this training may be quite limited (Gordon and Grommers, 1962, ch. 8). Even in an industrial country the foreign subsidiary may offer the domestic labour force some unique opportunities for training in association with the 'differentiation' advantage that makes the direct investment profitable in the first place. This training would presumably be in managerial and technical or scientific lines. Finally, the chances seem reasonably high that a subsidiary, especially if establishing a production activity new to a country, would invest in labour training *ex post* to an extent greater than that which maximizes its private profits. This is so because of asymmetry in the risks of running short of skills, on the one hand, and overestimating personnel turnover, on the other. If this asymmetry exists (and if employees underinvest in training on their personal initiative), then net social benefits from training will increase with the mobility of the labour force out of the foreign subsidiary. This mobility in turn will increase with the following factors: the number of domestic firms producing goods or using processes similar to those of the foreign firm; the extent to which the training is not specific to the subsidiary's particular processes or activities; and the physical proximity of the subsidiary to domestic employers.[36]

High productivity in a subisidiary, if captured in the firm's profits, yields no direct social benefit to the host country apart from the extra tax revenue. The empirical studies do suggest, however, a number of ways in which the subsidiary may fail to

36. In Britain, American subsidiaries show some tendency to move into depressed areas, where labour-training benefits might be significant, but to bid away trained employees from domestic firms rather than train their own. See R. M. Jones (1968) and Steuer *et al.* (1970, pp. 43–4). Substantial net benefits could still accrue in this case, since the elevated skill wages confer a rent to skilled employees, and the domestic firms may be induced to undertake socially productive training programmes.

capture the full value of its social product. One instance overlaps with the factor of labour training. To the extent that the firm instructs in unique skills, particularly for managerial labour, employees who switch to domestic firms may transplant knowledge that provides a basis for imitative productivity gains there without real resource cost. Productivity gains may leak out from subsidiaries by channels other than the transfer of personnel, however. Studies of United States subsidiaries in both Britain and Australia have shown that they sometimes take the lead in improving the productivity of their domestic suppliers or the domestic distribution channels through which they sell, passing along techniques of inventory and quality control, standardization and the like (Brash, 1966, ch. 8; Dunning, 1958, ch. 7). In markets where the domestic firms engage in gentlemanly competition, the arrival of a foreign subsidiary may spur greater efforts to raise productivity among the local firms if, as was suggested above, the subsidiary does not find its profits maximized by conforming to existing patterns of restricted competition (Scitovsky, 1960, ch. 18). These gains may accrue either through copying the subsidiary's production or marketing techniques or through an increased outlay of managerial effort in response to shrivelled profits.[37] Finally, even without induced productivity gains, increased competition triggered off by the subsidiary will convey a benefit in the form of increased consumers' surplus.

Any net social benefits to the host country from labour training or productivity spillovers would weigh in the balance with all other factors in determining whether a tax or subsidy for foreign investment might be appropriate. Since these sources of social benefit may prove large in some cases, however, it is worth inquiring whether their accrual to the host country is likely to deny equivalent benefits to the home country, when equity capital moves abroad rather than choosing the best available domestic alternative.[38] The industrial analysis offered above suggests a negative answer. The international firm probably already occupies a significant share of its domestic market. Its competi-

37. W. M. Corden (1969) has recently explored the economic implications of a relation between profits and efficiency.

38. For a theoretical analysis of adverse effects on the lending country, see Marvin Frankel (1965).

tive impact and any external benefits that may result from its presence there have already been unleashed. In any case, in an oligopoly market there is no reason to expect that denying it the opportunity to invest abroad will lead it to raise output in its main product line at home, driving down its rate of return in the process. Diversification into other home industries is more likely but its presence in other domestic industries may yield fewer positive externalities than its presence abroad in its principal line of activity, for the same reasons that it enjoys the advantage of lowered barriers to entry in horizontal expansion to a new foreign market.

This section has so far addressed itself primarily to horizontal direct investments. In closing, let me consider briefly the special features of vertical foreign investments in the extraction and processing of raw materials for export as they relate to the sources of benefit to the host country.

One difference arises in the welfare significance of taxation by the host country of subsidiaries' profits, because the (accounting) profits of the extractive subsidiary are likely to include both a pure return to capital and an intra-marginal rent on the natural-resource deposit which it exploits. If the rent is not separately captured by a native holder of resource rights for the domestic income stream, a case exists for taxing the subsidiary's profits even if equity capital (as a separate factor of production) is in perfectly elastic foreign supply. The large scale of resource deposits which attract foreign investments and the fewness of potential bidders for rights mean that great uncertainty will constrain the ability of the resource owner (private or public) to strike a prior agreement that will succeed in capturing all forthcoming rents. This poor bargaining position of the native resource-holder would naturally cause resentment and thus it is not surprising that American firms with extractive subsidiaries abroad report much greater concern over expropriation than do firms with horizontally related manufacturing subsidiaries (Barlow and Wender, 1955, p. 128).

Spillover benefits to the domestic economy from extractive subsidiaries while not totally absent, are likely to be smaller than for horizontal investment in manufacturing. The subsidiary is likely to be capital-intensive, offering fewer opportunities for the training of the local labour force for an equivalent amount of capital transferred. It sells largely on world markets and buys few local inputs, so that little pressure for efficiency gains is put on competing or supplying domestic firms. Its physical location is likely to be remote from the locations of domestic firms which might be favourably affected by its presence. Its remoteness may convey an advantage, however, if its draft on the labour supply in a thin local market generates significant rents for its employees.[39]

References

AITKEN, H. G. J. (1961), *American Capital and Canadian Resources*, Harvard University Press.

BAIN, J. S. (1956), *Barriers to New Competition*, Harvard University Press.

BAIN, J. S. (1966), *International Differences in Industrial Structure*, Yale University Press.

BALDWIN, R. E. (1966), *Economic Development and Export Growth: A Study of Northern Rhodesia 1920–60*, University of California Press.

BARLOW, E. R., and WENDER, I. T. (1955), *Foreign Investment and Taxation*, Prentice-Hall.

BEHRMAN, J. N. (1969), *Some Patterns in the Rise of the Multinational Enterprise*, Graduate School of Business, University of North Carolina.

BRASH, D. T. (1966), *American Investment in Australian Industry*, Australian National University Press.

BRECHER, I., and REISMAN, S. S. (1957), *Canada–United States Economic Relations*, Studies for Royal Commission on Canada's Economic Prospects, Ottawa.

BREWSTER, K. (1958), *Antitrust and American Business Abroad*, McGraw-Hill.

BURENSTAM-LINDER, S. (1961), *An Essay on Trade and Transformation*, Wiley.

CHAKRAVARTY, S. (1961), 'A structural study of international capital movement', *Economia internazionale*, vol. 14, pp. 377–402.

CHAMBERLIN, E. H. (1933), *The Theory of Monopolistic Competition*, Harvard University Press.

COMANOR, W. S., and WILSON, T. A. (1969), 'Advertising and the advantages of size', *Amer. econ. Rev.*, vol. 59, pp. 87–98.

CORDEN, W. M. (1967), 'Protection and foreign investment', *Econ. Rec.*, vol. 43, pp. 209–32.

39. Kindleberger (1969, pp. 107–10) and Stonehill (1965, pp. 151–2). For an excellent study of the effects of extractive foreign investment in a less-developed country, see R. E. Baldwin (1966).

CORDEN, W. M. (1969), 'The efficiency effects of trade and protection', Paper presented to Conference on International Trade, Monash University, 11–13 September.

DE CHAZEAU, M. G., and KAHN, A. E. (1959), *Integration and Competition in the Petroleum Industry*, Yale University Press.

DRÈZE, J. (1960), 'Quelques reflexions sereins sur l'adaptation de l'industrie Belge au Marché Commun', *Comptes rendues des Travaux de la Société Royale d'Economie Politique de Belgique*, no. 275.

DUESENBERRY, J. S. (1949), *Income, Saving and the Theory of Consumer Behavior*, Harvard University Press.

DUNNING, J. H. (1958), *American Investment in British Manufacturing Industry*, Allen & Unwin.

DUNNING, J. H. (1969), 'The role of American investment in the British economy', *PEP Broadsheet*, no. 507.

EASTMAN, H. C., and STYKOLT, S. (1967), *The Tariff and Competition in Canada*, Macmillan, Toronto.

EDWARDS, C. D. (1960), 'Size of markets, scale of firms and the character of competition', in E. A. G. Robinson (ed.), *Economic Consequences of the Size of Nations*, St Martin's Press.

ENGLISH, H. E. (1964), *Industrial Structure in Canada's International Competitive Position*, Canada Trade Committee Publications, Montreal.

FRANKEL, M. (1965), 'Home *v.* foreign investment: a case against capital export', *Kyklos*, vol. 18, pp. 411–33.

GATES, T. R., and LINDEN, F. (1961), *Cost and Competition: American Experience Abroad*, National Industrial Conference Board, New York.

GORDON, L., and GROMMERS, E. L. (1962), *United States Manufacturing Investment in Brazil: The Impact of Brazilian Government Policies, 1946–1960*, Harvard University Press.

GRUBER, W., MEHTA, D., and VERNON, R. (1967), 'The R & D factor in international trade and international investment of US industries', *J. polit. Econ.*, vol. 75, pp. 20–37.

HAMADA, K. (1966), 'Strategic aspects of taxation on foreign investment income', *Q. J. Econ.*, vol. 80, pp. 361–75.

HINES, H. H. (1957), 'Effectiveness of "entry" by already established firms', *Q. J. Econ.*, vol. 71, pp. 132–50.

HORST, T. O. (1969), 'A theoretical and empirical analysis of American exports and direct investment', unpublished Ph.D. dissertation, University of Rochester.

HYMER, S. H. (1960), 'International operations of national firms – a study of direct foreign investment', unpublished Ph.D. dissertation, Massachusetts Institute of Technology.

JOHNSON, H. G. (1968), *Comparative Cost and Commercial Policy Theory for a Developing World Economy*, Wicksell Lectures, Almqvist & Wiksell, Stockholm.

JOHNSON, H. G. (1970), 'The efficiency and welfare implications of the international corporation', in C. P. Kindleberger (ed.), *The International Corporation*, MIT Press.

JONES, R. M. (1968), 'The direction of industrial movement and its impact on recipient regions', *Manchester School*, vol. 36, pp. 149–72.

JONES, R. W. (1967), 'International capital movements and the theory of tariffs and trade', *Q. J. Econ.*, vol. 81, pp. 1–38.

JONES, R. W. (1971), 'A three-factor model in theory, trade and history', in J. Bhagwati (ed.), *Trade, Balance of Payments and Growth: Essays in Honour of C. P. Kindleberger*, Wiedenfeld, Amsterdam.

KEMP, M. C. (1966), 'The gains from international trade and investment: a neo-Heckscher–Ohlin approach', *Amer. econ. Rev.*, vol. 56, pp. 788–809.

KINDLEBERGER, C. P. (1969), *American Business Abroad*, Yale University Press.

KRAINER, R. E. (1967), 'Resource endowment and the structure of foreign investment', *J. Fin.*, vol. 22, pp. 49–57.

KRAUSE, L. B., and DAM, K. W. (1964), *Federal Tax Treatment of Foreign Income*, Brookings Institution, Washington, D.C.

LACROIX, R. (1970), 'Pour une théorie de l'investissement direct étranger dans l'industrie manufacturière', unpublished MS, University of Montreal.

MIKESELL, R. (ed.) (1962), *US Private and Government Investment Abroad*, Oregon University Press.

MODIGLIANI, F. (1958), 'New developments on the oligopoly front', *J. polit. Econ.*, vol. 66, pp. 215–32.

PENROSE, E. T. (1968), *The Large International Firm in Developing Countries: The International Petroleum Industry*, MIT Press.

REDDAWAY, W. B., POTTER, S. J., and TAYLOR, C. T. (1967–8), 'The effects of UK direct investment overseas: final report', *University of Cambridge, Department of Applied Economics, Occasional Paper*, no. 15.

REUBER, G. L., and ROSEMAN, F. (1969), 'The takeover of Canadian firms, 1945–61: an empirical analysis', *Economic Council of Canada, Special Study*, no. 10, Ottawa.

ROSENBLUTH, G. (1970), 'The relation between foreign control and concentration in Canadian industry', *Canad. J. Econ.*, vol. 3, pp. 14–30.

SAFARIAN, A. E. (1966), *Foreign Ownership of Canadian Industry*, McGraw-Hill.

SAFARIAN, A. E. (1969), *The Performance of Foreign-Owned Firms in Canada*, Canadian National Planning Association.

SCITOVSKY, T. (1960), 'International trade and economic integration as a means of overcoming the disadvantages of a small nation', in E. A. G. Robinson (ed.), *Economic Consequences of the Size of Nations*, St Martin's Press.

SERVAN-SCHREIBER, J. J. (1968), *The American Challenge*, Hamish Hamilton.

SHEARER, R. A. (1964), 'Nationality, size of firm and exploration for petroleum in Western Canada, 1946–1954', *Canad. J. Econ. polit. Sci.*, vol. 30, pp. 211–27.

STEUER, M. D. (1969), *American Capital and Free Trade: Effects of Integration*, Atlantic Trade Study, Trade Policy Research Centre.

STEUER, M. D., *et al.* (1970), 'The economic effects of inward investment in the United Kingdom: a preliminary report', unpublished Government document.

STEVENS, G. V. G. (1969), 'Fixed investment expenditures of foreign manufacturing affiliates of US firms: theoretical models and empirical evidence', *Yale econ. Ess.*, vol. 9, pp. 137–200.

STONEHILL, A. (1965), 'Foreign ownership in Norwegian enterprises', *Samfunnsokonomiske Studies*, no. 14, Oslo.

US DEPARTMENT OF COMMERCE (1960), *US Business Investments in Foreign Countries*, Office of Business Economics.

US SENATE (1967a), *International Aspects of Antitrust*, Hearings pursuant to S. Res. 191, Committee on the Judiciary, Subcommittee on Antitrust and Monopoly, Washington, DC.

US SENATE (1967b), *International Aspects of Antitrust*, Hearings pursuant to S. Res. 26, Committee on the Judiciary, Subcommittee on Antitrust and Monopoly, Washington, DC.

VERNON, R. (1966), 'International investment and international trade in the product cycle', *Q. J. Econ.*, vol. 80, pp. 190–207.

WELLS, L. T., Jr (1969), 'Test of a product cycle model of international trade: US exports of consumer durables', *Q. J. Econ.*, vol. 83, pp. 152–63.

WHEELWRIGHT, E. L. (1963), 'Overseas investment in Australia', in A. Hunter (ed.), *The Economics of Australian Industry*, Melbourne University Press.

Part Five
Foreign Investment, Trade and the Balance of Payments

For many years it has been clear that a close relationship exists between foreign investment and trade. Cairncross (1953), Hobson (1914) and others have explored the nature of this relationship for the nineteenth century, and the fact that a quarter of the manufacturing exports of the US and UK firms are now dispatched to their foreign affiliates gives some idea of the current linkages. In his contribution (Reading 12), Raymond Vernon traces a possible theory explaining the relationship between trade and investment within particular industries; his essay also sheds some light on the evolution of foreign direct investment in a world economy strongly dominated by technology, yet where there are barriers to the free trade in goods.

The other contributions in this Part are concerned with assessing the effects of inward or outward investment on a country's balance of payments and economic welfare. David Robertson (Reading 13) discusses the trade effects associated with overseas direct investments including export generation, import generation and export displacement. He also summarizes the research findings of Hufbauer and Adler (1968) and Reddaway, Potter and Taylor (1967–8). This subject continues to fascinate economists as witnessed by major research projects now being conducted by the National Bureau of Economic Research and the US Tariff Commission.

Reading 14 by Snider is a timely reminder that no answer of use to policy can be separated from examining alternative ways of tackling the balance of payments problem. Indeed, some economists refuse to recognize that the effect of foreign investment on the balance of payments is a relevant question to ask. According to them, the only important economic issue at stake is its impact on national real income; any adverse balance of payments repercussions should be put right by policies least damaging to this goal, and quite independently of the cause of these repercussions. Nevertheless, it is useful to be able to value the trade-off between balance of payments and income goals; and also the timing of balance of payments effects. Studies by Moffat (1967), Penner (1966) and Steuer *et al.* (1970) acknowledge this. Each of these indicate that income effects of inward investment far outweigh the direct balance of payments effects and that any attempt to relate inward capital to outflow of profits and dividends (as some of the developing countries are inclined to do) can give seriously misleading answers.

References

CAIRNCROSS, A. K. (1953), *Home and Foreign Investment, 1870–1913*, Cambridge University Press.

HOBSON, C. K. (1914), *The Export of Capital*, Constable, reissued 1963.

HUFBAUER, G. C., and ADLER, F. M. (1968), 'Overseas manufacturing investment and the US balance of payments', *US Treasury Tax Research Policy Document*, no. 1.

MOFFATT, G. G. (1967), 'The foreign ownership and balance of payments effects of direct investment from abroad', *Austral. econ. Pap.*, vol. 6, pp. 1–24.

PENNER, R. G. (1966), 'The benefits of foreign investment in Canada, 1950/56', *Canad. J. Econ.*, vol. 32, pp. 172–83.

REDDAWAY, W. B., POTTER, S. J., and TAYLOR, C. T. (1967–8), 'The effects of UK direct investment overseas: final report', *University of Cambridge, Department of Applied Economics, Occasional Paper*, no. 15.

STEUER, M. D., *et al.* (1970), 'The economic effects of inward investment in the United Kingdom: a preliminary report', unpublished Government document.

12 Raymond Vernon

International Investment and International Trade in the Product Cycle[1]

Raymond Vernon, 'International investment and international trade in the product cycle', *Quarterly Journal of Economics*, vol. 80, 1966, pp. 190–207.

Anyone who has sought to understand the shifts in international trade and international investment over the past twenty years has chafed from time to time under an acute sense of the inadequacy of the available analytical tools. While the comparative cost concept and other basic concepts have rarely failed to provide some help, they have usually carried the analyst only a very little way toward adequate understanding. For the most part, it has been necessary to formulate new concepts in order to explore issues such as the strengths and limitations of import substitution in the development process, the implications of common market arrangements for trade and investment, the underlying reasons for the Leontief paradox, and other critical issues of the day.

As theorists have groped for some more efficient tools, there has been a flowering in international trade and capital theory. But the very proliferation of theory has increased the urgency of the search for unifying concepts. It is doubtful that we shall find many propositions that can match the simplicity, power and universality of application of the theory of comparative advantage and the international equilibrating mechanism; but unless the search for better tools goes on, the usefulness of economic theory for the solution of problems in international trade and capital movements will probably decline.

The present paper deals with one promising line of generalization and synthesis which seems to me to have been somewhat neglected by the main stream of trade theory. It puts less emphasis

1. The preparation of this article was financed in part by a grant from the Ford Foundation to the Harvard Business School to support a study of the implications of United States foreign direct investment. This paper is a by-product of the hypothesis-building stage of the study.

upon comparative cost doctrine and more upon the timing of innovation, the effects of scale economies, and the roles of ignorance and uncertainty in influencing trade patterns. It is an approach with respectable sponsorship, deriving bits and pieces of its inspiration from the writings of such persons as Burenstam-Linder (1961), Hoffmeyer (1958), Kindleberger (1950), MacDougall (1957) and Williams (1929).

Emphasis of this sort seems first to have appeared when economists were searching for an explanation of what looked like a persistent, structural shortage of dollars in the world. When the shortage proved ephemeral in the late 1950s, many of the ideas which the shortage had stimulated were tossed overboard as prima facie wrong.[2] Nevertheless, one cannot be exposed to the main currents of international trade for very long without feeling that any theory which neglected the roles of innovation, scale, ignorance and uncertainty would be incomplete.

Location of new products

We begin with the assumption that the enterprises in any one of the advanced countries of the world are not distinguishably different from those in any other advanced country, in terms of their access to scientific knowledge and their capacity to comprehend scientific principles.[3] All of them, we may safely assume, can secure access to the knowledge that exists in the physical, chemical and biological sciences. These sciences at times may be difficult, but they are rarely occult.

It is a mistake to assume, however, that equal access to scientific principles in all the advanced countries means equal probability of the application of these principles in the generation of new products. There is ordinarily a large gap between the knowledge of a scientific principle and the embodiment of the principle in a marketable product. An entrepreneur usually has

2. The best summary of the state of trade theory that has come to my attention in recent years is Bhagwati (1964). He refers obliquely to some theories which concern us here; but they receive much less attention than I think they deserve.

3. Some of the account that follows will be found in greatly truncated form in Vernon (1962). The elaboration here owes a good deal to the perceptive work of Hirsch (1965).

to intervene to accept the risks involved in testing whether the gap can be bridged.

If all entrepreneurs, wherever located, could be presumed to be equally conscious of and equally responsive to all entrepreneurial opportunities, wherever they arose, the classical view of the dominant role of price in resource allocation might be highly relevant. There is good reason to believe, however, that the entrepreneur's consciousness of and responsiveness to opportunity are a function of ease of communication; and further, that ease of communication is a function of geographical proximity.[4] Accordingly, we abandon the powerful simplifying notion that knowledge is a universal free good and introduce it as an independent variable in the decision to trade or to invest.

The fact that the search for knowledge is an inseparable part of the decision-making process and that relative ease of access to knowledge can profoundly affect the outcome are now reasonably well established through empirical research (see, e.g., Aharoni, 1966; Cyert and March, 1963, esp. ch. 6). One implication of that fact is that producers in any market are more likely to be aware of the possibility of introducing new products in that market than producers located elsewhere would be.

The United States market offers certain unique kinds of opportunities to those who are in a position to be aware of them.

First, the United States market consists of consumers with an average income which is higher (except for a few anomalies like Kuwait) than that in any other national market – twice as high as that of Western Europe, for instance. Wherever there was a chance to offer a new product responsive to wants at high levels of income, this chance would presumably first be apparent to someone in a position to observe the United States market.

Second, the United States market is characterized by high unit labor costs and relatively unrationed capital compared with practically all other markets. This is a fact which conditions the demand for both consumer goods and industrial products. In the case of consumer goods, for instance, the high cost of laundresses

4. Note C. P. Kindleberger's (1962, p. 15 *passim*) reference to the 'horizon' of the decision maker, and the view that he can only be rational within that horizon.

contributes to the origins of the drip-dry shirt and the home washing machine. In the case of industrial goods, high labor cost leads to the early development and use of the conveyor belt, the fork-lift truck and the automatic control system. It seems to follow that wherever there was a chance successfully to sell a new product responsive to the need to conserve labor, this chance would be apparent first to those in a position to observe the United States market.

Assume, then, that entrepreneurs in the United States are first aware of opportunities to satisfy new wants associated with high income levels or high unit labor costs. Assume further that the evidence of an unfilled need and the hope of some kind of monopoly windfall for the early starter both are sufficiently strong to justify the initial investment that is usually involved in converting an abstract idea into a marketable product. Here we have a reason for expecting a consistently higher rate of expenditure on product development to be undertaken by United States producers than by producers in other countries, at least in lines which promise to substitute capital for labor or which promise to satisfy high-income wants. Therefore, if United States firms spend more than their foreign counterparts on new product development (often misleadingly labeled 'research'), this may be due not to some obscure sociological drive for innovation but to more effective communication between the potential market and the potential supplier of the market. This sort of explanation is consistent with the pioneer appearance in the United States (conflicting claims of the Soviet Union notwithstanding) of the sewing machine, the typewriter, the tractor, etc.

At this point in the exposition, it is important once more to emphasize that the discussion so far relates only to innovation in certain kinds of products, namely to those associated with high income and those which substitute capital for labor. Our hypothesis says nothing about industrial innovation in general; this is a larger subject than we have tackled here. There are very few countries that have failed to introduce at least a few products; and there are some, such as Germany and Japan, which have been responsible for a considerable number of such introductions. Germany's outstanding successes in the development and use of plastics may have been due, for instance, to a traditional concern with her lack of a raw materials base and a recognition that a market might exist in Germany for synthetic substitutes.[5]

Our hypothesis asserts that United States producers are likely to be the first to spy an opportunity for high-income or labor-saving new products.[6] But it goes on to assert that the first producing facilities for such products will be located in the United States. This is not a self-evident proposition. Under the calculus of least cost, production need not automatically take place at a location close to the market, unless the product can be produced and delivered from that location at lowest cost. Besides, now that most major United States companies control facilities situated in one or more locations outside of the United States, the possibility of considering a non-United States location is even more plausible than it might once have been.

Of course, if prospective producers were to make their locational choices on the basis of least-cost considerations, the United States would not always be ruled out. The costs of international transport and United States import duties, for instance, might be so high as to argue for such a location. My guess is, however, that the early producers of a new product intended for the United States market are attracted to a United States location by forces which are far stronger than relative factor-cost and transport considerations. For the reasoning on this point, one has to take a long detour away from comparative cost analysis into areas which fall under the rubrics of communication and external economies.

By now, a considerable amount of empirical work has been done on the factors affecting the location of industry.[7] Many of these studies try to explain observed locational patterns in conventional cost-minimizing terms, by implicit or explicit reference

5. See two excellent studies: Freeman (1963, pp. 22 ff.) and Hufbauer (1965). A number of links in the Hufbauer arguments are remarkably similar to some in this paper; but he was not aware of my writings nor I of his until after both had been completed.

6. There is a kind of first-cousin relationship between this simple notion and the 'entrained want' concept defined by H. G. Barnett (1953, p. 148). Albert O. Hirschman (1958, p. 68) also finds the concept helpful in his effort to explain certain aspects of economic development.

7. For a summary of such work, together with a useful bibliography, see John Meyer (1963).

to labor cost and transportation cost. But some explicitly introduce problems of communication and external economies as powerful locational forces. These factors were given special emphasis in the analyses which were a part of the New York Metropolitan Region Study of the 1950s. At the risk of over-simplifying, I shall try to summarize what these studies suggested.[8]

In the early stages of introduction of a new product, producers were usually confronted with a number of critical, albeit transitory, conditions. For one thing, the product itself may be quite unstandardized for a time; its inputs, its processing and its final specifications may cover a wide range. Contrast the great variety of automobiles produced and marketed before 1910 with the thoroughly standardized product of the 1930s or the variegated radio designs of the 1920s with the uniform models of the 1930s. The unstandardized nature of the design at this early stage carries with it a number of locational implications.

First, producers at this stage are particularly concerned with the degree of freedom they have in changing their inputs. Of course, the cost of the inputs is also relevant. But as long as the nature of these inputs cannot be fixed in advance with assurance, the calculation of cost must take into account the general need for flexibility in any locational choice.[9]

Second, the price elasticity of demand for the output of individual firms is comparatively low. This follows from the high degree of production differentiation or the existence of monopoly in the early stages.[10] One result is, of course, that small cost differences count less in the calculations of the entrepreneur than they are likely to count later on.

Third, the need for swift and effective communication on the

8. The points that follow are dealt with at length in the following publications: Hall (1959, pp. 3–18, 19 *passim*), Lichtenberg (1960, pp. 31–70) and Vernon (1960, pp. 38–85).

9. This is, of course, a familiar point elaborated in George F. Stigler (1939, pp. 305 ff.).

10. Hufbauer (1965) suggests that the low price elasticity of demand in the first stage may be due simply to the fact that the first market may be a 'captive market' unresponsive to price changes; but that later, in order to expand the use of the new product, other markets may be brought in which are more price responsive.

part of the producer with customers, suppliers and even competitors is especially high at this stage. This is a corollary of the fact that a considerable amount of uncertainty remains regarding the ultimate dimensions of the market, the efforts of rivals to preempt that market, the specifications of the inputs needed for production and the specifications of the products likely to be most successful in the effort.

All of these considerations tend to argue for a location in which communication between the market and the executives directly concerned with the new product is swift and easy, and in which a wide variety of potential types of input that might be needed by the production unit are easily come by. In brief, the producer who sees a market for some new product in the United States may be led to select a United States location for production on the basis of national locational considerations which extend well beyond simple factor cost analysis plus transport considerations.

The maturing product[11]

As the demand for a product expands, a certain degree of standardization usually takes place. This is not to say that efforts at product differentiation come to an end. On the contrary; such efforts may even intensify, as competitors try to avoid the full brunt of price competition. Moreover, variety may appear as a result of specialization. Radios, for instance, ultimately acquired such specialized forms as clock radios, automobile radios, portable radios, and so on. Nevertheless, though the subcategories may multiply and the efforts at product differentiation increase, a growing acceptance of certain general standards seems to be typical.

Once again, the change has locational implications. First of all, the need for flexibility declines. A commitment to some set of product standards opens up technical possibilities for achieving economies of scale through mass output, and encourages long-term commitments to some given process and some fixed set of facilities. Second, concern about production cost begins to take the place of concern about product characteristics. Even if

11. Both Freeman (1963) and Hirsch (1965) make use of a three-stage product classification of the sort used here.

increased price competition is not yet present, the reduction of the uncertainties surrounding the operation enhances the usefulness of cost projections and increases the attention devoted to cost.

The empirical studies to which I referred earlier suggest that, at this stage in an industry's development, there is likely to be considerable shift in the location of production facilities at least as far as internal United States locations are concerned. The empirical materials on international location shifts simply have not yet been analysed sufficiently to tell us very much. A little speculation, however, indicates some hypotheses worth testing.

Picture an industry engaged in the manufacture of the high-income or labor-saving products that are the focus of our discussion. Assume that the industry had begun to settle down in the United States to some degree of large-scale production. Although the first mass market may be located in the United States, some demand for the product begins almost at once to appear elsewhere. For instance, although heavy fork-lift trucks in general may have a comparatively small market in Spain because of the relative cheapness of unskilled labor in that country, some limited demand for the product will appear there almost as soon as the existence of the product is known.

If the product has a high income elasticity of demand or if it is a satisfactory substitute for high-cost labor, the demand in time will begin to grow quite rapidly in relatively advanced countries such as those of Western Europe. Once the market expands in such an advanced country, entrepreneurs will begin to ask themselves whether the time has come to take the risk of setting up a local producing facility.[12]

How long does it take to reach this stage? An adequate answer must surely be a complex one. Producers located in the United States, weighing the wisdom of setting up a new production facility in the importing country, will feel obliged to balance a number of

12. M. V. Posner (1961, pp. 323 ff.) presents a stimulating model purporting to explain such familiar trade phenomena as the exchange of machine tools between the United Kingdom and Germany. In the process he offers some particularly helpful notions concerning the size of the 'imitation lag' in the responses of competing nations.

complex considerations. As long as the marginal production cost plus the transport cost of the goods exported from the United States is lower than the average cost of prospective production in the market of import, United States producers will presumably prefer to avoid an investment. But that calculation depends on the producer's ability to project the cost of production in a market in which factor costs and the appropriate technology differ from those at home.

Now and again, the locational force which determined some particular overseas investment is so simple and so powerful that one has little difficulty in identifying it. Otis Elevator's early proliferation of production facilities abroad was quite patently a function of the high cost of shipping assembled elevator cabins to distant locations and the limited scale advantages involved in manufacturing elevator cabins at a single location (Phelps, 1963, p. 4). Singer's decision to invest in Scotland as early as 1867 was also based on considerations of a sort sympathetic with our hypothesis.[13] It is not unlikely that the overseas demand for its highly standardized product was already sufficiently large at that time to exhaust the obvious scale advantages of manufacturing in a single location, especially if that location was one of high labor cost.

In an area as complex and 'imperfect' as international trade and investment, however, one ought not anticipate that any hypothesis will have more than a limited explanatory power. United States airplane manufacturers surely respond to many 'noneconomic' locational forces, such as the desire to play safe in problems of military security. Producers in the United States who have a protected patent position overseas presumably take that fact into account in deciding whether or when to produce abroad. And other producers often are motivated by considerations too complex to reconstruct readily, such as the fortuitous timing of a threat of new competition in the country of import, the level of tariff protection anticipated for the future, the political situation in the country of prospective investment, and so on.

We arrive, then, at the stage which United States producers

13. John H. Dunning (1958, p. 18). The Dunning book is filled with observations that lend casual support to the main hypotheses of this paper.

have come around to the establishment of production units in the advanced countries. Now a new group of forces are set in train. In an idealized form, Figure 1 suggests what may be anticipated next.

As far as individual United States producers are concerned, the local markets thenceforth will be filled from local production units set up abroad. Once these facilities are in operation, however, more ambitious possibilities for their use may be suggested. When comparing a United States producing facility and a facility in another advanced country, the obvious production–cost differences between the rival producing areas are usually differences due to scale and differences due to labor costs. If the producer is an international firm with producing locations in several countries, its costs of financing capital at the different locations may not be sufficiently different to matter very much. If economies of scale are being fully exploited, the principal differences between any two locations are likely to be labor costs.[14] Accordingly, it may prove wise for the international firm to begin servicing third-country markets from the new location. And if labor-cost differences are large enough to offset transport costs, then exports back to the United States may become a possibility as well.

Any hypotheses based on the assumption that the United States entrepreneur will react rationally when offered the possibility of a lower-cost location abroad is, of course, somewhat suspect. The decision-making sequence that is used in connection with international investments, according to various empirical studies, is not a model of the rational process.[15] But there is one theme that emerges again and again in such studies. Any threat to the established position of an enterprise is a powerful galvanizing force to action; in fact, if I interpret the empirical work correctly, threat in general is a more reliable stimulus to action than opportunity is likely to be.

In the international investment field, threats appear in various

14. Note the interesting finding of Mordecai Kreinin (1965). Kreinin finds that the higher cost of labor in the United States is not explained by a higher rate of labor productivity in this country.

15. Aharoni (1966) provides an excellent summary and exhaustive bibliography of the evidence on this point.

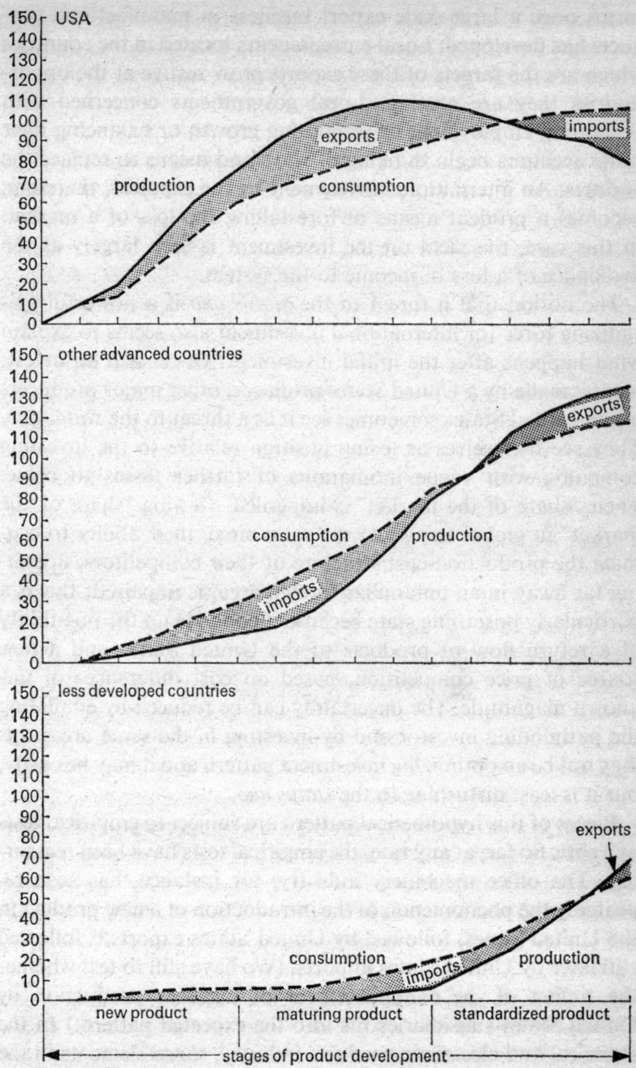
150
140
130
120
110
100
90
80
70
60
50
40
30
20
10
0
USA
production
exports
consumption
imports
150
140
130
120
110
100
90
80
70
60
50
40
30
20
10
0
other advanced countries
consumption
production
imports
exports
150
140
130
120
110
100
90
80
70
60
50
40
30
20
10
0
less developed countries
consumption
production
imports
exports
new product
maturing product
standardized product
stages of product development

Figure 1

forms once a large-scale export business in manufactured products has developed. Local entrepreneurs located in the countries which are the targets of these exports grow restive at the opportunities they are missing. Local governments concerned with generating employment or promoting growth or balancing their trade accounts begin thinking of ways and means to replace the imports. An international investment by the exporter, therefore, becomes a prudent means of forestalling the loss of a market. In this case, the yield on the investment is seen largely as the avoidance of a loss of income to the system.

The notion that a threat to the *status quo* is a powerful galvanizing force for international investment also seems to explain what happens after the initial investment. Once such an investment is made by a United States producer, other major producers in the United States sometimes see it as a threat to the *status quo*. They see themselves as losing position relative to the investing company, with vague intimations of further losses to come. Their 'share of the market' is imperiled, viewing 'share of the market' in global terms. At the same time, their ability to estimate the production-cost structure of their competitors, operating far away in an unfamiliar foreign area, is impaired; this is a particularly unsettling state because it conjures up the possibility of a return flow of products to the United States and a new source of price competition, based on cost differences of unknown magnitude. The uncertainty can be reduced by emulating the pathfinding investor and by investing in the same area; this may not be an optimizing investment pattern and it may be costly, but it is least disturbing to the *status quo*.

Pieces of this hypothetical pattern are subject to empirical tests of a sort. So far, at any rate, the empirical tests have been reassuring. The office machinery industry, for instance, has seen repeatedly the phenomenon of the introduction of a new product in the United States, followed by United States exports,[16] followed still later by United States imports. (We have still to test whether the timing of the commencement of overseas production by United States subsidiaries fits into the expected pattern.) In the electrical and electronic products industry, those elements in the pattern which can be measured show up nicely (Hirsch, 1965). A

16. Reported in US Senate (1960, pp. 130–39).

broader effort is now under way to test the United States trade patterns of a group of products with high-income elasticities; and here, too, the preliminary results are encouraging.[17] On a much more general basis, it is reassuring for our hypotheses to observe that the foreign manufacturing subsidiaries of United States firms have been increasing their exports to third countries.

It will have occurred to the reader by now that the pattern envisaged here also may shed some light on the Leontief paradox (Leontief, 1953, 1956). Leontief, it will be recalled, seemed to confound comparative cost theory by establishing the fact that the ratio of capital to labor in United States exports was lower, not higher, than the like ratio in the United States production which had been displaced by competitive imports. The hypothesis suggested in this paper would have the United States exporting high-income and labor-saving products in the early stages of their existence and importing them later on[18]. In the early stages, the value-added contribution of industries engaged in producing these items probably contains an unusually high proportion of labor cost. This is not so much because the labor is particularly skilled, as is so often suggested. More likely, it is due to a quite different phenomenon. At this stage, the standardization of the manufacturing process has not gotten very far; that is to come later, when the volume of output is high enough and the degree of uncertainty low enough to justify investment in relatively inflexible, capital-intensive facilities. As a result, the production process relies relatively heavily on labor inputs at a time when the United States commands an export position; and the process relies more heavily on capital at a time when imports become important.

This, of course, is an hypothesis which has not yet been sub-

17. These appear in a doctoral thesis at the Harvard Business School by Louis T. Wells, (1966.)

18. Of course, if there were some systematic trend in the inputs of new products – for example, if the new products which appeared in the 1960s were more capital-intensive than the new products which appeared in the 1950s – then the tendencies suggested by our hypotheses might be swamped by such a trend. As long as we do not posit offsetting systematic patterns of this sort, however, the Leontief findings and the hypotheses offered here seem consistent.

jected to any really rigorous test. But it does open up a line of inquiry into the structure of United States trade which is well worth pursuing.

The standardized product

Figure 1, the reader will have observed, carries a panel which suggests that, at an advanced stage in the standardization of some products, the less-developed countries may offer competitive advantages as a production location.

This is a bold projection, which seems on first blush to be wholly at variance with the Heckscher–Ohlin theorem. According to that theorem, one presumably ought to anticipate that the exports of the less-developed countries would tend to be relatively labor-intensive products.

One of the difficulties with the theorem, however, is that it leaves marketing considerations out of account. One reason for the omission is evident. As long as knowledge is regarded as a free good, instantaneously available, and as long as individual producers are regarded as atomistic contributors to the total supply, marketing problems cannot be expected to find much of a place in economic theory. In projecting the patterns of export from less-developed areas, however, we cannot afford to disregard the fact that information comes at a cost; and that entrepreneurs are not readily disposed to pay the price of investigating overseas markets of unknown dimensions and unknown promise. Neither are they eager to venture into situations which they know will demand a constant flow of reliable marketing information from remote sources.

If we can assume that highly standardized products tend to have a well-articulated, easily accessible international market and to sell largely on the basis of price (an assumption inherent in the definition), then it follows that such products will not pose the problem of market information quite so acutely for the less-developed countries. This establishes a necessary if not a sufficient condition for investment in such industries.

Of course, foreign investors seeking an optimum location for a captive facility may not have to concern themselves too much with questions of market information; presumably, they are thoroughly familiar with the marketing end of the business and are looking for a low-cost captive source of supply. In that case, the low cost of labor may be the initial attraction drawing the investor to less-developed areas. But other limitations in such areas, according to our hypothesis, will bias such captive operations toward the production of standardized items. The reasons in this case turn on the part played in the production process by external economies. Manufacturing processes which receive significant inputs from the local economy, such as skilled labor, repairmen, reliable power, spare parts, industrial materials processed according to exacting specifications, and so on, are less appropriate to the less-developed areas than those that do not have such requirements. Unhappily, most industrial processes require one or another ingredient of this difficult sort. My guess is, however, that the industries which produce a standardized product are in the best position to avoid the problem, by producing on a vertically integrated self-sustaining basis.

In speculating about future industrial exports from the less-developed areas, therefore, we are led to think of products with a fairly clear-cut set of economic characteristics.[19] Their production function is such as to require significant inputs of labor; otherwise there is no reason to expect a lower production cost in less-developed countries. At the same time, they are products with a high price elasticity of demand for the output of individual firms; otherwise, there is no strong incentive to take the risks of pioneering with production in a new area. In addition, products whose production process did not rely heavily upon external economies would be more obvious candidates than those which required a more elaborate industrial environment. The implications of remoteness also would be critical; products which could be precisely described by standardized specifications and which could be produced for inventory without fear of obsolescence would be more relevant than those which had less precise specifications and which could not easily be ordered from remote locations. Moreover, high-value items capable of absorbing significant freight costs would be more likely to appear than bulky items low in value by weight. Standardized textile products are, of course, the illustration *par excellence* of the sort of product

19. The concepts sketched out here are presented in more detail in Vernon(1963).

that meets the criterion, but other products come to mind such as crude steel, simple fertilizers, newsprint, and so on.

Speculation of this sort draws some support from various interregional experiences in industrial location. In the United States, for example, the 'export' industries which moved to the low-wage south in search of lower costs tended to be industries which had no great need for a sophisticated industrial environment and which produced fairly standardized products. In the textile industry, it was the grey goods, cotton sheetings and men's shirt plants that went south; producers of high-style dresses or other unstandardized items were far more reluctant to move. In the electronics industry, it was the mass producers of tubes, resistors and other standardized high-volume components that showed the greatest disposition to move south; custom-built and research-oriented production remained closer to markets and to the main industrial complexes. A similar pattern could be discerned in printing and in chemicals production.[20]

In other countries, a like pattern is suggested by the impressionistic evidence. The underdeveloped south of Italy and the laggard north of Britain and Ireland both seem to be attracting industry with standardized output and self-sufficient process.[21]

Once we begin to look for relevant evidence of such investment patterns in the less-developed countries proper, however, only the barest shreds of corroboratory information can be found. One would have difficulty in thinking of many cases in which manufacturers of standardized products in the more advanced countries had made significant investments in the less-developed countries with a view of exporting such products from those countries. To be sure, other types of foreign investment are not uncommon in the less-developed countries, such as investments

20. This conclusion derives largely from the industry studies conducted in connection with the New York Metropolitan Region study. There have been some excellent more general analyses of shifts in industrial location among the regions of the United States. See e.g., Victor R. Fuchs (1962). Unfortunately, however, none has been designed, so far as I know, to test hypotheses relating locational shifts to product characteristics such as price elasticity of demand and degree of standardization.

21. This statement, too, is based on only impressionistic materials. Among the more suggestive, illustrative of the best of the available evidence, see J. N. Toothill (1962).

in import-replacing industries which were made in the face of a threat of import restriction. But there are only a few export-oriented cases, similar to that of Taiwan's foreign-owned electronics plants and Argentina's new producing facility, set up to manufacture and export standard sorting equipment for computers.

If we look to foreign trade patterns, rather than foreign investment patterns, to learn something about the competitive advantage of the less-developed countries, the possibility that they are an attractive locus for the output of standardized products gains slightly more support. The Taiwanese and Japanese trade performances are perhaps the most telling ones in support of the projected pattern; both countries have managed to develop significant overseas markets for standardized manufactured products. According to one major study of the subject (a study stimulated by the Leontief paradox), Japanese exports are more capital-intensive than is the Japanese production which is displaced by imports (Tatemoto and Ichimura, 1959); this is what one might expect if the hypothetical patterns suggested by Figure 1 were operational. Apart from these cases, however, all that one sees are a few provocative successes such as some sporadic sales of newsprint from Pakistan, the successful export of sewing machines from India, and so on. Even in these cases, one cannot be sure that they are consistent with the hypothesis unless he has done a good deal more empirical investigation.

The reason why so few revelant cases come to mind may be that the process has not yet advanced far enough. Or it may be that such factors as extensive export constraints and overvalued exchange rates are combining to prevent the investment and exports that otherwise would occur.

If there is one respect in which this discussion may deviate from classical expectations, it is in the view that the overall scarcity of capital in the less-developed countries will not prevent investment in facilities for the production of standardized products.

There are two reasons why capital costs may not prove a barrier to such investment.

First, according to our hypotheses, the investment will occur in industries which require some significant labor inputs in the production process; but they will be concentrated in that subsector of the industry which produces highly standardized products capable of self-contained production establishments. The net of these specifications is indeterminate so far as capital-intensiveness is concerned. A standardized textile item may be more or less capital-intensive than a plant for unstandardized petrochemicals.

Besides, even if the capital requirements for a particular plant are heavy, the cost of the capital need not prove a bar. The assumption that capital costs come high in the less-developed countries requires a number of fundamental qualifications. The reality, to the extent that it is known, is more complex.

One reason for this complexity is the role played by the international investor. Producers of chemical fertilizers, when considering whether to invest in a given country, may be less concerned with the going rate for capital in that country than with their opportunity costs as they see such costs. For such investors the alternatives to be weighed are not the full range of possibilities calling for capital but only a very restricted range of alternatives, such as the possibilities offered by chemical fertilizer investment elsewhere. The relevant capital cost for a chemical fertilizer plant, therefore, may be fairly low if the investor is an international entrepreneur.

Moreover, the assumption that finance capital is scarce and that interest rates are high in a less-developed country may prove inapplicable to the class of investors who concern us here.[22] The capital markets of the less-developed countries typically consist of a series of water-tight, insulated, submarkets in which wholly different rates prevail and between which arbitrage opportunities are limited. In some countries, the going figures may vary from 5 to 40 per cent, on grounds which seem to have little relation to issuer risk or term of loan. (In some economies, where inflation is endemic, interest rates which in effect represent a negative real cost are not uncommon.)

These internal differences in interest rates may be due to a number of factors: the fact that funds generated inside the firm

22. See George Rosen (1958). Rosen finds that in the period studied, from 1937 to 1953, 'there was no serious shortage of capital for the largest firms in India'. Gustav F. Papanek (1967) makes a similar finding for Pakistan for the period from 1950 to 1964.

usually are exposed to a different yield test than external borrowings; the fact that government loans are often floated by mandatory levies on banks and other intermediaries; and the fact that funds borrowed by governments from international sources are often reloaned in domestic markets at rates which are linked closely to the international borrowing rate, however irrelevant that may be. Moreover, one has to reckon with the fact that public international lenders tend to lend at near-uniform rates, irrespective of the identity of the borrower and the going interest rate in his country. Access to capital on the part of underdeveloped countries, therefore, becomes a direct function of the country's capacity to propose plausible projects to public international lenders. If a project can plausibly be shown to 'pay its own way' in balance of payment and output terms at 'reasonable' interest rates, the largest single obstacle to obtaining capital at such rates has usually been overcome.

Accordingly, one may say that from the entrepreneur's viewpoint certain systematic and predictable 'imperfections' of the capital markets may reduce or eliminate the capital-shortage handicap which is characteristic of the less-developed countries; and, further, that as a result of the reduction or elimination such countries may find themselves in a position to compete effectively in the export of certain standardized capital-intensive goods. This is not the statement of another paradox; it is not the same as to say that the capital-poor countries will develop capital-intensive economies. All we are concerned with here is a modest fraction of the industry of such countries, which in turn is a minor fraction of their total economic activity. It may be that the anomalies such industries represent are systematic enough to be included in our normal expectations regarding conditions in the less-developed countries.

Like other observations which have preceded, these views about the likely patterns of exports by the less-developed countries are attempts to relax some of the constraints imposed by purer and simpler models. Here and there, the hypotheses take on plausibility because they jibe with the record of past events. But, for the most part, they are still speculative in nature, having been subjected to tests of a very low order of rigorousness. What is needed, obviously, is continued probing to determine whether the 'imperfections' stressed so strongly in these pages deserve to be elevated out of the footnotes into the main text of economic theory.

References

AHARONI, Y. (1966), *The Foreign Investment Decision Process*, Harvard University Press.

BARNETT, H. G. (1953), *Innovation: The Basis of Cultural Change*, McGraw-Hill.

BHAGWATI, J. (1964), 'The pure theory of international trade', *Econ. J.*, vol. 74, pp. 1–84.

BURENSTAM-LINDER, S. (1961), *An Essay on Trade and Transformation*, Wiley.

CYERT, R. M., and MARCH, J. G. (1963), *A Behavioral Theory of the Firm*, Prentice-Hall.

DUNNING, J. H. (1958), *American Investment in British Manufacturing Industry*, Allen & Unwin.

FREEMAN, C. (1963), 'The plastics industry; a comparative study of research and innovation', *Nat. Inst. econ. Rev.*, vol. 26, pp. 22–62.

FUCHS, V. R. (1962), *Changes in the Location of Manufacturing in the United States since 1929*, Yale University Press.

HALL, M. (ed.) (1959), *Made in New York*, Harvard University Press.

HIRSCH, S. (1965), *Location of Industry and International Competitiveness*, Harvard Business School.

HIRSCHMAN, A. O. (1958), *The Strategy of Economic Development*, Yale University Press.

HOFFMEYER, E. (1958), *Dollar Shortage*, North-Holland Publishing Co.

HUFBAUER, G. C. (1965), *Synthetic Materials and the Theory of International Trade*, Duckworth.

KINDLEBERGER, C. P. (1950), *The Dollar Shortage*, Wiley.

KINDLEBERGER, C. P. (1962), *Foreign Trade and the National Economy*, Yale University Press.

KREININ, M. (1965), 'The Leontief scarce-factor paradox', *Amer. econ. Rev.*, vol. 55, pp. 131–9.

LEONTIEF, W. (1953), 'Domestic production and foreign trade: the American capital position re-examined', *Proc. Amer. Phil. Soc.*, vol. 97, pp. 332–49.

LEONTIEF, W. (1956), 'Factor proportions and the structure of American trade: further theoretical and empirical analysis', *Rev. Econ. Stat.*, vol. 38, pp. 386–407.

LICHTENBERG, R. M. (1960), *One-Tenth of a Nation*, Harvard University Press.

MACDOUGALL, D. M. (1957), *The World Dollar Problem*, Macmillan.

MEYER, J. (1963), 'Regional economics: a survey', *Amer. econ. Rev.*, vol. 53, pp. 19–54.

PAPANEK, G. F. (1967), *Pakistan's Development: Social Goals and Private Incentives*, Harvard University Press.
PHELPS, D. M. (1963), *Migration of Industry to South America*, McGraw-Hill.
POSNER, M. V. (1961), 'International trade and technical change', *Oxf. econ. Pap.*, vol. 13, pp. 323–41.
ROSEN, G. (1958), *Industrial Change in India*, Free Press.
STIGLER, G. F. (1939), 'Production and distribution in the short run', *J. polit. Econ.*, vol. 47, pp. 305–27.
TATEMOTO, M., and ICHIMURA, S. (1959), 'Factor proportions and foreign trade: the case of Japan', *Rev. Econ. Stat.*, vol. 41, pp. 442–6.
TOOTHILL, J. N. (1962), *Inquiry into the Scottish Economy*, Scottish Council.
US SENATE (1960), *Hearings on Foreign Commerce*, Interstate and Foreign Commerce Committee.
VERNON, R. (1960), *Metropolis, 1985*, Harvard University Press.
VERNON, R. (1962), 'The Trade Expansion Act in perspective', in *Emerging Concepts in Marketing*, American Marketing Association, pp. 384–9.
VERNON, R. (1963), *Problems and Prospects in the Export of Manufactured Products from the Less-Developed Countries*, UN Conference on Trade and Development, 16 December (mimeographed).
WELLS, L. T. (1966), 'Product innovation and direction of International trade', unpublished doctoral thesis, Harvard Business School.
WILLIAMS, J. H. (1929), 'The theory of international trade reconsidered', *Econ. J.*, vol. 39, pp. 195–209.

13 David Robertson

The Multinational Enterprise: Trade Flows and Trade Policy

Excerpts from David Robertson, 'The multinational enterprise: trade flows and trade policy', in J. H. Dunning (ed.), *The Multinational Enterprise*, Allen & Unwin, 1971, pp. 169–203.

Introduction

Historical observation establishes that there are irrefutable links between trade flows and overseas investment. What is more difficult to determine is the nature of the relationships between different types of foreign direct investment and international trade flows. With the rapid proliferation of transnational operations by large companies, where investment decisions become interwoven with transfers of technical knowledge, management expertise and skilled labour, relationships between investment and trade have become even more complex.

Until quite recently foreign direct investment was closely associated with trade interests.[1] Early merchants were concerned with obtaining supplies of essential raw materials and primary products to sell in their home country and with establishing new outlets for domestic production. The former often led to investments in plantations or mines, although in many cases this trade originated without much direct control over harvesting or extraction, for example, tea and spices from the orient. Subsequently the search for new outlets for home produce frequently led to investments, too, in selling organizations and agencies.

These early overseas investments engendered trade which was founded on absolute advantage in production. When overseas investment extended to cover overseas assembly plants or the manufacture of products that competed with exports from the investing country, then trade displacement resulted; products

1. Frequently, portfolio investment was also associated with trading interests, for example, the investment of British capital in the nineteenth century in pioneering railways in North and South America.

assembled or fabricated locally were substituted for imports. A further stage has been reached with the rapid development of the multinational enterprises which are concerned with control over production rather than flows of direct investment, which represent only one of the many instruments available to implement their aims (Kindleberger, 1969). New overseas projects may be financed by an outflow of capital from the parent company or by retentions of profits by a subsidiary. But with increasing frequency they are financed also by drawing on local savings. [. . .]

The way in which a multinational producing enterprise (MPE) exercises its control over overseas subsidiaries can have substantial effects on trade flows in addition to the traditional links associated with international investment flows. Multinational operation can involve international planning of production, of purchasing policies for materials and components and of marketing strategy in order that the enterprise operating as an entity is able to optimize its objective function. The extent of the control exercised by the management of the parent company and the amount of control retained by local management varies from one enterprise to another, and it often differs even between subsidiaries of the same enterprise. The degrees of centralization and integration of functions such as production, finance and marketing depend on many considerations, including the equity structures of subsidiaries, the bargaining power or boardroom skills of directors at different levels, the nature of the industry, the market situation of the subsidiaries and even the attitude of host countries' governments. To a greater or lesser extent all large multinationals are anxious to show good citizenship in all countries where they operate, which has some influence on management decisions. Nevertheless, the fact that decisions taken within multinational enterprise lead to international flows of materials, components, finished goods, production resources, technical knowhow, etc. means that the external economic positions of countries where these enterprises have operations are influenced and altered, both directly and indirectly. [. . .]

The balance of payments approach

Until recently attention has been focused principally on the effects of foreign direct investment on a country's balance of payments either as the investing country or as the recipient country. Perhaps the overriding concern with this aspect of the subject is a consequence of the external payments difficulties in recent years of the most important overseas investors, the United States and Britain. (These two countries also happen to be the only ones that publish detailed statistics on investments suitable for analysis!)

The usefulness and, indeed, the validity of isolating one section of a country's balance of payments for investigation appears questionable. The balance of payments represents the outcome from an aggregation of the net external effects from all types of internal and external transactions involving residents of the reporting country. It is not possible to isolate the external consequences for an economy of a particular item of its balance of payments. To say that certain changes would have occurred in the absence of a particular outflow or inflow of capital necessitates assumptions about the alternative position and the net effects on production, employment, prices, etc. – in fact, all economic variables. Moreover, national economies are interdependent through trade so that the consequences for other countries also have feedback effects on the reporting country.

The net effect of a foreign investment flow on the balance of payments should be considered in the same way as the balance of payments effects of any other disturbance affecting economic equilibrium. This section discounts any 'loss' of community well-being associated with nationalistic feelings about the increase in foreign ownership or control of production. An inflow of foreign investment creates a flow of incomes in the future, which accrues to owners of domestic factors of production and to foreigners, in the same way as a stimulation of domestic output through lower taxes or increased government expenditure. The incomes generated lead to higher imports and, assuming sufficient unemployed resources are available in the recipient country, higher domestic output and employment too.

The magnitudes of these increments depend on the nature as well as the size of the initial changes. If the foreign investment simply replaced an investment that would have been undertaken by a resident firm anyway, then the increments in total output, employment, etc. depend on how the domestic funds it releases are utilized. If they are not employed elsewhere, a net increase in output only occurs in as far as the foreign investor achieves higher productivity than the domestic competitor would have shown, through better organization or superior production methods. If the released funds are invested elsewhere, there is a larger increase in the value of output, even though the return on the domestic investment would be less in this alternative use compared with the preferred use. If the foreign investment represents additional resources, then the whole value of output, employment, etc., represents an increment.

The foreign investment may also be a takeover of existing plant. In this case, as above, the outcome depends on how the released capital resources are employed and how much more efficient the foreign company proves to be.

The changes induced by the foreign investment inflow differ from a shift in a purely domestic variable only because the foreign investment brings a net addition to the recipient country's foreign exchange reserves, equivalent to the inflow of capital funds less any expenditure on imported capital equipment. Over time the flow of repatriated profits, fees, etc. to the parent company will affect the current account position too, but so will flows of imported inputs for production and exports from the foreign-owned plant. Whether the postulated change involves foreign investment or a domestic change affecting incomes, output, etc., it involves adjustments in economic policy if the original economic objectives are maintained. The net effects of either type of change for the balance of payments can be compensated by policy adjustments, even within the present system of fixed exchange rates and limited foreign exchange reserves.

Similarly, an outflow of investment has repercussions for domestic incomes, employment, etc., over time. Assuming the outflow results in a reduction in investment at home, the initial effect is a decline in the flow of expected incomes; unless full employment existed already, in which case it would help to maintain an acceptable level of aggregate demand in the investing country, acting from a balance of payments point of view in the same way as a disinflationary policy of increased taxation or tighter credit. Future repatriations of profits, fees, etc. and export displacements or import increases resulting from the project also affect future incomes. Again, adequate economic management can resolve the net balance of payments effects within the normal operation of the economic system.

The balance of payments is a residual and it cannot be treated as an end in itself. In so far as inward or outward investment affects the balance of payments, therefore, it must be interpreted within the framework of economic policy adjustments necessary to achieve basic objectives on employment, prices, economic growth, social equity in income distribution and so forth. It remains necessary, though, to determine the types of effect that can be expected to result from overseas investment flows and the operation of multinational enterprises. To operate effective national policies, the impact of existing policies on decisions by MPEs and the impact of the growing presence of these organizations on the general environment needs to be understood. The interdependence of separate national policies in these circumstances must also be recognized.

Trade considerations

Although balance of payments considerations have dominated much of the debate on national policies with regard to the impact of foreign investment by multinational enterprises, there are several more fundamental aspects of transnational operating that deserve attention.

In the first place, MPE is concerned with the allocation of resources between different countries. In the case of a multi-product or a vertically integrated enterprise there is also the question of distributing resources among the different stages of production in order to optimize its objective function. International trade seeks to extend specialization in production by enlarging the sizes of markets and by widening the choices available to consumers. Under conditions of free trade, resources are employed such that the value of world output is maximized; this situation does not prevail in practice. When an MPE invests in an overseas plant and introduces new methods of organization and production, it affects the allocation of resources between countries in a variety of ways. In consequence, it also affects potential trade and the maximum value of world output under conditions of free trade. In assessing the implications for international trade flows of the operations of MPEs, therefore, it is necessary to employ an adequate analytical model of international trade and investment. Only if the model allows the types of change in resource allocations between countries that are affected by multinational enterprises can it help to explain their consequences for real output and consumption.

The situation is more complicated in practice because it is not possible to achieve a first best allocation of resources owing to distortion. Free trade does not exist. The many distortions that prevent the attainment of optimum welfare, even in the theoretical model, mean that only second-best solutions are possible (see Lipsey and Lancaster, 1956). Restrictions on trade and factor movements exist for natural reasons, such as geographical distance and non-tradeability, or for reasons of national economic policy. These interferences mean that the activities of MPEs may improve, or worsen, the allocations of available resources within or between some countries and achieve an increase, or decrease, in real outputs and incomes. But, because we are dealing with second-best solutions where resource allocations are subject to distortions, it is not possible to state with certainty whether the reallocations brought about by the activities of MPEs will raise or lower real outputs and incomes in a given situation. Equally the effects on trade among countries cannot be specified. Furthermore, trade policy and other aspects of national economic policy affect not only resource allocations within countries but also decisions made by MPEs about allocations between countries of resources under their control In other words, the policies of MPEs are influenced by both the overall effect of national economic policies on the worldwide allocation of resources and the differences between these policies with regard to their own specific activities.

Little attention has been given to the effects of MPEs on international trade or to the manner in which they take account of national economic policies. Basically, these are questions concerned with the effects of the operations of MPEs on the international allocation of resources. Is the MPE an instrument which extends the international division of labour?

A theory of trade and investment for a changing world

The operations of MPEs cannot be examined or discussed within the framework of a static theory of international trade. According to conventional theory, differences in comparative costs between countries are caused by differences in relative factor endowments, which are fostered by school and cultural differences between nations, and augmented by deliberate government policies. In addition, differences in the relative economic sizes of national markets create differential opportunities to exploit economies of scale in certain industries. Comparative advantage founded on these differences is maintained by the many natural and government-designed barriers to trade, and the fundamental assumption that factors of production are not free to move among countries.

MPEs seek to grow and earn profits by transferring the means of production from one location to another. This requires a dynamic theory of trade in which productive resources of all forms are mobile. Several major contributions to a theory of trade for a changing world have evolved in recent years from attempts to verify or extend the scope of certain aspects of neo-classical theory. Harry Johnson (1969) has attempted a synthesis of these contributions into a comprehensive theory of comparative advantage in a changing world.

Barriers to trade which emphasize comparative advantage among countries provide the basis for a dynamic theory. Johnson specifies three broad categories of trade barriers:

1. The influence of geographic distance and the transport costs of overcoming it.

2. Differences of political and legal systems, culture and language which divide the world into separate national markets.

3. The obstacles to international trade created by governments, such as tariffs and other trade policy instruments, exchange rate policies, taxation policies, etc.

These barriers create a *raison d'être* for MPEs. On the one hand, barriers to trade promote the location of production in the country where the market exists for the product. On the other hand, they inhibit producers from transferring production from a high-cost location to a lower-cost location in another country. MPEs seek to take an advantage possessed in one country and to transfer it to other lower-cost locations by overcoming barriers to trade and barriers against movement of productive resources. In the case of backward vertical investments the motive is still to overcome trade barriers but of a rather different or potential kind. Uncertainty about supplies means producers feel it necessary to invest in the highly capital-intensive processing of raw materials which are often located in remote and poor countries.

The differences which give rise to comparative advantage in in the first place – natural endowments of various factor inputs, geographical location, etc., and acquired differences such as differences in the stock of physical capital, the stock of production and technical knowledge, skills embodied in labour, management, etc. – also provide the basis for change. A comparative advantage is vested in a nation's industry. Individual firms or groups of producers discover new types of product and new techniques of production to meet the needs of their insulated domestic markets. As income levels rise, consumption patterns become more capital-intensive and less time-intensive. New products are created to meet new wants; washing-machines, dish-washers and easily maintained furniture become available at prices consumers can pay. Labour resources become more expensive relative to capital as incomes rise and this stimulates industry to find less labour-intensive methods. Labour-saving machinery is developed; tractors and combine harvesters for extensive farming methods, fork-lift trucks and conveyor belts to facilitate in-plant movements of materials, components, etc. Past investments in the acquisition of highly specialized human knowledge can obviously facilitate the rate of innovation to meet new wants, which is again a reflection of the wealth of a country since education is an expensive process in terms of short-term opportunity costs (Hufbauer, 1965).

The strongest incentives to introduce new products and new techniques are felt in the largest and richest countries where new wants manifest themselves most obviously. This largely accounts for the technological lead of the United States in the past hundred years. But innovation is not the prerogative of the largest and richest. Each country's producers in responding to their own market situations may discover innovations that can be marketed in other countries. Burenstam-Linder (1961) has observed that such innovations are most likely to be exported to countries with similar demand patterns, as represented by average income levels. Moreover, smaller countries cannot provide economies of scale from their own markets, so that these countries tend to specialize in internationally traded goods whereas larger countries can specialize in nationally differentiated products, because their large home markets give the opportunity to achieve low unit costs of output.

Once a competitive advantage is procured over local producers, or a new market has been created for an innovated product, it is possible for the innovator to gain further benefits by selling it abroad. In terms of Raymond Vernon's (1966) theory of the product cycle the first stage of expansion into overseas markets is by means of exports. This has been referred to as 'technological gap' trade (Hufbauer, 1965; Posner, 1961). Because countries are at different stages of economic development, new markets are readily available to receive new products through the demonstration effect from richer countries. And more important perhaps for MPEs, the value of labour time differs between countries so that by shifting production towards lower-cost locations they may manufacture at lower costs and extend their markets further.

During the development stage, the production of the innovated product is likely to remain within the market for which it was designed, according to Vernon. In the early stages, costs of production are probably relatively unimportant because of the monopoly position of the producer. Another reason for early immobility is that while commercial production is being developed, the innovator needs close contacts with both customers and suppliers of components, machinery, etc., for as the product's market expands the methods of production employed and possibly the materials and components may be adapted and improved. When the product stabilizes into a standard form, production costs become more important as competing products are evolved and because expansion of sales is likely to depend on price reductions. It is at this stage that the innovator may look overseas for lower-cost locations and for new markets. This is particularly the case for American companies. Innovators from smaller, European countries may first look towards higher-cost locations in the large and rich United States' market in order to raise sales volume for a new product and thereby reduce unit costs.

In the classical and neo-classical theories of international trade, the innovatory advantage once acquired remains as a permanent source of exports to other countries; factors of production are not transferable between countries. In practice, however, production is eventually transferred from the country of innovation. It may occur only in the long run when the proprietary knowledge giving the advantage becomes generally available; for example, if a patent lapses or if the commercial value of the knowledge disappears through competition or it is superseded. Competing firms at home and abroad may decide to invest resources in acquiring the knowledge to imitate the innovator (Hufbauer, 1965; Posner, 1961). This is likely to be expensive and some guarantee against the risk is probably required in the form of protection of the home market or the prospect of lower labour costs. Both these forms of transfer involve substantial time lags during which the gap will be filled by trade.

The role of MPEs in the transfer of production is expounded in Vernon's theory of the product cycle. In this case, the technology is retained under the control of the innovating firm. Its first option is to sell or lease the productive knowledge to overseas producers. In this way the innovating firm achieves additional income from its invention without having to bear the risks attached to producing and marketing in a foreign country, where it may be unfamiliar with the legal system and accepted business practices. Moreover, it avoids the uncertainty of whether a profitable volume of sales can be achieved. The disadvantage of this approach is that a competitive advantage is given up either permanently or temporarily. Even when a licence lapses the foreign licensee is usually aware of the necessary knowledge and he may even have so improved on the original that the innovator is at a competitive disadvantage. If the innovator considers his real advantage is in research and development rather than production and marketing, then, of course, lease or sale of proprietary knowledge may be the most profitable course to follow, since he expects to retain a technical lead over his rivals.[2]

The second option is to invest in an overseas subsidiary. When exports reach a sufficient level, the first concern is likely to be for support services, such as a distribution network and after-sales servicing. This may later extend to an assembly plant. If new capacity is required, the decision may be taken to invest in an overseas plant close to major markets or potential markets. The decision may be encouraged by trends in competition at home or abroad. Lower production costs may be available abroad, both because factor inputs are less expensive and because additional economies of scale may be obtained by allocating production of components to different plants, permitting longer production runs. International programming of production of components and assembly plants can offer substantial economies of scale for some products.

In general, horizontal investment abroad can be justified for any unique asset or advantage possessed by an enterprise that differentiates it, or its product, from competitors. Typically multinational enterprises operate in oligopolistic market situations where product differentiation is characteristic. Differentiation may be derived from the nature of the product, the methods employed in its production, or special attributes of the producing firm, such as marketing ability, management or research and development strength. Any attribute that differentiates its position on the home market may be exploited by a firm on foreign markets. In the first place this is likely to be by means of exports. Investment in overseas production will be undertaken only when the investor is convinced it is possible to earn higher profits than local competitors on that market; the differential must compensate for extra expenses and inconvenience of operating in an unfamiliar environment and the greater risk that implies.

The mechanisms for the transfer of production, in which the multinational enterprise plays an important role, provide a basis

2. Technological lead depends on research and development effort, which in turn usually depends on sales and profit performance of an enterprise. The importance of R & D to United States trade and investment has been shown by Gruber, Mehta and Vernon (1967); also Dunning (1969a).

for a dynamic theory of comparative cost. Technical improvements generated in response to rising living standards and changing relative costs of capital and labour yield initial comparative advantage which is lost by diffusion through the world economy in response to economic incentives provided by differences, ultimately, in relative costs of human labour time, themselves the result of international differences in capital accumulated per unit of labour time availability, and the immobility especially of labour.

Thus, except for trade in primary commodities which depends primarily on natural resource endowments, most trade depends on comparative advantage, that is, international differences. But comparative advantage is temporary and after a time it is likely to be eroded away. Multinational enterprises, therefore, may be able to contribute to general world welfare and to raise real incomes by accelerating the diffusion of more efficient processes of production and more advanced types of products. That is, they extend the international division of labour within the economic system in as far as they are able to overcome barriers to trade and factor movements. [. . .]

The nature of trade effects

The specific effects on merchandise trade flows of the operations of MPEs are complex. Discussion is usually restricted to the effects caused by foreign direct investments. Yet not all overseas direct investment is undertaken by MPEs, neither is all the foreign investment undertaken by multinationals recorded as international flows. The latter is probably the more serious qualification because local savings are being increasingly employed by multinationals, whereas the proportion of total foreign direct investments not undertaken by companies with transnational activities is quite small. Other decisions by MPEs have a bearing on trade flows, too, such as production programming on an international scale and the allocation of export markets among particular subsidiaries. No attempt has been made to measure these less quantifiable influences, as the trade effects discussed in this survey are restricted to those derived from investments by MPEs.

Direct investment flows concerned with manufacturing are of

principal interest because the expansion of the activities of MPEs in this area has had most influence on trade patterns. Investment in the production of primary products and raw materials is less relevant to the present interest. Although such investments may be important for vertical integration within the large company and in some cases they may cause changes in trade flows, especially substitutions between sources, they are not greatly affected by considerations of trade policy; most advanced industrial countries have low or zero tariffs and few other restrictions on raw material imports.

Following the formal theoretical sequence of investment decisions for an enterprise's overseas expansion, set out by Vernon and described in a previous section, it is evident that effects on trade flows vary in intensity according to the nature of the product and the form of the investment; for example, whether a complete production plant is established or only a sales and servicing organization to promote export sales. It is possible, however, to specify certain general trade effects that can be associated with overseas direct investments.

Export generating effects result from additional sales of finished goods, components, raw materials or capital equipment from the investing country. These may be direct exports from the parent or other subsidiaries. They may also be indirect exports from other suppliers in the investing country to the new subsidiary, resulting from established links fostered by the parent company. After a time lag similar exports may arise as competitors in the foreign market learn of superior or cheaper techniques, components, machines or materials which they decide to adopt.

Import generation results if the foreign subsidiary begins to export components or finished products back to the market of the parent company. Increases of imports into the investing country in this manner are in accordance with the product cycle theory. There are several reasons why such trade flows may occur. It may be a management decision to specialize production in plants in several countries which would involve flows of materials, components and finished goods between countries. Or, lower labour costs or other factor inputs may enable the subsidiary to manufacture at lower costs once a particular scale of output has been achieved. These reasons may be present together in such trade flows. If a company is interested in maximizing its profits internationally it is rational that it should place its sources of supply in the most efficient locations and programme its production in such a way as to obtain all cost reductions available from economies of scale and from minimizing transport costs, tax payments, tariffs, etc.

Export displacement effects result if output from an overseas subsidiary replaces exports from the parent company's factories, or exports from a competitor in the investing country, or exports from another affiliated company, either in the local market or in a third country market. Such changes do not increase international trade flows necessarily, but by affecting the pattern of trade there are, of course, further induced effects on national income levels and trade flows.

These three effects – export generating, import generating and export displacement – constitute what one might call a net trade balance effect for the investing country. The net trade balance effect together with other income remittances, from profits, licence fees, royalties, service charges, etc. represent the flow of incomes to the investing country resulting from the initial investment decision.

For the recipient country the net trade balance effect is composed of the same effects, but they are reversed. Imports are generated by the capital inflow to provide necessary materials and components; these may be supplied by the parent company or other affiliates, or suppliers with whom the parent has close association or from independent producers in third countries. In addition, the presence of the local plant may attract to the market imports of other finished products from the parent company and affiliates. Local production also replaces purchases of similar products previously imported. And if the new plant also exports its output, either back to the country of the parent company or to third country markets, new exports are generated for the recipient country. On the other side of the ledger, the local subsidiary would have to make various external payments profits, licence fees, service charges, etc., to the parent and dividends to other foreign creditors.

Having established the three types of trade effects of international investment flows – export generating, import generating and export–import displacement – it must be pointed out that these are direct trade effects.[3] These changes in trade flows also alter income levels in the countries involved, which induce further changes in trade flows according to the multiplier; changes that eventually dissipate themselves throughout all international trade. (This reverts back to the basic problem of balance of payments effects of foreign investment flows.)

Measuring even the direct trade effects of foreign investment flows is very difficult and the multiplier effects have so far received little attention.[4] One basic problem of measurement concerns time. When an investment decision is taken, several time lags influence developments. If the investment is to create new plant there is a delay before production commences; and a further delay before full-capacity output is achieved. Furthermore, even if the parent company has been exporting to the local market, it is likely to take some time before sales in the local market can be expanded to absorb a substantial proportion of potential output from the new plant. Similarly, breaking into overseas markets with exports only occurs after a time lag. All these lags in developing markets also influence imports of materials and components, and up to a point even imports of capital equipment will be affected by output requirements.

Empirical evidence

The only evidence available on the effects of MPEs on international allocation of resources and trade flows is restricted to empirical studies on the effects of overseas investment flows on particular countries' balances of payments. The two most detailed studies of the effects of direct overseas investment are the Hufbauer–Adler report (1968) for the United States and the Reddaway report (1967–8) for the United Kingdom. Work on the effects of inward investment has been done by Safarian (1969) for Canada, Brash (1966) for Australia and Dunning (1969b) for

3. The system of valuation may distort the effects. Intra-firm transfers may not be made at arm's-length prices if another system of valuation could benefit the company, in terms of lower taxes or as a means of transferring liquid funds between countries.

4. The multiplier effects are examined rather unsuccessfully in the Hufbauer–Adler report; see below.

the United Kingdom. Although these studies provide useful indications of the trade effects of direct overseas investment, even they do not show the full impact on trade flows. They are concerned with the bilateral effects of direct investment flows between the investing country and the recipient; exports of capital equipment, components and parts and finished products from the former to support the investment project, and the reverse flow of imports of finished goods from the new overseas plant to the investing country. In order to understand the full trade effects of an investment flow, it is necessary also to examine the consequences for third countries; the extent to which their exports of finished products and components to the investment-receiving country might be curtailed or increased by the construction of a new plant; or the extent to which imports into the recipient country of materials and components might be increased; or the impact of exports from the new plant on other countries' exports to third markets or the investing country.

The Hufbauer–Adler and Reddaway reports show that the results of such studies are highly dependent on the specific assumptions adopted. Comparisons between the results of these studies are difficult because of the different assumptions, the different basic approaches to the empirical investigations (the Reddaway report relying principally on information collected from firms while the Hufbauer–Adler study used published statistics) and differences in the time-periods covered.

Studies of this kind are concerned with comparing what actually happened with what might have happened in alternative circumstances. It is necessary, therefore, to make an assumption about the alternative position. The Reddaway report works from a reverse classical assumption that a given foreign investment substitutes for investment in the host country without decreasing the capital formation in the investing country. Another possibility is a classical assumption which postulates that a given foreign investment causes a net addition to capital formation in the host country but an equal decline in capital formation in the investing country. Both these involve no change in total capital formation for the world as a whole. The third alternative is the anti-classical assumption that foreign investment leads to an increase in capital formation abroad without reducing capital investment in the investing country. The Hufbauer–Adler report investigates all three alternatives.

For practical purposes the best alternative will depend on other assumptions. For example, if full employment exists in the host country, an inflow of foreign investment must substitute for local investment (anti-classical assumption or reverse classical) or equilibrium in that economy will be disturbed, bringing structural changes. Which of these two assumptions is most suitable will then depend on the position in the investing country. If full employment equilibrium is maintained there, then an anti-classical assumption is most suitable. A reverse classical assumption would disturb the investment-saving relationship in the investing country. If the full-employment assumption is released, of course, then an increase in capital formation in the recipient country would stimulate economic growth through the multiplier. This latter possibility is not followed in either the Hufbauer–Adler or Reddaway studies.[5]

The concern in this chapter is to examine the trade effects revealed by these studies without going into their full conclusions. For this reason the results following the reverse classical assumption are used for direct comparison of the two reports. Two types of trade effect can be distinguished: the initial effect, which will not be repeated, and the continuing effect over time once the investment has been implemented. In discussing the estimates from these studies it must be understood that the figures refer to average global figures and that wide differences exist between the results for particular industries and particular countries. Details about the range of results given in each study can be obtained in the references given below.

The initial effect is concerned principally with the exportation of suitable plant and machinery for the investment project from the investing country. For Britain this was estimated at an average of 11 per cent of the value of the overseas direct investment in manufacturing. Wide variations were revealed between industries; estimates as high as 21 per cent were found for the vehicle industry compared with 1 per cent for the paper industry (Reddaway, Potter and Taylor, 1967–8, table XIV 1, p. 374). An

5. For a fuller discussion of the different implications of the alternative assumptions, see a review of the two reports by Dunning (1969c).

important consideration, of course, is the suitability and availability of the right kind of equipment in different countries. Higher estimates of the intial effect were made for the United States in the Hufbauer–Adler report, an average estimate of 27 per cent of the value of overseas direct investment in manufacturing. Account must be taken, though, of the potential exports of plant and equipment to independent foreign producers. Hufbauer and Adler show that the United States is a much more important supplier of machinery to world markets than Britain. They go on to show that the direct effects on British exports of capital equipment are more favourable than for the United States (Hufbauer and Adler, 1968, app. B); that is, if the investment were made by a non-British company, very little equipment would be likely to be purchased from Britain. On the other hand, the high level of American exports of capital equipment probably includes an indirect benefit from the size of American overseas investment through a 'demonstration effect'. Facing competition from American overseas subsidiaries, local companies may be forced to buy American equipment if it is more efficient.

In addition to the once-for-all effect of initially equipping a new plant, there are continuing trade effects. Established overseas subsidiaries may continue to import components and parts from the parent company, or from independent suppliers in the investing country. Again the estimated purchases of input items from Britain by British overseas manufacturing subsidiaries were lower than for American companies; 3·2 per cent of total subsidiary sales compared with 4·2 per cent for the United States (Hufbauer and Adler, 1968, table 3.7; Reddaway, Potter and Taylor, 1967–8, table VI 2, p. 365). Yet, as in connection with exports of capital equipment, British exports appear to be more favourably influenced by direct overseas investment than American exports, because United States industry is a more important supplier of these items anyway to independent foreign companies.

Establishing an overseas subsidiary can affect existing production patterns in the investing enterprise in a variety of ways too. A foreign assembly or production plant may stimulate exports of finished products or components from the parent company. In the former case the goods of the parent company become identified with the local branch and there is probably an improvement in sales effort and servicing. If components or semi-manufactures are available from the parent company (or another subsidiary for that matter) there is a profit incentive for the vertically integrated international company to buy through its own facilities, thereby retaining the profit element in the cost of components, as well as the obvious advantages of direct control over stocks, quality, etc.

Evidence on the expansion of exports in this way is incomplete. The Reddaway report (see p. 367 and Interim Report) found that purchases of goods from Britain for resale by overseas subsidiaries represented around 6 per cent of their total sales; possibly 10 per cent if transport costs are added. A large proportion of these purchases for resale were reported as being from the parent group. What was also clear, however, was that the importance of this business declined over the period of the study, 1955–64. The Hufbauer–Adler study found a similar proportion for 'associated exports', 4·5 per cent of subsidiary sales (Hufbauer and Adler, 1968, p. 30). A later survey by the Office of Business Economics suggested a somewhat higher figure of 5·3 per cent in 1965. In that year $4·5 billion of exports by American parent companies were channelled through foreign affiliates, and $2·5 billion consisted of goods exported and sold without further processing. On the other hand, the same group of international companies covered in this survey also exported $4 billion to independent purchasers. The total of $8·5 billion exported by these companies represented one-third of total United States merchandise exports; 45 per cent of non-agricultural merchandise exports.

Assigning the importance of overseas direct investment to these exports of finished goods is a difficult task. Given the large volumes of exports by the parent companies to non-affiliated buyers, it is likely that a substantial share of these exports would have taken place anyway, without the investment flow. That is, they could be marketed through normal marketing channels. Hence, by no means all these exports could be considered as a trade effect of the investment flows. It is questionable, too, how long such exports will continue. In many cases they may be used to 'fill a gap' until local production is expanded to cover the full range of products marketed by the company. When a suitable market has been created locally by means of imports from the parent, local manufacture will be initiated.

Parent company exports are also displaced by overseas production. The extent to which this occurs depends largely on the assumptions about the alternative position. Following the reverse classical assumption, overseas direct investment causes little export displacement because in the absence of the investment flow from one country, a competitor, either local or from another country, would have made a similar decision and displaced the exports of the first country. Supporters of foreign investment as competing with exports adopt a classical assumption: that the investment flow creates capital plant in a country where it would never have existed while it deprives the investing country of that investment. The Hufbauer–Adler report (pp. 33–43) after some complex regression analysis concludes, under a reverse classical thesis, that increased output by an overseas subsidiary causes the output of local competing firms to be reduced. Reddaway, on the same assumption, asserts that displacement of British exports of finished goods by overseas direct investment would be small: around 2½ per cent per additional £100 of operating assets. Export displacement appears to be greater for Britain, however, than the United States and it greatly reduces the net effects on continuing exports (Reddaway, Potter and Taylor, 1967–8, p. 299, and Interim Report, p. 110). The explanation given for this is that British production abroad frequently involves models and brands identical to those exported from Britain.

Following direct overseas investment it is possible also that the new subsidiary may be able to export its output back to the investing country. Given that investment in overseas manufacturing plant may be stimulated by relative cost advantages, it is distinctly possible that the subsidiary's output of finished goods or components may be imported. The Reddaway report (p. 345) 'found virtually no trace . . . of imports into the UK of manufactured goods produced by overseas subsidiaries'. The Hufbauer–Adler report, on the other hand, found substantial effects: 4·3 per cent of sales by subsidiaries. The explanation of this probably rests with the size and value of the American market, which has encouraged investment in lower-wage countries where American techniques are used to produce at low cost for export throughout the world. For Britain, imports from subsidiaries are mainly materials which would have had to be imported anyway.

Countries receiving an investment inflow experience additional trade effects. Apart from trade flows generated by the close association with the country of the parent company, there are also likely go be new trade flows created with third countries. In the first place there may be imports of capital equipment from third countries if the items required are not available in the host country or from the country of the parent, or if suitable equipment is only available at higher delivered prices. More significant, however, may be the continuing effects on trade with third countries. Imports of materials or components from independent suppliers may be essential inputs for the manufacturing process, or the finished products may substitute for some items previously imported from third countries. Similarly, exported output may create new trade or displace exports from competitors in third countries, or from an affiliated company, if lower production costs, lower transport costs or preferential trading arrangements, such as the European Economic Community, enable the subsidiary to penetrate new markets.

For an integrated MPE, new trade flows may evolve directly from policy decisions. International programming of production to obtain maximum economies of scale from long production runs may lead to substantial movements of component, semi-processed goods and finished goods between manufacturing and assembly centres and markets. Equally, if particular markets are allocated to specific subsidiaries, the potential trade flows may be curtailed, although if profit maximization is the assumed objective for the company as a whole this is only likely in the short-run.

It is difficult to arrive at reasonable estimates of these potential trade flows. Figures for 'associated exports' in the Reddaway and Hufbauer–Adler reports do not cover intra-company transfers between overseas subsidiaries. They are concerned only with transactions with the parent company. The *Board of Trade Journal*, 16 August 1968, estimated that in 1966 around 22 per cent of Britain's merchandise exports were accounted for by transactions between related concerns. Out of this total, approximately 12 per cent were exports by British-owned companies to their overseas affiliates. Of the remaining 10 per cent which were controlled from outside Britain, 7 per cent were from American-owned companies. Unfortunately, the survey does not indicate the proportion of those intra-company transfers[6] that are for resale by the affiliates, which may be high as they include selling organizations; neither does it show what proportion is for further processing. Wide variations in the values of those transfers were indicated between different industries. Exports by the motor vehicles industry to affiliates were particularly important, representing one-third of the total value of those related exports and more than half of total motor vehicle exports from Britain; the proportion for subsidiaries of American companies was 80 per cent, compared with 37 per cent for exports of British companies to overseas affiliates. Other industries showing a high proportion of exports to affiliates included chemicals and electrical engineering.

More detailed figures are available for exports from United States parent companies to overseas affiliates in a survey by the Office of Business Economics of the US Department of Commerce (Bradshaw, 1969). The basic figures from this study were mentioned earlier (see page 344 above). A somewhat smaller proportion of total American exports than Britain's exports went to overseas affiliates in 1965: around 17 per cent. (Figures are not available, though, for exports of companies controlled by non-residents of the United States. These are probably small but would raise the total figure closer to the British estimate.) Out of these intra-company transfers, just over half were finished goods for resale and the remainder were for further processing. Variations between industries were again significant. Approximately 68 per cent of exports of motor vehicles were channelled through foreign affiliates; around 55 per cent were exports for further processing. Other industries showing a high proportion of exports to foreign affiliates included chemicals, rubber products, non-electrical machinery and professional and scientific instruments.

These estimates indicate the importance of intra-company

6. The article does not consider the valuations placed on these intra-firm shipments and it accepts the declarations.

transfers across frontiers, and these flows have probably increased greatly since these surveys were carried out. It must be recognized, of course, that in the absence of MPEs a substantial proportion of this trade would have occurred between independent companies in those countries, simply on a basis of relative cost differences. Hence, the whole of this trade cannot be treated simply as an effect of the operation of the multinationals.

Some investment-receiving countries have become worried about the effects on their economies of the performances of foreign-owned firms, that is, whether foreign ownership inhibits exports and stimulates excessive imports. Safarian (1969, ch. 4) found that there was little evidence to suggest this was true for Canada. American-owned enterprises in Canada exported around 20 per cent of their output in 1965, about the same proportion as for American subsidiaries in Europe. This represented 48 per cent of manufactured exports from Canada in that year, while residents of the United States controlled 46 per cent of capital invested in Canadian manufacturing investment. Safarian found, too, that there was no tendency for firms to export less as the number of overseas affiliates increased. Some foreign-owned subsidiaries exported through their parent company's sales organization. In many cases this assisted exports, but in a few cases, where markets were allocated among the affiliates, some limitation might occur; usually, however, relative production costs were thought to be the major constraint on exports. Imports into Canada by foreign-owned subsidiaries were found to be smaller in value than their exports. The proportion of imported inputs used by these firms varied widely from one industry to another; the impact of the Canadian–American Automotive Agreement is mentioned specifically. In general, Safarian found that subsidiaries established abroad commenced as partial alternatives to imports, but it was a common experience that once a subsidiary became established it tended to raise the domestic content of production. This was supported by evidence that, of the firms under foreign control, the largest firms had the lowest import content in their production. Statistical investigation showed that foreign-owned subsidiaries in Canada were more import-oriented than purely domestically controlled firms; in part, Safarian considered this was due to Canadian tariffs, and for the remainder it reflected the opportunities for improved specialization within the MPE.

Australian experience indicates a much smaller share for exports of manufactures for American-owned companies than in Canada or Britain. Brash (1966, pp. 203–40) considers this not surprising because many direct investments in manufacturing in Australia were made to get behind high-tariff barriers. The need for the tariff indicates that the industries are not competitive by world standards, a view supported by the statements from export companies that Australian production costs are high. In general, Brash arrives at the same conclusions as Safarian. Foreign affiliation often aids the export activities of subsidiary companies and, although market allocation by the parent company may limit exports, the main consideration in exports appears to be the inability of the Australian subsidiary to compete abroad. The import content of production by American-owned subsidiaries in Australia has declined in recent years under the influence of tariff policy.

Implications for trade policy

A review of recent investigations into the effects of foreign direct investment yields some guidance as to the magnitude of the changes in merchandise trade flows that result from the rapidly expanding activities of MPEs. But this is only part of the picture. No measurement has so far been attempted of the consequences of overseas direct investment for the trade of third countries, although these effects could cause significant changes in trade patterns. Similarly, feedback effects through the various multipliers have received only cursory treatment. Furthermore, it must be emphasized that investment is only one aspect of the activities of the MPE that affects trade flows. The location of production plants, the planning of output and the allocation of specified markets to subsidiaries must also alter trade patterns.

Even the evidence gleaned from studies not intended specifically to measure trade effects, however, indicates the powerful influence that the activities of MPEs can have on trade flows. United States direct investment represents around two-thirds of the total overseas investment stake; at the end of 1968, this was valued at $65 billion (Devlin and Cutter, 1969). Hence, figures relating to United States output and exports may be used to provide a crude estimate of the relationships for all overseas investments. For 1965, it was estimated that exports accounted for over 18 per cent of total sales by foreign manufacturing affiliates of United States companies;[7] this export–sales ratio was higher for Europe (23·5 per cent) and Canada (19 per cent) than for less-developed countries; there were also wide variations in this ratio between different industries. In addition, it has been established that in the same year around 17 per cent of total United States merchandise exports (and more than a quarter of manufactured exports) were directed through foreign affiliates (Bradshaw, 1969). Unfortunately, similar figures are not available for other countries. The importance of the operations of the multinationals, however, can be illustrated by Dunning's (1969b) estimate that, by 1981, 25 per cent of British exports will be controlled by American companies. He also shows that American subsidiaries in Britain tend to export a higher proportion of their output than competing domestic companies, which corroborates the conclusions drawn by Safarian and Brash (see previous section). This suggests a general interpretation that multinational companies are more interested in international trade than national companies, although this may also be a function of size.

Some commentators conclude from such estimates that the influence that foreign-controlled companies can exert on a country's trade balance through their subsidiaries can be harmful to the interests of the host country, and they often recommend that government supervision is necessary. There appear to be two origins to this line of argument. First, the common nationalistic approach to international transactions. Fortunately, this is under attack from several quarters, yet it persists in attitudes towards trade in spite of the rapid extension of international cooperation in the economic sphere. Second, a misunderstanding of the underlying economic model within which the activities of MPEs should be considered. Too often because MPEs cannot be comprehended within the static neo-classical theory of international trade, their activities are condemned as necessarily being contrary to the interests of the community.

7. See Safarian (1969, p. 25), derived from *Survey of Current Business*, November 1966.

The problem of nationalism extends far beyond the present area of discussion. Johnson and others have indicated how nationalistic goals can be included in an assessment of trade policy, but at an economic cost. Some aspects of the activities of MPEs are principally political, however, and fall outside the economic field altogether. Problems of extra-territoriality, for example, are clearly a political issue. In this case, policy decisions made by one national government may be insidiously imposed on another country through the commercial links between a parent and its overseas subsidiaries.[8]

Within the context of trade and investment flows, however, critics of the development of MPEs are prepared to accept the national benefits derived from the operations of foreign-owned subsidiaries: the financial aspect of a capital inflow, the extra employment and incomes generated within the country, the availability of superior technology and management, the increased exports for the trade balance, and so forth. Offsetting increases in imports of materials and components, and remission of profits, fees, dividends, etc. to the parent company are reluctantly accepted. National rivalry really comes to the forefront, though, in connection with the allocation of a new investment or a division of overseas markets between different national subsidiaries of an MPE. Then the claim is that a national company would have acted differently. It would have expanded its production at home or it would have successfully penetrated an overseas market with exports, regardless of competition. The implication is that the foreign-owned subsidiary has in some way acted against the national interest; some kind of 'loss' is involved.

Much of this discussion proceeds in a balance of payments context without reference to the general equilibrium of the national economy; and, moreover, without questioning whether if the foreign-owned subsidiary had been a national company it would have achieved the same degrees of success to have warranted expansion anyway. The international aspect of resource allocation is ignored in this neo-mercantilist approach. In the

8. United States regulations on supplying strategic materials to Cuba and China are direct examples; the impact of United States Anti-Trust Laws may have direct consequences also.

case of the division of overseas markets, reference is not usually made to whether the local subsidiary has sufficient capacity to sell in the bespoken market. In the case of investment in new capacity, the aggregate demand position in the economy, the likely pressure it would create on existing resources – labour, capital goods industries, etc. – is not considered. An MPE makes its decision in its own best interests, but these need not diverge from the national interests. If investment in one country would create inflationary pressures, then it would not be in the interest of an MPE to invest there, where it would have to compete for scarce resources in order to operate the new plant. Similarly, such investment would be against the interests of the national economy if it created inflationary pressures.

It is possible that in some circumstances an MPE may act in a manner that is discordant with the best interests of a particular country, as defined by its government. But this cannot be asserted generally in economic terms. Within a multinational enterprise it can be assumed that economic resources are allocated rationally. Non-economic factors may influence decisions, such as political stability or the record of industrial disputes. But within the framework of its objectives, an MPE can be expected to allocate its resources according to economic criteria.

A fundamental problem, therefore, is the adoption of an economic theory that permits analysis of the impact of the activities of MPEs on international flows of trade and investment. An outline of a dynamic theory of comparative advantage is sketched in this survey. It is within this type of framework that the problems of resource allocation induced by MPEs, within and between nations, must be considered.

Trade theory is usually couched in terms of exchanges of final goods, embodying primary factors of production, between a buyer in one country and a seller in another. In practice, trade involves transfers of goods at all stages of fabrication; that is, raw materials, components, intermediate goods and finished products. Some components may pass across frontiers many times before they reach the final consumer. MPEs are specifically concerned with this kind of trade at many stages of processing. This has given cause for concern about the values attached to intra-enterprise transfers across national frontiers.

Transfer prices for goods passing between affiliated companies in different countries can be adjusted in a manner that permits financial resources to be shifted from one country to another. It may suit an MPE to take its profit in a country with low taxes and, therefore, to invoice exports of components to that country at manufactured cost without a normal profit element, and possibly to invoice exports from that country at inflated prices to reduce profit margins earned in other markets. Motives for this kind of manipulation include exploiting differences between tax regimes, avoiding exchange controls, or simply a method of transferring funds. (Inter-affiliate credit or unusually long delays in payments for goods received – leads and lags – have similar effects on international monetary movements.)

Whatever the motive, the effect will be to distort the values of trade flows between countries involved in such transactions; one country's exports may be undervalued, hence another country's imports will be undervalued; alternatively, the value of a trade flow may be overvalued. If this device is employed to maximize profits in one country, then a subsidiary there may have its imports undervalued and its exports overvalued. In terms of interest in national trade balances, this country benefits at the expense of its trading partners.

In theory this device appears to offer considerable opportunities, especially as inter-affiliate transfers become more intricate. But, in practice, the opportunities are probably more limited. Customs officials are aware of import and export values of invoiced items, either because similar products pass in trade between other independent companies or because the supplying subsidiary also sells to non-affiliated companies at full commercial prices. Moreover, the managements of subsidiaries of multinationals are generally anxious to achieve the best possible financial results for presentation to the parent company's board. Rivalry between subsidiaries will tend to establish transfer prices at commercial rates. The only case where this may not provide a safeguard would be in a highly integrated and centrally controlled multinational, and few of these exist so far.

The stratification of trade over many stages of production towards the final good has also introduced special problems in trade policy. Following the same lines as traditional trade theory, tariffs were considered as protection for final goods. But, in fact, goods passing in international trade depend on inputs of raw materials and components that may themselves be imported. It is necessary, therefore, to differentiate *nominal* tariffs from *effective* rates of protection afforded to specific processes; that is, rates of protection on value added in a process, which takes into account tariffs on inputs (Corden, 1966). Effective rates of protection may differ greatly from nominal rates contained in national tariff schedules (Balassa, 1965). It is assumed throughout the discussions on trade policy in this paper that MPEs are aware of effective rates of protection and act on these. This seems to be the most realistic assumption since by definition MPEs are concerned with the distribution of different stages of production in relation to markets. The issues raised by effective rates of protection are all part of the same problem of resource allocation in a changing world.

A simple reading of the position would suggest that national trade policy, especially tariffs, has a far greater impact on national-based companies, relying on exports for overseas sales, than on MPEs which can allow for differences in national trade policies. If this is the case, it must bring into question whether the principal aims of national trade policies are being thwarted. The trade effects of decisions taken by MPEs have a direct bearing on the effectiveness of trade policy instruments because both are concerned with the international allocation of resources. In these changed circumstances, the selection of policy instruments designed to achieve a particular objective must be re-examined and probably altered. A more fundamental problem is whether the objectives of a national trade policy should be adjusted and how one country's policy selection is influenced by another's choice.

Already the development of MPEs has raised questions about certain aspects of traditional international economic policy and helped to bring change. Exchange control regulations intended to isolate national money markets have been exploited by transnational enterprises. Control over capital movements was conceived as a means of insulating financial markets from external influences. An MPE, however, has access to several capital markets and, in many cases, it is able to transfer funds, directly or indirectly, between subsidiaries or between subsidiaries and the parent company. Through a system of fixed exchange rates this acts as a link between capital markets, which weakens the impact of monetary policy as a domestic economic instrument. A tight credit policy in one country can be overcome by a suitable strategy of borrowing and transferring funds between subsidiaries or between subsidiaries and the parent company. The insulation sought through exchange controls can be overcome by selective borrowing and transferring of funds because the enterprise operates within the segregated national parts of the economic system. Taken a stage further, of course, this same mechanism of financial control by MPEs can be used for speculative purposes during times of exchange rate uncertainty.

The managed exchange rate system, which involves large discreet adjustments at infrequent intervals, plays into the hands of the MPEs because they are able to benefit from the actions of separate decision-taking segments of the system, that is, national monetary authorities. Governments show increasing recognition of the weaknesses of the managed exchange rate system in the presence of MPEs and they seek to overcome difficulties with greater cooperation in monetary policy and by changing the system. This is witnessed by the open discussion and growing support for a change towards greater flexibility of exchange rates.

International monetary relations could be cited, therefore, as one area of policy in which the operations of MPEs have helped to elicit changes. Perhaps the growing international economic interdependence, of which the development of MPEs is one aspect, will also induce national authorities to review and reassess the effects of present trade policy measures in the light of revised policy objectives for the changed environment.

References

BALASSA, B. (1965), 'Tariff protection in industrial countries: an evaluation', *J. polit. Econ.*, vol. 73, pp. 573–94.

BRADSHAW, M. T. (1969), 'US exports to foreign affiliates of US firms', in *Survey of Current Business*, US Department of Commerce, May.

BRASH, D. T. (1966), *American Investment in Australian Industry*, Australian National University Press.

BURENSTAM-LINDER, S. (1961), *An Essay in Trade and Transformation*, Wiley.

CORDEN, W. M. (1966), 'The structure of a tariff system and the effective protective rate', *J. polit. Econ.*, vol. 74, pp. 221–37.

DEVLIN, D. T., and CUTTER, F. (1969), 'The international investment position of the United States: developments in 1968', in *Survey of Current Business*, US Department of Commerce, November.

DUNNING, J. H. (1969a), 'European and US trade patterns, US foreign investment and the technological gap', paper read at the International Economic Association Conference, Algarve, Portugal, August.

DUNNING, J. H. (1969b), 'The role of American investment in the British economy', *PEP Broadsheet*, no. 507.

DUNNING, J. H. (1969c), 'The foreign investment controversy', *Bankers' Mag.*, May and June.

GRUBER, W., MEHTA, D., and VERNON, R. (1967), 'The R & D factor in international trade and international investment of United States industries', *J. polit. Econ.*, vol. 75, pp. 20–37.

HUFBAUER, G. C. (1965), *Synthetic Materials and the Theory of International Trade*, Duckworth.

HUFBAUER, G. C., and ADLER, F. M. (1968), 'Overseas manufacturing investment and the US balance of payments', *US Treasury Tax Research Policy Document*, no. 1.

JOHNSON, H. G. (1969), *Comparative Cost and Commercial Policy Theory for a Developing World Economy*, Wicksell Lectures, Almqvist & Wiksell, Stockholm.

KINDLEBERGER, C. P. (1969), *American Investment Abroad*, Yale University Press.

LIPSEY, R. G., and LANCASTER, K. J. (1956), 'The general theory of second best', *Rev. econ. Stud.*, vol. 24, pp. 11–32.

POSNER, M. V. (1961), 'International trade and technical change', *Oxf. econ. Pap.*, vol. 13, pp. 323–41.

REDDAWAY, W. B., POTTER, S. J., and TAYLOR, C. T. (1967–8), 'The effects of UK direct investment overseas: final report', *University of Cambridge, Department of Applied Economics, Occasional Paper*, no. 15.

SAFARIAN, A. E. (1969), *The Performance of Foreign-Owned Firms in Canada*, Canadian–American Committee, Washington and Montreal.

VERNON, R. (1966), 'International investment and international trade in the product cycle', *Q. J. Econ.*, vol. 80, pp. 190–207.

14 D. A. Snider

The Case for Capital Controls to Relieve the US Balance of Payments

D. A. Snider, 'The case for capital controls to relieve the US balance of payments', *American Economic Review*, vol. 54, 1964, pp. 346–58.

It is doubtful that many economists would disagree that one of the two or three current major economic problems of the United States is the reduction and ultimate elimination of the balance of payments deficit and the accomplishment of this without restraining growth of the domestic economy. Presumably no one would contest the grave seriousness of a failure to show a marked improvement in the balance of payments over the course of the next three or four years or the necessity of reducing the deficit without serious adverse side effects.

It is evident, however, that there is no consensus among economists of what, if anything, should be done to meet the problem. There are two kinds of divergences of opinion: first, between those who believe nothing in the way of positive new policy measures should be undertaken and those who advocate various specific policy remedies; second, among the latter, differences as to what specific measures would be optimal. The primary purpose of this paper is to examine the second issue – what specific measures would be optimal, with the case for measures to reduce the outflow of private capital given special attention.

Interest in measures to reduce the outflow of private capital has been stimulated by the Administration's proposal, now before the Congress, to levy a tax on the purchase of securities from foreigners (HR 8000). I shall not be concerned in this paper with this or any other specific types of measures to reduce outward capital movements, nor with the problems – some of which may be formidable – attending the implementation of such measures. I shall instead concentrate on the theoretical aspects of capital controls, with 'controls' understood to embrace any kind of measure, direct or indirect designed to reduce private capital outflows. Finally, the analysis applies only to long-term capital movements, the special case of short-term movements being excluded from consideration.

Before entering into the discussion of alternative policy measures to correct the US balance of payments deficit and of the case of capital controls as the least undesirable alternative, a brief comment on the first issue mentioned above – whether any kind of specific balance of payments policy is called for – is in order.

Market correction of the deficit

Whether or not it would be wise for specific policy measures to be adopted to relieve the balance of payments depends upon the probability that market forces – operating under present policies – will correct the deficit within a reasonable period of time and without interfering with policies to expand the domestic economy. Fortunately, the option of relying on market forces is still open, since the reserve position of the United States, together with the various swap agreements and other arrangements among central banks, permit a continuation of the deficit for some time without leading to a crisis situation.[1]

The thesis that market forces can be expected to work in the direction of eliminating the US balance of payments deficit, even though (and in part *because*) domestic policies succeed in accelerating the rate of growth in the United States, has been most ably supported by the recent Brookings study under the direction of Walter Salant (1963). However, the study's optimistic projections are based on several assumptions which may or may not be realized. Most critical among these is the assumption that US costs and export prices will fall relatively to those of Western Europe. Because of the large degree of uncertainty underlying this assumption, together with the uncertainty involved in extrapolating into the future functional relationships derived from past behavior, the present writer, as well as numerous others, has argued that the Brookings study's projections are not a sufficiently solid base on which to arrive at policy con-

1. One must also assume, however, that the deficit does not continue unimproved for so long that fear of eventual drastic measures induces widespread destabilizing speculative actions.

clusions (US Congress, Joint Economic Committee, 1963). This is, of course, a personal judgement, based on the subjective weighing of how much confidence can be placed in balance of payments projections in comparison with the consequences of failure of the projections to be actually realized.

Apart from the question of whether one can confidently expect market forces satisfactorily to solve the payments problem without the aid of additional discretionary policy measures, there is the second question of what particular policy measures would be appropriate and acceptable. If there are acceptable policies that could be adopted to relieve the deficit, the case for relying on market forces to do the job is weakened; if not, the case is strengthened.

The criteria of acceptable policies

The crux of the matter, of course, is what constitutes 'acceptable' policies. There are three general economic criteria to which, it is believed, most economists would agree. These may be briefly identified as effectiveness, employment and efficiency. In addition, there is a fourth criterion, essentially noneconomic in nature, that I shall call institutional.

The three economic criteria are rather obvious and require only summary explanation. Effectiveness refers strictly to the balance of payments repercussions of a measure. It is clearly a primary desideratum, any measure failing substantially to reduce the payments deficit being ineligible for consideration at the outset.

The employment criterion refers to the effects of a measure on domestic employment – or, more generally, on economic growth. Regardless of how effective a given measure might be in reducing the payments deficit, it would be objectionable if it caused serious domestic unemployment or if it was inconsistent with domestic policies for full employment and a reasonable growth rate.

The criterion of efficiency relates to the allocation of resources. Any measure that would tend to interfere with the optimum use of resources or that would aggravate an already existing deviation from the optimum pattern of resource use would violate the efficiency criterion.

Finally, the institutional criterion refers to the possibility of a policy in the context of the contemporary world and the historical position of the United States in that world. Even though this aspect of policy has no theoretical interest to the economist, *qua* economist, any serious discussion of policy requires its consideration. A policy may not be feasible, in the sense employed here, either because it conflicts with noneconomic objectives that have priority or because it requires institutional changes that for political or other reasons are not acceptable.

An ideal policy would completely satisfy all four of the above criteria.[2] If there were such a policy available, presumably the issue of whether to rely on (uncertain) market forces to correct the payments deficit would disappear. Obviously, however, there is no such 'ideal' policy. But there surely are different policies whose degree of fulfillment of the stated criteria vary by wide margins. The question, therefore, remains of whether there are particular measures sufficiently satisfactory to deserve consideration as an alternative to reliance on market forces.

Alternative payments policies

In pursuing this question, we may begin by listing the major policies, each of which, alone or in combination with others, could conceivably be effective in reducing a payments deficit. The list is as follows:

1. Internal deflation of real income and/or prices.
2. Devaluation and establishment of new fixed dollar exchange rates.
3. Abandonment of fixed dollar exchange rates and acceptance of free or floating rates.
4. Quantitative limitation of imports or increased tariffs.
5. Export subsidies or other devices (tax rebates, etc.) directly to stimulate exports.
6. Reduced foreign military expenditure.
7. Reduced foreign aid.
8. Limitations or penalties on private capital outflows.

The list includes only those policies over which the deficit country has some control and excludes such potentially effective

2. I am assuming that other welfare critera – such as those relating to income distribution – are not significantly involved.

policies on the part of other countries as upward revaluation of currencies, expansionary monetary and fiscal policies, control over capital inflows, etc.

It may appear that one very important possible approach to reducing the payments deficit has been omitted – namely, measures to increase productivity while holding the line on wage and profit increases. In the Brookings study (Salant, 1963), this is the principal avenue of the projected improvement over the forthcoming years in the balance of payments.

While it cannot be denied that increases in productivity, accompanied by relatively stable money-wage rates and profit margins, would indeed tend to contribute significantly to improving the balance of payments and, further, would fully meet the other criteria of acceptability, unfortunately such a method is not amenable to discretionary policy determination, at least in the short run. It is true, of course, that different policies may influence differently the rate of productivity increases and the level of factor prices, and that particular policies might be identified as more contributive to economic growth at stable prices than are other policies. But the influence of policies in this area is uncertain, marginal and, in any event, long-run. It is fairly easy through discretionary policies to *retard* the rate of growth and *increase* money wages and profit margins; it is much more difficult to accelerate the rate of growth while restraining wage rates and profit margins.

These comments do not argue against the pursuit of policies most likely to influence favorably growth with price stability; they only argue against the view that such policies can be expected to have a significant impact within the space of the next few years during which the balance of payments problem must in some fashion be solved.

Effective but otherwise objectionable measures

The first point suggested by an examination of the alternative policies listed is that those which best meet the criterion of effectiveness are the worst from the point of view of one or more of the other criteria. For sheer effectiveness in reducing a payments deficit, internal deflation, abandonment of fixed exchange rates and quantitative limitation of imports rank at the top.

Deflation is the most serious violator of the employment criterion, quantitative limitation of imports is the most serious violator of the efficiency criterion, and abandonment of fixed exchange rates is objected to mainly on the basis of the one noneconomic criterion, institutional. Undoubtedly this is the reason why there is a consensus among economists opposing deflation and import controls but far from a consensus opposing free exchange rates. Disagreement over the abandonment of fixed rates as a method of eliminating the payments deficit arises in part out of differences in opinion as to the merits of fixed rates versus free rates in encouraging an optimum level of world trade and investment (Friedman, 1953; Houthakker, 1962; Meade, 1951, ch. 15; Sohmen, 1961). But this is an economic argument, whereas the more definitive consideration so far as policy making is concerned is essentially noneconomic in character, embracing such questions as the effect of abandoning fixed rates on the financial and economic (and perhaps political?) leadership of the United States in the Free World. Whatever the economic merits of the case, it would appear that fundamentally changing the system of pegged exchange rates is not at present a feasible choice so long as alternative measures involving a smaller departure from established institutions and practices continue to be available.

Devaluation

If abandonment of pegged exchange rates is not feasible, what about devaluation of the dollar and its repegging at a lower gold content? The employment and efficiency criteria are as well satisfied as they are with floating rates, but the institutional criterion is violated to nearly the same extent as it is with floating rates and, in addition, devaluation carries the risk of being ineffective in eliminating the payments deficit.

The institutional criterion is not met by devaluation because it would involve a fundamental shock to the present international monetary system based on a gold- and dollar-exchange standard. The status of the dollar as an international monetary 'anchor' would in all probability be destroyed if the weight of the anchor were to be allowed to change.

The second objection to devaluation is its potential ineffectiveness. It may be ineffective for either one of two kinds of reasons.

The first is that it may evoke counterdevaluations by other countries, especially Western European countries and the United Kingdom, which are the chief international competitors of the United States, and Canada, which is the largest market for US exports.

Assuming the problem of counterdevaluation is overcome, the second reason devaluation may be ineffective is more strictly economic in character, relating to the difficulties of selecting the right degree of change in the international value of the dollar. Various estimates of the amount of overvaluation of the dollar have been made (Vanek, 1962), and although these may be reasonable, there is no known way of being certain they do not contain a large margin of error. The danger of too small a degree of devaluation can be reduced by choosing the amount of devaluation indicated by the higher ranges of estimated overvaluation. However, in this case, the opposite danger is run of ending up with an undervaluated dollar, thereby increasing the probability of counteraction by other countries, either in the form of devaluation of their currencies or in the form of various import restrictions. Again, the special international position of the dollar leaves less room for mistakes than in the case of other currencies.

Reduction of foreign military expenditure and aid

If, as I have so far concluded, there are strong objections to deflation, import controls, abandonment of fixed exchange rates and devaluation, the field of choice is considerably narrowed. It can immediately be further narrowed by eliminating two other possible measures – reduction of military expenditure and reduction of foreign aid.

There is one common ground on the basis of which both of these latter measures are rendered unacceptable as a means of correcting the payments deficit – they are autonomously determined by noneconomic objectives. They are both instruments of foreign policy and therefore not appropriately determined by balance of payments considerations.

A second, though subsidiary, consideration applicable to foreign aid is the ineffectiveness of reductions in significantly contributing to eliminating the payments deficit. Because aid recipients tend to spend most of their grant and loan dollars directly on US exports, reinforced by the government policy of tied aid, only a fraction of any reduction in aid would be reflected in improvement in the US balance of payments (Salant, 1963, pp. 155 ff.).

Export subsidies

Theoretically, exports could be increased just as effectively through subsidies – direct or indirect – as through devaluation. Indeed, a uniform subsidy for all exports would be tantamount in effect to a 'half' devaluation. (The effect could be made 'full' by simultaneously imposing a uniform *ad valorem* tariff on all imports.) However, the efficiency and institutional criteria are seriously by-passed by export subsidies and, in addition, the effectiveness criterion is not likely to be met.

Export subsidies are the counterpart of import duties and, like them, distort international cost-price comparisons which underlie the optimum allocation of resources internationally. And, again like import tariffs, subsidies go counter to the prevailing and generally accepted code of commercial conduct. Finally, the balance of payments effectiveness of subsidies is rendered doubtful because of probable retaliation by other countries, either in the form of increased import tariffs against the subsidizing country's goods or in the form of subsidies on their own export goods.

Capital controls

The last remaining measure to investigate is control over capital outflows. While there are certainly serious objections to this policy, there are reasons to believe they may be less serious, in the context of the present balance of payments problem of the United States, than any of the other alternatives available. This conclusion is supported by examining capital controls from the point of view of each of the four criteria of acceptability.

Effectiveness criterion

Starting with the effectiveness criterion, the first question is to what extent the payments deficit is attributable to private capital movements. In view of the interrelationships among the various items in the balance of payments, it is practically impossible to identify with precision the net role of any one item. But theoretical considerations, plus empirical studies, permit conclusions as to the general nature and direction of the balance of payments effect of capital movements.

There are many different possible approaches to explaining the reasons for the US payments deficit and nearly all of them have been cited (US Congress, Joint Economic Committee, 1962). Different approaches may serve different purposes. If the purpose of the analysis is to find appropriate policy measures to correct the deficit, approaches may be broadly classified according to whether the emphasis is on enlarging the current-account surplus or on reducing the autonomous capital-account (including unilateral transfers) deficit.

In terms of the *causes* of the deficit, there is no basis for choosing between these two approaches. One may equally well say either that the deficit is caused by the failure of the 'transfer' mechanism or that it is caused by a too large capital outflow. These are saying the same thing, for a 'too large' capital outflow can be meaningfully identified only in terms of a 'too small' current-account surplus, and likewise 'failure' of the transfer mechanism can be identified only in terms of an insufficiently large current-account surplus.

Capital outflow contributes to a payments deficit to the extent that the outflow does not, directly or indirectly, lead to an equivalent current-account surplus. Conversely, a reduction in capital outflow contributes to eliminating a deficit to the extent that it does not lead, directly or indirectly, to an equivalent reduction in the current-account surplus.

On theoretical grounds, the influence of capital flows on the current account of the balance of payments is in the direction of an accomodation. In the absence of countervailing policies, and with fixed exchange rates, a capital movement tightens money and discourages spending in the capital-exporting country and eases money and encourages spending in the capital-receiving country. However, there is no *a priori* way of knowing whether these prices and income effects will be sufficiently strong in any particular case to bring about a real transfer equal to the money transfer. Either underadjustment or overadjustment may occur, depending upon numerous conditions – such as reserve positions, propensities to spend, institutional ties, etc. – which are a matter for empirical determination (Meade, 1951, part 2). Moreover, and perhaps most important in the modern world, the transfer mechanism may be either reinforced or completely swamped by discretionary policies on the part of monetary and fiscal authorities.

In the case of the United States in recent years, the strain on the adjustment mechanism from capital outflow has been great and the evidence indicates its failure fully to meet the challenge.

A sharp change in the volume of private long-term capital movements out of the United States occurred in 1956. Compared to an annual outflow averaging about $0·8 billion during the preceding five years, beginning in 1956 and continuing through 1962 the outflow reached an annual average of about $2·7 billion (Salant, 1963, pp. 278–9).

The nearly two billion dollars of added annual payments on account of private long-term capital outflow from 1956 onward did not, of course, contribute an equivalent net amount to the payments deficit. Even in the absence of indirect adjustment processes, the outflow of capital can be expected directly to cause an increase of exports of goods and services, especially in the case of direct foreign investments, which ordinarily involve the capital-exporting country's shipment of equipment and materials, the receipt of management fees, etc. Some portfolio investments have similar direct effects – as, for example, when the recipient is a capital-hungry underdeveloped country with close trade ties to the United States.

In addition to contributing to the sending-country's exports, a capital outflow also contributes to current receipts in the form of interest and dividends, and, for direct investments, other 'invisible' receipts. However, the benefits of such return flows are received only after some delay, the length of which depends upon various circumstances. The balance of payments 'payoff' period for US direct investments has been estimated as between four to seven years (Bell, 1962, pp. 412–13; Salant, 1963, pp. 142–6), though under some assumptions with respect to investments in Europe and Canada the payoff period may be as long as ten to fifteen years (Bell, 1962, p. 413). In the case of portfolio investments, at average rates of return received in recent years, 'it will be a very long time before even a single investment outflow is recouped in cumulative interest and dividend receipts' (Bell, 1962, p. 416).

While the lack of complete information on all the relevant variables and functions makes it impossible to specify with precision the net balance of payments effect of the outflow of US capital, a careful econometric investigation by Philip W. Bell (1962, p. 458) led to the general conclusion that 'Shifts in the flow of private capital, in particular in US private capital flowing overseas, have been a major cause of our deteriorating balance of payments position since 1956.'

From a long-run point of view, after taking into account return flows, capital movements out of the United States may have a net favorable balance of payments effect. Thus, as frequently noted, in recent years US income receipts from past foreign investments have exceeded the annual outflow of new capital. But this is not a particularly relevant consideration if the immediate problem is to reduce the balance of payments deficit within the course of the next few years. Receipts from past investments would presumably continue unabated regardless of the level of future capital flows. Any reduction in new capital outflows can therefore be expected to have a favorable balance of payments impact during the period for which such a result is critical.

For the purposes of the remaining discussion, I shall assume the balance of payments of the United States could be substantially improved over the course of the next four or five years by reducing the outflow of private capital.

Employment criterion

Turning now to the second criterion of acceptable policy – the employment criterion – control over capital movements falls in between the adverse effects associated with internal deflation and the favorable effects associated with such measures as devaluation. A reduction in capital outflow would cause an adverse effect on domestic employment to the extent that exports are reduced by the diminished outflow of capital. On the other hand, employment would be increased to the extent that domestic investment expenditure is substituted for foreign investment. Neither effect is likely to be very significant, however, and for practical purposes it is fairly safe to regard the net domestic employment effect as neutral.

There are advantages to balance of payments policies that do not directly increase (or decrease) domestic employment. Any policy that simultaneously improves the balance of payments and increases domestic employment is very likely to *decrease* employment in other countries. Thus, devaluation, to the extent that it succeeds in reducing the deficit by decreasing imports and increasing exports, exerts a deflationary impact on other countries. Besides being unfortunate on its own grounds, such foreign effects increase the probability of countervailing measures abroad that would negate the initial favorable balance of payments effect.

It may be argued, however, that reduction in the payments deficit inherently involves an adverse foreign employment effect, regardless of the means employed to bring about the reduction. To the extent that the payments deficit is eliminated by increasing the current-account surplus, this is necessarily true. But if the deficit is attacked via the capital account it is a different matter.

Looking at it from the point of view of the capital-recipient countries, a distinction should be drawn between those countries whose rate of domestic investment expenditure is significantly dependent upon foreign capital inflow and those where such is not the case. Generally, the former consists principally of underdeveloped economies and the latter of developed economies. A decreased inflow of foreign capital may well cause decreased investment in underdeveloped countries and thereby reduced employment opportunities. It is much less likely that total domestic investment expenditure would be significantly affected by diminished capital inflow into already developed countries, such as those of Western Europe.[3]

The unfavorable foreign employment effect of capital controls could be largely eliminated by confining restrictions to capital flows going to developed countries. Since the adverse balance of

3. Of the major recipients of U S capital, Canada may be an exception to this general rule. If so, consideration might be given to including Canada in the exemption referred to in the next paragraph.

payments effect of capital flows is probably highly concentrated in these particular movements, such selective application of controls would not greatly reduce their effectiveness in improving the balance of payments.

There remain for discussion the efficiency and institutional effects of capital control. Because of the larger issues involved in the former, I shall reserve discussion of it until after the institutional criterion is examined.

Institutional criterion

It must be admitted forthwith that one of the strongest objections to capital control by the United States is the violation it would cause to the principle of freedom in international economic relations. This principle has two aspects, one domestic and the other international.

From a domestic point of view, the United States has a long-established principle that individuals and businesses should be free to invest as they see fit, both at home and abroad. This is part and parcel of a more general philosophy of government and economics, and deviations cannot be taken lightly. Justification for restricting freedom of international investment may nevertheless be found on at least two grounds.

The first is based on another equally valid and accepted principle – namely, that when the national interest demands it, the interests of particular individuals become secondary. I think it can be maintained that the balance of payments problem of the United States is one of critical importance and, if left unsolved, it could cause great harm to both the domestic and international economy. Therefore, measures that otherwise would be unacceptable may become acceptable, provided they would effectively contribute to its solution.

Support for this position is strengthened by the fact that failure to correct the payments deficit in itself results in a loss of freedom that is in some respects much more serious and extensive than the loss of freedom to invest abroad without restriction. Freedom is of very limited meaning if opportunities for exercising it are absent. The presence of a payments deficit imposes constraints upon the domestic policy which, in turn, reduce opportunities for *domestic* investment. Specifically, the payments deficit directly restrains growth of the domestic economy and prevents the adoption of expansionary monetary and fiscal policies which would be capable of creating greater investment opportunities at home.

Turning now to the international aspect of capital controls, again there is the objection that they would go counter to the principle of freedom which the United States has vigorously espoused. However, there are two points to be noted in the connection.

The first is that, unlike quantitative trade controls, control over capital movements is recognized as a legitimate exception to the general principle of freedom of international economic relations. This acceptance is formalized in the 'codes' of conduct set out in the charter of the International Monetary Fund.[4]

The second point is that nearly all other countries are currently, or have in the recent past, employed control over capital movements as a device for correcting or protecting their balances of payments. In short, it is a policy both accepted in principle and sanctioned by practice and therefore not subject to legitimate criticism by other countries.

Efficiency criterion

Finally, we arrive at the examination of capital control from the standpoint of the efficiency criterion. From a strictly economic point of view, this is where the most important issues arise, for freedom of capital movements is strongly embedded in the tradition as a necessary part of the market mechanism allocating resources in an optimal fashion. If it can be shown that capital controls would seriously interfere with the optimum allocation of resources, the economic case against them might be decisive.

The theory of gain from long-term capital movements is well known and requires only brief summary (Meade, 1955). The optimum allocation of capital resources requires that the marginal net rate of return be equalized in alternative uses, both at home and internationally. If the marginal rate of return is higher in country B than in country A, world output and the

4. Section 3 of Article VI of the Articles of Agreement of the International Monetary Fund states t hat 'Members may exercise such controls as are necessary to regulate international capital movements. . . .'

national income of A and B are increased by the movement of capital from A to B until the marginal rate of return is equalized in the two countries.[5]

Under ideal conditions, the flow of capital from areas of lower marginal yield to areas of higher marginal yields will take place in response to market forces. In the real world, these ideal conditions are never completely fulfilled and, indeed, may under particular circumstances fall so far short as to cause a *perverse* movement of capital. The absence of ideal conditions is not, *per se*, a reason for concluding that actual capital movements are undesirable from a welfare point of view or that capital controls are justified. It depends upon the extent and seriousness of deviations from the ideal in particular cases.

In the case of the United States, there is a strong presumption that over the long run she should be a net exporter of long-term capital. But there is a serious question of whether the large increase in capital outflow of recent years can be justified on welfare grounds. Leaving aside the distortion caused by imperfect markets, differential rates of taxation and of subsidies, and similar factors that are always present to some degree, special elements have arisen in the last few years to weaken the presumption that uncontrolled capital movements are desirable.

The first of these special elements is the slowdown in the rate of economic growth of the United States, accompanied by above-normal unemployment, in conjunction with extraordinarily high growth rates and below-normal unemployment in Western Europe. There is little room for doubting that the increased flow of capital – especially in the form of direct investment – to Western Europe has been stimulated by the relative boom conditions there compared to the United States.

Now it can be argued that an outflow of capital induced by more prosperous conditions abroad than at home is perfectly rational and economically desirable from the points of view of both the sending and recipient countries. The sending country finds productive employment for some of its 'excess' saving and

5. The marginal test may not be adequate in those cases where large flows of capital are economic, even though smaller movements are not, such as movements to underdeveloped countries to finance 'social overhead' and infrastructure investment.

the receiving country is supplied with additional resources to relieve the strain on its economy. Even if it actually works this way (see discussion below), however, the benefits derived are not those stemming from a more efficient allocation of resources but rather from a fuller use of resources.

An outflow of long-term capital caused by differences in cyclical stages at home and abroad cannot be defended on the basis of the efficiency criterion. Higher rates of return abroad are in this case not an indication of a relatively greater scarcity. Presumably, such differences in return are temporary and would tend to be eliminated, *without* a flow of capital, as recovery in the capital-exporting country occurs.

In short, the comparison of marginal rates of return is relevant as a guide to proper resource allocation only when the rates are those emerging under full employment both at home and abroad. Such has not been the case during much of the time of the great increase in capital outflow from the United States in recent years.

The second special element that weakens the objection to capital controls on efficiency grounds has been the distorting influences exerted by the European Economic Community. If it is true, as commonly asserted, that US capital has been attracted to Western Europe in order to get 'under' the common tariff wall being erected there, the adverse efficiency effects of tariffs may be only compounded by the movement of capital into the area. If we suppose that capital would not have moved into Europe if a discriminatory tariff wall were not to be created, the actual capital movement cannot be regarded as contributing to the more efficient use of resources.

The third special element interfering with the process of optimum allocation is institutional in character. Compared to the financial markets in the United States, in most other countries they are 'thin'. It is considerably easier to float new issues in New York than in most other financial centers. The apparent lack of any significant relationship between interest rates in New York and in other centers and the floating of new foreign issues (Bell, 1962, pp. 419–20) suggests that the attraction of New York as a capital market has to do less with the cost of borrowing than the availability of credit and the ease of acquiring it. To the extent that the latter is a function of more developed financial institutions rather than simply of capital supply, there is no assurance that the flow of capital is desirable on welfare grounds.

Finally, I turn to what is perhaps the most important point of all. In order for a money capital movement to result in a more efficient allocation, it must lead to or be accompanied by a *real* capital movement. Real capital movements take the form of net current-account balances. To the extent that a net current-account balance of equal amount (but of opposite sign) to a money capital movement fails to develop, the capital movement aborts. In such cases, the capital outflow is accompanied by a reverse movement of short-term capital of an accommodating character and/or by an outflow of gold. If these are temporary movements, they are normal stages in the process of adjustment, but when they persist it is an indication that adjustment and a real transfer have failed to occur.

It will be observed that the failure of real capital to move with money capital is tantamount to one variety of balance of payments disequilibrium. What we are saying, then, is that, if a country incurs a deficit disequilibrium accompanying an outflow of long-term capital, control over the capital outflow cannot be regarded as contrary to the efficiency criterion, for real capital is not in fact being reallocated.

The issue runs deeper than this, however, for it might be argued that if there is an autonomous long-term capital movement out of a country, what is required, on welfare grounds, is not suppression of the movement but rather adjustment of the balance of payments to the movement. This argument is applicable, of course, only on the assumption that the marginal productivity of capital is higher abroad than at home. But even with this assumption, is it a valid argument?

References

BELL, P. W. (1962), 'Private capital movements and the US balance of payments position', in *Factors Affecting the United States Balance of Payments*, US Congress, Joint Economic Committee, Washington.

FRIEDMAN, M. (1953), 'The case for flexible exchange rates', in *Essays in Positive Economics*, University of Chicago Press.

HOUTHAKKER, H. S. (1962), 'Exchange rate adjustment', in *Factors Affecting the United States Balance of Payments*, US Congress, Joint Economic Committee, Washington.

MEADE, J. E. (1951), *The Theory of International Economic Policy: I. The Balance of Payments*, Oxford University Press.
MEADE, J. E. (1955), *The Theory of International Economic Policy: III. Trade and Welfare*, Oxford University Press.
SALANT, W. S. (1963), *The United States Balance of Payments in 1968*, Brookings Institution, Washington.
SOHMEN, E. (1961), *Flexible Exchange Rates*, University of Chicago Press.
US CONGRESS, JOINT ECONOMIC COMMITTEE (1962), *Factors Affecting the United States Balance of Payments*, Washington.
US CONGRESS, JOINT ECONOMIC COMMITTEE (1963), *Factors Affecting the States Balance of Payments*, Washington.
VANEK, J. (1962), 'Overvaluation of the dollar: causes, effects and remedies', in *Factors Affecting the United States Balance of Payments*, US Congress, Joint Economic Committee, Washington.

Part Six
Foreign Investment, Technology and Economic Development

The key feature of foreign direct investment is that it provides the recipient country with a package of knowledge, capital and entrepreneurship. It thus is likely to have a key influence on its country's economic development. Technology is one of the most important ingredients of growth. It can be generated internally or bought from abroad in a varicty of ways. Both developing and developed countries import technology; in this respect, Canada and Australia have been no less dependent on foreign investment than Nigeria and Malaysia. But the problems posed are rather different.

Reading 15 by Dunning deals with the transfer of technology from the US to Europe via the operation of US companies. As shown at the end of the article there is a considerable literature developing on this subject. Several international agencies, e.g. OECD, UNCTAD, have produced or are commissioning studies on the subject. The problems facing the developing countries have been examined *inter alia* by Jack Baranson (1966, 1969). Various case studies of the transfer of technology are given in a recent volume edited by Raymond Vernon (1970).

The other essays in this section deal with the impact of foreign investment on developing countries. Gerald Meier (Reading 16) summarizes the main contribution of private investment. More recent thinking on this subject is contained in Paul Streeten's contribution (Reading 17). Here he highlights some of the alternatives to foreign investment. The reader is is also invited to consult the writings of Hirschman (1969), Penrose (1970) and Vernon (1968).

References

BARANSON, J. (1966), 'Transfer of technical knowledge by International corporations to developing economies', *Amer. econ. Rev., Proc.*, vol. 55, pp. 260–66.

BARANSON, J. (1969), *Industrial Technologies for Developing Economies*, Praeger.

HIRSCHMAN, A. O. (1969), *How to Divest in Latin America and Why*, Princeton University Press.

PENROSE, E. T. (1970), 'International economic relations and the large international firm', in P. Lyon and E. T. Penrose (eds.), *New Orientations: Essays in International Relations*, Cass.

VERNON, R. (1968), 'Conflict and resolution between foreign direct investors and less developed countries', *Pub. Pol.*, vol. 17, pp. 333–51.

VERNON, R. (1970), *The Technology Factor in International Trade*, Columbia University Press.

15 John H. Dunning

Technology, United States Investment and European Economic Growth

John H. Dunning, 'Technology, United States investment and European economic growth', in C. P. Kindleberger (ed.), *The International Corporation*, MIT Press, 1970, pp. 141–76.

Introduction

The subject of this paper is technology and economic development, with particular reference to the contribution made by US direct investment to European economic development since 1950. For the purposes of most of our arguments, we shall think of economic development in terms of the growth rate of real national output per person employed (Denison, 1967) and shall pay only passing attention to its composition or its distribution between factors inputs.

Association between US investment and growth in European output per head

We first start with one or two fairly well-known observations. First, a casual inspection of Table 1 reveals a generally close association between US direct investment (i.e. the increase in US direct capital stake) and European development between 1950 and 1965.[1] Roughly the same picture emerges for later years and from other cross-sectional studies. In particular, US manufacturing investment in Europe has been directed to those countries that have increased their manufacturing output the most rapidly, while Krause (1968) has shown that such investment in the EEC has also been largely concentrated in the faster growing manufacturing sectors.

Such data as these, of course, may imply no causal relationship. Both US investment and economic development in individual

1. Switzerland is an exceptional case. Most US (and other foreign) investment there is of a 'window dressing' character and much of it is immediately reexported to other countries, particularly Italy (EFTA, 1969).

Table 1 United States Direct Investment in Europe and Economic Development, 1960 to 1965

	Increase in US direct capital stake			*Increase in gross national product per capita*		
	1950/58 1950 = 100	*1958/65 1958 = 100*	*1950/65 1950 = 100*	*1950/58 1950 = 100*	*1958/65 1958 = 100*	*1950/65 1950 = 100*
Europe (total)	275·2	320·6	882·3	132	131	173
EEC	303·0	351·1	1064·0	144	134	193
Belgium and Luxemburg	400·0	298·0	1192·0	117*	132	154
France	251·2	318·6	800·5	133	130	173
W. Germany	330·2	389·6	1286·3	165	135	223
Italy	532·0	369·2	1964·0	147	138	203
Netherlands	280·3	344·7	966·3	127	133	169
EFTA	258·6	299·1	773·5	120	127	152
United Kingdom	261·5	248·6	650·0	116	123	143
Denmark	148·4	434·8	645·2	116	138	160
Norway	226·1	292·3	660·9	118	135	159
Sweden	196·4	291·7	572·8	120	134	161
Switzerland	316·7	1473·6	4667·2	122†	128	156

* Estimated on basis of 1953/8 data.
† Estimated on basis of 1954/8 data.
Sources: OECD, *Statistics of National Accounts*, 1950/61, 1956/65, Paris; US Department of Commerce (1960, 1966a).

European countries (or industries) may be the result of other factors. One might have hoped that a time-series approach – particularly with the introduction of time lags – might help settle this issue, but in this case (as Bandera and White, 1968, have shown) it does not. The level and distribution of US investment appear to both influence, and be influenced by, European growth. One difficulty, of course, is that investment (and particularly the net capital outflow component of it) is discontinuous, while its effects are spread over many years. When first differences, i.e. the rate of change of investment, are related to growth variables, the results are inconclusive (Bandera and White, 1968). Our impression is that one can waste a lot of time trying to manipulate and refine the few macrostatistics that are available. As they are, they are broadly suggestive, but insufficiently detailed or reliable to help us test any but the very simplest of propositions.

On the other hand, it is not difficult to formulate theories of *why* US direct investment has been attracted to certain countries and industries in Europe and of how this might have affected their development. There would seem little doubt that in the early 1950s American firms were prompted to begin, or expand, manufacturing and petroleum refining operations in Europe, partly by the prospects of growth (both absolute and relative to that in the United States) and the profits likely to be associated with such growth; and that, after 1958, this was accentuated by forces making for *more* growth, for example, the impact of the EEC. This holds good for both aggressive and defensive investment, and is most clearly seen in the shift of American interest away from the United Kingdom to the EEC at a time when the supply conditions for US investment were most favorable.[2] Between 1957 and 1966, for example, plant and equipment expenditure by US firms in the EEC rose by eight times while in the United Kingdom it increased by only two and a half times.

In the last two or three years, the pace of new US investment in Europe has slowed down a bit, partly due to the resurgence of the US economy, partly to the curbs placed on outward US

2. It will be noted, however, that even in the United Kingdom the increase of plant and equipment expenditure by US firms has continued to outpace that of their UK competitors.

investment and partly to the decline in the profitability of capital in European economies, both absolutely and relatively to the United States. There is, indeed, evidence that in various directions the European economy is catching up with the US economy. This, coupled with the cyclical boom in the United States, explains why, relative to domestic investment, the rate of US investment in Europe is now about three-quarters of that of the early 1960s.

The growth contribution of inward investment: some macroeconomic considerations

Part of the difficulty in calculating the impact of US direct investment, on either overall European economic development or that of individual economies, is that, in relation to domestic capital formation it is still quite small and there are so many other determinants of growth. Table 2 shows that the proportion of gross domestic fixed capital formation in various EEC countries and the United Kingdom accounted for by the expenditure of US subsidiaries on plant and equipment ranged, in 1965, from 4 per cent in France to 10 per cent in the United Kingdom. If one could assume that this capital (and any local expenditure generated by it) represented a net addition to resource formation in the host countries, then the value of sales of US firms (less imports and remitted profits), might be said to represent their direct contribution to the growth of European output. The second part of Table 2 expresses the sales of US manufacturing subsidiaries in selected European countries in relation to the gross national product of these countries in 1957 and 1965 and the increase in sales to the increase in gross national product between these years. These calculations, however, ignore the technological multiplier effect of US investment on the output of competitors, suppliers, customers, and so on (Quinn, 1968).

If the alternative assumption of full employment in the host-countries is made, then US investment must replace either other domestic expenditure or imports (unless capital imports rise by the same amount). If it replaces other investment, then its net effect on economic development is the difference between the level of output actually produced and that which would have otherwise been produced by domestic firms. If it replaces con-

Table 2 Relative Significance of Plant and Equipment Expenditure and Sales of US Firms in Selected European Countries, 1957 to 1965

	*Plant and equipment expenditure by US subsidiaries as % of all gross domestic fixed capital formation**					*Manufacturing sales of US subsidiaries as % of GNP*			*△ in sales/△ in GNP, 1957 to 1965*
	1957	*1959*	*1961*	*1963*	*1965*	*1957*	*1963*	*1965*	
Belgium	2·2	2·6	3·3	3·8	4·5	†	†	†	†
France	1·8	1·9	2·1	3·0	4·0	1·4	2·5	2·8	4·7
W. Germany	1·8	2·9	4·2	3·9	4·1	2·2	3·3	3·9	5·3
Italy	2·0	1·3	2·9	4·1	5·0	0·9	1·8	2·2	3·4
Netherlands	2·6	1·2	3·2	5·4	4·8	2·3	3·4	4·4	6·5
EEC	2·2	2·6	3·3	3·8	4·5	1·7	2·8	3·5	4·6
United Kingdom	7·8	5·7	7·4	7·9	10·0	5·9	6·9	7·5	9·7

* In machinery and equipment.

† Included in Netherlands.

Sources: OECD, *Main Economic Indicators*, various issues; United Nations (1967, p. 67); US Department of Commerce (1966b, p. 8).

sumption, then, because the savings ratio has been raised, the long-term benefits will be equal to the investment/net output ratio.

What, too, of the effect of inward investment on the balance of payments, terms of trade and prices of goods and services? In the main, our analysis will omit consideration of these and the impact any changes in their value are likely to have on resource allocation, utilization and growth. However, depending on the assumption one makes about government policy, for example, whether a country operates a flexible exchange or fixed exchange rate, it is possible that the indirect impact of US investment on European development could be more important than the direct impact (Powie, 1969). But I fear that if we went much further along these lines we would soon stray from our brief, which is less to evaluate the overall contribution of US investment to Europe's economy, and more the extent to which it has advanced growth and development, through supplying additional factor inputs and knowledge. And here macrodata are not very helpful. We have, instead, to turn to data on individual sectors of the economy and/or on the components of growth and development.

In his book *Why Growth Rates Differ*, Edward Denison (1967) sets out the main determinants of European growth between 1950 and 1964. How far has the participation of US affiliates contributed to this growth? Basically there are three ways in which such a contribution might have been made. First, US firms might have used (or have caused to be used) resources that would otherwise have remained unemployed. Second, they might have brought about (directly or indirectly) an improvement in resource allocation, by redirecting resources from slow-growing to fast-growing industries. Third, by the injection of new technology and more progressive managerial attitudes, they might have helped raise the efficiency of production in whatever sectors they invest and/or speeded their rate of growth. The first two of these effects essentially arise from the (money) 'capital' component of US investment and the efficiency with which US enterprises choose their European outlets; the third arises from the 'knowledge'-component – though, in practice, the two effects cannot easily be separated.

One way in which some idea might be obtained of the relative significance of the second aspect of growth is by use of shift and share analysis (Dunning, 1969a; Thirlwall, 1967). Let us illustrate from the data in Table 3. Between 1957 and 1964, the total manufacturing sales[3] of US subsidiaries in Europe rose by 160·2 per cent compared with an increase of 45·3 per cent for all European firms.

To calculate what part of this differential growth is due to differences in the structure, or industrial mix, of US investment and what part to the faster rate of growth of US affiliates within particular industries, one can first estimate what the average rate of growth would have been in US affiliates had their rate of growth in each group of products been that of European firms. This works out at 51·7 per cent ($\sum$ column 1/$\sum$ column 4). The difference between this and their actual rate of growth (108·5 per cent) measures the differential sector growth component, and that between the adjusted rate of growth and the actual rate of growth of European firms (7·6 per cent), the structural or composition shift effect. In the present example, it can be seen that almost all of the faster growth of the output of US firms is explained by the former effect. What part of this, in turn, reflects differences in the efficiency of US affiliates and European firms cannot be adduced without further data on the inputs of the two groups of firms.

The 'knowledge' capital ingredient of direct investment

It is now, I think, generally accepted that the main distinction between portfolio and direct foreign investment is that the latter incorporates knowledge and entrepreneurship, which the former does not – and which, moreover, is unlikely to be possessed by local competitors. This may take various forms, as outlined by Kindleberger (1969), and includes not only technical expertise but attitudinal advantages as well. These – through what Quinn (1968) and others have called the 'technological' multiplier – affect the productivity and growth of particular sectors in the host country, as both new markets are opened up and production processes improve.[4] When a firm in a technically progressive industry

3. Of those considered in the table.

4. Edwin Mansfield (1968) cites the electronic computer as an example of an investment with an exceptionally high technological multiplier and illustrates some of the ways it has affected the production function of various firms and industries.

Table 3 Sales of US Affiliates in Europe and all European Firms

	All European firms			*US affiliates*			
	(1)	(2)	*(3)*	*(4)*	(5)	(6)	(7)
	1957	*1964*	*1957/64 1957 = 100*	*1957*	*1964*	*1957/64 1957 = 100*	*Col. 4× Col. 3*
Food products	34,183	44,796	131·1	734	1308	178·2	962
Paper and allied products	7188	10,846	150·9	34	148	435·2	51
Chemicals	18,310	34,039	185·9	822	2273	276·5	1533
Rubber products	2451	3697	150·8	262	517	197·3	395
Nonelectrical machinery	19,420	26,807	138·0	1009	2735	271·1	1392
Electrical machinery	10,802	16,958	157·0	678	1968	290·2	1064
Metal products	32,868	42,634	129·7	435	1115	256·3	564
Transportation equipment	20,506	31,956	155·8	1700	4700	276·5	2649
Total	145,728	211,733	145·3	5674	14,764	260·2	8610

Sources: All European firms: Hufbauer and Adler (1968). United States firms: US Department of Commerce (1960, 1966b).

in an advanced industrial country invests in a less-advanced industrial country, but one that is gradually assimilating the economic structure of the advanced country, it follows not only that the knowledge content of the investment is likely to be significant, but that it will be directed to growth sectors. This explains why many US firms have been able to gain a foothold in the newer European industries – simply because they were first in the field in America. Once established, by a judicious reinvestment policy, they are able to grow rapidly.

The product-cycle thesis of Hirsch (1967) and Vernon (1966), tested by Wells (1969), Wilkinson (1968), and others, is now familiar to most economists. This suggests very strongly that certain types of international investment are inherently growth oriented, not only because they are directed to industries supplying products, the demand for which increases proportionately to the growth in GNP per head (Wells, 1968), but because of the various advantages, for example, access to knowledge and markets, size, integration and finance, possessed by the investing companies over their host competitors. Even the most cursory glance at the structure of US firms in Europe reveals that their activities are heavily concentrated in two sectors: first the science-based, or research-intensive, industries supplying both producer and consumer goods, and second, industries subject to economies of scale and producing products with a high income elasticity of demand. Between 1958 and 1964, for example, the four most research-intensive industries in the United States spent two and a half times the amount on new plant and equipment in Europe than fourteen other industries (Gruber, Mehta and Vernon, 1967). Moreover, these same 'knowledge' industries (e.g. computer, instruments, electronics, chemicals, etc.), by providing a kind of infrastructure of knowledge, create substantial spillover effects and act as a catalyst for growth which may far outweigh the initial demand-stimulating effects.[5]

5. This technological multiplier of an investment is achieved by *inter alia* – (a) increasing the productivity of the sectors in which it is employed; (b) lowering the factor costs of those who use the output of that sector and releasing their resources for other purposes; (c) stimulating responsive innovations in customers, suppliers or competition; (d) encouraging research and development to derive the maximum benefit from the new innovations (Quinn, 1968, p. 11).

The determinants of economic growth in Europe

Having briefly described the character of US investment in Europe, I now want to examine the sources of economic development to see how far the ingredients of one are common to the other. Several economists, notably Beckerman *et al.* (1965), Denison (1967), Lamfalussy (1963) and Maddison (1964), have tried to pinpoint the reasons for differential growth rates in Western Europe in the last two decades or so. Their explanations differ according to the emphasis they place on supply- and demand-oriented factors – and also to the techniques used. Our purpose in using these theories in this paper is simply to identify the main components of growth which one might reasonably expect to be affected by the international transfer of capital and knowledge.

We shall concentrate mostly on Denison's results because his classification of the sources of growth is more appropriate to our interests than that of the other writers. His approach is based on an accounting scheme that estimates total factor inputs by weighting the individual factor inputs by their respective prices. Similarly, growth in total factor inputs is derived by weighting the individual factor inputs by their respective shares of all inputs. An increase in aggregate output resulting from increased input is then separated from growth resulting from increased output per unit of input (i.e. total factor productivity). Changes in total factor productivity are, in turn, explained by (a) intersectoral resource shifts,[6] (b) economies of scale, and (c) a residual, advances in knowledge.

A summary of Denison's findings is given in Table 4, from which it is clear that increases in total factor productivity were the main component of economic growth in the period 1950 to 1962 (cf. line 3/line 1). Some of the items in this table require explanation since they have a special relation to inward technology. First, however, it should be observed that the table refers to relative growth rates in national income *per person employed.* This explains the small contribution of labor inputs and the corresponding large contribution of capital inputs to that part of growth which is explained by increased factor inputs.

6. The following four paragraphs lean heavily on an approach adopted by Scarfe (1969).

Table 4 Sources of Growth of Total National Income per Person Employed, 1950 to 1962*

	US	*Germany*	*UK*	*France*	*Italy*	*Netherlands*	*Belgium*	*Denmark*	*Norway*
1. Growth rate (2+3)†	2·15	5·15(2)	1·63(8)	4·80(3)	5·36(1)	3·65(4)	2·64(6)	2·56(7)	3·27(5)
2. Total factor input	0·79	0·72	0·45	1·13	1·07	0·86	0·62	0·62	0·86
(a) Labor	0·22	−0·12	0·10	0·37	0·54	0·09	0·36	−0·11	0·02
(b) Capital	0·60	0·93	0·37	0·76	0·57	0·78	0·28	0·77	0·85
(c) Land	−0·03	−0·09	−0·02	0·00	−0·04	−0·01	−0·02	−0·04	−0·01
3. Output per unit of input	1·36	4·43(1)	1·18(8)	3·67(3)	4·29(2)	2·79(4)	2·02(6)	1·94(7)	2·41(5)
(a) Advances in knowledge	0·75	0·75	0·75	0·76	0·76	0·75	0·76	0·75	0·76
(b) Economies of scale	0·36	0·69	0·27	0·51	0·62	0·54	0·40	0·42	0·45
(c) Adjustments and other	−0·04	0·26	−0·09	0·22	0·01	0·21	0·17	0·15	−0·02
(d) Improved allocation of resources	0·29	1·00(2)	0·12(8)	0·95(3)	1·42(1)	0·63(6)	0·51(7)	0·67(5)	0·92(4)
(e) Changes in the lag in the application of knowledge	0·00	0·83(2)	0·04(7)	0·74(3)	0·88(1)	0·43(4)	0·07(6)	−0·27(8)	0·18(5)
(f) 'Economies of scale' associated with income elasticities	0·00	0·90(1)	0·09(8)	0·49(3)	0·60(2)	0·23(4)	0·11(7)	0·22(5)	0·12(6)
4. Residual sources of growth (3d+3e+3f)‡	0·29	2·73(2)	0·25(8)	2·18(3)	2·90(1)	1·29(4)	0·69(6)	0·62(7)	1·22(5)
5. Difference from US in 4	—	2·44	−0·04	1·89	2·61	1·00	0·40	0·33	0·93
6. Growth of US capital/stake (1950 = 1·00)		7·24(2)	3·85§(7)	4·74(3)	8·79(1)	4·48(4)	4·15(6)	3·63(8)	4·42(5)

* *Sources:* Denison (1967, pp. 298–317); Scarfe (1969). (Figures in parentheses are rankings, excluding the United States.)

† The following growth rates of *gross national product* per person employed over the period 1950 to 1962 are given by Beckerman *et al.* (1965, p. 15): US 2·0; Germany 5·1; UK 2·0; France 4·2; Italy 4·7; Netherlands 3·5; Belgium 2·5; Denmark 3·2; Norway 3·4; Japan's rate of growth has outstripped all of these.

‡ This item does not appear in Denison's tables, but is derived directly from them as indicated.

§ Excluding increased investment by Ford US in Ford UK in 1961.

According to Denison, most of the contribution of improved resource allocation (3d) to productivity growth arises from a shift of resources from agriculture to secondary industry. In this connection, it is worth observing that four-fifths of US direct investment in Europe since 1950 has been concentrated in manufacturing and petroleum refining, and that its growth has been particularly marked in countries that have recorded the largest gains in intersectoral productivity. Moreover, *within* manufacturing industry, investment has been directed to above-average growth sectors (Krause, 1968). In the United Kingdom, for example, nearly 80 per cent of US investment is concentrated in industries – the output per unit of input has risen *above the average* in the last ten years (Dunning, 1969a).

Next, Denison considers the contribution of knowledge to increased output per unit of input under two headings, viz., advances in knowledge (3a) and changes in the lag in the application of knowledge (3e). The first of these is simply his estimate of the same component's contribution to US growth during these years; the second is his evaluation of the extent to which advances in knowledge in Europe are greater or less than this rate – the implication being that if they are greater, the technological gap is being narrowed; if they are less, for example, as in the case of Denmark, it is being widened. Clearly one would expect this source of economic growth in Western Europe to be particularly closely associated with technology importation from the United States. It will be observed, however, that it has been very uneven in its impact among the Western European countries, contributing most to productivity in Germany, Italy and France, and least in Denmark, the United Kingdom and Belgium.

The contribution of economies to scale to European economic development has also been divided into two parts, the first of which (3b) is associated in a straightforward manner with the growth of markets. The second part (3f), which is no less important, requires further elucidation. Essentially, it arises from the index-number problem of international comparisons of real national income and consumption levels. The technical implications of this need not concern us here. What is important is the fact that the overall growth rates of real national income of the various European countries are higher if individual commodities are weighted by appropriate domestic prices than if they are weighted by US prices. Denison argues that this phenomenon is a result of the interaction of income elasticities and increasing returns to scale. With the growth of incomes in Europe, increased consumption has been concentrated on those commodities such as automobiles and consumers' durables, which have high income elasticities of demand (Wells, 1968), but which, in 1950, were sold in Europe at relatively high prices (in comparison with the United States). The increase in demand made profitable the introduction of new and more mechanized methods of production which could be readily borrowed from the United States. As Europe's output of these products rose, so their unit costs fell and prices moved more in line with those in the United States.

It follows, then, that the significance of 'economies of scale associated with income elasticities' as a growth variable depends upon three elements: (a) the existence of other growth-producing mechanisms; (b) the ability to borrow technology from abroad and, hence, to decrease the lag in the application of knowledge to economic processes; and (c) the ability to adjust the structure of production and to reallocate resources between various productive sectors (Scarfe, 1969). Since the process through which this is achieved cannot easily be separated from that arising from the improved allocation of resources and changes in the lag in the application of knowledge, a case may be made for combining the three components, 3d, 3e and 3f, into the category 'Residual sources of growth'.

If we now compare the increase in the US capital intake[7] with these various sources of growth (particularly 3d, 3e, 3f and 4), we see a pretty close correlation in each case, although the marginal contribution of US investment to European growth appears to be a declining function. Moreover, with one or two notable exceptions, both reinvested profits and net capital outflows appear to be equally well associated with the growth variables. On the other hand, there is little connection between the absolute size of the increase in US capital stake or its share in the capital formation and of various European countries and their rates of growth (Bandera and White, 1968). For example, in the period 1957/65, US investment in Britain was $3224 million compared with

7. Either total or in manufacturing industry and petroleum.

$1836 million in Germany and $720 million in Italy. As a proportion of gross fixed domestic capital formation, the plant and equipment expenditure of US firms over this time was 9·7, 5·3 and 3·4 per cent, respectively. This, of course, may simply reflect the fact that Britain invests less (as a per cent of GNP) than Italy and Germany or that her industrial structure is less geared to growth. It could also mean that the composition of US investment or its productivity was somewhat less growth stimulating than that in other countries.[8] Furthermore that new investment reflects the size of existing investment and the profits earned on these. A better measure of investment might be net capital outflows or plant and equipment expenditure, though it is not difficult to think of situations in which these need not have any marked impact on productivity.

The technological gap and technological transplants – their economic implications

So much by way of broad introduction, which suggests not only that the rate of US capital inflows is positively associated with economic development in Europe, but that, in those areas in which such investment is likely to make the most pronounced contribution, the relationship seems particularly close. One result of this technological borrowing – which we have dealt with in another paper (Dunning, 1969b) – is the convergence of the composition of European and US exports. But the questions to which this paper addresses itself are, first, the extent to which host countries (either singly or collectively) maximize the net benefits of US investment and, second, whether or not the net benefits (particularly the technological benefits) associated with this investment could be obtained by other, and cheaper, means. Before discussing these questions, a word about US investment and the so-called 'technological gap'.

The fact of the technological gap between US and Europe, measured in terms of technology actually produced, is hardly debatable – although its extent is easily exaggerated. We would

8. This hypothesis is supported by Chase Manhattan Bank statistics of the industrial structure of new US companies setting up in Europe in recent years. See their *Report on Western Europe*, March–April 1966.

make simply four observations to illustrate this point. First the latest available data show a five-to-one advantage ($264 million to $46 million annually) for the United States in receipts from technological royalties from four European countries[9] (OECD, 1968a). Second, the United States spends about four times as much on research and development as Western Europe combined (although Europe's population is larger) and about twice as much in proportion to gross national product (OECD, 1968b). Third, the United States tends to dominate world trade most in those industries that are the most research-intensive (Keesing, 1967). Fourth, the contribution of US subsidiaries in Europe (as a proportion of output produced) is most pronounced in the science-based industries (Behrman, 1969; Servan-Schreiber, 1968). (75 per cent of the computers sold in Europe and an even larger proportion of integrated electronic circuits come from US companies; so do one-half the pharmaceuticals bought by the UK national health service.)

The economic implications of the technological gap and the associated managerial gap (Diebold, 1968) are, however, by no means clear. It seems to be widely regarded as a bad thing and is frequently cited as the main cause of Europe's economic backwardness. Since technology and growth are closely linked (Williams, 1967), then, so the argument runs, those countries that are most behind in the production of technology must necessarily be the slowest growers. This is a *non sequitur*. It is not the production of technical or managerial knowhow (or even the production of the goods that incorporate this knowhow), but the extent to which this knowhow is used which is the important determinant to economic development. In theory, it is possible for one country to be entirely parasitic on another for technology; and providing the tradeoff between technology and other goods and services is worthwhile, it is right and proper this should be so. Indeed, of the eight countries with the highest output per head in the world, only the United States has a surplus on its technological balance of payments account, and only the United States, the United Kingdom and Switzerland are currently net exporters of direct capital account.

Most countries then, find it worthwhile to import most of the

9. United Kingdom, Germany, France and Italy.

technology they need or to import technology-embodied products. But the comparative advantage of being a technology producer, technology borrower or importer of technology-embodied goods varies over time between countries and sometimes in the same country, and is strongly influenced by the ease with which both factors and goods are traded. Most discussion of Europe's economic future seems to assume that Europe must assimilate the US techno-economic structure to reach its standards of living. Occasionally, it is recognized that some specialization of activity within particular manufacturing is desirable but, for the most part, the popular belief seems to be that only by adopting US production methods and producing US-style products can this objective be achieved. That this could be the best way of advancing Europe's growth, we do not wish to deny, but, as a first-best solution, this has by no means been proved. It is, at least, arguable that the United Kingdom could advance her growth and benefit her balance of payments more by investing £100 million in building hotels and encouraging US tourism to the Bahamas, than by spending the same money trying to prop up her aircraft industry to meet US competition.

In the final analysis, economic welfare and economic growth are measured by the rate of growth of consumer goods and services produced and, in some cases, foreign technology is best transferred in finished goods traded between countries. Indeed, where there are substantial barriers to factor movements, this is the *only* way it can be transferred. But it may not always be the cheapest or the most practical way of transferring knowledge; where costs favor local production or where trade in goods is deliberately restricted, the international migration of technology is better accomplished by other routes. It is important, when trying to assess the effects of inward direct investment on the technology of the host country, to be clear about the assumptions one is making about the conditions of trade and exchange rates. The classical theory of trade presupposed a perfect and instantaneous transmission of knowledge (indeed it either virtually ignored it or assumed it to be a free good), and that, irrespective of its country of origin, production would immediately be shared between those countries (comparatively) best suited to the task. Nowadays, not only is technological innovation generally recognized as one of the main components of growth (Denison, 1962, asserts 'advances in knowledge' accounted for 40 per cent of the total income per person employed in the United States between 1929 and 1957), its production is costly in both manpower and capital. But the 'correct' distribution of the production of goods embracing new technologies, from the viewpoint of world economic welfare, may well depend upon freedom of such knowledge to move across boundaries. For, because of different resource endowments, it by no means follows that the best country (or countries) for a firm to research or innovate in will necessarily be the best country (countries) for it to produce or market in. If there are differences in comparative advantages of this kind, then international investment is a prerequisite of, or at least complementary to, international trade – a fact that multinational corporations are not slow to emphasize to governments wishing to curb their foreign activities.

Summarizing then, there are three ways a nation can benefit from the fruits of world technology.

1. By importing the products of technology, be they capital or consumer goods.
2. By importing the technological knowhow and producing technology-embodied products.
3. By producing the technological knowhow itself.

Switzerland and New Zealand obtain their technology mainly in the first way, Japan and Germany in the second, and the United States the third. As we have seen, the popular conception of technological 'gap' refers essentially to the amount of technology indigenously produced. It implies that (a) a country's growth is best served by the encouragement of competitive production of products with a high technological content; (b) it is better to produce the technology itself rather than import it.

I do not wish to argue the case for or against the first proposition, but simply to reiterate the obvious point that present-day restrictions on trade of both factors and goods, by distorting the best distribution of product-embodied technology and technological borrowing throughout the world, make it difficult to estimate what this best distribution should be.

On the second point, I have seen no reasoned economic assessment of why technological borrowing is, by its nature, against the interest of host countries, and it is better for a nation to be as technologically independent (or at least technologically competitive) as possible. This is not to deny that there could be some genuine costs to the host country – both economic and non-economic – involved in technological borrowing (which will, in part, depend on the form of the borrowing) which must be set against its benefits. These we will consider in a later part of this paper. Again, the problem is conceptually simple. Is the European economy likely to grow faster (or more efficiently) by borrowing technology (or particular kinds of technology) from the United States and using its resources in other directions, or by sacrificing the obvious gains to be derived from knowledge transplants, and allocating more resources to education and research and development to produce this knowledge itself? Part of the answer must obviously depend on the efficiency of knowledge creation in Europe and the United States. To argue that it is better for France to operate an independent computer industry implies that, once it has had a chance to build up its own technological infrastructure, the industry can serve the needs of the French economy better and/or more cheaply than by importing the technology direct from the United States. Or should Europe aim at developing a more specialized technological strategy and exchange the output of its own research and development for that of a different kind originating from US laboratories?

Unfortunately, this is not a matter that can be left to market forces to resolve, simply because technological advances are powerfully influenced by the policies of public authorities toward higher education, on the one hand, and the support of research and development activities, on the other. Servan-Schreiber (1968) acknowledges this in *The American Challenge* and argues that the only way for Europe to escape US domination is for it, or more particularly a supranational authority acting on its behalf, to make a massive investment in both lines of activity. I am by no means persuaded that this should be the main thrust of European policy, particularly if it adds to, rather than reduces, the brain drain across the Atlantic.

However, let me try to be more specific and tackle the question from the viewpoint of the costs of acquiring technology from abroad. Now, technology can be transferred between nations in a variety of ways. Sometimes the technology is owned (or controlled) specifically by particular institutions – we shall call such technology 'proprietary technology'. It is mainly transmitted by (a) direct investment of multinational corporations and (b) licensing of patents, and a variety of manufacturing or technical service agreements, and some kinds of consultancy services. 'Nonproprietary technology' includes not only the results of new knowledge contained in the technical literature, but

1. Direct purchases of hardware or services, such as new machinery and equipment, test devices, computer software and related consulting services.
2. Technical-service activities backing up these sales or introducing new products.
3. Demonstrations of modern management technologies at seminars, conferences, exhibitions, etc.
4. Technical assistance to suppliers and customers on special problems.
5. Observation and imitation of nonproprietary technologies (Quinn, 1968).

Each of the above kinds of technological transfer has led to the development of whole industries in specific countries. For example, shipbuilders in Norway and Sweden simply observed the new construction techniques developed in the United States during the Second World War and at once applied them, after using surplus (US) government equipment. More recently, the Japanese have been very adept at observing and imitating US technologies in a variety of knowledge industries, particularly consumer electronic products.

In this paper, we shall be primarily concerned with the dissemination of proprietary technology via the medium of the multinational corporation. We illustrate our argument from the experience of the United Kingdom.

The technological impact of US investment in the United Kingdom

There are, in general, two views of the technological impact of US investment in the United Kingdom. The first of these, which prevailed up to 1960 or thereabouts, and still holds in some quarters, is that this is entirely beneficial. By the presence of US firms, so the argument goes, Britain is able to tap the flow of technological (and managerial) knowledge of the US economy, valued at many times the amount she spends on indigenous research and development each year at a cost – in the form of royalties, fees, profits and interest – considerably lower than that which she would have had to pay to produce the knowledge herself.

The costs are of two kinds. First there are the actual costs associated with US investment in the United Kingdom; these deducted from the benefits give the technological net return to the host country of inward investment. Second, there is opportunity cost of this net return in terms of net returns that could have been gained by obtaining this knowledge in a different way. We deal with each of these costs in turn.

The main cost of inward investment arises wherever it weakens the host country's competitive position in the world economy. Here, America is seen as a technological competitor to the United Kingdom, with the power to retard as well as to accelerate its rate of development. If, by their activities in the United Kingdom, US firms can add to their stock of technology, skilled labor and ideas – at the expense of the United Kingdom – then the technological gap may widen rather than close. For example, for a very small financial investment in the United Kingdom, US companies could (a) gain access to the results of UK research and development which they may be able to exploit more profitably than the firms originating such research and development; (b) stifle indigenous research and development, and polarize it to the United States, thus increasing the technological dependence of the United Kingdom on the United States; (c) use their presence to monitor human capital back to the United States and, in so doing, encourage the brain drain from the United Kingdom. Were these policies widely practised, then the technological costs of inward investment could well be high, *unless* these gains were properly reflected in the price paid by

US firms for them[10] (Dunning and Steuer, 1969). Not only would her rate of development become even more dependent on that of the United States than it is now, but she would have borne the costs of producing technology without receiving any of its benefits. A separate, though related argument, is that when the 'knowledge-producing' operations of multinational subsidiaries are centrally controlled, then there is always the possibility that these might be diverted from the United Kingdom to other countries (Dunning, 1969a). But, equally, the United Kingdom might be the beneficiary of such shifts and, in any case, multinational firms of UK parentage might find it profitable to act in a similar way.

There has been no systematic measurement of these costs (or potential costs), though it is known that they have arisen in a number of cases. On the other hand, the fact that some US firms do little research in the United Kingdom has been argued as being beneficial to the host economy, since it releases scarce skilled personnel for other activities. Much depends here on the state of the (UK) market for research workers. If, as we are often led to believe (Peck, 1968), this type of human capital is in short supply in Britain, US firms might be doing the United Kingdom a service by undertaking no research. On the other hand, there is no doubt that American companies have helped create a demand for certain types of scientists and engineers, which otherwise might have found no suitable employment in the United Kingdom. The fact that there *is* quite a substantial brain drain to the United States (Chorafas, 1968) suggests there is no room for additional sources of employment in the United Kingdom and that this latter hypothesis is as likely to be as true as the former.[11]

The evidence on the amount of research and development undertaken by US firms is a little conflicting. On the one hand, a report of the Stanford Research Institute (1963) indicated that,

10. For example, in the takeover of a UK firm by a US enterprise.

11. This is an example of a reverse flow of technology from the United Kingdom to the United States. The difference between this and US investment in the United Kingdom is that, while the latter remains the property of the exporting country and earns it a return, the migration of skilled manpower is essentially a gift from the exporting to the importing country.

while one-half of a sample of 200 American firms undertook research and development in Europe, most spent 4 per cent or less of their research and development budget there. The report went on to say that many US firms regarded their European operations primarily as a means of steering the results of European research and development back to the United States and of gaining entry into the European scientific community. On the other hand, US manufacturing firms in Britain tend to spend more on research and development than their UK competitors, and more often than not, it seems, when American firms take over UK enterprises, they increase rather than diminish the research and development activity.

I have dealt with some of the wider implications of inward foreign investment which are complementary to the technological implications in the PEP paper mentioned earlier (Dunning, 1969a), and a good account of them is given in the Watkins Committee report on foreign ownership in Canadian industry (Watkins *et al.*, 1968). However, in Canada, the technological issue is not the central issue surrounding the costs and benefits of US investment. Rather it is the extent to which such investment may impinge upon national political and cultural autonomy. The same is probably true of the attitudes of most developing countries to foreign ownership and control. But these nations can hardly hope to be technologically competitive to the United States in the way Europe can – and it is for this reason (and the fact that technological dependence may be the first step along the road to political and cultural dependence) that the views of Servan-Schreiber have been so widely acclaimed.

Maximizing the net benefits of US investment

It may be, of course, that European host countries (individually or collectively) are neither gaining the benefits from US investment that they should, nor are geared effectively to coping with the economic power associated with it. That the technological costs may be too high and the technological advantages may not be exploited or disseminated as efficiently as they might, may reflect some weakness in the institutional or competitive structure of the local economies. (Here a distinction needs to be made between the position of individual European economies and an integrated European community). In its report, the Watkins Committee repeatedly emphasized the point that, in the absence of effective competition to inward investment, most of the benefits will simply accrue to the investing rather than the recipient country. Only a quick glance at the economy of Europe reveals that, at the moment, it is not organized to take full advantage of inward investment. In general, her research and development effort is too uncoordinated and her industries and her markets too fragmented to offer the competition needed to combat US giant firms; and, because of obstacles in framing a rationalized merger and fiscal policy and updating company law, one cannot see an effective industrial strategy developing for some years.

From a cost viewpoint, the type of market structure most suited to the type of US firms now operating in Europe is oligopolistic in character. At least, it is oligopolistic in the United States, with markets several times the size of most individual European countries. The firms are generally research- and capital-intensive and able to benefit from economies of scale. In most European countries, one firm could comfortably supply the total market. This means that the firm first in the field often creates its own barriers to entry, which sometimes can be overcome only by firms of comparable size. At the moment, these are few and far between in Europe, for what is sometimes overlooked is that, from a technological viewpoint, European firms are competing against the facilities of US corporations and not just those of their European subsidiaries. Compared to eighty-two US firms with a sales turnover of more than $1 billion in 1967, there were twenty-eight European firms – and most of these are not concentrated in the science-based industries. In the motor vehicles industry, the combined assets of the three largest European producers are still smaller than that of the third largest US firm. Of the largest ten mechanical engineering firms in the world, only one is European. In the pharmaceutical industry there are ten US firms with assets of over $100 million; in Europe the largest specialist pharmaceutical company has assets of less than one-half this amount. The combined assets of the six largest European aircraft companies are still smaller than the Boeing company of the United States (Behrman, 1969).

It is outside the scope of this paper to examine the extent to which size confers advantages. Most comparisons that economists have so far made (which, on the whole, play down the size advantage) are not really helpful for our purposes. Very rarely is like compared with like and usually the industrial (and sometimes the size) classification chosen is far too broad. Moreover, size is correlated with profitability and not with growth. But, in so far as research and development expenditure tends to be closely correlated with size, and there do appear to be marked economies of scale in this sector (Mansfield, 1968), it would seem to follow that the growth potential of large firms is likely to be greater than that of small firms. The fact that some large European firms have expanded faster than the largest US firms in recent years (Dunning and Pearce, 1969) in no way invalidates this hypothesis, since much of the growth has been accomplished by merger and acquisition.

The United Kingdom has probably gone further with rationalizing its industrial structure than other European countries, the best-known mergers being the BMC/Leyland merger in the automobile industry, the Plessey, English Electric and ICT merger in the computer industry, and the General Electric and AEI merger in the electrical industry. Most mergers in recent years have been horizontal rather than vertical by nature (Utton, 1969). The larger of these rationalization schemes are often backed by the government (through the Industrial Reorganization Commission), who also uses other forms of countervailing power to help British industry combat US competition.

But, one cannot help feeling that, in the end, corporate alliances by firms within a country are not likely to be sufficient to counteract the American invasion and, in any case, sooner or later one comes up against local antitrust legislation. (In parenthesis, one might make the point that the growth of economic power of US corporations in the world economy has gone hand in hand with the internationalization of their activities. The United Kingdom might do well to note this fact at a time when policy is actively directed to discouraging foreign direct investment.) When one looks at the practicability of intracountry corporate mergers, or a 'European' industrial policy, one runs into all sorts of difficulties – such as those already mentioned – relating to company law, taxation, fiscal policies, patents and standards. There has been only one merger between two European firms in recent years, that between Agfa – a subsidiary of West Germany's Bayer Corporation, producing photographic equipment – and Gevaert, a Belgian company.[12] This was a classic case of Europe's response to the challenge of American size: in this case, the Kodak company. Neither of the two leading European companies could, by itself, raise the financial resources to meet the US company's advanced technology. At the time of the merger, Kodak's expenditure on research and development was roughly equivalent to Gevaert's entire turnover (Layton, 1969).

In his book *European Advanced Technology*, Christopher Layton examines some of the difficulties facing Europe in her attempts to pool her resources and to rationalize her industrial structure and the measures required for her to challenge effectively US competition. There are, of course, many other aspects of American strength besides size. Indeed, some authorities feel that the provision of risk capital to dynamic small firms in advanced technology is an equally important need, together with the further development of the European capital market. Nevertheless, I think that a European research director, quoted by Layton, put the matter very succinctly when he said, 'If America wishes to close the technological gap with Europe, all she needs to do is erect fifty-one different sets of customs barriers, tax systems, space and defence programmes, science policies and public buying arrangements; the gap will be gone in a year!' (Layton, 1969, p. 50).

To some extent, the success of European competition with US investment will affect the attitudes of host countries to the technological character of such investment. For example, to encourage US firms to establish research and development laboratories may bring with it beneficial effects where there is little or no competition either for the skilled manpower used by such firms or their end products. These firms would then add to the research and development input of the host country. Where, however, US subsidiaries siphon off skilled personnel from other parts of the

12. We should, however, observe that at an official or semiofficial level there has been a great deal of intra-European technical cooperation of which the European Nuclear Energy Research Organization (CERN) has been an outstanding example.

economy, the effect, depending on the relative efficiency of US and UK firms, may be to weaken indigenous research. The same sort of argument applies to the encouragement of foreign firms to install fully integrated production facilities, to hire local nationals, to use local suppliers and to encourage joint ventures. In some cases, this kind of resource allocation might raise efficiency and make for faster growth: in others not so, and while this may be an acceptable price to encourage the full involvement of foreign countries, it may be only a second-best policy to some other alternative, for example, the extension of licensing agreements and the encouragement of more effective domestic competition in the first place.

An alternative course of action for Europe is to try and specialize in certain areas of research and development for which it has (or is likely to have) a comparative advantage *vis-à-vis* the United States. Some economists, notably J. B. Quinn of Dartmouth College, strongly favor a selective economic/technological strategy in Europe. At the moment, national growth efforts tend to be scattered 'with a little bit for everyone'. Not enough resources are committed to any sector for it to achieve economic viability in world terms. Nations may well learn from firms. Many a small enterprise has exploited 'holes in the armor' of their larger competitors by concentrating its research and development efforts in a particular field.

Here we would offer just three comments. First, assuming Europe were able to integrate her individual economies effectively in the way earlier suggested, and that she continued to have a comparative advantage in labor costs, then one would expect her to gain most by concentrating her attentions on relatively labor-intensive *vis-à-vis* capital-intensive activities. This holds good even if factor endowments are tending to converge with those of the United States, as long as Europe does not completely catch up with the United States.

Second, one must be careful not to exaggerate the importance of proprietary technology in economic development. Industries that spend more than 1·5 per cent of their net output on research and development still only account for a fairly small proportion of total manufacturing output. And the contribution of manufacturing output to GNP has for some years been steadily declining. It is true, as we have argued, that advances in technology in one industry often act as a catalyst to growth in others but, again, these can often be obtained from abroad by other means than direct investment. It may be that Europe should be encouraged to specialize in trading goods that have a high income elasticity of demand, but whose knowledge content is of a kind which, while utilizing substantial amounts of skilled labor does not require the scale of research and development expenditure (e.g., on laboratory facilities) which can only be undertaken by large firms. Examples include unstandardized and high-income furniture, clothing, metal products, electrical fittings, etc.[13]

Third, one can foresee that there may be more specialization, not only in the end products produced by multinational companies in various countries, for example, horizontal specialization, but also in the stages of production processes as well, for example, vertical specialization. In this instance, in genuine geocentric companies (Perlmutter, 1969), there is a minimum of nationalism in the way the company operates. (Incidentally it is sometimes felt that many of the problems arising from the presence of US firms in Europe are due to the nationality of their parent companies – and if only there could be more geographical diffusion of ownership, these would disappear. This is a fallacy. It is true that European citizens would share in the profits earned by such companies; it is not necessarily the case that if companies broadly seek the same aims, for example, maximization of profits, the geographical structure of the activities of these companies would be very different. In other words, the nation-state/multinational company conflict would still arise.)

It is a fact that many of the larger multinational companies are tending to concentrate their output of particular products and research and development facilities in certain countries and practicing specialization of stages of production process. I mentioned this back in 1958 in *American Investment in British Manufacturing Industry* and I believe this trend has become more pronounced over time. The theory is simply that, where it is in

13. It is perhaps interesting to note that, relative to US exports, European exports of these products have grown particularly in recent years. See Dunning (1969b).

the best interest of a firm to distribute geographically the various stages of its production process, this will be done on the basis of factor costs and productivity, and the cost of transporting inputs and outputs between countries. Since the early stages of knowledge-producing are very labor-intensive, then assuming equal efficiency of research personnel, Europe rather than the United States may be a better place to do this: the knowledge commercialization process, through to the pilot stage of production, is more capital-intensive and may need the facilities of large centralized laboratories and testing plants, and may be better done in the United States. The costs of the actual manufacturing process will be largely dependent upon the structure of wage rates, rents and material prices, but where these are cheaper in Europe – and sufficient to outweigh any differences in marketing costs which may favor a US location – it may pay to specialize at least manufacturing operations in Europe and export the goods to markets previously served by the United States.

I have not put this theory to the test in any systematic way, but the growing international specialization of multinational firms and the quite substantial development of sponsored research in Europe by US controlled companies certainly seems to lend support to it. It is also consistent with the product-cycle theory of international trade.

Alternatives to inward investment

So far I have been discussing some of the actual (or possible) technological costs and benefits associated with inward investment. Some of the costs I have suggested are inherent in the operations of multinational companies irrespective of their nationality; some could be minimized or even eliminated by freer international trade, an appropriate research and development strategy, and institutional reform on the part of host governments.

What now of the alternatives to inward investment as a means of obtaining proprietary foreign technology? First, and most obvious, are licensing agreements, covering, for example, grants of patents, trademarks, technical assistance, franchises, etc. It is sometimes argued that, from the licensee's viewpoint, the main merit of licensing agreements is that they do not (or may not) involve any interference by the licensor in his policy and decision-taking activities – in the same way as may happen with direct investment. This is obviously true, up to a point. For one thing, many of the activities of the licensee will be completely untouched by the agreement; for another, there is likely to be little or no impact on the managerial practices of the licensee: for a third, even the methods of production may not be affected. Indeed, in some cases, all that is being purchased is 'paper' knowledge, for example, formulas, specifications, drawing designs, etc. On the other hand, the licensor may seek to impose certain controls on the buying and selling outlets of the licensee. He may limit the sale of the final product to the licensee's country and/or influence the choice of suppliers. Even the license itself may only be granted for a specified period or be subject to withdrawal at short notice (Bonin, 1967).

At a macrolevel, there is a possibility that the more a country licenses knowledge from abroad, the less it tends to undertake research and development itself. This, *vis-à-vis* direct investment, probably increases rather than diminishes its dependence on foreign technology. That this may still be the fastest and possibly cheapest way to grow may still be true, and for a country wishing to concentrate its research resources in particular sectors, such a complete dependence for other forms of knowhow – providing there is adequate 'software' – supporting research and development facilities may be the best thing. It is interesting that Italy and Germany, both of which have relied on this type of technological borrowing rather more than the United Kingdom in the post-war period, have grown so much faster. Likewise with Japan; but the particularly fascinating thing about Japan is the way she has gone about acquiring *non*proprietary technology, for example, by sending teams of scientists and technologists over to the United States to gain knowledge at firsthand. Japan has long been a first-class imitator, but in recent years she has become an important competitor to the United States in high-technology products, for example, in the field of consumer electronics. One observes that the industries in which Japanese exports have increased most are precisely those in which Japan has endeavored to absorb Western technology in the way I have suggested. She is now building both her own indigenous research and development and allowing inward investment on this quite firm technological infrastructure.

To the licensed firm, there are two important benefits of licensing agreements. First, the access to new technology while remaining free to produce the products or engage in the methods of production it chooses, and second the savings realized in research costs, enabling it to market the product more speedily than if it had been forced to depend entirely on its own resources or on a purely national technology. This latter advantage is becoming more important as the time lag between the discovery of new product is becoming less and the need to keep up with one's competitor is that much greater.

Direct investment, on the other hand, is likely to be favored whenever the expertise most required is of a kind that cannot be easily incorporated into a licensing agreement and where 'on the spot' managerial involvement is especially valued. It is not unusual to come across two firms with technologically nothing to choose between them, but one much better managed than the other. One suspects that such differences – which are partly a reflection of managerial attitudes – are at least as important a cause of the difference in profit rates of US subsidiaries and their UK competitors in Europe as any technological differences. One further possible advantage of knowledge transmittance via direct investment is that the parent company may charge its subsidiary less than the market price for the knowledge it transmits. Should this be passed on to the local consumer in the form of lower prices, the host economy gains as it does, indeed, if the foreign subsidiary could produce more efficiently than the licensee. And if profits are higher than they would be otherwise, the local exchequer gains from additional tax revenue.

Such empirical data as we have suggest that, as a percentage of gross or net output, US subsidiaries are charged considerably lower royalties and fees than European firms under license to US firms. On the other hand, any wholesale transfer or assimilation of US technology by their European subsidiaries may, because of differences in market and/or prices of factor inputs, be ill suited to local conditions. In Canada, for example, Safarian found that foreign companies were often at a disadvantage because of their 'inability to buy or develop products, designs or machinery more suitable to Canadian market conditions' (Safarian, 1966). Where the licensing agreements enable European companies to obtain (or maintain) a technology better suited to their needs, this would represent an important benefit. At the same time, the secondary or technological multiplier effects of licensing are likely to be less than those arising from direct investment, even if the immediate technological benefits and costs may be broadly comparable. It is difficult to give an *a priori* assessment here. Among the factors to be considered are (a) the amount and direction of existing foreign investment in the country, (b) the strength of local competition, (c) the national importance of industries in which foreign investment is concentrated, and (d) the availability of research and development personnel.

If, as has been suggested, the eventual aim of Europe is to create a viable technology of its own and to reduce the technological gap between itself and the United States by adopting a selective program of research and development, then, in so far as licensing agreements economize in research personnel, this is all to the good. On the other hand, if European industrial strategy is geared to competing across the board with the United States, then licensing agreements have more limitations than direct investment. Indeed, the more complex the running of a business enterprise becomes, the less the knowledge content can be embodied in licensing agreements (which essentially enable standardized 'knowhow' to be transmitted), and the more important are the techniques of decision making and managerial judgement (which cannot be embodied in formulas, drawing, specifications, etc.).

Joint ventures

Joint equity ventures represent a midway house between the fully owned subsidiary and licensing agreements. It is not our purpose to examine the advantages and disadvantages of these, but simply to observe that these are an alternative way of obtaining technology to those already mentioned and at (generally) a lower cost involved than that of the fully owned subsidiary. Basically speaking, their contribution to technology is the same as in the fully owned subsidiary, although the extent of management involvement may be rather less. However, there is likely to be a better appreciation of local economic conditions and needs, and less likelihood that the foreign company will use the host company's technology to meet its own ends. Joint ventures also generally make for good relations with host governments and the more nationalistic sectors of the host country.

On the other hand, there are certain well-known problems in the operation of joint companies, for example, the disposal of profits, organization of production, staff transfers, etc. (Bonin, 1967). These often involve high costs, but again, in some cases, the net technological benefits to the host country may be higher than those offered by alternative schemes.

Other forms of obtaining technology

These are the days of experimentation of different forms of the international dissemination of technology. There are many models and proposals – particularly as they relate to the growth of LDCs. These vary from technical assistance and coproduction agreements to jointly public and privately financed enterprises, and the observation and imitation of product technologies. Mass production in cars, techniques for welded ship construction, mathematical systems for production, and quality control are examples of high-impact technologies transferred through these latter means by Japan and Italy. Each type of technology transference has its particular costs and benefits: though certain principles can be laid down as to which is likely to be the best method or mix, under which conditions of assimilation, far more research is necessary before any definitive answer can be given from the particular standpoint of Europe.

Conclusions

We have seen in this paper that Europe has leaned heavily on the United States for technology since the war and that conditions in Europe have generally favored the transfer of this technology in the form of direct investment and licensing agreements. Partly this simply reflects the fact that European economy has gradually moved more in the direction of the US economy and that the products the demands for which are growing most rapidly are those first produced in the United States.

The share of US investment in Europe's industries is still small but strongly concentrated in the research-intensive and growth sectors. This implies a strong technological impact, the costs and benefits of which we have sought to examine and appraise. Chief among the benefits is that Europe's *per capita* real income has grown more rapidly than otherwise would have been the case and certainly faster than that of the United States. This is partly because (a) the technological improvements have been largely embodied in new vintages of capital goods; (b) Europe was, at the beginning of our period under review (1950), less well endowed with capital equipment than the United States; and (c) during those years Europe has increased capital per head at a faster rate than the United States. The result has been that the effects of changes in technology and changes in factor proportions have worked together to yield not only convergence in patterns of production but also a higher growth rate in Europe along with the process of adapting to the borrowed technology. Given that it is desired to attract technology by direct investment, the problem of European economies is to maximize the resulting technological multiplier and to minimize its costs. We have suggested ways in which this may be done and certain obstacles in the way of doing it.

References

BANDERA, V. N., and WHITE, J. T. (1968), 'US direct investment and domestic markets in Europe', *Economia internazionale*, vol. 21, pp. 117–33.

BECKERMAN, W., *et al.* (1965), *The British Economy in 1975*, Cambridge University Press.

BEHRMAN, J. N. (1969), 'Some patterns in the rise of the multinational enterprise', *University of North Carolina, Graduate School of Business, Research Paper*, no. 18.

BONIN, B. (1967), 'Licensing and joint ventures as alternatives to direct investment', study prepared for the Task Force on the Structure of Canadian Industry, unpublished.

CHORAFAS, D. N. (1968), *The Knowledge Revolution*, Allen & Unwin.

DENISON, E. (1962), *The Sources of Economic Growth in the United States*, Committee for Economic Development, New York.

DENISON, E. (1967), *Why Growth Rates Differ*, Brookings Institution, Washington.

DIEBOLD, J. (1968), 'Is the gap technological?', *For. Aff.*, vol. 46, pp. 276–91.

DUNNING, J. H. (1958), *American Investment in British Manufacturing Industry*, Allen & Unwin.

DUNNING, J. H. (1969a), 'The role of American investment in the British economy', *PEP Broadsheet*, no. 507.

DUNNING, J. H. (1969b), 'European and US trade patterns, US foreign investment and the technological gap', paper read at the International Economic Association Conference, Algarve, Portugal, August.

DUNNING, J. H., and PEARCE, R. D. (1969), 'The world's largest enterprises: a statistical profile', *Bus. Ratios*, vol. 3, pp. 4–30.

DUNNING, J. H., and STEUER, M. (1969), 'The effects of US investment on UK technology', *Moorgate and Wall Street*, Autumn, pp. 5–33.

EFTA (1969), *Foreign Investment*, Geneva.

GRUBER, W., MEHTA, D., and VERNON, R. (1967), 'The R & D factor in international trade and international investment of United States industries', *J. polit. Econ.*, vol. 75, pp. 20–37.

HIRSCH, S. (1967), *Location of Industry and International Competitiveness*, Clarendon Press.

HUFBAUER, G. C., and ADLER, F. M. (1968), 'Overseas manufacturing investment and the US balance of payments', *US Treasury Tax Research Policy Document*, no. 1.

KAUFMAN, R. H. (1968), 'Strategies for Atlantic technological development', background paper for the Atlantic Institute Conference, Paris, April.

KEESING, D. (1967), 'The impact of research and development on United States trade', *J. polit. Econ.*, vol. 75, pp. 38–48.

KINDLEBERGER, C. P. (1969), *American Business Abroad*, Yale University Press.

KRAUSE, L. B. (1968), *European Economic Integration and the United States*, Brookings Institution, Washington.

LAMFALUSSY, A. (1963), *The United Kingdom and the Six: An Essay on Economic Growth in Western Europe*, Macmillan.

LAYTON, C. (1969), *European Advanced Technology*, Allen & Unwin.

MADDISON, A. (1964), *Economic Growth in the West: Comparative Experience in Europe and North America*, Twentieth Century.

MANSFIELD, E. (1968), *The Economics of Technological Change*, Norton.

OECD (1968a), 'Technological gaps: their nature, causes, effects', *OECD Observer*, vol. 33, pp. 18–28.

OECD (1968b), *The Level and Structure of Europe's Research and Development Effort*, Paris.

PECK, M. (1968), 'Science and technology', in R. Caves (ed.), *Britain's Economic Prospects*, Brookings Institution, Washington.

PERLMUTTER, H. V. (1969), 'The tortuous evolution of the multinational corporation', *Canad. J. world Bus.*, vol. 4, pp. 9–18.

POWIE, T. L. (1969), 'The influence of international capital flows on the effectiveness of domestic policy instruments', in R. Caves and G. Reuber (eds.), *Canadian Economic Policy and the Impact of International Capital Flows*, University of Toronto Press.

QUINN, D. (1968), 'Scientific and technical strategy at the national and major enterprise level', paper for UNESCO Symposium on the Role of Science and Technology in Economic Development, Paris.

SAFARIAN, A. (1966), *Foreign Ownership of Canadian Industry*, McGraw-Hill.

SCARFE, B. (1969), 'Capital accumulation and comparative advantage: a critical appraisal', unpublished Ph.D. thesis, University of Oxford.

SERVAN-SCHREIBER, J. J. (1968), *The American Challenge*, Hamish Hamilton.

STANFORD RESEARCH INSTITUTE (1963), *Long Range Planning Report 198*.

THIRLWALL, A. P. (1967), 'A measure of the proper distribution of industry', *Oxf. econ. Pap.*, vol. 20, pp. 46–58.

UNITED NATIONS (1967), *Economic Bulletin for Europe*, vol. 19, no. 1, Economic Commission for Europe.

US DEPARTMENT OF COMMERCE (1960), *US Business Investments in Foreign Countries*, Washington.

US DEPARTMENT OF COMMERCE (1966a), *Survey of Current Business*, Washington, September.

US DEPARTMENT OF COMMERCE (1966b), *Survey of Current Business*, Washington, November.

UTTON, M. A. (1969), 'Diversification, mergers and profit stability', *Bus. Ratios*, vol. 3, pp. 24–8.

VERNON, R. (1966), 'International investment and international trade in the product cycle', *Q. J. Econ.*, vol. 80, pp. 190–207.

WATKINS, M., *et al.* (1968), *Foreign Ownership and the Structure of Canadian Industry. Report of the Task Force on the Structure of Canadian Industry*, Queen's Printer, Ottawa.

WELLS, L. T., Jr (1968), 'A product life cycle for international trade', *J. Market.*, vol. 32, pp. 1–6.

WELLS, L. T., Jr (1969), 'Test of a product-cycle model of international trade: US exports of consumer durables', *Q. J. Econ.*, vol. 83, pp. 152–62.

WILKINSON, B. (1968), *Canada's International Trade: An Analysis of Recent Trends and Patterns*, Private Planning Association of Canada, Montreal.

WILLIAMS, B. (1967), *Technology, Investment and Growth*, Chapman & Hall.

16 G. M. Meier

Private Foreign Investment

Excerpts from G. M. Meier, 'Private foreign investment', in *The International Economics of Development*, Harper & Row, 1968, pp. 131–61.

Although the international financing of development has been dominated by foreign aid, there is now reawakened interest in the potential role of private foreign investment. Unlike earlier historical episodes of international investment, however, the widespread practice of national economic planning in developing countries is moving the problems of foreign investment into a new context. To appreciate more fully the issues that are emerging, we need an analytical framework for appraising how a less developed country might attain the double policy objective of encouraging a greater inflow of private foreign capital while, at the same time, obtaining from this capital a more substantial contribution to the country's development program. This chapter attempts to provide such a framework.

Our concern throughout is with 'direct' private investment and with the national regulations of such investment by the capital-recipient countries.[1] The experience of the past two decades has made it increasingly evident that policies of the capital-receiving countries are more decisive in determining the quantity and quality of the private capital inflow than are the measures taken by the capital-exporting countries to encourage and protect foreign investment.[2] For the host country has con-

1. The justification for considering only investments in which the foreign investor exercises managerial control is that portfolio investment is now of negligible quantitative importance for newly developing countries and can be expected to remain so.

An illuminating discussion of the differences between present-day and nineteenth-century international investment is provided by Ragnar Nurkse (1954).

2. In an attempt to promote a larger flow of private capital to less developed countries, several capital-exporting countries have adopted a

trolling power as the ultimate policy maker and can neutralize action taken initially by the investing country.[3] Controls exercised by the host country over the conditions of entry of foreign capital, the operation of foreign enterprises, and the remittance of profits and repatriation of capital are of crucial importance in determining the flow and contribution of external private capital.

By shifting the emphasis to the policies connected with development planning in the recipient countries our discussion might focus more directly on the primary determinants of the flow and contribution of foreign private capital. We shall, therefore, begin by sorting out the various benefits and costs of private foreign investment from the viewpoint of a national development program. Against this conceptual background, we may then appraise the effects of policy measures being taken by developing countries to encourage an inflow of private capital and to regulate the operation of the foreign enterprise in conformity with developmental objectives.

Even though only a small amount of private capital, relative to government loans and grants,[4] has gone to poor countries, the belief persists that capital from official sources is only a transitional arrangement and that foreign economic aid should be gradually replaced by a flow of private financial resources. To this end, considerable interest is being shown in measures that might promote foreign investment and allow it to contribute more effectively to the development of the recipient countries.[5]

---

range of measures that include tax incentives, State guarantees and financial assistance to private investors. For a sampling of the extensive literature on these measures, see generally, Barlow and Wender (1955), Behrman (1962), von Neuman Whitman (1965).

3. American businessmen have consistently believed that the overall role of the United States government in impeding or promoting profitable private foreign investment is minor compared with the role of foreign governments and with market and economic forces outside the control of the investor's government: National Industrial Conference Board (1965, pp. 39–42), US Department of Commerce (1964).

4. For summary statistical data on the flow of official and private long-term capital to less developed countries, see OECD (1966, tables 3–8), *IMF Balance of Payments Yearbook*, annual editions, Pizer and Cutler (1966).

5. US Agency for International Development (1965); see also the recommendations of earlier special Presidential commissions: the Gray

When one examines the policies taken by the developing countries, however, they reveal a mixed picture of restrictions and incentives. On the one side, the foreign investor's freedom of action may be constrained by a variety of governmental regulations that exclude private foreign capital from certain sectors of the economy, impose limitations on the extent of foreign participation in ownership or management, specify conditions for the employment of domestic and foreign labor, limit the amount of profits and impose exchange controls on the remission of profits and the repatriation of capital. And yet, during recent years, a progressive liberalization of policy toward private foreign investment has occurred and a number of investment incentive measures have been recently adopted or are under consideration. These incentive devices include establishment of overhead facilities such as in industrial estates, protective tariffs on imports that compete with local commodities produced by foreign enterprise, exemptions from import duties on necessary equipment and materials the granting of exchange guarantees or privileges, tax concession schemes for the encouragement of desired new investments, and special legislation for the protection of foreign capital.

The current trend toward greater encouragement of private foreign investment reflects, in part, a retrenchment from the earlier post-war reliance on a 'heavy' comprehensive type of detailed economic planning to a 'lighter' framework type, in which there is greater scope for the private sector and, in part, a growing awareness that a community of interest might be established between the foreign enterprise and host country.

More directly, many countries have come to realize that an inflow of private capital can offer some unique qualitative advantages over public capital. For no problem of productive use arises with foreign direct investment: by its very nature, a foreign investment necessarily entails the identification of an economic opportunity, the formulation of a productive project and its efficient implementation. Especially significant is the merit that foreign direct investment has in carrying with it an integral ingredient of technical assistance – the managerial and technical knowledge which are usually in even shorter supply than capital.

Report (1950), Rockefeller Report (1951), Paley Commission Report 1952) and the Randall Commission Report (1954).

As an instrument for transmitting technical and organizational change, integrating technical and financial assistance, and helping to overcome the skill and management limitations in development, the private foreign investment has a distinct advantage over foreign public capital.

If recipient countries have assumed a more positive attitude toward foreign enterprise, so too have foreign investors come to appreciate that the practice of development planning need not in itself be inimical to the promotion of a larger inflow of private capital. Development planning now involves much more than a public investment program, and the practice of planning is not to be confused with the issue of public ownership and control. The essence of development planning is the formulation and coordination of a set of policies to achieve explicit objectives. In doing this, a plan may stress the complementary relationship between the public and private sectors and may include policies designed to induce and assist action in the private sector. Although a development plan reserves some areas of investment for the public sector, there is at least, on the other side, a clear statement of policy regarding areas in which private investment is desired. A development plan can be of service to the foreign investor when it expressly defines the particular role assigned to the private sector, indicates clearly the existence of investment opportunities, facilitates advance calculation, and reduces the foreign investor's uncertainties regarding his position *vis-à-vis* the domestic private and public industrial sectors.

An American government report, for example, lists several advantages that private enterprise may gain from the emphasis on national planning by developing countries:

1. Competent development planning, by emphasizing statistical information and a quantitative framework for future targets and goals, creates a more dependable environment for evaluating business opportunities and risks than now exists in many less developed countries.

2. Planning may define exactly and more reliably the fields of activity in which government and private business, respectively, are expected to provide the main leadership and activity.

3. Careful planning facilitates the timely provision of publicly financed installations, such as roads, irrigation facilities or power plants, which are important to the growth of private investment. To the extent that development planning improves the use of resources for development, the basic facilities to support a vigorous private sector are provided more rapidly and effectively.

4. The planning process forces the planners to recognize the size of the requirements for sustained economic growth and the consequent necessity of enlisting the forces of private enterprise in helping to meet these requirements (U S President's Task Force on Foreign Economic Assistance, 1961, pp. 102–3).

Although development planning does not necessarily limit the scope for private activity and may actually promote more attractive business opportunities, it does mean that private investors must share with the government a common interest in accelerating development. The tasks of development require both more effective governmental activity and more international investment. But the private investor must be aware of the developmental objectives and priorities of the host country in order to determine how his investment will fit into the country's development strategy. As long as the host country remains serious about accelerating its development, the continued beneficial economic performance of foreign investment (in terms of our analysis, a high benefit–cost ratio) will be the decisive determinant of the investment's security.

No longer is it simply a matter of private investors dismissing investment prospects with the complaint that a 'favorable climate' does not exist; the meaning of a 'favorable climate' calls for reinterpretation in terms of development planning. Nor need host countries contend that an inflow of private capital entails nothing but 'foreign domination'; in the context of development planning, the effects of foreign investment need no longer be feared as being a repetition of the undesirable features in the history of colonialism. Development planning now allows the government to influence the performance of private foreign investment, but in doing this, the government should appreciate fully the potential contribution of this investment, and should devise policies that will encourage a greater inflow of private capital and gain the maximum contribution toward the achievement of the country's development. This calls for more intensive analysis of the consequences of foreign investment and for more thought and ingenuity in devising new approaches that favor the mobilization of private foreign capital while ensuring its most effective 'planned performance' in terms of the country's development program.

To provide an analytical basis for understanding the rationale and effects of foreign investment policies in the host countries, we should weigh the benefits of foreign investment against its costs.[6] After assessing what difference the presence of foreign-owned capital might make to the real income of the recipient country, we may then appraise existing policies.

Just as we have already noted for public foreign capital, an inflow of private capital contributes to the recipient country's development program in two general ways – by helping to reduce the shortage of domestic savings and by increasing the supply of foreign exchange. To this extent, the receipt of private foreign investment permits a more rapid expansion in real income, eases the shortage of foreign exchange, and removes the necessity of resorting to a drive toward self-sufficiency and the deliberate stimulation of import-substitution industries out of deference to foreign exchange considerations.

Beyond this initial contribution, the essence of the case for encouraging foreign investment is that in time, as the investment operates, the increase in real income resulting from the act of investment is greater than the resultant increase in the income of the foreign investor. There is a national economic benefit if the value added to output by the foreign capital is greater than the amount appropriated by the investor: social returns exceed private returns. As long as foreign investment raises productivity, and this increase is not wholly appropriated by the investor, it follows that the greater product must be shared with others, and there must be some direct benefits to other income groups. These benefits can accrue to (a) domestic labor in the form of higher

6. Much of the following analysis has been suggested by G. D. A. MacDougall (1960), also see Paul Streeten (1964, ch. 5).

real wages, (b) consumers by way of lower prices and (c) the government through expanded revenue. In addition, and of most importance in many cases, there are likely to be (d) indirect gains through the realization of external economies. [. . .]

The presence of foreign capital may not only raise the productivity of a given amount of labor; it may also allow a larger labor force to be employed. This may be especially significant for heavily populated countries where the population pressures are taken out through unemployment or underemployment in the rural sector. If, as is frequently contended, a shortage of capital limits the employment of labor from the rural sector in the industrial sector where wages are higher, an inflow of foreign capital can make possible more employment in the advanced sector. The international movement of capital thus serves as an alternative to the migration of labor from the poor country: when outlets for the emigration of 'surplus' labor are restricted, the substitution of domestic migration of labor into the advanced sector becomes the most feasible solution. The social benefit from the foreign investment in the advanced sector is then greater than the profits on this investment, for the wages received by the newly employed exceed their marginal productivity in the rural sector; and this excess should be added as a national gain.[7]

Some benefits from foreign investment may also accrue to consumers. When the investment is cost-reducing in a particular industry, there may be a gain not only to the suppliers of factors in this industry through higher factor prices but also to consumers of the product through lower product prices. If the investment is product-improving or product-innovating, consumers may then enjoy better quality products or new products.

In order that labor and consumers might gain part of the benefit from the higher productivity in foreign enterprises, the overseas withdrawal by the investors must be less than the increase in output. But even if the entire increase in productivity accrues as foreign profits, there will still be a national benefit

7. Balogh and Streeten (1960, p. 220), MacDougall (1960, pp. 21, 35). But it should be noted that even if rural labor is in disguised unemployment, the social cost of transferring labor to the advanced sector is not zero.

when the government taxes these profits or receives royalties from concession agreements.[8]

From the standpoint of contributing to the development process, the major benefits from foreign investment are likely to arise in the form of external economies. Besides bringing to the recipient country physical and financial capital, direct foreign investment also includes nonmonetary transfers of other resources – technological knowledge, market information, managerial and supervisory personnel, organizational experience, and innovations in products and production techniques – all of which are in short supply. By being a carrier of technological and organizational change, the foreign investment may be highly significant in providing 'private technical assistance' and 'demonstration effects' that are of benefit elsewhere in the economy. New techniques accompany the inflow of private capital and by the example they set, foreign firms promote the diffusion of technological advance in the economy.[9] Technical assistance may also be provided to suppliers and customers of the foreign enterprise. In addition, foreign investment frequently leads to the training of labor in new skills, and the knowledge gained by these workers can be transmitted to other members of the labor force or the newly trained workers might be later employed by local firms.

Private foreign investment can also stimulate additional domestic investment in the recipient country. If the foreign capital is used to develop the country's infrastructure, it may directly facilitate more investment. Even if the foreign investment is in one industry, it may still encourage domestic investment by reducing costs in other industries; profits may then rise and lead to expansion in the other industries. Since there are so many specific scarcities in a poor country, it is common for investment to be of a cost-saving character by breaking bottlenecks in production. This stimulates expansion by raising profits in

8. If the borrowing country is party to a double-taxation agreement with the investing country, with full credit allowed on foreign taxes, it may enjoy this fiscal benefit by taxing the earnings of imported capital up to the rate of taxation in the investing country without impeding the inflow of capital.

9. For a broader discussion of the process by which new techniques are transferred from one country to another, see A. K. Cairncross (1962, ch. 11).

all under-utilized productive capacity and by allowing the exploitation of economies of scale that had previously been restricted.

There is also considerable scope for the initial foreign investment to create external investment incentives by raising the demand for the output of other industries. The foreign investment in the first industry can give rise to profits in industries that supply inputs to the first industry, or that produce complementary products or that produce goods bought by the factor-owners who now have higher real incomes as a result of the inflow of foreign capital. A foreign investment that is product-improving or product-innovating may also have similar effects. A whole series of domestic investments may thus be linked to the foreign investment.

These external effects raise production outside the foreign enterprise, but the foreign investor cannot appropriate this additional output. The spillover goes unpriced and constitutes an uncompensated service. To the extent that the foreign investment yields an external economy, the marginal social net product of the foreign capital is greater than its marginal private net product. According to the criterion of national economic benefit, the case for governmental encouragement of private foreign investment is then strong.

Against these benefits, however, there are a number of costs to foreign investment that may be detrimental to the host country's development plan. These costs may arise from (a) special incentives and concessions offered by the host country, (b) adverse effects on domestic saving, (c) deterioration in the terms of trade and (d) pressure on the country's balance of payments.

To attract foreign capital, the government of the host country may have to provide special facilities, undertake additional public services, extend financial assistance or subsidize inputs to the foreign enterprise. These have a cost in absorbing governmental resources that could be used elsewhere. Tax concessions may also have to be offered and these may have to be extended to domestic investors, since the government may not be able to discriminate, for administrative and political reasons, in favor of only the foreign investor. In encouraging foreign investment, there is thus a fiscal cost through increased government expenditure or forgone revenue.

Once foreign investment has been attracted, it should lead to a higher level of real income and hence to an increase in domestic saving. This effect may be offset, however, by a redistribution of income away from domestic capital if the foreign investment competes with home investment and reduces profits in domestic industries. The consequent reduction in home savings would then be another indirect cost of foreign investment.

The possible effects of foreign investment on the terms of trade are usually related to the transfer problem – the terms of trade normally tend to improve with an inflow of capital, then tend to worsen when there is, subsequently, a return flow of capital from the borrowing country. We shall consider these effects as part of the broader problem of balance of payments adjustment.

Aside from these transfer effects, foreign investment may also affect the terms of trade through structural changes associated with the pattern of development that results from the capital inflow. If foreign investment leads to an increase in the host country's rate of development without any change in the terms of trade, then the country's growth of real income will be the same as its growth of output. Only under exceptional conditions, however, is this likely. Instead, it is to be expected that the terms of trade will alter – improving or worsening, depending on various possible changes at home and abroad in the supply and demand for exports, import-substitutes and domestic commodities. We have already considered in chapters 2 and 3 [not included here] under what conditions the commodity terms of trade will turn against a country when it accumulates capital. The same analysis can be applied to an inflow of foreign capital when it results in a higher rate of capital formation.

If the pattern of development associated with foreign investment involves a deterioration in the country's commodity terms of trade, then the net gain from foreign capital will be diminished. It is improbable, however, that foreign investment would cause any substantial deterioration. For if an unfavorable shift resulted from an export bias on the side of consumption, it would probably be controlled through import restrictions. And if it resulted from private direct investment in the export sector, this inflow of foreign capital would diminish as export prices fell, thereby limiting the deterioration in the terms of trade. Moreover, if the deterioration comes through an export bias in production, it is possible that the factoral and the income terms of trade might still improve even though the commodity terms worsen.

The most significant costs of foreign investment tend to be associated with balance of payments adjustment. We have already considered in the preceding chapter [not included here] the burden of debt servicing. A similar problem arises when the return outflow of interest, profits and dividends on the accumulated investments and repatriation of capital put pressure on the developing country's balance of payments.[10] Again, when the country is not currently earning sufficient foreign exchange to cover the external servicing of the foreign investment, the adverse effects of measures designed to reequilibrate the balance of payments will entail indirect costs of foreign investment, to be added to the direct costs of the foreign payments.

We have now classified the major consequences of foreign investment into those benefits or positive gains that contribute to the developing country's objective of increasing real income and those costs or negative effects that involve some sacrifice of the objective. The rational approach to the economic regulation of foreign investment would be to ensure that each foreign investment project meets the criterion of yielding a benefit–cost ratio greater than unity.[11]

10. It might be thought that, if foreign private investment is in export industries, direct investment payments would be correlated with fluctuations in export receipts and hence not be so burdensome. The correlation is absent, however, if the investment is in import-substitute industries: export earnings may decline, but profit remittance on direct investments may rise.

11. It would be a misconception to express the criterion as 'maximum benefit with minimum cost'; there is no policy that will meet the criterion of simultaneously maximizing gains while minimizing costs. See Roland McKean (1958, pp. 34–49).

For a more refined analysis, we should consider the time-stream of benefits and the time-stream of costs, and then discount these two streams down to the present value excess of benefits over costs. The rate of discount to be used depends on when it is most desired that the benefits should accrue, i.e. 'social time preference'.

With the foregoing conceptual framework in mind, we may now evaluate the investment laws and regulatory measures of developing countries. No attempt will be made to present in detail the variety of policies that are being used to affect the import of private investment capital. But the foregoing analysis might help us concentrate on the essential features of these measures and gauge their effectiveness in fulfilling the benefit–cost criterion.

The host country's regulatory measures over foreign investment are embodied for the most part in investment statutes, tax laws, controls over foreign trade and foreign exchange regulations. Although these measures have generally arisen in an unsystematic and *ad hoc* fashion, rather than as a closely coordinated set of policies, we can conveniently analyse the consequences of these policies in terms of an 'allocation effect', a 'distribution effect' and a 'balance of payments effect'. By considering alternative investment policies in terms of these effects, we shall be able to evaluate the effectiveness of these policies in increasing benefits or decreasing costs.

The 'allocational effect' of investment policies has two aspects: the inducement of foreign investment to one country rather than to another country and, within the recipient country, the allocation of the investment to one activity rather than to another. Most of the developing countries have now consolidated legislation regarding foreign investment in an investment statute which sets forth both the privileges and obligations of foreign investors and specifies the administrative procedures, rules and regulations governing the entry and operation of foreign investment.[12] The statute attempts to encourage an inflow of foreign capital through the use of tax exemptions, tariff concessions, relaxation of exchange controls, some guarantee of nonexpropriation and nondiscrimination, and assurances for the repatriation of earnings or capital.

12. For a recent list of investment laws, see Unesco, *The Promotion of the International Flow of Private Capital*, annex IV, 1961. Texts of investment statutes are also periodically available in US Department of Commerce, World Trade Information Service.

Indicative of the objectives sought by the legislation, these statutes – some of which may relate to domestic private capital as well as foreign – are variously called 'industrial incentive law', 'pioneer industries law', 'export industry encouragement law' or 'production development law'.

From the economic standpoint, an investment statute is effective in encouraging foreign investment when its provisions reduce nonbusiness risks, lower costs, or result in an increase in the net rate of return. To this end, tax concessions represent the major legislative effort to promote private investment. These concessions take three principal forms: relief from income and other taxes to 'new and necessary industries', partial or complete exemption from duties on the importation of essential equipment and materials, and liberal depreciation allowances in the calculation of company taxes.

It is commonly believed that these concessions have provided some incentive to foreign capital. But their use can be overdone. For this type of legislation imposes costs on the government in the form of some loss of government revenue, new differentials in tax burden distribution and additional burdens upon administrative facilities. A central issue is whether these revenue, equity and administrative costs outweigh the advantages that the use of the incentives may afford to a developing country. In examining this question, a major study concluded that for many countries the tax system is relatively unimportant in inducing investment, compared with other factors impeding investment, and that tax relief seems to be of only secondary importance in creating conditions conducive to industrial growth, especially when the objective is to increase the level of new investment instead of merely to promote reinvestment (Heller and Kauffman, 1963, pp. 60–66). Given the low utility of tax incentives, the costs of tax concessions may commonly outweigh the advantages.[13]

The provision of tax holidays or reduced rates of taxable income is effective, of course, only when the investment yields substantial taxable profits. The assistance provided by tax exemption is, in fact, inverse to need: as long as a firm experiences losses

13. See also, Taylor (1957, pp. 143–9). Taylor concludes that tax exemption may serve as an irrational or purely psychological inducement in the sense that it may be instrumental in encouraging the initiation of the inducement or the need for the assistance and the amount of subsidy actually received. There is little evidence to indicate that tax exemption has been an important incentive leading to the expansion of existing Puerto Rican firms. It is also contended that many of the new firms that use labor-intensive methods of production would have come to Puerto Rico even without tax exemptions.

and needs assistance, it receives no income-tax subsidy; but the more successful and independent of aid it becomes, the more subsidy it enjoys.

Moreover, the foreign investor in a newly developing country is less likely to be attracted by the prospect of receiving an exemption after a profit is made than he is by being sure of a profit in the first instance. To raise profit expectations, the government may have to undertake additional public expenditures, particularly in providing public utilities, developing industrial sites, expanding labor training facilities and furnishing statistical and information services. Governmental measures that increase labor productivity and help to stabilize the labor force are especially helpful in lowering the otherwise high marginal labor cost for a firm. With the same effect on the government's budget, these expenditures could be a more effective inducement for private investment than tax reduction. They would also reveal more directly the real cost of encouraging foreign investment. But governments have preferred the alternative of forgoing future tax revenue rather than incurring greater present expenditures.

Finally, it can be contended that a developing country might actually be offering excessive concessions to foreign capital. When confronting large foreign enterprises and competing among themselves for the short supply of foreign capital, small countries might well be providing more by way of inducement than is necessary – especially when the concessions do not affect the total of investment forthcoming, but only its intercountry allocation. Some types of foreign investment (for instance, those to secure a necessary raw material or mineral) would go to one developing country or another, regardless of inducements; but the foreign enterprise may 'shop around' and attempt to secure the most favorable terms from each possible source of supply. Special concessions in this case have no appreciable effect in raising the total flow of international investment, but they can affect the allocation between one recipient country or another. Countries that are potential recipients compete among themselves and the competing concessions will largely cancel out – to the benefit of no one country. Competitive tax subsidies among developing countries, for example, may result in a process in which few of the advantages but most of the disadvantages of tax subsidies would remain (Taylor, 1957, p. 149). Negotiating independently, each developing nation offers greater concessions than it would if all the countries could act under a collective agreement regarding the maximum concessions that will be made. In this situation, there is a case for international discussion possibly leading to conventions or agreements that would eliminate the excessive competition (Kaldor, 1965, p. 185; Seers, 1963). It is to the interest of developing countries as a group that the tax treatment should be as uniform as possible and that individual countries should not offer extra concessions except in agreement with the others.

Overconcessions are also made when, in order to avoid discriminatory policies, already existent investments are granted the same concessions that are necessary to encourage new capital. There is also the danger that the temporary preferential treatment offered by concessions will attract the quick, speculative type of foreign investment that makes no long-run contribution to the economy, but simply takes advantage of the concessions. Even for a desired foreign investment that initially has a high benefit–cost ratio, concessions may be extended for too long a time: if the benefits come within a short period of time, then prolongation of the concessions beyond this period is not justified. The cost of 'overencouraging' certain types of foreign investment can be considerable. The problem, therefore, is not simply to consider the relative costs of different incentive devices, but also to devise sufficiently flexible instruments to allow selectivity in the conferral of concessions. The adoption of a selective investment statute, however, assumes that a necessarily high level of administrative capability exists to allow the conferring of broad discretionary powers on administrators who must be able to interpret the purposes of the law and its relationship to the country's development program (Heller and Kauffman, 1963, pp. 50–56).

If the attraction of foreign investment to the country is one objective of an investment statute, another is to channel the investment into fields of high priority within the country. By a denial of concessions or absolute prohibition, developing countries now commonly screen foreign capital away from certain sectors of the economy that are reserved for public enterprise or domestic capital. Governmental grants of permits, licenses, leases and concessions are important means of controlling the acquisition and the extent of rights of foreigners in the country's natural resources. In many countries, authorization or official approval is not granted for foreign investments in the traditional areas of mining, plantations and public utilities which are now reserved for national capital, either exclusively or by prescribing a share in ownership control for nationals. Instead of supporting a continuation of the historical pattern of foreign investment, developing countries have shifted their emphasis to the encouragement of foreign capital in industries that process agricultural products, manufacture for export or produce import substitutes. More and more the channeling of foreign capital appears predicated on a desire to stimulate industrialization, exercise sovereignty over natural resources, avoid the granting of monopoly positions to foreign enterprises and protect domestic competitors.

Beyond the negative controls of outright exclusion, the positive inducements to attract foreign investment into desired channels fall into three main categories: (a) tax exemptions or privileges for 'approved investments', (b) a tariff structure that induces 'tariff factories' to replace imports and that provides high protection on the final stages of production while reducing or removing tariffs on imported components and (c) the use of foreign exchange controls (especially multiple exchange rates and exchange licensing) in order to subsidize specific exports, favor the importation of necessary materials for approved investments and allow a large remittance of earnings on desired investments.

Although their effects may be indirect and not readily apparent, import restrictions and exchange controls are now extremely important in determining the pattern of foreign investment. For the effects of a differentiated tariff structure and multiple exchange rates are equivalent to those of a scheme of subsidies and taxes, affecting the rate of return on foreign investment. When the country imposes prohibitive tariffs, or other import restrictions, against foreign manufactures, the foreign manufacturer may be induced to escape the controls against his product by establishing a branch plant or subsidiary behind the tariff wall. Although the protection would have little effect in attracting supply-oriented industries, the inducement may be significant for the creation of 'tariff factories' in market-oriented industries. It is particularly effective in encouraging the final stages of manufacture and assembly of parts within the tariff-imposing country when there is an import duty on finished goods while raw materials or intermediate goods remain untaxed.

Turning to the 'distribution effect', we are now interested in how regulatory measures may affect the contribution of the foreign investment to local income. This contribution depends on the value of total output attributable to foreign investment and the proportionate share of local participation in the value of that output. Tax measures – consisting mainly of taxes on income and profits and export duties – are, of course, the major policies for reducing the share of the gross domestic product accruing to nonresidents. Under double-taxation agreements, the investee country receives the first share of profits taxation. To raise the share of local participation, however, additional measures are also now taken to control the operation of the foreign investment. Thus, many of the developing countries require domestic partnership with the foreign investors and stipulate that a percentage of the capital in certain industries should be locally owned. The employment and training of nationals is also frequently sought by requiring a certain percentage of the labor force of foreign-owned enterprises to be composed of nationals or by designating that a fixed percentage of the payroll should go to nationals. Minimum wage requirements and social welfare benefits are also designed to ensure a certain return to domestic labor from the operation of the foreign enterprise. There may also be an insistence on the local production or purchase of components and supplies. Finally, there are commonly restrictions on the amount of profit that can be earned or limitations on the distribution of profits.

All these measures are intended to give domestic factors of production a larger share of the total value of the foreign enterprise's output. This intention, however, may conflict with the objective of attracting foreign investment in the first place. If domestic partnership limits the management and control of the enterprise, labor legislation is onerous and allowable profits are not sufficiently attractive, then foreign investment will not be forthcoming and the concessions previously discussed will be of no avail. It is difficult to determine just when measures aimed at increasing the share of domestic income are more than offset by a loss in total income resulting from a decline in the inflow of foreign capital; but at some point, policies designed to raise the benefit–cost ratio may result in no benefit whatsoever as foreign investment ceases.

Special attention should be given to the third kind of effect of foreign investment measures – that on the balance of payments. If the development program is not to be constrained by a shortage of foreign exchange, policies must be instituted to ensure that the deficit is as small as possible and that the remaining irreducible deficit is accommodated by external financing. It is therefore important to analyse how policies affecting external private investment might lessen the pressure on the recipient country's balance of payments.

The initial inflow of foreign capital provides foreign exchange and this is a benefit. But as noted previously, the outward flow of interest, profits and dividends may require balance of payments adjustments that involve some cost. The return flow of capital is a charge on domestic real income that has to be transferred abroad either by increasing exports, decreasing imports or receiving additional capital from overseas. To avoid or reduce this cost, local equity participation is frequently required. Many developing countries also exclude foreign investments that will not contribute to an increase in exports or a replacement of imports, allowing entry only for investments which it is believed will earn sufficient foreign exchange to service their own transfers. Through exchange controls and taxation, the developing country may also limit the maximum transferable return on foreign capital, by restricting the transfer of profits to some per cent of direct investment capital per annum or by allowing earnings up to some percentage of registered foreign capital to be remitted at a lower official exchange rate and the remainder at only a higher free market rate. More severe exchange restrictions are generally applied to the repatriation of capital. A number of countries also attempt to limit transfer of income abroad by imposing a tax on dividends paid to nonresidents. By these means of an absolute ceiling on income and capital transfers, unfavorable exchange rates and increased taxation, the host country seeks to encourage the reinvestment of profits rather than the withdrawal with consequent pressure on the balance of payments.

On the surface, these measures seem sensible; but when examined more closely, they too are subject to some criticism. As previously noted in connection with foreign aid, an investment may ease the balance of payments even if it does not occur in an export- or import-replacing industry. What ultimately matters for the balance of payments is the productivity of investment and the impact of the investment on the total use of resources; the concern with the direct stimulation of exports or direct replacement of imports is a policy of misplaced concreteness.

The emphasis on reinvestment of profits may also be shortsighted. If the initial investment is of value in itself, but the foreign investor does not wish to reinvest his profits in the country, then an attempt to force him to do so is more likely to result simply in a smaller inflow of foreign investment instead of any additional contribution from the reinvestment of profits. There is then a loss to the economy equal to the amount by which real national income would have risen from the investment less the real value of dividend payments abroad. Those firms that will not be deterred by the reinvestment requirement will be precisely those that would expect reinvestment to be profitable anyway, and reinvestment would occur without the governmental requirement.

Moreover, while the insistence on reinvestment does reduce the immediate demand for foreign exchange to pay dividends abroad, it raises, at the same time, the amount of foreign investment on which further dividends may be earned and transferred in the future. The equity interest of the foreigner is increased, without new funds flowing in from abroad. If the intangible benefits – the managerial technical assistance – from the original investment are realized within a short period of time, then the continued expansion of the foreign enterprise through retained earnings ceases to make any special contribution to the economy (Penrose, 1956, 1962). But the ploughing back of profit is tantamount to new foreign investment which expands the base on which profits may be made and causes the country's foreign service charges to become ever greater as the foreign equity increases. It may therefore be submitted that to restrain the rise in foreign service charges, the developing country should attempt to have as much of the subsequent expansion as possible financed from local equity sources. Alternatively, instead of encouraging further expansion of the initial investment, the host country may find it more desirable in the interests of diversification of the economy to encourage the investment of profits in other activities in the economy. To the extent that the initial investment gives rise to future investment elsewhere in the economy, the benefits of foreign investment become more widespread.

Out of concern for the 'balance of payments effect' and also the 'distribution effect', many countries have attempted to secure local equity participation from the very beginning of the investment by excluding the foreign investor in certain industries unless the investment is in the form of a joint international business venture. *Ceteris paribus*, an equity joint venture does allow more positive 'distribution' and 'balance of payments effects' than would 100 per cent foreign ownership, but these advantages should not be overemphasized. There are also several disadvantages which may combine in certain cases to make it undesirable to encourage or enforce an equity joint venture.

If a foreign investor believed it was advantageous to participate in a joint venture, he would seek its establishment without the requirement of a foreign investment law. To the potential investor, the requirement cannot encourage more foreign investment than would have been forthcoming without the requirement; it can only operate in the direction of discouraging foreign investment. A joint venture will not be attractive to the foreign investor when the foreign enterprise has adequate capital and does not need local equity capital, there is no need to have a local partner to supply local knowledge, or when the participation of a local partner would affect the freedom of operation of an internationally integrated company. Given the foreign investor's disinclination to engage in a joint venture, the developing country's insistence on this form of investment will simply diminish the inflow of foreign capital.

From the standpoint of the recipient country's interests, there are also conditions under which the joint venture cannot be considered as the preferred form of foreign investment. To require domestic participation is, of course, to tie the amount of foreign investment to the amount of domestic investment that will be forthcoming; even if the foreign investor were willing to invest in a joint venture, the foreign investment will be lost if domestic investors do not respond. Assuming there is adequate response, there is still a problem connected with the means of financing the domestic participation. If, on the one hand, local savings do exist, and these are mobilized by local participation in the foreign investment, the result may simply be to replace domestic investment which would otherwise have been made; the joint venture then has an opportunity cost by way of the forgone domestic investment. If, on the other hand, a significant supply of local savings is not already existent, but the joint venture presents an attractive opportunity for investment and the local investor borrows the necessary funds, then the joint venture has simply led to credit creation and inflationary financing of the local equity participation; this, in turn, will induce imports which are uncovered by an inflow of foreign exchange. The joint venture might also arise through the acquisition of a pre-existing domestic firm – in this case, actual or potential competition will be diminished, and an undesirable concentration of economic power may result. To the extent that joint ventures tend to predominate in large-scale enterprises, there is also less scope for the imitation of the joint venture's production techniques elsewhere in the economy; the external economies from a large-scale joint venture may thus be less than from a number of smaller scale foreign enterprises which in the aggregate involve no greater amount of foreign equity than is present in the single large-scale joint venture.

Finally, the true alternative to the joint venture is not complete foreign ownership but rather no foreign equity participation at all. To the host country, the advantage of a joint venture is the acquisition of the intangible benefits and the nonmonetary transfer of resources associated with foreign investment without incurring the costs of 100 per cent foreign equity. But along a scale of different forms of foreign investment, the equity joint venture is only one of several alternative arrangements for securing the international transfer of technology and the acquisition of managerial skills. At one extreme on the scale is the foreign investment without local participation and without a time limit on its duration. This may be modified by a requirement that after the initial foreign investment, any subsequent expansion of the enterprise must come through local participation, in order to reduce the proportion of foreign equity over time; or a limited time duration may be imposed, after which the foreign enterprise must be sold to local investors. The joint venture extends this principle by limiting the amount of foreign equity and securing local participation at the outset. Compared with the alternative of a time limit on foreign investment and the eventual bringing of the foreign investment under local ownership and control, the joint venture is clearly less costly, in so far as the equity shares of the foreign enterprise will appreciate, and the repatriation of the sales proceeds imposes a foreign exchange burden.

If, however, the foreign knowhow, managerial talent and training facilities could be acquired without the foreign equity from the start, the developing country would then completely escape the costs of foreign financial involvement. To this end, contractual devices involving engineering and construction agreements, technical services agreements, management contracts or license or franchise arrangements may be superior to the equity joint venture. These contractual devices provide an extremely flexible means of directly transferring specialized technical and managerial knowledge of a proprietary nature from a foreign enterprise, which is the outstanding – and the early – benefit of foreign investment, without the higher costs – which mount over time – of a foreign equity interest.

In the light of development planning, it is significant that not only is a new pattern of international investment emerging, but also that the developing countries are seeking a less costly mix of public and private foreign capital and public and private technical assistance. Instead of overemphasizing the institution of an equity joint venture, the less developed countries might be better advised to seek the following mix: for the securing of foreign exchange – foreign public sources of capital that can supply funds in the form of long-term low-interest loans and grants-in-aid; for the stimulation of the private sector – the relending of these funds to domestic enterprise through intermediate credit institutions, such as local development banks or domestic finance corporations;[15] for technical knowledge and business methods – more extensive use of contractual devices with foreign supplying enterprises. Through such a combination of public foreign capital with management contracts or technical collaboration agreements, the developing country may obtain both the capital and the technical, managerial and training services at a lower cost than by insisting on an equity joint venture. The higher rate of return required for a direct equity investment is in essence a payment for foreign knowledge and if this can be acquired through contractual devices while the foreign capital is received from governmental sources at a low rate of interest, then there is a distinct advantage in shifting the emphasis to management and service contracts. If developing countries are attempting to depart from the traditional pattern of private foreign investment, so too is there a compelling need to seek new methods of foreign partnership to gain the benefits of 'jointness' at reduced cost. The potentialities for thus combining local ownership with technical assistance from private foreign enterprise and financial aid from public sources can become of considerable practical importance.

References

BALOGH, T., and STREETEN, P. (1960), 'Domestic versus foreign investment', *Bull. Oxf. Univ. Inst. Stat.*, vol. 22, pp. 213–24.

BARLOW, E. R., and WENDER, I. T. (1955), *Foreign Investment and Taxation*, Harvard Law School.

BEHRMAN, J. N. (1962), 'US government encouragement of private direct investment abroad', in R. Mikesell (ed.), *US Private and Government Investment Abroad*, Oregon University Press.

BOSKEY, S. (1959), *Problems and Practices of Development Banks*, Johns Hopkins Press.

CAIRNCROSS, A. K. (1962), *Factors in Economic Development*, Allen & Unwin.

15. For an elaboration of the role that these institutions can perform in providing long-term finance to private industry, see generally, Boskey (1959), Diamond (1957, 1965), Mikesell (1966).

DIAMOND, W. (1957), *Development Banks*, Johns Hopkins Press.

DIAMOND, W. (1965), 'Development finance companies', *Fin. Devel.*, vol. 2, pp. 97–102.

HELLER, J., and KAUFFMAN, K. M. (1963), *Tax Incentives for Industry in Less Developed Countries*, Harvard Law School.
KALDOR, N. (1965), 'The role of taxation in economic development', in E. A. G. Robinson (ed.), *Problems in Economic Development*, Macmillan Co.
MACDOUGALL, G. D. A. (1960), 'The benefits and cost of private investment from abroad: a theoretical approach', *Econ. Rec.*, vol. 36, pp. 13–35.
MCKEAN, R. (1958), *Efficiency in Government through Systems Analysis*, Wiley.
MIKESELL, R. (1966), 'Public foreign capital for private enterprise in developing countries', *Essays in International Finance*, no. 52, Princeton University.
NATIONAL INDUSTRIAL CONFERENCE BOARD (1965), *Obstacles and Incentives to Private Foreign Investment, 1962–1964*, report no. 115.
NURKSE, R. (1954), 'The problem of international investment today in the light of nineteenth-century experience', *Econ. J.*, vol. 64, pp. 744–58.
OECD (1966), *Development Assistance Efforts and Policies, 1966 Review*, Paris.
PENROSE, E. T. (1956), 'Foreign investment and growth of the firm', *Econ. J.*, vol. 66, pp. 220–35.
PENROSE, E. T. (1962), 'Some problems of policy toward direct private foreign investment in developing countries', *Mid. East econ. Pap.*, pp. 135–6.
PIZER, S., and CUTLER, F. (1966), 'Foreign investments, 1965–1966', *Survey of Current Business*, US Department of Commerce, Washington.
SEERS, D. (1963), 'Big companies and small countries', *Kyklos*, vol. 16, pp. 601–3.
STREETEN, P. (1964), *Economic Integration*, A. W. Sythoff, 2nd edn.
TAYLOR, M. C. (1957), *Industrial Tax Exemption in Puerto Rico*, University of Wisconsin Press.
US AGENCY FOR INTERNATIONAL DEVELOPMENT (1965), *Foreign Aid through Private Initiative*, Advisory Committee on Private Enterprise in Foreign Aid.
US DEPARTMENT OF COMMERCE (1964), *Factors Limiting United States Investment Abroad: II*, Washington.
US PRESIDENT'S TASK FORCE ON FOREIGN ECONOMIC ASSISTANCE (1961), *Act for International Development: Summary Presentation*, Office of Public Services, Washington.
VON NEUMAN WHITMAN, M. (1965), *Government Risk-Sharing in Foreign Investment*, Princeton University Press.

17 P. Streeten

New Approaches to Private Investment in Less Developed Countries[1]

P. Streeten, 'Nouvelles manières d'aborder le problème de l'investissement privé dans les pays en boie de dèveloppement', *Revue de la Société d'Études et d'Expansion*, vol. 238, 1969, pp. 909–24.

The role of private investment in the process of development needs rethinking in the light of fundamental changes in the world economy. Much of our present thinking and many of our institutions are still dominated by the experience and the doctrines of the nineteenth century and are therefore ill-adapted to the altogether different circumstances and needs of the second half of the twentieth.

Foreign private enterprise has an important part to play in assisting the progress of the developing countries. At the same time, a number of obstacles stand in the way of greater participation of private overseas investment in the development process. New thinking, new policies and new institutions can contribute to overcoming these obstacles.

The obstacles are partly economic, arising from the difficulties of operating in countries with shortages of skilled manpower, foreign exchange and basic utilities, and partly political. The latter include the sometimes ambivalent attitudes of the governments of developing countries and the resulting political risks faced by private enterprise.

There are a number of features which distinguish modern private foreign investment from that in the last century (Rosenstein-Roden, 1967). First, whereas in the nineteenth century 70 per cent of world foreign investment took the form of bonds and only 30 per cent that of equity, today bond investment is small (although it has in recent years risen) and, disregarding trade credits, the majority is in direct equity. This implies that the

1. I am grateful to Mrs Frances Stewart and Mr J. P. Hayes for many ideas and comments.

rates of return and the services rendered have changed. Second, equity investment in the nineteenth century carried the risks to cyclical fluctuations. In bad years no dividends would be paid out. Such fluctuations are less important today, in spite of continued fluctuations in export earnings, and there is, therefore, less justification for a reward to this kind of risk bearing.[2] Third, in the nineteenth century the transfer of capital was accompanied by the migration of skilled people, in whom aptitudes and attitudes geared to development were incorporated. Today, traditional attitudes have to be transformed and skills have to be created. Fourth, as a result of the more rapid spread of knowledge, certain, although by no means all, types of technological knowledge are nowadays more widespread and standardized than they were in the nineteenth century. It is sometimes cheaper to hire foreign engineers and to borrow capital at fixed interest rates than to invite equity investment. In those areas where hired skills plus fixed interest borrowing can achieve the samc results more cheaply than foreign equity investment, the latter puts an excess burden on the host country. There are other industries in which technical and managerial knowhow is not so readily available and where high returns are justified. In particular, the most difficult problem frequently is to sniff out profitable opportunities as well as, having selected projects, to execute and run them. This sniffing out can be done by foreign capital which acquires in return the right to exploit fully these opportunities. But there are many other arrangements which may serve the same purpose, some of which impose a smaller burden on the host country. It would, for instance, be possible to offer a management contract to a foreign investor who may also be permitted to hold a substantial minority of shares (Rosenstein-Rodan, 1967). The foreign investor would construct and manage the plant and would receive a management fee. This fee can take the form of a percentage both of profits and of foreign exchange savings realized. At the same time the managing firm may be expected to offer a credit at a fixed rate of interest to the local firm.[3] This credit should cover either the foreign exchange costs or a certain

2. On the question of political risks, see below.

3. Hans Singer calls this a form of direct bond investment. See Rosenstein-Rodan (1967, p. 182).

proportion of the total investment costs of the project. The duration of the loan would be the same as the duration of the management contract.

Drawbacks of private overseas investment

Private overseas investment (POI), since about 1950, has played a smaller part in the transfer of resources to underdeveloped countries than official aid. Between 1956 and 1967 the net flow of private (including portfolio) investment and private export credits to poor countries fluctuated round an annual rate of over $3 billion, while private investment by rich countries in rich countries was considerably larger and increased substantially. Private investment in poor countries reached a peak of $4329 million in 1967, to which it rose from a trough of $2544 million in 1963. The average annual flow is about half that of official net DAC disbursements, but it is obviously less easily controlled or predictable. The British contribution to this fluctuated between $310 million in 1963 and $726 million in 1957. In 1967 it was $377 million.

Private overseas investment, with all its merits, can probably not achieve a large and sustained transfer of foreign exchange resources to developing countries. Yet this is one of the needs today. Only if the percentage rate of growth of foreign capital is higher than the rate of return on old capital is there a current net addition to the foreign exchange resources available for development

It might be argued that this formulation of the foreign exchange contribution of POI refers only to the minimum of the transfer and that the maximum is given by all additional sales made possible by the investment project, minus the imported inputs into the project. This would be a true maximum if all resources employed in the project were previously unemployed, all sales were either exports or import substitutes, and all additional income generated were saved, or if the marginal propensity to import were zero or if fiscal policy kept consumption constant. Otherwise, there will be some reduction in the maximum foreign exchange earnings and savings, depending on the amount of extra imports or reduced exports. The lower limit of the maximum would then be no change in the balance of trade, as the marginal propensity to save becomes zero or the marginal propensity to import unity.[4]

But there are two faults in this analysis. First, the characteristic peculiar to POI, as distinct from domestic investment, is that privately owned foreign exchange first flows in for the construction of the project and later flows back in the form of remitted profits. The indirect effects described in the previous paragraph arise from *any* investment, not specifically from POI.

Thus, if, say, Tanzania wishes to build a cement factory, she can invite Portland Cement to do it for her, or she can build it herself, hiring experts and managers, hiring or buying machinery, borrowing capital, etc. Or she may do without the cement for a time. It may, of course, be that the foreign investor will erect and manage a factory more efficiently or more cheaply than if it had been all done at home or if it had been done by borrowing capital and hiring skills. (Though it can also work the other way.) Then the differences in costs and returns should be credited (or, in the opposite case, debited) to POI. But the economics of investment is not the same as the economics of POI and to credit all indirect effects to POI is to confuse the two. Historically, POI may often have been the only way of getting the investment and it would then be correct to identify the total effects with the differential effects.[5] But analytically (i.e. for the purpose of analysis) and operationally (i.e. for the purpose of policy), the two are quite distinct.

The second flaw of the analysis is that it assumes not only that the resources employed in the project were previously unused (and, as the previous paragraph showed, unusable), but also that

4. The improvement in the balance of trade is given by the expression

$$I_{VA}\left(1-\frac{1}{1+s/m}\right),$$

where I_{VA} is the domestic value added by POI, s is the marginal propensity to save and m the marginal propensity to import, because the increase in imports equals

$$m\Delta Y = \frac{mI_{VA}}{sm},$$

when Y = national income.

5. Perhaps the typical case here is investment in oil. The oil exports would not have occurred had it not been for the foreign company's investment and total oil export earnings should therefore be credited to the balance of payments contribution of the investment.

they represent *net* additions in that they do not replace resources in other sectors of the economy. Even where supply is freely available, demand may be such that previously employed resources now become unemployed. The production may neither earn nor save foreign exchange, but simply displace other resources, which now become unemployed or underemployed.

There is a further objection, not to the analysis but to the assumption of unemployment. If any of the resources employed in the project are taken away from activities which earn or save foreign exchange, it is quite possible that the foreign exchange contribution becomes negative.

Finally, this type of analysis makes no allowance for the complex political effects of the pressures of POI upon the general policies conducted by the host country. In a world in which no longer, as in the nineteenth century, a handful of countries confronts hundreds of businesses but where, instead, hundreds of countries confront a handful of companies, the repercussions upon a host of policies pursued by a government which admits POI are considerably more important than the above analysis which assumes these policies to be unaffected.

But the analysis which runs in terms of capital inflow and profit outflow, crude though it is, has still a certain logical validity and operational use and can be defended against the criticism that it neglects the so-called indirect effects of POI.

We can, therefore, return to this analysis without too many scruples. It is sometimes said that additional new investment and the retention of current profits in the host country can indefinitely offset and more than offset the return flow of profits and dividends on old capital and of capital repatriation. But if the rate of return on foreign capital exceeds the rate of growth of national income – a quite realistic assumption because the former is likely to be at least 10 per cent and the latter at most 5 per cent – the rate of growth of foreign capital must be higher than that of national income. This implies, assuming a constant ratio between capital and output for foreign and for domestic capital, that foreign capital ownership grows at a faster rate than domestic capital and therefore an ever increasing proportion of the domestic capital stock will be owned by foreigners. This is particularly serious if, initially, little locally owned capital exists, as in many African countries. Even if such alienation of the capital stock were politically acceptable, the process must come to an end when all capital is owned by foreigners, beyond which further postponement of repatriation and remittances will not be possible.

Remittances abroad may also, sooner or later, grow faster than export earnings, since these are not likely to grow much faster than income. For a constant investment base, remittances may be expected to be constant and therefore, with growing export earnings, represent a shrinking proportion. But fixed interest-bearing capital may be raised locally and the growing gearing ratio may be reflected in a rising profit rate. Then growing profits will be remitted on a constant investment stake. Growing remittances may also reflect growing investment in the past and may place a growing future burden on the balance of payments.

For these reasons, private investment is not likely to make a sustained and substantial net contribution to the transfer of foreign exchange resources. To say this in no way implies that foreign investment may not make a contribution to economic growth. Numerous factors which accelerate growth lead to a deterioration of the balance of payments. It is, for example, quite possible that the worsened balance of payments position occurs at a higher level of foreign trade and real income than would have been attainable without the foreign investment. All that is argued here is that no large and sustained net contribution to foreign exchange can be expected.

But even during the period when a net inflow of foreign exchange is possible, because the rate of growth of foreign capital exceeds the rate of return on foreign capital, less developed countries are faced with a dilemma: either they permit or even encourage this growth of foreign capital, in which case they will be faced with growing foreign ownership of their capital stock; or else they limit this process of alienation, in which case a part of their export earnings will be mortgaged to remitting profits and repatriating capital. It is small wonder that this ineluctable dilemma has led to ambivalence and hostility towards foreign investment.

Inability to earn profits and repay debt has, in the past, led to bankruptcies, which relieve debtor countries of the need to repay capital or remit profits and which have facilitated the transfer to local ownership. The effective rate of return *ex post* has therefore been much smaller than would appear on paper. Today bankruptcies are much rarer and default is considered a much more serious matter. This implies that softer terms should be recognized in the terms of loans and that an institutional equivalent for the transfer through bankruptcies should be created.

Foreign companies are sometimes accused of sacrificing the national development of the country to their desire for profits. It would be both unreasonable and possibly undesirable to expect foreign companies to act altruistically in promoting local development. Within the constraints set by competition, legislation, morality and public opinion, there is a presumption that they are best employed in seeking profits, as long as they take a long-term view, not giving excessive weight to quick profits at the expense of future profits and as long as they assess correctly the constraints set by political action and public opinion.

More serious is the charge that the local company sacrifices its own profits to the interests of the parent company or sister companies in an advanced industrial country and that this, rather than any lack of nationalism, charity or altruism, damages local development. Such restrictions on local profit maximization can have different reasons. The company may charge higher prices for its products in order to prevent the elimination of inefficient sister or parent companies in the investing country. But the reverse may also be true: the parent company pricing its products so as to keep an inefficient subsidiary in business. In the former case the high prices may lead to faster innovation in synthetic substitutes, in which the parent company may be engaged. The problem here is not monopoly pricing by the subsidiary, for price reductions would increase local profits, but the foreign locus of ownership and control. Profits may be minimized rather than maximized, by underpricing output and overpricing inputs, if by this device tax liabilities can be shifted from a high-tax country to a low-tax country, or losses can be set off against highly taxed gains. Another cause of trouble is to be found in the high wages and fringe benefits which the foreign company can offer to local workers and which do not reflect the cost of alternative uses of the labour forgone. While this policy ensures that some of the profits of foreign enterprise are retained by citizens of the host country, it can play havoc with the wage structure in the rest of the economy, aggravate social inequality, encourage the wasteful use of capital and, above all, increase unemployment.

These considerations, quite apart from political fears of domination or foreign influence, suggest that a framework should be created which would reduce the costs of foreign investment to the host country, without reducing its benefits. A high share of equity investment imposes two kinds of burden on the host country. First, a high share of the increase in production, which the investment makes possible, must return to the foreign investor in the form of profits. Secondly, these resources must be transferred through additional foreign exchange earnings or foreign exchange savings. In view of the limitations of contemporary international trade, this secondary transfer burden, superimposed on the first, can be heavy.

Political risks, such as expropriation without adequate compensation, restrictions on repatriation of profits and capital, or devaluation are often cited as factors which make it necessary to earn high rates of profit to compensate for these risks. The high rates earned then cause suspicion and hostility in the host country, which feels that the firm is taking out much more than it puts in, and tend to lead to those dreaded events, which the high profits seek to compensate for. This leads to the demand for even higher profits and the vicious spiral is given another twist. High profits, required because of risks, also impose a heavy balance of payments burden, tending to lead to restrictions on remittances and repatriation, and once again strengthen the demand for higher profits to compensate for the risk of the imposition of such restrictions.

It is clear that mutual gains could be derived from measures which lower these risks, lighten the balance of payments burden, reduce the rate of profits required by the company and dispel fear and suspicion. Private investment in uncertain conditions is not a zero-sum game and both investor and host country can gain from such mutually agreed 'disarmament'.

Advantages of POI

Private investment is frequently lumped together with official aid as a quantum with which to fill the 'resource gap', and with official aid and receipts from visible and invisible trade as a quantum with which to fill the 'foreign exchange gap'. It has been argued above that private investment cannot be expected to make a substantial contribution over a sustained period of time to filling the foreign exchange gap. But while the additions to the *volume* of total available foreign exchange may not be substantial, private investment may provide capital in a particularly productive form, so that the *efficiency* of the resources transferred is high. The particular contribution of private investment may lie, not in the transfer of foreign exchange so much as in helping to lay the foundations for further growth in the economy and in strengthening the base from which domestic savings and foreign exchange are generated. In particular, private overseas investment can bestow substantial benefits on the host country where domestic management skills and entrepreneurship are embryonic and there is no other way of organizing large-scale manufacturing industry.

Its merits then lie not so much in contributing to filling the *foreign exchange gap*, or even the *savings gap*, as in the following:

1. It may contribute indirectly to filling the savings and the foreign exchange gaps by contributing to tax revenue. This contribution to filling the *budgetary* gap is particularly important in countries where effective taxation of the domestic sector is difficult. It can, however, be eroded by tax concessions extended by less developed countries to attract foreign companies.

2. It helps in the *transfer* of technology (knowhow) and skills.

3. It provides management and training of local managers.

4. It can help in the *training* of workers and the creation of indigenous skills in administration, marketing and other business techniques.

5. In appropriate forms and with appropriate safeguards, it can contribute to the growth of local entrepreneurship, by subcontracting, by the encouragement to repair shops and other ancillary enterprises, etc.

6. It may, by changing the market structure, contribute to more vigorous competition.

7. It helps in establishing contacts with overseas banks, capital markets, markets for products, sales organizations and other institutions and it opens a previously closed society to world-wide influences.

8. It may create, directly and indirectly, employment opportunities.

9. It may raise domestic wages or improve the terms of trade.

While all these contributions are possibilities rather than certainties, since under each heading negative as well as positive results can be listed, they point the way to solutions which will maximize the net gains. Thus if it were found that the net foreign exchange contribution is small but the contribution to management large, methods and institutions should be devised to raise the foreign exchange contribution.

The organizational structure and motivation of the international corporation, with subsidiaries and branches in many countries, which can militate against the interests of development in a particular country, is for the same reason capable of responding more effectively to technological, political and economic changes in switching to new products, closing down inefficient lines, cutting costs by shifting to new sources of supply, etc. The pressure for greater local participation in ownership and control may impede or prevent these operations in much the same way in which nationalism and autarky prevent the most efficient international specialization. Adam Smith's invisible hand has a strong cosmopolitan bias. It ignores nationalistic aims and, in seeking profits wherever they arise, transcends national boundaries. Whatever may be true of the *national* corporation, what is good for international General Motors is *not* always good for America. It is this dilemma between, on the one hand, international allocation in the service of efficiency and, on the other greater local participation and commitment, which must be resolved.

The role of POI

Any operational assessment of the potential contribution of POI must start from an assumption about the alternatives. If a country wishes to evaluate the costs and benefits to be derived from setting up an additional cement plant, it is irrelevant to compare the established plant with the situation before its establishment. What is relevant is a comparison between the following possibilities:

1. To raise the capital and other resources domestically and set up an indigenous cement plant.
2. To borrow money abroad, hire engineers and managers and buy the knowhow.
3. Any partial combination between 1 and 2, including joint ventures, management contracts, etc.
4. Not to carry out the investment now but to import the cement or do without it for the time being.

A clear formulation of the alternatives is an essential prerequisite to the proper appraisal of the value of foreign enterprise. The important point for planners is to free themselves from ideological bias and historical precedent, and to exercise their *institutional imagination* upon the various alternatives, against which any *operational* assessment has to be made.

Areas of common interest

A policy which aims at maximizing the positive impact on development of private foreign enterprise may begin by tracing the interest spheres of the foreign company and attempt to identify areas of common interest, where progress benefits both the foreign company and the host country, and areas of interest clashes, where bargaining encroaches upon the interests of either party.

The foreign investor is interested in profits and growth. His risks are reduced by clear terms, informed negotiators, speedy decisions. That way the companies who come know what they are coming to, the companies who do not come make their decision with the minimum of hard feelings. The charge for risk comes down, the charge for risks which exist only in the investor's imagination disappears.

Both foreign company and host country have an interest in growth, which adds to production, and in higher profits, though their division between taxes and dividends raises interest conflicts. Both are interested in a growing, skilled labour force and better trained local managers who replace expensive overseas personnel. Both are interested in reducing risks due to subjective fears in the mind of the investor. Such risk reduction lowers the required rate of return on foreign investment and, as a result, removes some of the forces that may justify the fears. Several measures contribute to risk reduction: investment guarantees, free remittance of profits, ready availability of information, speedy administration of licences. As risks are reduced, the required rate of return falls; and as the rate of return falls, the burden on the balance of payments of foreign remittances falls or the rate of growth of foreign ownership falls and the contribution of the foreign enterprise to the domestic economy rises.

On the other hand, there are areas in which the company's gain is the country's loss or vice versa. In this area, the task will be, once it has been decided to attract the foreign company, to negotiate so that that share of profits is permitted to accrue to the company which induces it to remain and expand and encourages new companies to enter, while the remainder accrues to the government as taxes and other forms of government revenue.

Suggestions for planners

The following suggestions are illustrative only. The main point of this paper is to emphasize the need for exploring new institutional approaches, which should attempt to combine the best features of public and private operations.

Increased role of the private sector in the planning processes

The private sector's commitment to national development is likely to be far greater if some of their numbers are consulted both in the formulation of the development plan and in occasional exploratory discussions of new policies affecting foreign exchange control, reinvestment, trade and transport regulations, etc. Small, informal exchanges are likely to be most fruitful. Sometimes the private sector's understanding of what is needed and why, and the willingness to contribute to it is likely to be enhanced with such participation. The private sector can in turn provide the government with information about their plans for existing and potential productive resources, present and anticipated market demands, inventory accumulations, prospective need for capital and credit, and bottlenecks including government regulation. In every development plan, much is required of the private sector: it may be wiser, therefore, to plan with and not for them and to exchange ideas. Private sector planning has often been the weakest link in the chain of planning.

Training for planners/civil servants on negotiating a new enterprise

In many developing countries, there are few on government staff who have had experience in developing and negotiating a project with the private sector and relatively low priority has been given to this exercise. This experience is often accompanied, understandably, by suspicion of the motives of the 'outsider', on the one hand, and of the competence of the government, on the other: attitudes which do not work toward amicable negotiations. Frequently the civil servants need background information on how such enterprises have worked in other countries, where to obtain assessments of foreign firms, what points need to be covered in analysing and negotiating a private project and where to collect information on specific types of industry.

Encouragement to public and private enterprises to develop local entrepreneurs for their ancillary supply, service and distribution activities

Far too few local or foreign enterprises, private or public, have undertaken to build up local entrepreneurs or cooperatives who could provide their supplies or service their equipment. More have trained distributors and retailers of their products. Such an effort requires the establishment of specifications, training in how to meet these, help in defining and maintaining quality control, possible assistance in opening links to overseas suppliers and obtaining local sources of credit, etc. All of this requires considerable expenditure of time and is unlikely to be undertaken by the larger enterprise unless specifically encouraged by government.

Partners in development

Even in sectors and in industries in which foreign equity investment is the best form of promoting development, political considerations suggest that partnerships and joint ventures, in which local capital and knowhow participate, are often preferable. A private firm could establish a joint enterprise with a local government or a government agency, such as a local development corporation. The foreign firm should put up not more than 49 per cent of the capital, but enough to benefit if the enterprise succeeds and of course suffer if it fails. It should have a substantial minority interest, while the local government or agency has the dominant interest.

Such a holding would often be sufficient to secure a decisive role in management. But it might be possible to arrange in special circumstances that, in the initial phase, the foreign investor should hold a higher percentage of the equity, as long as the arrangement for eventual transfer to local ownership is clearly stated. The foreign firm might also provide some of the money on a fixed interest basis or in the form of preference shares.

The equity interest of the foreign firm would be bought out by the local government at the end of a prearranged period. This period could be ten years, with provision each year after, say, seven years to extend for a further five years up to, say, fifteen years or longer in the case of, for example, plantation enterprises. Other forms of rolling extensions could be devised, such as periodic reviews with stated period of extension. Alternatively, the period might be longer, but there could be options at fixed points when either the local government can buy out or the firm can sell out. An evaluation procedure to determine the price would have to be agreed.

Managerial and technical staff would initially be provided almost exclusively by the foreign firm, perhaps under a management contract, but with the obligation to train local replacements within the specified period before buy-out. The rate of replacement could not be specified contractually, but the local government would be able to use its representation on the board to ensure that it went forward at a satisfactory pace.

Housing and other community services should be provided by the local government or appropriate local statutory body set up for the purpose. In view of the relatively short period of ownership participation, the foreign firm's capital should be concentrated on directly productive activities.

Official aid may provide the finance for participation of the local government. It might be possible to provide a long-term loan on soft terms to enable a host government to participate in a venture. No subsidy to a particular private firm would be involved, for the government's terms of on-lending could be commercial. Only the secondary foreign exchange burden would be lightened. Governments can also support such joint ventures with buying-out options either by investment guarantees or by including a clause in the contract of the loan that in case of expropriation without proper compensation the whole outstanding loan would fall due for repayment immediately. The force of such a clause would lie in the fear of loss of credit standing if default occurred.

Arguments against such proposals are based partly on the need to repatriate capital paid to buy out a firm and the consequential strain on the host country's balance of payments, and partly on the fear that limited participation is bound to reduce the involvement of the foreign firm in the host country and to reinforce its enclave nature.[6] The reply to both points is that companies should be encouraged to reinvest their funds in new ventures in the same country. Where this is impossible, the costs of repatriation and short-term involvement would have to be compared with the benefits of increased local participation.

Arrangements of the kind sketched out above would attract foreign capital and knowhow to the activities where they are most useful, but would release them, when the host government buys out the firm, for new ventures elsewhere. Thus good use would be made of the finance and experience of foreign companies by keeping them in a revolving fund. Teams could be kept working together and political friction and transfer burdens would be minimized.

The climate for international investment and for new forms of joint ventures would be greatly improved if a set of rules for the remittance of profits, capital and capital gains could be agreed upon and obeyed. It is important that profits earned by

6. See Hans Singer in Rosenstein-Rodan (1967, p. 185).

foreign capital should be allowed to be remitted home. Restrictions, except those imposed temporarily in emergencies, would only discourage the future flow of investment and are as much against the interests of the investor as they are against those of the host country. But if the foreign firm borrows local capital, which it can often do very cheaply in view of its good credit standing, profits earned on this local capital need not enjoy the same freedom. The same rules should apply to these profits as those which apply to local firms.

While it may be sensible to aim at a certain proportion of equity to fixed interest investment for foreign capital in an underdeveloped economy as a whole, the proportions of specific sectors and firms may, of course, vary widely from the country-wide average. Some sectors, like transport and power, can be wholly financed on a fixed interest basis. Others, where entrepreneurial initiative is important, may be financed wholly by direct equity investment, while others again may show a variety of gearing ratios of equity to bond capital. Again, a variety of arrangements can be made for the transfer and adaptation of knowhow. Individuals can be hired, management contracts can be concluded and participation in profits can be arranged. It is the purpose of such arrangements to minimize both the cost to the host country of the transfer of capital and knowhow, and political frictions, while safeguarding the interests of those who are willing to conduct this transfer.

If our main concern is the social and economic development of less developed countries, the contribution of private overseas investment must be assessed in the light of a variety of methods of mobilizing indigenous resources, skills and knowhow. Our task is to explore the most effective and the cheapest way of attracting foreign resources, skills and knowledge and the best way of combining them in order to bring about such a mobilization. This requires the examination of new institutions, arrangements and forms of contract.

The objectives of the new arrangements are, first, to reduce the political tensions that arise from large foreign-owned enclaves in less developed countries and the fears of expropriation which deter foreign enterprise by an agreed upon and institutional form of divestment, which would replace the cataclysmic form of the past; second, to establish a framework which would change the policies of foreign companies so that they do not necessarily subordinate the policies of the local companies to the interests of the parent companies; third, to induce spread effects, so that the beneficial activities of the foreign companies spill over into the less dynamic sectors of the rest of the economy; fourth, to set free, after a period, the scarce foreign capital and skills so that these can be re-employed in pioneering new ventures rather than continuing to be employed in existing activities.

Reference

ROSENSTEIN-RODAN, P. N. (1967), 'The philosophy of international investment in the second half of the twentieth century', in J. H. Adler (ed.), *Capital Movements and Economic Development*, Macmillan.

Part Seven
International Investment and Economic Welfare

International direct investment sometimes gives rise to a conflict of interests between the agents of such investment, for example, the companies concerned, and the Nation States of which they are part – and sometimes, indeed, between the participating Nation States. While this volume does not examine these conflicts in depth, Professor Johnson's contribution (Reading 18) is of sufficiently general interest to warrant a place in it. In his essay Johnson deals with some of the general principles underlying effects of the flow of direct investment on the welfare of the participating, and particularly host, nations.

18 H. G. Johnson

The Efficiency and Welfare Implications of the International Corporation

H. G. Johnson, 'The efficiency and welfare implications of the international corporation', in C. P. Kindleberger (ed.), *The International Corporation*, MIT Press, 1970, pp. 35–56.

Monopolistic competition in knowledge

Direct foreign investment by the large international corporation, and especially by the large American international corporation, has become an increasing source of political concern in countries where such investment has been significant since the Second World War and particularly in the past decade or so; and there has been much discussion, and some practice, of the application of restrictions to such investment. Much of the concern about direct foreign investment has merely expressed xenophobic or nationalistic sentiments of a type that cannot readily be reasoned with; but there are obviously theoretical possibilities that the consequences of such investments may be adverse, either by comparison with the situation as it would be in their absence or, less stringently and more plausibly, by comparison with alternative methods of handling the transference of knowledge, which is the crux of the direct investment process. These possibilities of adverse effects have usually been discussed – as exemplified by C. P. Kindleberger's (1969) contribution to a recent seminar in Chicago – in terms of the standard arguments for tariff protection, together, more recently, with considerations drawn from the analysis of market organization and competition, due particularly to the work of Stephen Hymer (1960, 1966, 1967, 1968). This paper will be concerned with essentially the same possibilities as other authors have noted, but it seeks to place the issues in a broader and more fundamental perspective by relating them to the welfare economics of technological and managerial knowledge as a factor of production.[1]

1. For an earlier and in some respects more detailed treatment, see H. G. Johnson (1968).

As has long been known from the economic analysis of the patent system, the production and utilization of knowledge in a private enterprise system poses an insuperable dilemma from the point of view of welfare maximization. The dilemma arises from the fact that the creation or development of new productive knowledge requires an investment of resources which must be recompensed if there is to be an incentive for private investment in knowledge creation, but that once new knowledge has been created it has the character of a public good, in the sense that use of such knowledge by one person does not preclude use of it by another, so that optimality requires that it be made available to all potential users without charge. Ideally, therefore, the production of useful new knowledge should be financed collectively through the government and the results made available to potential users free of charge. This is the practice with respect to some sectors of the economy, most notably agriculture; but for the most part a private enterprise system relies on private enterprise for the production of commercially useful knowledge. Private production of commercially useful knowledge is encouraged by granting or allowing its producer a temporary monopoly in the use of it. Formerly, an explicit grant of a temporally limited monopoly through the patent system served this purpose; in contemporary conditions, public tolerance and legal protection of commercial secrecy has become more important than the patent system. The practice of rewarding the production of commercially useful knowledge by the right to charge a monopoly price for the product for a period limited either legally or by the natural erosion of commercial secrecy necessarily tends to generate economic inefficiency in at least four major ways.

First, as long as the temporary monopoly enables price to be set above marginal cost of production, the implicit tax on the use of the knowledge restricts such use below the socially optimal level.

Second, the reward to the private producer of new knowledge is less than the social gain from its existence, both the actual gain enjoyed from it in the presence of monopolistic restriction on use and the potential gain that could be derived if the knowledge were made available free of charge.

These two points are illustrated in Figure 1. In the figure, *DD′*

is the demand curve for a new product, this demand curve being assumed to be latent in the utility functions of consumers but not expressed in the market because until it is introduced the new product has an infinite price; to avoid certain obvious complications, either DD' must be defined as a compensated demand

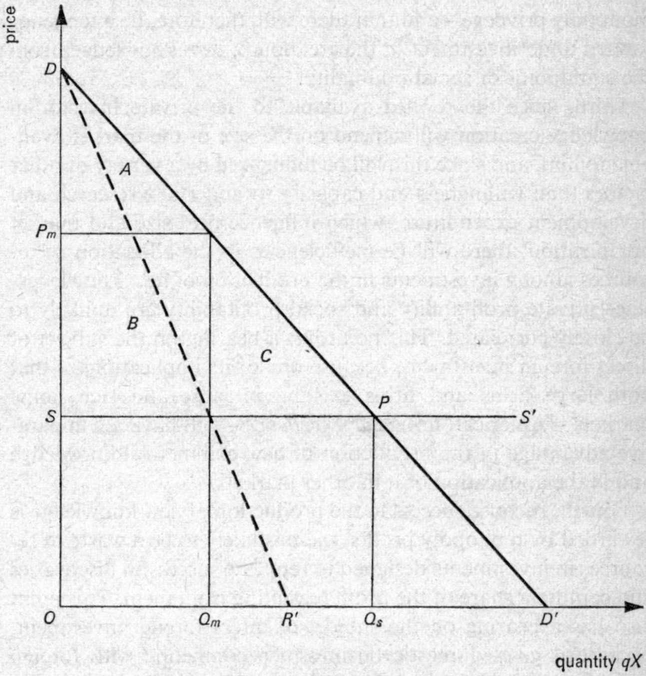

Figure 1 Optimal and monopoly pricing of a new product

curve or the effect of introducing the new product must be assumed to be too small to affect the marginal utility of income. Once the new product has been invented, socially optimal policy would require it to be sold at its cost of production (shown by SS', constant cost being assumed for simplicity). From the equilibrium output Q_s that would result, society would derive a consumers' surplus DSP, composed of triangles A and C and the rectangle B. Monopoly would result in the price OP_m, with a monopoly profit of rectangle *B* and a total social gain of triangle *A* plus rectangle *B*.

The first point implies that existing knowledge will be used to a suboptimal extent. The second implies that the private return from the creation of new knowledge will be less than the social return – a further reason for this is the temporal limitation of the monopoly privilege – and that there will, therefore, be a tendency toward underinvestment in the creation of new knowledge, from the standpoint of social optimality.

Third, since the reward available to the private investor in knowledge creation will depend on the size of the market available to him, and since this will be influenced by a variety of other factors than willingness and capacity to undertake research and development expenditure, which influence firm size and market organization, there will be inefficiencies in the allocation of resources among investments in the production of new knowledge, since private profitability and social profitability are unlikely to be closely correlated. This point has a bearing on the subject of direct foreign investment, because one of its implications is that both large firms and firms existing in large and rich home markets – American firms *par excellence* – will have a comparative advantage in the production of new commercial knowledge and in the application of it in other markets.

Fourth, because success in the production of new knowledge is rewarded by monopoly profits, there is likely to be a waste of resources in investments designed to replicate successful discoveries and capture a share of the profits resulting from them. This point also has a bearing on the subject of direct foreign investment, because it gives domestic businessmen competing with foreign firms incentives to try to get their government either to invest public resources in helping them to develop the knowledge necessary to enable them to compete, or to impose restrictions on foreign investment either to give themselves protection or to force the foreign firms to let them in for a share of the profits generated by the foreign firms' superior knowledge.

Exploiting technological monopolies in foreign investment

The foregoing points are perfectly general observations about the welfare effects of entrusting the production of commercially useful knowledge to private enterprise and competition, in so far as no reference is made to differences of nationality between producers and consumers. But they do help to put in perspective some of the common reactions in host countries to direct foreign investment in them, if we identify such investment – which involves overcoming the cost disadvantages of operating production and distribution facilities in an unfamiliar environment – as being motivated by the opportunity to profit by the application of superior commercial knowledge.

In the first place, while it is generally recognized that the transplantation of superior technical and managerial knowledge is most probably beneficial to a country receiving foreign direct investment, complaint is frequently made about the high profits derived by the foreign companies from their investments. Usually this complaint is a simple case of wanting to have one's cake and eat it too, that is, specifically, of wanting to have the benefits of knowledge developed by others without contributing anything to defraying the costs they have incurred in developing it. High measured rates of profit on capital, often taken as an indication of 'exploitation', may in fact not be so, since the 'excess' profits may represent a return on past investments in creating capital in the form of knowledge, which does not appear on the firm's books as an addition to material capital. Of course, if the foreign firm has been given heavy protection in the domestic market to induce it to establish operations there, its profits may reflect an element of monopoly profit, but that will be a consequence of the excess protection awarded it, and presumably remediable.

There is, however, more to the issue than that. On the one hand, resentment of the high profits earned by advanced foreign enterprises may be credited with a vague understanding of the theoretical point that, for welfare optimality, existing knowledge should be made available as a free good, to maximize the social benefits from it, rather than monopolized and charged for. This argument leaves unanswered the question of how the production of additional knowledge is to be motivated and so is inconsistent and incomplete as a basis for policy. It can be argued, however, that for most of the countries in the world, and especially the less developed countries, the contribution that the opportunity to earn a profit in their markets makes to the encouragement of investment in the creation of new commercial knowledge is negligible, so that any profit they allow to be earned from the command of advanced technology is for them a short-run loss with no compensating long-run gain from the encouragement of technical progress. To make the point somewhat differently, playing the rules of allowing monopoly gains to be made from economically useful knowledge involves the cost of paying for foreign knowledge that would probably be available anyhow, in the hope of a gain from the reciprocal obligation on foreign countries to pay monopoly profits on the use of knowledge commanded by your own producers; and since most developing countries are unlikely for a long time to be in the position of holding substantial direct foreign investments made by their own domestic firms, they are unlikely to obtain sufficient *quid* to justify the *quo*. In short, there might be a good case for the less advanced countries to insist on playing by a different set of rules. Apart from that, if the need for recompensing those who make investments in the development of new knowledge is accepted, it does not necessarily follow that recompense through monopoly profits on the use of the knowledge is the ideal arrangement for the host country. On the contrary, the principles of Pareto-optimality suggest a lump-sum payment by the government of the host country in return for the knowledge and the placing of the knowledge at the free disposal of all firms, foreign as well as domestic, operating in the economy.

On the other hand, given that productive knowledge has the character of a public good, one would expect a firm possessing it to behave as far as possible like a discriminating monopolist: since any additional earnings obtained by applying the knowledge in an additional market will be a net addition to its profits from the initial investment in creating the knowledge, the firm will have an incentive to extend its operations to any market that offers a positive profit and to fix the price it charges for the use of its knowledge so as to maximize profit in each market. This implies, incidentally, that, because poorer and less developed countries are likely to have more elastic demands curves for knowledge-intensive products than richer and more advanced countries, the former are likely to pay less, and the latter more, than their *pro rata* share of the costs of development of the knowledge; in other words, there is a general presumption that discriminating monopoly redistributes real income from the rich to the poor. However, the fact that the firm will gain from any positive profit on the knowledge that it is able to make means that there may be an opportunity for governments to squeeze the firm's profits, to the firm's loss but to the social gain. In the second place, foreign firms have frequently been criticized for failure to develop technologies and products appropriate to the factor-price relationships, income levels and local conditions of the countries in which they operate. This complaint overlooks the two considerations of the cost of developing new technologies and the need for an appropriate payoff. It is presumably cheaper to transplant an already known technology to a different environment to which it is not entirely appropriate, paying some extra cost in terms of inferior efficiency, than to develop a new technology more appropriate to that environment; otherwise firms would not engage in the practice and there would be no direct foreign investment.

Third, foreign firms have frequently been criticized for employing their own nationals, rather than residents, especially in top positions. Since this is typically relatively expensive, it is presumably explained by the superior competence of the individuals in question in applying the firm's superior knowledge efficiently, rather than by discrimination on behalf of nationals.

Fourth, there is considerable resentment and dismay over the domination of the American corporation in the most technologically advanced sectors of industry. That dominance, however, is a natural reflection of comparative advantage, in two senses. First, the large rich market, high wage level and relative abundance of capital of the United States tend to give American firms a comparative advantage in the production of new technology; in particular, the United States economy provides strong incentives for labor-saving innovations, either in production processes to economize on the use of workers' time or in new consumption goods to economize on the use of consumers' time. Second, the high wage levels in the United States relative to other countries imply that if the United States is to have a comparative advantage, either in exporting or in establishing and operating productive enterprises to compete in foreign and unfamiliar markets, it cannot be in unskilled-labor-intensive and technologically standardized industries: it must be in technically advanced and technologically dynamic industries. Other countries may well resent this, but it is questionable whether their own market sizes, income levels and availabilities of scientifically trained personnel would permit them to invest with profit in the development of rival advanced technologies.

Fifth, there has been concern, especially in recent years, over the preference of foreign companies for raising as much capital as they can on the domestic market, thereby competing in that market with domestic companies and minimizing the direct foreign exchange gain from such investment. Apart from questions of minimization of foreign exchange risk, the explanation may well be that the comparative advantage of these companies lies in their possession of superior technology rather than in access to a cheaper source of capital than is available to their domestic competitors, and that this advantage enables them to raise capital on the same terms as their domestic competitors without impairing their competitive ability.

Welfare effects of direct investment

To turn specifically to the question of the welfare effects of foreign direct investment, and whether restriction of inward investment might in some cases be desirable, it is convenient to idealize such investment as involving an increase in the country's capital stock and an improvement in its technology. The standard theory of trade and growth suggests that, as far as the capital inflow is concerned, the country's terms of trade will tend to improve if its imports are relatively capital intensive and worsen if its exports are relatively capital intensive, the latter case carrying with it the possibility of 'immiserizing growth' (Bhagwati, 1958), especially when the welfare of the resident population is at issue and remissions of interest and dividends to foreign owners of capital are excluded. More recently, Murray Kemp (1962a, 1962b, 1966) and Ronald Jones (1967) have investigated the concept of an optimal tax on international capital movements, parallel to the concept of the optimum tariff, and Jones has developed conditions for optimization of welfare with respect to both the tariff and the capital tax. It turns out that in some cases a subsidy rather than a tax on either goods flows or capital flows (but not both simultaneously) may be necessary to maximize national welfare. Similarly, technical progress in the export industry will tend to turn a country's terms of trade against it and in the import industry to turn the terms of trade in its favor.[2] Undoubtedly there is an optimum tax on technological transplants, or on inward foreign investment as a mixture of capital inflow and technological transplant, waiting to be analysed by a mathematical trade theorist. However, it does not seem worthwhile to dwell on the point, both because it is an obvious one and because it is hard to believe that actual national policies are governed sufficiently closely by consideration of possibilities of national gain of this kind. It is worth remarking, however, that just as the optimum tariff argument is the only economic argument that leads to restrictions on international trade, as the first-best policy solution, all other arguments being either noneconomic arguments or economic arguments in which tariffs figure as a second-best solution that may or may not improve welfare, depending on the empirical circumstances, so the optimal capital tax argument is the only economic argument that leads to restrictions on international capital flows as a first-best solution. (As such, it suggests restrictions on such flows by both capital-importing and capital-exporting countries, in their own national interests.) Henceforward this paper ignores both terms-of-trade and terms-of-borrowing arguments for intervention in direct international investment.

Host-country gains

Before we proceed to an analysis of the second-best arguments for restriction of inward private foreign investment, something must be said about the presumptive gains to the nation from such investment. Technical progress such as is brought by inward foreign investment is generally assumed to be beneficial by definition. But, assuming constant terms of trade, this is true in general only to the extent that technical progress is a free good. If the return on the superior technology brought by foreign investment is entirely absorbed by the foreign companies, prices

2. See, for example, Johnson (1955) and Findlay and Grubert (1959).

of commodities to consumers and the prices of factors of production in the economy remaining unchanged, there is no direct benefit to the economy. The only benefit it gets, though it may be a quantitatively important one, is the right under double taxation agreements to tax the earnings of the foreign capital invested in it, earnings which will include both the earnings of the capital as such and the earnings of the 'technological capital' represented by the superiority of the foreign firm's technology and its consequent ability to earn profits higher than those earned by domestic firms. Apart from this tax benefit – which will be ignored in what follows, despite its possible significance – the residents of the country gain only to the extent that the benefit of the superior technology is passed on either in lower commodity or factor prices or both. This point provides a rationale for the insistence of the Watkins Committee (Watkins, 1968) on the desirability of maximizing the benefits and minimizing the costs of foreign investment in Canada. This is really a meaningless statement, since what is to be maximized is net benefit, and this is not usually achieved by separate maximization of gross benefit and minimization of cost. Presumably, it means minimizing the rents that foreign firms derive from their possession of superior knowledge. This in turn implies attempting to obtain for Canadian capitalists and Canadian labor a share of the monopoly profits derived by foreign enterprises from their superior knowledge, and attempting to force the benefits of this knowledge to be transferred to the Canadian consumer in the form of lower prices.

Redistributive effects

It is an interesting theoretical point that, if, as may seem plausible in spite of much recent work on the Leontief paradox,[3] direct foreign investment tends to flow into the more capital-intensive sectors of the economy, and if the failure or prevention of the extraction of the whole of the monopoly rent on superior knowledge is reflected in changes in the general levels of factor prices, rather than in premium prices for the factors employed

3. Cf. Gruber, Mehta and Vernon (1967). These authors find that the technologically advanced sectors of American industry are not exceptionally intensive in material capital.

by the foreign companies, the effect of the inflow of foreign capital will be to raise the rate of return on capital and reduce the wages of labor. This point is illustrated in Figure 2, where *XX* and *YY* are the isoquants for the two sectors of the economy as they are before the foreign investment, and $X'X'$ is the isoquant for the situation after the introduction of the foreign technology. If the foreign companies absorb the whole benefit of their superior efficiency in profits on the technology, factor prices remain unchanged and they derive a profit on their technological superiority as a proportion of cost at the rate MM'/OM'. If they pass it on to the consumers completely, in the form of a price reduction proportional to their technical superiority, the price of *X* falls by MM' in terms of capital and factor prices are unchanged; if they keep commodity prices unchanged and let the benefits be absorbed by the community through altered factor prices, the new factor-price ratio is the slope of *NN*, which implies a relative and absolute increase in the price of the services of capital and an absolute and relative decline in the price of the services of labor. This point may explain the otherwise rather implausible fact that in Britain the employers are favorably inclined toward American investment in the country, while the trade unions are generally hostile towards it. (Dunning, 1969). One would expect labor to favor direct foreign investment as bringing in more capital to compete for the services of labor and so to raise real wages, and the owners of capital contrarily to be opposed to inward foreign investment; but if the effect of inward investment by foreign firms is to increase the demand for capital and reduce the demand for labor, these class reactions are understandable. (Of course, views on the desirability of capitalism may play a more important part than assessments of probable class gain or loss from particular phenomena.)

Justifications for restrictions

It would appear from the foregoing analysis that, first-best effects of foreign investment on the terms of trade and the terms of borrowing, and second-best effects on the distribution of national income between owners of labor and owners of capital, apart, inward foreign direct investment cannot harm a country and may confer substantial benefits upon it. What, then, are the arguments against freedom of foreign direct investment and in favor of restriction on it? As already mentioned, such arguments must be either noneconomic arguments, that is, arguments directed at the maximization of something other than the privately consumable

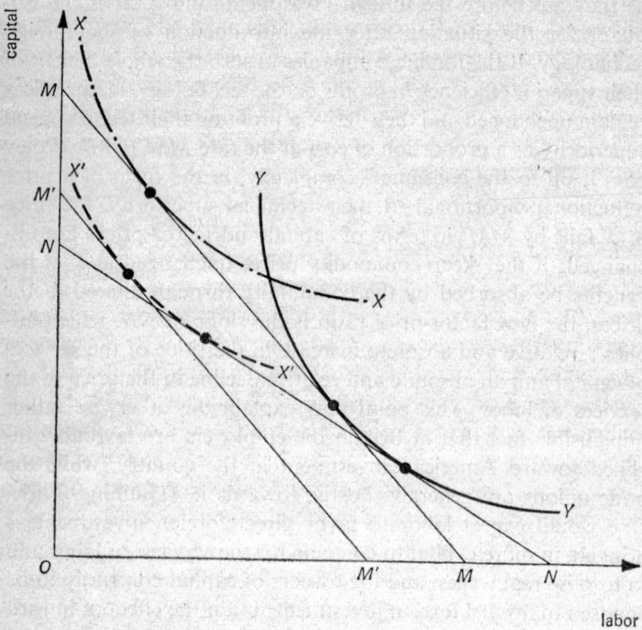

Figure 2 Redistribution of factor income from direct investment

flow of goods and services, or arguments that produce the policy of restriction on inward private foreign investments as a second-best (possibly third-best) policy with an uncertain effect on the achievement of the desired economic aim.

The classical example of a noneconomic argument for protection is the national defense argument: the argument for protecting those industries that supply military equipment, foodstuffs and materials vital in times of war. In principle, the economist cannot debate the necessity of national defense – though in recent years economists have in fact been arguing the necessity of relating defense policy to the kinds of wars that have a non-zero probability of occurring – but he can legitimately raise the question of whether protection of domestic output (as contrasted, say, with stockpiling) is the cheapest form of investment in future defense capability. As applied to the question of restrictions on domestic investment and production by foreign firms, however, the national defense argument would seem to have very little in it. By establishing branch enterprises in a country, the foreign firm gives a hostage to fortune which can be only too readily imprisoned in the event of war or the prospect of war. The only risks a country runs in allowing foreign enterprises in defense industries are:

1. The risk of espionage: this is so obvious as to be probably unimportant in practice.

2. The risk that top personnel in the enterprise will refuse to operate it in time of war if their country of origin is on the opposite side: this is unlikely to be a major problem both because few people are prepared to endure prolonged idleness in prison for the sake of principle and because it is unlikely that the foreign enterprise will be so closely controlled by nationals of an enemy State that substitutes for uncooperative foreigners cannot be found among residents employed either by the foreign firm or by other domestic competitors in the same industry.

3. The risk that, because the foreign firm will be relying in part on research and development conducted in the parent country, the country will be cut off from the results of on-going research, even though it is not cut off from the existing knowledge embodied in the foreign firm's current production techniques: this point cuts both ways, since the presence of the foreign firm will, up to the point of a serious prospect of war, make more information on production technology available to the country than it otherwise would have.

These risks are likely to be of negligible importance by comparison with the costs of developing a modern weapons system on a national economic base, for the vast majority of countries, especially since the countries capable of and politically obliged to develop such systems are likely to provide the results of their investment in them at a subsidized price to friendly countries.

Nationalism as a public good

In the contemporary world, the national defense argument is more likely to appear in the more general form of a 'national independence' argument: that is, the argument that it is valuable to have at least certain kinds of production controlled by resident nationals rather than by foreigners. Albert Breton (1964), and following him myself (Johnson, 1965a, 1965b), have developed a theory for this situation, in which nationalism figures as a collective consumption good that can be invested in by sacrifice of private consumption in order to increase the collective consumption of nationalism. This theory explains many of the phenomena of nationalist economic policies. In the context of direct foreign investment, it explains the desire, reflected in a variety of policies, to have technologically advanced industries controlled by national rather than foreign enterprises, as a facet of the desire to demonstrate national competence in an internationally competitive game. (Backward countries take inordinate pride in success in Olympic sports and invest resources in achieving it; advanced countries take inordinate pride in success in the international basic research and technological progress races and are prepared to invest resources on a large scale in achieving it.) Again, in this context, the economist cannot in principle dispute the public tastes, though he can question whether the policies adopted are well designed to secure their ostensible objectives, and stress the need for examination of alternative methods of securing those objectives.

In the course of a correspondence distinguished by its terse ambiguity, C. P. Kindleberger has attempted to induce me to treat nationalism as a producers' good rather than a consumers' good. I find it difficult to understand the distinction he seeks to draw. From one point of view, the distinction is merely semantic: nationalist policies directed at the production of more of the collective consumption good of nationalism clearly generate a producers' good, the capacity to supply the collective consumption good of nationalism. From another point of view, the implication is that investment in nationalism, i.e. national rather than foreign control of productive enterprises, somehow increases future income from both collective consumption of nationalism and private consumption of goods and services.

For this to be the case, it must be assumed that there are externalities from national ownership and control of productive enterprises, as compared with foreign ownership and control, which raise the productivity of other national enterprises above what it would otherwise be. The only possibility of this that I can see is that somehow superior productive knowledge possessed by nationals is communicated more readily and rapidly to other nationals than is superior productive knowledge possessed by foreign enterprises. This proposition in turn assumes that, for sociological reasons, businessmen are more ready to confide their commercial secrets to fellow nationals than to foreigners – a not entirely credible proposition. In any case, treating nationalism nonsemantically as a producer's good involves reintroducing second-best economic arguments for protection.

Second-best arguments

I now turn to the second-best economic arguments for protection of domestic firms against the intrusion of foreign direct investment. One of these, just mentioned, is that national rather than foreign ownership of certain industries conveys externalities that are valuable enough to be worth subsidizing at public expense. This argument, which entails permanent subsidization of the industries in question, is to be distinguished from the standard infant-industry argument, which calls for temporary subsidization of a given industry during the period it takes to get the industry established.[4]

The infant-industry argument for protection, as is well known, requires that there be an opportunity for investment in the acquisition of productive knowledge that is socially profitable but privately unprofitable. For this purpose, it is not sufficient that the protected industry will eventually become competitive with foreign suppliers; it must eventually either be able to charge prices low enough to the domestic consumer or to pay prices high enough to the owners of domestic factors of production (including profits on domestic capital invested) to yield a socially adequate rate of return on the investment involved in the initial

4. For this distinction, and a full analysis of second-best arguments for protection, see H. G. Johnson (1965c).

protection. Nor is it sufficient that an initial loss must be incurred as an investment in obtaining the ultimate gains. If private entrepreneurs could capture the gains in the form of profits greater than those prevalent elsewhere in the economy, they would be led to undertake the investment required if it were socially profitable and to avoid it if it were socially unprofitable – at least on the assumption that the cost of capital to them is the social alternative opportunity cost of capital. What is required is that the social benefits of investment in the acquisition of productive knowledge exceed the private benefits. In this connection, it is necessary to observe that the argument commonly used – that the infant industry trains labor, which is then available for other firms at a wage lower than the true cost of production of the trained labor, the training being paid for by the infant industry but not recompensed by the use of the trained labor – is fallacious. In a well-organized market system, training that is freely transferable to other employers will not be paid for by the initial employer who provides the training, but will instead be paid for by labor itself through an appropriate apprenticeship system which pays the employee under training a wage lower than his current marginal product to the extent of the training costs incurred by the employer.

The infant-industry argument for insisting on confining participation in an industry to domestic firms must therefore rest on the assumption that there are social benefits from investment in the creation of new knowledge which are not capturable by the firm undertaking investment in the creation of such knowledge, *and* which are greater in the case of a domestically owned firm than in the case of a foreign-owned firm. This is a doubtful proposition from at least two points of view. First, in so far as the external effects of the development of advanced technology are a 'demonstration' or 'public goods' effect – that is, in so far as superior knowledge developed by a firm can be understood and applied by other firms without their having to incur the costs of developing the knowledge for themselves – it should make no difference whether the firm providing the external effects is domestically or foreign owned. Second, since the foreign firm is likely to be using knowledge that has already been developed, and is immediately applicable for a rental price that is likely to be lower than a fair rate of return on the cost of developing it for the reasons explored earlier in this paper, insistence on development of a substitute for this knowledge by domestic firms is likely to be a poor social investment, first because it will delay the development of the knowledge yielding the externalities and second because the national enterprise will have to obtain an adequate rate of return on the investment in knowledge creation, whereas by relying on foreign enterprises the country may only have to pay a rate of return on knowledge creation which is substantially below the country's alternative opportunity cost of capital.

It is for this reason that the restriction of inward foreign direct investment in order to subsidize the acquisition of technological knowledge by domestic firms is a second-best argument. In so far as the difference between foreign-controlled and domestically controlled enterprise is relevant to the determination of the extent of non-privately-capturable benefits from the availability and application of superior knowledge, optimal policy consists in securing that the knowledge is available to and applied by domestic rather than foreign firms, at the least possible acquisition cost. This would normally require arranging for the requisite knowledge to be acquired by domestic firms from foreign sources, through licensing or partnership arrangements or, optimally, through outright purchase by the State, rather than excluding foreign firms from the domestic market as a means of giving domestic firms an incentive to invest in replicating the knowledge of foreign firms – an incentive to which they may not find it profitable anyway to respond, given the protection provide d them.

Another and very obviously second-best argument for excluding foreign firms is that the products they provide are 'socially undesirable' – either 'luxury goods' for the despised rich or 'recreation goods' for the resented idle of all classes. First-best policy here would involve either changing the overall income distribution by taxes and transfers, if it is the prevailing income distribution that it is sought to alter, or putting consumption taxes on the goods in question, if it is the consumption of these particular goods that is regarded as socially undesirable. A second-best policy of doubtful efficacy would be to prohibit all production of the disfavored goods, whether by domestic or foreign firms. Prohibition of investment and production by foreign firms only will, unless only foreign firms have the knowhow to produce the product and they are unwilling to make it available to domestic firms at any price (which would be irrational on their part, in view of the preceding analysis of the economics of knowledge as a monopolized public good), have the paradoxical result of encouraging domestic firms to invest one way or another in acquiring the knowhow to produce goods considered socially undesirable or noncontributory to economic growth, and diverting scarce domestic capital and entrepreneurial talent from industries considered to be socially desirable or to be socially productive.

The balance of payments

Another type of second-best argument for restricting foreign direct investment in a country concerns the balance of payments. Any such argument must be either a second-best argument – because the balance of payments is determined by macroeconomic relationships and should be controlled by macroeconomic policy instruments (specifically the exchange rate and monetary and fiscal policy) rather than by microeconomic policies (which in any case are of very doubtful efficacy) – or it must be a subtle and unacknowledged version of the terms-of-trade argument for capital taxes. One version of this argument – that the balance of payments cost of the earnings on a foreign direct investment will be 'too high' to justify the investment – reflects partly the resentment previously mentioned against paying the price of acquiring foreign productive knowledge, and partly the possibility that overvaluation of the currency coupled with import controls and domestic inflation has made the money profits earnable by foreign investors artificially high [by comparison with (a) what they would be if the exchange rate were an equilibrium rate and there were no import restrictions; (b) the real alternative opportunity cost of capital to the country].

Another version of the balance of payments argument for restricting foreign direct investment is that the country will be unable, when the investment has occurred, to generate the foreign exchange earnings required to service the investment, through increasing exports or reducing exports. This argument assumes either an unwillingness to devalue the currency and restrict aggregate demand sufficiently to balance the balance of payments, or that balancing the balance of payments requires a worsening of the terms of trade, whose adverse effect on domestic real income more than wipes out any gains from the foreign investment captured by the country through lower product prices, higher factor prices or receipts from the taxation of foreign capital and foreign knowledge. In the latter case, what is at issue is the optimal capital tax argument, which is a first-best argument excluded from the analysis of this paper.[5]

Monopoly

A final second-best argument for restriction of foreign direct investment, popularized by Stephen Hymer, is motivated by the possibility that the presence of foreign enterprises may increase monopoly and thus affect the social welfare adversely. This is a second-best argument, because the intrusion of foreign enterprises may either increase or decrease competition in the domestic economy, and if more competition is desired it can be achieved more reliably by domestic antitrust policy, or still more reliably, by reducing the tariff protection enjoyed by industries where the presence of monopoly can be verified. Moreover, the question of whether foreign ownership of part of industry leads to social loss through increased monopoly requires more careful analysis than it has usually received. Social loss would seem to require either an increase in prices to consumers above what they would otherwise be, or additional wastes of resources on the nonprice aspects of monopolistic competition. Higher profits derived from the superior efficiency of foreign firms are not evidence of such loss, but rather the contrary from a cosmopolitan point of view, reflecting the saving of resource costs through greater efficiency; and from the national point of view, there is a gain to the extent that prices to consumers are lowered, prices of domestic factors of production are raised or the nation shares in the increased profits of the foreign firms through taxation.

5. Kindleberger (1969, pp. 8–9) concedes this case for restriction of foreign direct investment without, apparently, realizing that it involves the analog of the optimum tariff argument that earlier in his paper he dismisses as 'unrealistic in policy terms'.

It has been suggested that, to maximize the chances of preserving and increasing competition when inward foreign direct investment occurs, takeovers of existing domestic firms should be discouraged and the construction of new domestic production facilities encouraged instead. This rule of thumb seems poorly grounded in economic analysis, since for the foreign firm the choice between the two alternatives of takeover and new construction is a matter of relative cost of entry into domestic production and reflects nothing of the purpose for which that firm wishes to establish itself as a producer in the market (that is, whether its purpose is to compete or to organize more effective monopoly arrangements). It should be remarked also that if takeovers are forbidden, foreign entry via new construction will probably mean capital losses for domestic firms if the foreigner intends to compete vigorously, whereas entry by takeover, since it requires payment of a price for the domestic firm higher in the owners' eyes than the capitalized value of their prospective future profits under existing management, gives those owners the capitalized value of a slice of the profits the foreign firm expects to make through the application of its superior technology. The same consideration probably applies to the case where the foreigner enters to organize a more effective monopoly.

In conclusion, it is evident that with sufficient analysis one can construct cases in which there is a second-best argument for restriction of inward foreign direct investment. The fundamental problem is that, as with all second-best arguments, determination of the conditions under which a second-best policy actually leads to an improvement of social welfare requires detailed theoretical and empirical investigation by a first-best economist. Unfortunately, policy is generally formulated by fourth-best economists and administered by third-best economists; it is therefore very unlikely that a second-best welfare optimum will result from policies based on second-best arguments.

References

BHAGWATI, J. (1958), 'Immiserizing growth: a geometrical note', *Rev. econ. Stud.*, vol. 25, pp. 201–5.

BRETON, A. (1964), 'The economics of nationalism', *J. polit. Econ.*, vol. 72, pp. 376–86.

DUNNING, J. H. (1969), 'The role of American investment in the British economy', *PEP Broadsheet*, no. 507.

FINDLAY, R., and GRUBERT, H. (1959), 'Factor intensity, technological progress and the terms of trade', *Oxf. econ. Pap.*, vol. 11, pp. 111–21.

GRUBER, W., MEHTA, P., and VERNON, R. (1967), 'The R & D factor in international trade and international investment of United States industries', *J. polit. Econ.*, vol. 75, pp. 20–37.

HYMER, S. H. (1960), 'The international operations of national firms: a study of direct investment', unpublished doctoral dissertation, MIT.

HYMER, S. H. (1966), 'Direct foreign investment and national interest', in P. Russell (ed.), *Nationalism in Canada*, McGraw-Hill.

HYMER, S. H. (1967), 'Antitrust and American direct investment abroad', in *International Aspects of Antitrust*, Hearings before the Subcommittee on Antitrust and Monopoly, Committee on the Judiciary, US Senate, 89th Congress, 2nd session, Washington.

HYMER, S. H. (1968), 'The impact of the multinational firm', in M. Bye (ed.), *La politique industrielle de l'Europe integrée*, Presses Universitaires de France, pp. 167–85.

JOHNSON, H. G. (1955), 'Economic expansion and international trade', *Manchester School*, vol. 23, pp. 95–112.

JOHNSON, H. G. (1965a), 'A theoretical model of economic nationalism in new and developing states', *Polit. Sci. Q.*, vol. 80, pp. 169–85.

JOHNSON, H. G. (1965b), 'An economic theory of protectionism, tariff bargaining and the formation of customs unions', *J. polit. Econ.*, vol. 72, pp. 256–83.

JOHNSON, H. G. (1965c), 'Optimal trade intervention in the presence of domestic distortions', in R. E. Baldwin (ed.), *Trade, Growth and the Balance of Payments: Essays in Honor of Gottfried Haberler*, Rand-McNally, pp. 3–34.

JOHNSON, H. G. (1968), *Comparative Cost and Commercial Policy Theory for a Developing World Economy*, Wicksell Lectures, Almqvist & Wiksell, Stockholm.

JONES, R. W. (1967), 'International capital movements and the theory of tariffs and trade', *Q. J. Econ.*, vol. 81, pp. 1–38.

KEMP, M. C. (1962a), 'Foreign investment and the national advantage', *Econ. Rec.*, vol. 38, pp. 56–62.

KEMP, M. C. (1962b), 'The benefits and costs of private investment from abroad: comment', *Econ. Rec.*, vol. 38, pp. 108–10.

KEMP, M. C. (1966), 'The gain from international trade and investment: a neo-Heckscher-Ohlin approach', *Amer. econ. Rev.*, vol. 56, pp. 788–809.

KINDLEBERGER, C. P. (1969), 'Restrictions on direct investments in host countries', discussion paper for the University of Chicago Workshop in International Business, 5 March.

WATKINS, M. (1968), *Foreign Ownership and the Structure of Canadian Industry*, Queen's Printer, Ottawa.

Further Reading

The reader is also invited to consult the reference lists at the end of the introduction to each Part.

J. H. Adler (ed.), *Capital Movements and Economic Development*, Macmillan, 1967.

Y. Aharoni, *The Foreign Investment Decision Process*, Harvard University Press, 1966.

D. T. Brash, *American Investment in Australian Industry*, Australian National University Press, 1966.

A. K. Cairncross, *Home and Foreign Investment, 1870–1914*, Yale University Press, 1953.

Central Office of Information, *Britain's International Investment Position*, HMSO, 1971.

R. S. Deane, *Foreign Investment in New Zealand Manufacturing*, Sweet & Maxwell, 1970.

J. H. Dunning, *American Investment in British Manufacturing Industry*, Allen & Unwin, 1958.

J. H. Dunning, *Studies in International Investment*, Allen & Unwin, 1970.

S. Hirsch, *Location of Industry and International Competitiveness*, Clarendon Press, 1967.

C. K. Hobson, *The Export of Capital*, 1914, Constable, reissued 1933.

T. O. Horst, 'A theoretical and empirical analysis of American exports and direct investment', unpublished Ph.D. dissertation, University of Rochester, 1969.

G. C. Hufbauer and F. M. Adler, 'Overseas manufacturing investment and the US balance of payments', *US Treasury Tax Research Policy Document*, no. 1.

H. Hughes and You Pol Seng, *Foreign Investment and Industrialization in Singapore*, University of Wisconsin Press, 1969.

S. H. Hymer, 'The international operations of national firms: a study of direct investment', unpublished doctoral dissertation, MIT, 1960.

C. Iversen, *International Capital Movements*, Oxford University Press, 1936.

L. H. Jenks, *The Migration of British Capital in 1875*, 1927, Cape, revised 1938.

A. W. Johnstone, *United States Direct Investment in France*, MIT Press, 1965.

M. Kemp, *The Pure Theory of International Trade and Investment*, Prentice-Hall, 1969.

M. Kidlon, *Foreign Investment in India*, Oxford University Press, 1965.

C. P. Kindleberger, *American Investment Abroad*, Yale University Press, 1969.

C. P. Kindleberger, *The International Corporation*, MIT Press, 1970.

C. Lewis, *America's Stake in International Investment*, Brookings Institution, Washington, 1938.

C. Lewis, *The United States and Foreign Investment Problems*, Brookings Institution, Washington, 1948.

I. A. Litvak and C. J. Maule, *Foreign Investment and the Experience of Host Countries*, Praeger, 1970.

H. K. May, *The Contributions of US Private Investment to Latin America's Growth*, Council for Latin America Inc., Washington, 1970.

R. Mikesell, *US Private and Government Investment Abroad*, Oregon University Press, 1962.

P. B. Musgrave, *United States Taxation of Foreign Investment Income*, Harvard University Press, 1969.

E. T. Penrose, *The Large International Firm in Developing Countries: The International Petroleum Industry*, MIT Press, 1968.

W. B. Reddaway, S. J. Potter and C. T. Taylor, *The Effects of UK Direct Investment Overseas: Interim and Final Reports*, Department of Applied Economics, University of Cambridge, 1967–8.

G. L. Reuber and F. Roseman, 'The takeover of Canadian firms, 1945–61: an empirical analysis', *Economic Council of Canada, Special Study*, no. 10.

A. S. Safarian, *Foreign Ownership of Canadian Industry*, McGraw-Hill, 1966.

D. Stikker, *The Role of Private Enterprise in Investment and Promotion of Exports in Developing Countries*, United Nations, New York, 1968.

A. Stonehill, *Foreign Ownership in Norwegian Enterprises*, Oslo Central Bureau of Statistics, 1965.

M. Watkins, *Foreign Ownership and the Structure of Canadian Industry*, Queen's Printer, Ottawa, 1968.

Acknowledgements

Permission to reproduce the Readings in this volume is acknowledged from the following sources:

1 International Economic Association, Macmillan and R.N. Cooper
2 Lloyds Bank Ltd
3 Harvard University Press
4 Royal Economic Society and A. E. de Jasay
5 *Economic Record*, Melbourne
6 *Economic Record*, Melbourne
7 Edizioni Cedam, Padua
8 *American Economic Review* and H. G. Grubel
9 Royal Economic Society, Macmillan and B. Thomas
10 Royal Economic Society and E. T. Penrose
11 *Economica*
12 *Quarterly Journal of Economics* and R. Vernon
13 George Allen & Unwin Ltd, Frederick A. Praeger Inc. and D. Robertson
14 American Economic Association and D. A. Snider
15 MIT Press
16 *Harper & Row*
17 Société d'Études et d'Expansion, Liège
18 MIT Press

Author Index

Subject Index